William White

Pioneer Victorian Architect

William White

Pioneer Victorian Architect

Gill Hunter

Spire Books Ltd

PO Box 2336, Reading RG4 5WJ
www.spirebooks.com

Spire Books Ltd
PO Box 2336
Reading RG4 5WJ
www.spirebooks.com

CIP data:
A catalogue record for this book is available
from the British Library
ISBN 978-1-904965-26-8

Designed and produced by John Elliott
Text set in Bembo

Frontispiece: The only known portrait of William White, undated, but post-1864 when he became a member of the Society of Antiquaries [*Royal Institute of British Architects*].

Jacket: Bishop's Court, Exeter (*Chris Chapman*).

CONTENTS

For Peter, who made it possible

ACKNOWLEDGEMENTS

The publication of this book could not have been achieved without the support of the Marc Fitch Fund, the Scouloudi Foundation in association with the Institute of Historical Research, and the Society of Architectural Historians of Great Britain, which awarded a Dorothy Stroud Bursary. I am very grateful to them all.

There is insufficient space to mention individually the many people who have shown me such kindness and been so helpful in the researching of this book. Geoff Brandwood, John Elliott, Tom Gretton and Frank Salmon have been enthusiastically and critically supportive over many years. Michael Kerney has shared his knowledge of White's stained glass, and Andrew Saint has passed on the results of his research into White's buildings in Battersea. Alex Bremner, Tim Brittain-Catlin, David Brownlee, Peggy Day, Graham Daw, Graham Fuller, Clive Glover, Michael Hall, Paul Joyce, the late Kenneth Major, Hugh Meller, Stefan Muthesius, James Rothwell, Paul Snell and Brenda Watkin have also been generous with information. I am very grateful to Jo Cox, who allowed me to look through Chris Brooks's notes, and to Susan Dalton for her hospitality and for allowing me to search through and reproduce some of Christopher's photographs; also to Jane Wainwright for Clive's pictures of Bishop's Court, to Tim Grevatt for his; and to Martin Charles for his Wantage photograph. Thanks are also due to Dale Jones for family information; to René Lachal for photographs of Madagascar Cathedral, and Malcolm Edwards for asking him; to John Turnbull who allowed me to go through the Grey papers; to Philip and Christine Kestell-Cornish for access to their family archive; to Viscount Ashbrook for permission to use the Arley Hall Archive, and to Charles and Jane Foster who made me so welcome there. A research grant from the Paul Mellon Foundation allowed me to visit South Africa, where Melvyn Wallis-Brown, Paul Murray and all the staff at Bishops made me very welcome. Ingrid Andersen at St Bart's and staff at the Cory Library, Albany Museum, Amathole Museum and Cape Town University Library have all been generous with their time.

Staff at the Bodleian Library, Exeter Local Studies Library, Lambeth Palace Library, Keble College Library, the RIBA Library, and the National Monuments Record, together with John Bevan at Church House, and Philip Gale at the Church of England Record Centre, have all been unfailingly helpful. Janet Seeley made me very welcome at the library of the Council for the Care of Churches. I have benefited from particular assistance from Angela Broome at the Royal Institution of Cornwall, Robin Darwall-Smith at Magdalen College, Peter Meadows at Cambridge University Library, and Natalie Mees at Gilbert White's House, Selborne. I am very grateful for the help and interest shown by staff at many record offices: particular mention must be made of David Thomas at Cornwall Record Office, and the staff at Oxford Record Office, where the Kimberley Archive is deposited.

I have been made very welcome at many schools: Toby Parker, archivist at Haileybury (although we found no evidence of White's involvement there); Terry Rogers, archivist at Marlborough College; the late Anthony Money, archivist at Radley; and James Lawson, archivist at Shrewsbury School; Mike Critchlow, estates bursar at Repton; John Wells, works bursar at Winchester; and house masters at all these schools, and at Eton, have all given generously of their time. Adrienne Reynolds has shared her extensive research on Forest School. Busy school secretaries have answered questions and found information. Similarly, incumbents, churchwardens and parishioners have opened their churches and searched their records. Particular thanks are due to Pam Braithwaite, Geoffrey Bamsey, Doris Butler, Pam Cantle, Vanessa Cato, Jeremy Dowding, Joan Endean, George Morris, Pam Perry, Gordon and Sally Steel, Betty Smith, Ken Stanhope, Richard and Georgina Tregoning, Brian Tremain, Paul Trend, Leonard Tridgell, Ron Watkins and Joan Walton.

Owners of houses designed by White have been enthusiastic to know more about the architect and generous in allowing me access to their homes. Especial thanks to Shaun Atkins, Frances Balasuriya, Jamie Brown, Mr and Mrs Clements, Heather and Michael Clews, Nicholas and Anne Graham, Jill Hale, David Harvey, Barry and Suzie Kelley, John and Mercedes Leonard, Colette McGarry and David Hunt, Peter Molyneux, Paul Hacking, Martin and Angela Ould, Mrs Radford, Richard and Avril Read, Mr and Mrs Roche, Jane and Murray Rose, and Enid Wormald.

Finally, I must thank my family and friends, particularly my husband, for their interest, support and practical help – for accommodation on research trips, drawing up plans, proof-reading, and assisting with illustrations – and for tolerating the intrusion of William White into my affections.

Gill Hunter
Reading
January 2010

INTRODUCTION

> Let us, I say, give all the encouragement we can to ... the advancement of true art, and the consequent well-being and happiness of ourselves, our families, and our fellow-countrymen.

These stirring words were met with loud cheering from the members and friends of the Architectural Museum gathered in the lecture theatre of the South Kensington Museum (now the Victoria and Albert Museum) on the evening of 9th January 1861.[1] The speaker was the successful 35-year-old architect, William White, whose practice at 30a Wimpole Street, London, was receiving a constant stream of commissions for churches, parsonages, schools, commercial premises and private houses, not only from Cornwall to Aberdeen but also abroad.

White's buildings express the talent of this great-nephew of the naturalist Gilbert White, author of *The Natural History of Selborne*. An enquiring mind and knowledge of science and the natural world enlivened his deep Christian faith and adherence to the Church of England. Although a member of the Ecclesiological Society, White's buildings never conformed to the strictures expressed in their publication, *The Ecclesiologist*. Neither did they consist of sketchbook details culled from travels at home and abroad. A follower of Pugin, White believed that a successful modern style could only be achieved if architects were persuaded to 'analyse the remains, to fathom the principles' of medieval builders and apply them to nineteenth-century requirements.[2] He eschewed an architecture that was a 'vortex of Eclecticism, or a Museum of Antiquarianism', calling for 'some rational and feasible system' to acquire that 'pure dignity with perfect repose' achieved by both classical and medieval builders.[3] His practice, spanning the entire latter half of the nineteenth century, began with the vigour of the Gothic Revival, but always recognised a gentler, English vernacular idiom. His later buildings anticipated the Queen Anne movement and the Arts and Crafts style. All his designs are expressive of a thoughtful, inventive and lively personality.

White was a prolific writer of letters, papers, articles and pamphlets on many disparate topics that give an insight into a man whom Charles Eastlake recognised for his 'ingenuity and vigour in design'.[4] This inventiveness was wide-ranging: in 1871 he patented his 'porte knapsack', the frame rucksack that was not in general production until the second half of the twentieth century. But architecture was White's principal concern and in his writings can be found the dichotomy of the age – the sensibility of the Romantic and the practicality of the scientist.

Although he defended the sentiment inherent in a love of antiquity, White consistently promoted the science of architecture. His many innovations included double-glazing at All Saints', Notting Hill, *c*.1851, to keep out 'cold and noise', a method he believed 'might be adopted with advantage more often than it is at present.'[5] For the same church he devised a system so that the large Gray and Davison organ would be partly in the north transept and partly in the south one. The organist, sitting at a keyboard in the choir, would have 'perfect control ... by means of electric wires'.[6] In 1858 he proposed using concrete faced with brick for the walls at St Michael's, Lyndhurst, a method he was eventually permitted to employ at St Mark's, Battersea Rise in London in 1872. White incorporated a revolving serving hatch in the dining rooms of many of his parsonages and houses to allow the easy serving of food without associated cooking smells. Fumbling in dark cupboards was overcome by White's 1853 specification of glass slates to the roof above the closets of the new vicarage for Holy Trinity, Halstead. An alternative was the tiny square windows he designed to light the cupboards on the first floor of his isolation block for Winchester Sanatorium thirty years later.

In 1858 *The Ecclesiologist* drew attention to White's system of laying solid wood blocks for flooring at his school at Little Petherick, Cornwall. It was termed 'a very admirable plan, as it ensures warmth and dryness, as well as great solidity.'[7] *Parquet*, employing various hardwoods to form patterned floors, had been used in wealthy homes since the seventeenth century, but White adapted this system, using plain rectangular wooden blocks set in a herringbone pattern on a concrete bed. The moderate cost enabled him to employ it in churches as well as secular buildings. White claimed to have invented this form, but refused to take out a patent, claiming 'that it was far too useful for anyone to be debarred from using it.'[8]

Like many of his contemporaries, White condemned iron construction, although he realised its advantages for 'extensive works, to be built with vast accommodation and at moderate cost, or within a short limited space of time.'[9] He cited as an example the Crystal Palace, which, he believed, was without almost all 'characteristics of Architecture-proper', classing it as 'a piece of Constructional Engineering'.[10] Even in 1880, White still held to his view that because it lacked 'the massiveness, the bulk, the play of light and shadow', iron architecture could only be regarded as 'ferrotecture'.[11] He recognised the mutual interests and skills of architects and civil engineers: rather than a fusion that he believed would be 'unnatural and impossible', White advocated a 'fraternal relation[ship]', such as existed between surgeons and physicians.[12]

On the question of iron, White was in agreement with John Ruskin, whom he must have known through their mutual membership of the Hogarth Club and the Mediaeval Society. However, White disagreed fundamentally with Ruskin's belief that freedom should be given to the workman. White 'did not want a man who would think in his own way ... but he wanted a man to learn and take in *his* way of thinking instead of his own.'[13] Of course, Ruskin's view was not 'the sort of dream that such eminent professionals as Street and Waterhouse could have had any sympathy with', but they quietly ignored it rather than antagonise such a powerful critic.[14]

White, either naïvely or foolishly, published details of his correspondence with that 'eminent amateur' (Ruskin), concerning the study of the laws of proportion. White was writing on 'Systematic Proportion in Architecture' and advocating the study of laws 'of order or harmony' that might 'form the basis of a School of Architecture. [For] Architecture without a school is as language is without grammar.'[15] Ruskin derided the teaching of any laws, other than those of construction, and declared that 'it is no use my reading anything on this matter, my mind being conclusively made up about it.'[16] Not content, White retorted that the ancient laws of proportion had been practised by medieval builders, and that, before publication of *The Stones of Venice*, he had observed 'similar variation of spacings, etc., in English Early Architecture'.[17] White also pointed out that 'some of the greatest composers ... have continued a lifelong study of counterpoint ... for the sake of *enabling themselves to develop and perfect their own harmonies.*' 'Thank you for your letter. I agree to all it says' was Ruskin's terse reply, 'but the thing to be done is to get your nation into a musical ... mind', for, he warned, 'if you begin with mathematical laws you will stay there.'[18] But White was adamant, calling for 'colleges of education, not schools of instruction'. He asked why 'the study of construction be allowed and the study of proportion disallowed?' and, if so, 'how then should there have been three valuable volumes written merely upon the old stones found in an out of the way decayed city, in a gulf of the Mediterranean, with a view to illustrating the principles of their design?'[19] There was no reply from Ruskin.

White also disagreed with Ruskin's advocacy of variety, pointing out that,

> A revulsion from the stilted uniformity of the last century has set in, and the reaction seems likely not merely to carry men beyond the grounds of a fitting irregularity and diversity into an extravagant crookedness, and quaintness, but to lead them to view in a wrong light the very nature and purpose of uniformity, as an element of architectural beauty.[20]

White held more balanced views than many of his Gothicist contemporaries, for he claimed that repetition was not proof 'of poverty or incapacity in a design' but 'may be, and often is, a proof of power', citing the Parthenon as an example.[21]

In his first known paper White identified '*breadth*' as the 'first quality to be obtained in every building', pointing out that 'verticality is *a*, but it is not *the*, characteristic feature in the construction of a proper building ... horizontalism is equally with verticality an emblem of beauty ... [which] symbolizes repose'.[22] In this he differed from Pugin, who admired the great height of European medieval churches rather than the majority of

English Gothic cathedrals that are broad and relatively low. White applied his demand for broadness not only to outline but also to details: 'it is very desirable, on almost every account, to get *breadth* of window.'[23] His small, broad windows, often tucked under the eaves, were adopted by Voysey, while those that he wrapped round corners were used by Lutyens.

White argued particularly, as he did on that January evening in 1861, for more colour in buildings. It is not surprising that colour was so important to him, for although the White family was based in Hampshire, William White was born and bred in Northamptonshire, a county known for the rich diversity of colour of its stone.

1

Early Years

William White was born on 12 April 1825 at Blakesley, Northamptonshire, the fifth child and third son of the curate and schoolmaster, the Rev. Francis Henry White, and his wife Elizabeth Master. William's paternal grandfather, Henry (Harry) White, was the youngest brother of Gilbert White, author of *The Natural History and Antiquities of Selborne*. In 1762 Harry became rector of Fyfield, Hampshire, where, to supplement his income, he ran a successful academy to prepare young gentlemen for entrance to Oxford University. Like his famous sibling, Harry also kept a diary in which he recorded his observations of the natural world.[1] His death in 1788, when Francis Henry was only seven, left his widow in 'straightened circumstances', but financial support from his two elder brothers, each of whom obtained curacies, allowed Francis Henry to follow them to Oxford University.[2] After three years as a chaplain in the navy and a period as curate of Fyfield, Francis Henry moved to Blakesley, Northamptonshire. There he enjoyed country life, shooting, hare coursing and dining with his brother Sampson, rector of nearby Maidford, and the local gentry. Sampson's diaries reveal that their companions included Cornelius Ives, rector of Bradden, and William Master, fellow of New College and son of the late rector of nearby Paulerspury.[3] Cornelius Ives and Sampson White, the trustees of Blakesley Grammar School, appointed Francis Henry as master of the school with an income of £100 per annum. On 4 May 1818 Francis Henry White and Elizabeth Master, William's sister, were married. Children followed in quick succession: Frances Elizabeth in 1819, Henry Master in 1820, Emily in 1822, Francis Gilbert in 1824, William in 1825, Lucy Anne a year later, Mary in 1828, Harriet in 1829, and finally John Edward in 1832.[4]

The school at Blakesley had been established in 1669 for the education of 'all the masculine Children of the Parish in grammar, free of expense, from the age of *seven* years to *fourteen* inclusive'.[5] However, by the nineteenth century most scholars were the sons of the local farmers and labourers who did not want to be taught Greek and Latin grammar, so the Rev. White appointed an assistant 'who under his direction, now teaches all the boys of the Village, writing, reading, and arithmetic.'[6] This allowed the Rev. White, who was also vicar of Blakesley from 1838 to 1843, to teach William and his brothers for two hours from 6 am every morning.[7] From William's writings we can conclude that besides a detailed knowledge of the Bible and the rubrics of the established church, they were taught Latin, Greek and mathematics, as well as history, French and botany. Henry Master, the eldest son, and later John Edward, the youngest, went on to Winchester College and then to New College, Oxford. Francis Gilbert gained his degrees at Lincoln College, Oxford. Their education was made possible by family money, particularly from the estate of William Van Mildert, bishop of Durham, a relation of their mother, and from Anne Barker on their father's side.[8]

William did not follow in his brothers' academic footsteps, but, at the age of fifteen, was apprenticed for five years to Daniel Goodman Squirhill, an architect and surveyor, who had been admitted to the Royal Academy Schools in 1829 at the age of 21, and had been established in Leamington, Warwickshire, since 1837.[9] He was possibly the son of Charles Squirhill, an architect and surveyor in Northampton.[10] There is no record of D.G. Squirhill's commissions during the period of White's time with him, but in 1847 he designed the Warwickshire Proprietary College, Leamington, in the Tudor style that was considered appropriate for schools.[11] William later wrote that although taught 'some of the principles of construction, of quantities, and of the supervision of work', Squirhill had little to offer 'in the way of design or drawing', which he had to acquire for himself.[12]

It seems likely that William's choice of career was influenced by a near neighbour. About three miles west of Blakesley lies the estate of Canons Ashby, seat of the Dryden family since the sixteenth century. Francis Henry White had conducted the burial of Sir John Edward Dryden, the 2nd baronet in 1818, and Sampson White recorded travelling with Sir Henry, the 3rd baronet, to a musical party in 1820.[13] In 1837 the estate was inherited by the latter's nineteen-year-old son, also Henry, who became known as 'the Antiquary' for his regard for archaeology, architecture and local history. Sir Henry seems to have taken a close interest in the White family, and in 1849 appointed the Rev. F.H. White, now vicar of Pattishall, as his personal chaplain. (Sir Henry presented a writing table to H.M. White for being 'the first Wykhamist [sic] commoner to achieve a double first at Oxford'.)[14] Dryden produced his own architectural designs in vernacular style for schools, barns and cottages on his estate. Dryden's encouragement of local choirs is reflected in William's interest in choral music; and correspondence regarding scientific solutions to church heating and ventilation demonstrates their easy familiarity.[15]

In 1835 the Rev. Thomas Scott, rector of Wappenham, a village three miles south of Blakesley, had died, prompting his son, George Gilbert, to establish himself as an independent architect. With his partner, W.B. Moffatt, G.G. Scott successfully competed in numerous competitions for the design of workhouses to be built as a result of the Poor Law Amendment Act of 1834. Despite Scott's assertion that his parents' evangelicalism meant they had little social life, they were reported to be 'intimate friends' of the High Church Whites of Blakesley, and so it was that William White joined Scott's London practice as an 'improver' in 1845.[16] Another 'improver', who had joined Scott the previous year, was George Edmund Street, and he, together with George Frederick Bodley, who began his architectural training with Scott (a relation by marriage) in 1845, became White's close friends.

It was in 1841, on reading Pugin that Scott suddenly found himself 'like a person awakened from a long feverish dream' and 'became a new man'.[17] From the end of the eighteenth century Romanticism, particularly the novels of Sir Walter Scott, had popularised an ornamental style of Gothic architecture. The curtailment of travel caused by the Napoleonic Wars had focused the attention of antiquarians on local medieval buildings. A.W.N. Pugin's drawings in his polemical treatise, *Contrasts*, of 1836, vividly illustrated earlier criticism of both the Reformation and the current state of the nation expressed by writers such as William Cobbett.[18] In *Contrasts*, Pugin introduced a moral dimension to architecture, claiming that only 'a restoration of the ancient feelings and sentiments' could restore the soul of revived Gothic buildings.[19] He expanded his theories in *The True Principles of Pointed or Christian Architecture*, 1841, stating

> that there should be no features about a building which are not necessary for convenience, construction, or propriety; ... [and] that all ornament should consist of enrichment of the essential construction of the building. ... the smallest detail should have a meaning or serve a purpose; and even the construction itself should vary with the material employed.[20]

Pugin was encouraged by the Oxford *Tracts for the Times*, seeing in them a desire to return to pre-Reformation spirituality. No doubt stimulated by Pugin's *Contrasts*, the Oxford Society for Promoting the Study of Gothic Architecture (later known as the Oxford Architectural Society) was established at the university in March 1839. The society was academic and antiquarian in its interests, its objective being to 'collect Books, Prints and Drawings; Models of the Forms of Arches, Vaults, Etc.; Casts of Mouldings, and Details; and such other Architectural Specimens as the Funds of the Society will admit.'[21] William's eldest brother, Henry Master White, was recorded as a life member.[22] H.M. White was later described by his daughter as 'deeply influenced by contact with the leaders of the Oxford Movement'.[23] It seems likely, therefore, that he would have been familiar with Pugin's writings, and have discussed them with William.

In May 1839 the Cambridge Camden Society was founded by young undergraduates at Trinity College, Cambridge, 'to promote the study of Ecclesiastical Architecture and Antiquities, and the restoration of mutilated Architectural remains.'[24] The Cambridge Camden Society's journal, *The Ecclesiologist,* quickly became the arbiter of Gothic Revival architecture, dogmatically insisting that church building and decoration should follow pre-Reformation precedent. G.G. Scott joined the society in 1842, Street in 1845 (the year that it was renamed the Ecclesiological Society), William White in 1848 and Bodley a year later.[25]

It is not surprising that Scott, having suffered criticism of his early church designs

1.1 St John the Baptist, Moulsford, Berkshire, restored by G.G. Scott, 1846-7. It has been suggested that it was a project by the young William White, then an improver in Scott's office.

1.2 St Mary's, Hawridge, Buckinghamshire, rebuilt by White, 1855-6, shows marked similarities with the work at Moulsford, particularly the bell-cote and the south porch.

in *The Ecclesiologist*, joined the Oxford Society in 1843. He quickly befriended Edward Freeman, a leading member and author of many papers. Freeman articulated the parallels between the gradual development of architectural styles and the theory of development of Christian doctrine propounded by John Henry Newman, an early member of the society.[26] Freeman rejected antiquarian copyism, believing that architects unconsciously reflected the spirit and feelings of their own age, and therefore, unlike the Camdenians, he accepted both early and late styles of Gothic architecture, as well as foreign examples.[27] It was no doubt a reflection of Freeman's liberalism that set Scott on a whirlwind tour to study German Gothic architecture in preparation for his entry to the international competition to rebuild the Nikolaikirche in Hamburg.

White joined Scott's practice in 1845 when it had just been awarded the commission for the Nikolaikirche, for which many of the drawings were prepared by George Edmund Street. This project was in addition to the numerous English commissions that occupied the articled pupils, draughtsmen, clerks and office boys in Scott's hectic offices in Spring Gardens, Westminster. The rapid growth of the railway system permitted countrywide and international travel, encouraging the use of a wide range of styles and different materials. The 'improvers' had a certain degree of autonomy in the projects they administered, and David Brownlee has suggested that Scott's restoration of the church of St John the Baptist, Moulsford, Berkshire, 1846–7, may have come from the 'gentler' hand of William White (**1.1**).[28] In its vernacular flint and brick construction and shingled western bell tower, it is certainly very similar to White's rebuilding of St Mary's, Hawridge, Buckinghamshire, ten years later (**1.2**).

Scott's practice, with its reliance on a large number of staff for the detailed drawings and administration of numerous projects, was very different from the personal attention that White aspired to give to every aspect of his designs. It is not surprising, therefore, that in 1847, after only two years, White left his lodgings in Craven Street, near Charing Cross, to establish his own practice in Truro, Cornwall.[29]

This remote county, in the mid-nineteenth century a hotbed of non-conformism, may seem a strange choice of location for an aspiring young architect. It formed part of the unwieldy diocese of Henry Phillpotts, bishop of Exeter, who supported Lord John Russell's 1847 Bill to establish four new bishoprics, including one for Cornwall. An early member of the Cambridge Camden Society, Philpotts was patron of the Exeter Diocesan Architectural Society, established in 1841, the first outside of the universities. A High Churchman, he had been chaplain to William Van Mildert, the last prince bishop of Durham, a relative of White's mother. Perhaps White felt that Van Mildert's support for Phillpotts' appointment to Exeter would work in his favour. Certainly Phillpotts encouraged the restoration and building of churches, together with parsonage houses and schools, providing fertile ground for architectural ambition. Many clergymen appointed to livings in the county would have known Henry Master White as a fellow and tutor at Oxford. Perhaps it was anticipation of work through these contacts that persuaded William to settle so far from his family home and from London.

While William White was living in Truro it is likely that he worshipped at the church of St Cuby at Kenwyn, a short walk up the hill from his lodgings at 50 Ferris Town.[30] The High Church rector of the large, well-endowed parish of Kenwyn and Kea since 1828 was the Rev. George James Cornish, who was a close friend of John Keble, J. T.

Coleridge and Thomas Arnold during their Oxford days together. Cornish was Vice-President of the Exeter Diocesan Architectural Society in 1844. His eldest surviving son, Robert Kestell, had attended Winchester College, but after an accident that resulted in the loss of his right eye, he was 'obliged to leave the school in the course of the first half year'.[31] Robert, like Henry Master White, was a life member of the Oxford Architectural Society. It is probable therefore that William would have had an introduction to the vicarage at Kenwyn.

St Michael and All Angels, Baldhu

When he died in 1841 the 1st earl of Falmouth left a site at Baldhu (which means 'Black Mine'), about four miles south-west of Truro and within the parish of Kenwyn and Kea, for a church to serve the employees of a mining enterprise (that never materialised). The incumbent was the Rev. William Haslam, graduate of Van Mildert's University of Durham, and a member of the Exeter Diocesan Architectural Society although not a High Churchman In May 1847 Haslam applied for a grant from the Incorporated Church Building Society (ICBS) towards the cost, estimated at £1,755, of building a new church at Baldhu, to designs by William White – his first known commission.

The simple design, approximately 90ft x 40ft, consists of unbuttressed nave and chancel under one roof, with a separately gabled south aisle, the two unbroken, parallel, roofs typical of the county. The walls are of silvery elvan (the local quartz-porphyry) rubble with Portland stone for the windows and arcade, under sombre Delabole slate roofs (**1.3**). Reporting on White's original plans, the ICBS demanded that the Decorated style of the splay-footed spire north-east of the nave (redolent more of Northamptonshire than of Cornwall) be followed in the window tracery. Their comment that the arches of the nave arcade 'should be two-centred instead of four-centred' demonstrates that White was proposing a Perpendicular style rather than the 'middle-pointed' advocated by the Camdenians. As patron of the living, the 2nd earl of Falmouth had agreed to pay half the cost, his generosity reflected in the B (for Boscawen, his family name) and F carved in the dripstone label stops to the windows and painted on some of the corbels inside the church. White's botanical interest is reflected in the carving of the arcade capitals depicting the lily, convolvulus, oak and vine. Oak leaves and acorns decorate the wall-plate of the arched-braced nave roof, while that in the chancel is carved with vine leaves and grapes. The corbels of the tower arch bear portrait heads of Bishop Philpotts and the young Queen Victoria, carved 'with a grace and delicacy which could hardly have been expected from a provincial sculptor too closely engaged in his ordinary work to allow him to devote much time to the higher branches of his profession'.[32] Colour was provided by the stained glass to the tracery and borders of the east window, by Beer of Exeter; the green cathedral glass (with white borders) in the remaining windows, and the buff, red and black floor tiles, as well as the 'rich crimson velvet' of the altar frontal 'beautifully embroidered by Mrs Haslam'.[33]

Henry Master White took a lively interest in William's work, presenting an ancient

1.3 St Michael and All Angels, Baldhu, Cornwall, 1847-8, from the south. Having been vandalised and boarded up for many years, the church has now been converted into two dwellings with the addition of the triangular dormers.

piece of silver as an alms dish and preaching the sermon on the evening of the consecration, Thursday 20 July 1848, the anniversary of the laying of the foundation stone. The Rev. Haslam reported that 'The Church is completed in a manner wh[ich] meets the approval and admiration of all who see it.'[34] It also shows that from his first commission William White was concerned with simple outlines, the articulation of mass using satisfying proportions, the employment of local materials, an attention to detail, particularly stone carving, stained glass and ironwork, and the inclusion of colour.

St Gerrent's, Gerrans

The earl of Falmouth also subscribed to the rebuilding of the parish church at Gerrans, on the east side of the Roseland Peninsula, south of Truro. The Rev. William Longlands, rector since 1844, had been awarded a grant by the ICBS for the rebuilding of his church in 1846 to plans by a Mr Pryor. Only the fifteenth-century west tower and spire were deemed worthy of preservation. Despite the propping of the cracked and mouldy walls and the rotting floors, the Rev. Longlands had to overcome the opposition of the ratepayers to restore the church, which was described as 'a dishonour to God, and a disgrace to the parish'.[35] A fire in 1848 that partly destroyed the roof may have been the spur, for in March 1849 Longlands applied again to the ICBS for a larger grant based on plans, and an estimate of £1,025 prepared by William White, 'the talented architect of Baldiu [sic] Church', that he considered 'much better than those originally sent'.[36]

In justification of his rebuilding White explained to the Secretary of the ICBS that

> The Reason for pulling down the old Church is that it is in such a state of dilapidation it <u>could</u> not be restored without it. The eastern walls being propped, and from ten to fourteen inches out of perpendicular, and the side walls from six to ten inches out. I think it necessary that the Character of the old Church should be preserved as no other proportions would be suitable to the Steeple which is still in substantial condition; and I consider it otherwise desirable to retain its present character because it contains some peculiarities of style which it would be wrong to destroy. I also consider that the nature of the material is such that for a Church in that neighbourhood it could not be improved.[37]

1.4 East end at Gerrans, Cornwall, 1849–50, showing the Perpendicular window to the vestry, and the jambs of some of the windows which are of monolithic stones.

1.5 White used variously coloured slatestones to form voussoirs to some of the windows at Gerrans.

This reflects White's antiquarian, picturesque aesthetic, as well as his appreciation of vernacular style and use of local materials that would imbue all his work. His 'literal rebuilding, the very stones of the almost Debased piers and arches having been replaced, and the old windows, so far as possible, used again' did not meet the approval of *The Ecclesiologist*, which decided that this 'was an instance where a wholly new church might have been expected.'[38]

At Gerrans White again employed a simple outline, with no buttresses, to the continuous nave and chancel, north transept and south aisle that are constructed of slatestone rubble. Dressings are of granite and freestone, some being single huge, vertical blocks to form the window jambs. The windows range from simple single lancets, 3-light windows in Decorated style, to a small Perpendicular light removed from the north chancel wall and inserted in the east wall of the new vestry, constructed to the north east of the chancel

1.6 Undisguised pegs and dowels in the construction of White's benches at Gerrans with their crisply rolled edges.

(**1.4**). The variety of these styles was to reflect the continued development of the building since its foundation in the thirteenth century. Around the heads of some windows White arranged thin pieces of slatestone, not unlike voussoirs, without disturbing the flatness of the wall surface (**1.5**).

The interior of the church is equally simple with plastered walls beneath a trussed rafter roof. Although the rood screen and font cover have now been removed, White's wooden altar rail with curving iron supports like bishops' crosiers fortunately remains. So, too, do White's oak benches with their rolled edges and simple pegged construction – described by Clive Wainwright as 'splendidly plain and solid' – which pre-date William Morris's massive furniture of 1856 onwards (**1.6**).[39]

Kea school

In 1849 the Rev. George Cornish donated a plot of land near the church at Kea, south-west of Truro, for a school 'for the Education of Children … of the labouring manufacturing and other poorer classes in the Parish'.[40] He commissioned William White to design a new school for the site - a simple, single-storied schoolroom with a large porch, constructed of shale rubble and granite dressings under a slate roof, with pivoting windows (**1.7**).[41] Cornish had previously applied for Kea School to be united to the National Society (for the Education of the Poor according to the Principles of the Church of England). Fear of political unrest in the wake of the French Revolution, together with dissenting and evangelical emphasis on self-improvement, had provoked the Church of England into establishing the National Society in 1811, with funding from the government. With legislation in 1833 prohibiting children under the age of nine from working in factories, there was an even greater need to provide an education that would supply a suitably educated and morally upright labouring class. The widespread expansion of the National Schools building programme, including provision for each new school to have a house for the master/mistress, for which government grants were introduced in 1843, afforded considerable opportunities to nineteenth-century architects.

As *The Ecclesiologist* of 1847 pointed out, unlike churches, there were no medieval precedents for the design of schools, since 'Worldly knowledge was not then necessary for the poor'.[42] However, 'the moral importance of impressing children with the dignity of education' demanded the highest aesthetic standards, and *The Ecclesiologist* recommended that the school should be 'the prettiest building in the village, next to the church'.[43] Henry Kendall Jr advised 'that the style of our old English Architecture seems especially adapted for School Building'.[44] This Tudor style was popular for academic buildings, since it reflected that Golden Age when many schools were established. Joseph Clarke, architect to various diocesan boards of education, believed that 'it need not any longer be deemed a ruinous expense to attempt to give our Village Schools that character and association which so naturally belongs to them.'[45] Both Kendall and Clarke were architects and antiquaries, whose interest lay mainly in the appearance of the buildings:

1.7 Single-celled Kea school, Cornwall, 1849-51, with its large entrance porch. White normally eschewed bargeboards, so these may be later additions.

it would be some time before educational theories became influential in the design of school buildings. White was a leader in this respect. His plans usually included a substantial east-facing window. Based on the experience of a clergyman 'for many years engaged in tuition' (perhaps his father or grandfather), White believed that 'the cheerfulness of the morning sun sets up scholars as well as master for the rest of the day.'[46]

St Columb Major rectory

Cornish's son-in-law, the Rev. William David Morrice, curate of Probus, less than five miles north-east of Truro, commissioned William White to design a school there (now demolished). Morrice was a founder member of the Cambridge Camden Society, and also belonged to the Exeter Diocesan Architectural Society. He may well have introduced White to the Rev. Dr Samuel Edmund Walker, also a member of both the Cambridge and the Exeter societies. Walker was the only son of Edmund Walker, a barrister and master of the Exchequer Office. He attended both Cambridge and then Oxford universities, before being instituted as rector of St Columb Major, Cornwall, in 1841, his father having bought the valuable benefice in 1826. The Rev. Walker was obviously deeply attracted to the Oxford Movement which resulted in his being,

> at daggers drawn …[with] the great body of his parishioners … in consequence of the Tractarian fooleries which the rev. gentleman has introduced into the services of the church, and the alterations he has taken upon himself to make in the interior of the sacred edifice, for the purpose of adapting it to his Popish notions of public worship.[47]

Knowing Bishop Phillpotts was anxious to establish a separate Cornish see, Walker

1.8 St Columb rectory, Cornwall, 'as rebuilt 1851', print by Leighton Brothers, 4 Red Lion Square, from an original drawing by White. The fireproof stone staircase is shown in the two lower drawings, separated by plans of the ground and first floors, together with a section.

hoped it would be based at St Columb, and in 1849 commissioned William White to 'restore' the moated parsonage there with that end in view. The building had been known as 'the college' because it had formerly accommodated not only the rector, but also priests and deacons in a collegiate type of school. This house had been destroyed by fire in 1701 but rebuilt to a similar quadrangular plan.[48] Although White's drawings and specification appear to have been lost, an engraving of his perspective view also includes a section and plans (**1.8**).[49] White's design followed the footprint of the old house, retaining the central courtyard, with the walls and roofs rebuilt where necessary, but with new carved stonework for the windows and arches.[50] It was described by *The Ecclesiologist* as 'very good indeed; it will look a very model of domestic religious architecture'. Unaware of Walker's intentions, this praise was qualified by the observation that 'it looks too large for the residence of any one priest'.[51]

Undoubtedly White's design, as with his restoration of the church at Gerrans, reflects his respect for the 'ancient shell' that he had 'to work upon and enlarge.'[52] The addition of numerous gabled dormer windows has since destroyed the simplicity and power of the building's outline that White believed so important. Similarly, the insertion of some new windows has spoilt the balance provided by areas of plain slatestone rubble walling to the heavily traceried windows of the main rooms (**1.9**). These changes have produced a more overtly picturesque building than White's original, with its strong rooflines and windows barely disturbing the surface of the wall plane. Although varied, the windows are not strictly indicative of the purposes of the rooms they illuminate: the great five-light cusped window at the northern end of the east entrance front is reminiscent of the original chapel in that position rather than the drawing room of White's design. However, together with the two gabled windows of the adjacent dining room and the oriel to the library on the south elevation (**1.10**) they illuminate a suite of public rooms suitable for a bishop. White ensured the safety of the occupants by providing a fireproof staircase; the sharp lines of its granite piers contrasting with the sinuous iron supports of the balustrade (**1.11**).

1.9 Several dormer windows have been inserted later at St Columb rectory, but the first-floor window on the extreme left appears to have been a variation to White's original scheme,

1.10　The library oriel at St Columb rectory. The column seems to have been added later for support. Philip Webb included a similar oriel at Red House for William Morris, 1858.

White also designed furniture for the Rev. Dr Walker's rectory. A surviving piece, now in the Victoria and Albert Museum, is a dining chair of oak with an octagonal back, inlaid with walnut, mahogany and ebony (**1.12**).[53] White developed and simplified this design, but still utilised circular as well as square sections, for dining chairs at Humewood (Chap. 6). At Bishop's Court (Chap. 5), he designed an even simpler frame, but as at Humewood an embossed, coloured and gilded family device ornamented the leather-upholstered backs.

Having allegedly spent more than £7,000 of his own money on the rebuilding of the rectory, Dr Walker proposed to give the advowson of the parish as an endowment for a Cornish see. He also offered his 'beautiful house erected in the best style of Medieval architecture – a house, indeed, singularly adapted for the residence of a Bishop, and always, as it now appears intended for that purpose.'[54] Although St Columb was unusual in the size of its parsonage house and the wealth of its patron, it was the first of many residences that White designed for Church of England clergy.

Parsonages in England

As Nikolaus Pevsner has pointed out, the grouping of church and parsonage is an English feature that has no parallel in Europe, and distinctive features denoting the function of parsonages were not employed until the Victorian era.[55] Before then, the parson's residence was indistinguishable from any other private house, either by its style or

1.11 The fireproof granite staircase at St Columb rectory seems 'modernist' in the simplicity of its stonework and the detailing of the iron supports for the handrail.

29

location. This period of transition at the beginning of the nineteenth century, excellently surveyed and analysed by Timothy Brittain-Catlin, demonstrates the economic and social changes taking place in the new century.[56] The parsonage houses that William White created reflect not only the development of the Gothic style in secular buildings, but also differences in the structure and operation of the established Church that were occurring as the nineteenth century progressed.

Medieval parish churches owned land for the support of the priest – the glebe – hence the farm buildings that often surrounded the incumbent's house. The 'living' was originally a payment to the priest by parishioners of one-tenth, a 'tithe', of the production of the parish. 'Great tithes', of corn, grain, hay and wood were paid to the rector, while 'small tithes' on all other produce went to the vicar. After the upheavals of the Reformation and the Civil War, the poor state of the remaining parsonage houses prompted the establishment in 1704 of a fund, known as Queen Anne's Bounty, to help to repair them or to build new residences. Progress was slow. For example, in his *Rural Rides* published in 1830, William Cobbett noted that, on his journey beside the River Avon in Wiltshire, in nine of the twenty-nine parishes through which he passed, the parsonage house was either so dilapidated as to be uninhabitable, or the parish was without one altogether.

The Ecclesiastical Commission was established in 1835 to instigate reform of the distribution of the revenues of the Church of England. A year later the Tithe Commutation Act established procedures for changing tithes into rent charges based on the average price of the three main cereal crops during the preceding seven years. Although many tithes had in practice been paid in cash, this confirmed a position where the clergy no longer shared the day-to-day and seasonal activities of their parishioners. When William White's paternal grandfather, Harry White, was rector of Fyfield, Hampshire (1762-1788), his glebe farm supported his family of ten children, as well as the young men who attended his little academy. Wheat was grown for bread and barley for beer, as well as fruit and vegetables, while livestock provided meat, and even tobacco was produced.[57] The rector of Fyfield was popular with all classes of society in the locality, being 'ever ready with quotations from the classic authors, and familiar with all country loving subjects', including coursing and hunting in which he participated.[58]

Through the early nineteenth century increased yields resulting from enclosure and more scientific farming methods, together with the Corn Laws to protect prices, enhanced revenues so that many livings were seen as suitable for younger sons of the gentry. No longer did the incumbent require barns, granaries, cow houses or piggeries, for most of his glebe was rented out with just sufficient retained to produce fodder for his horse. His house, which had previously comprised a parlour, kitchen and dairy with bedrooms above, now required a drawing room, dining room and study, or even a library. Increasingly the clergy were seen, and saw themselves, as country gentlemen, graduates of the universities, often men of private means employing a large domestic staff and inhabiting correspondingly ample parsonage houses.

The granting of full social and political rights to dissenters and the emancipation of Catholics weakened the hold of the Church of England. This increasing tide of liberalism and the government's proposal to abolish ten bishoprics in Ireland provoked John Newman, John Keble, Edward Pusey and others at Oxford University into publishing, from 1833, *Tracts for the Times*. Initially philosophical essays encouraging greater seriousness and spirituality, as well as more frequent celebration of the Eucharist and adherence to the Book of Common Prayer, they developed into polemical demands for the independence of the Church based on the theory of apostolic succession – the Oxford Movement. The Tractarian emphasis on spirituality and sacramentalism resulted in the gradual diminution of the role of the church for any purpose other than services. Parish meetings, confirmation classes, tea parties for the school children all tended to take place at the parsonage house, which became the hub of village cultural life. The parson was often also a source of medicines, clothes, and other essentials that were dispensed to

1.12 Oak chair, its octagonal back inlaid with mahogany, walnut and ebony in a star pattern with fleur-de-lys ends, designed by White for St Columb rectory, *c.*1851.

the needy of the village, necessitating increased storage space in the parsonage house.[59]

In 1830, the same year that *Rural Rides* appeared, Francis Goodwin, architect, published a series of designs, including plans for a parsonage house to be expressed 'in the cottage style, blended with the more imposing style of work which flourished in the middle ages'.[60] Like others, Goodwin believed that 'the old English domestic style' was not only capable of providing all modern, necessary conveniences, but allowed the architectural character of the Rectory to 'be in conformity with the church'.[61] Through his eldest brother, Henry, it is likely that White would have been aware of a paper on the design of parsonage houses that John Billing, architect of Reading and London, in whose office Philip Webb was articled (1849–52), read to the Oxford Architectural Society. Billing demonstrated that in 1850 Goodwin's ideas were still current, arguing that the incumbent's house should be within sight of his church and should be in

> strict accordance with those feelings which its consecrated character calls forth;
> old English Domestic Architecture, with its high-pitched roofs, and substantial

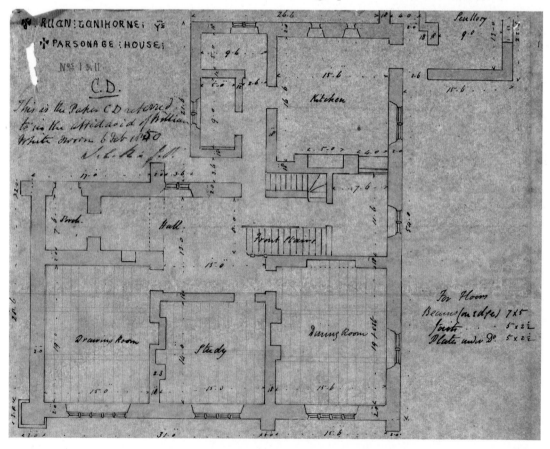

1.13 White often employed the L-shaped plan, allowing the principal rooms a mainly southerly aspect over the gardens, first seen here at Ruan Lanihorne rectory, Cornwall, 1850–1.

1.14 Cusped windows to the staircase and ventilators to the kitchen at Ruan Lanihorne indicate their varied functions as Pugin advocated.

character is best suited to fulfil this condition; it is also capable of being adapted to the peculiar materials of the respective localities, which should always be made use of, if possible, for economy and to avoid singularity.[62]

This support for the Picturesque was an endorsement of Pugin's demand that 'An architect should exhibit his skill by turning the difficulties which occur in raising an elevation from a *convenient plan* into so many *picturesque beauties*.'[63] It was reiterated by the Camdenians, who were 'more and more convinced that the true picturesque follows the sternest utility.'[64] White's buildings were very often described by *The Ecclesiologist* as picturesque. In fact, his first documented parsonage, at Ruan Lanihorne, Cornwall, was labelled by *The Ecclesiologist* as 'so irregular and picturesque … [it] might, in reality, appear exaggerated.'[65] It is possible that the criticism implicit in this comment was the result of White's individuality, his refusal to adopt wholeheartedly the Camdenians' preferred Middle Pointed style. Not for him the employment of details culled directly from medieval buildings, but his own interpretation and synthesis, based on practicalities and function.

Ruan Lanihorne rectory, Cornwall

The rector of Ruan Lanihorne, five miles south-east of Truro, appointed in 1849 was Henry Spencer Slight, a fellow of Corpus Christi College, Oxford. He had been senior dean and later bursar of his college and a select preacher to the university, and was, presumably, known to Henry Master White. The rector's accommodation was far from acceptable; in February 1850 White certified that the existing parsonage house was 'in a low and damp Situation ... is ill arranged and in a decayed and dilapidated condition.'[66] Allowing £30 for the value of old materials reused, White's design was estimated at £975 for the construction in 'Stone to be raised, and drawn from the quarry in the Parsonage field ... [with dressings] of good sound and durable St. Stephen's Granite.'[67] This L-shaped plan (**1.13**) became characteristic of White: the principal family rooms were arranged to take advantage of a generally southerly aspect, while the domestic offices and servants' quarters were contained in a north-easterly block, diminishing to a single storey, visually helping to anchor the building in the landscape. The staircase hall, with its fireplace and galleried landing, reflects that in Pugin's own home, The Grange, at Ramsgate and his parsonages at Rampisham and Lanteglos, described by Timothy Brittain-Catlin.[68] The hierarchy of social classes is evident in the provision of a first-floor water closet for the family but earth privies for the servants 'roofed with materials from the old house', and set well away from the main dwelling.[69]

Designs for the rectory at Ruan Lanihorne, dated January 1850, are an excellent

1.15 The massive offset entrance door of Ruan Lanihorne rectory. The smaller door in the angle gave parishioners access to the study.

1.16 Drip-moulds to the windows, heavy eaves and non-structural timber work have been added later to the garden elevation at Ruan Lanihorne.

example of White's belief that it is proportion and outline which define a building's purpose and character, rather than a reliance on details. This he expounded in his paper 'Upon Some of the Causes and Points of Failure in Modern Design' of 1851, and although he believed that the various functions of a dwelling should be 'almost distinguishable from the exterior', he did not advocate a '*needless* multiplicity of gables', nor conversely a square plan.[70] The entrance front here consisted of two lower gables of uneven heights and widths set between two higher gables (**1.14**). Although later alterations and additions have obliterated much of the original entrance facade, it is still obvious why it might have been regarded as 'so irregular' (**1.15**). Unfortunately the garden front has been stuccoed, giving this elevation a heavy regularity which detaches it from the rest of the building (**1.16**).

1.17 St Ive rectory, Cornwall, 1852-4, has an unusual kitchen window of local dark red sandstone, incorporating three ventilators above the four lancets.

St Ive rectory, Cornwall

Some similar features can be discerned in White's more mature design of 1852-4 for a new rectory at St Ive, near Callington, Cornwall. Again, the entrance is on the north elevation, so not requiring a porch for shelter from the prevailing winds, and is approached via the kitchen (**1.17**). The entrance door is at the eastern end of this elevation, below a massive gable, bare apart from a cusped lancet at first-floor level. The windows are flush with the surface of the rubble stone walls, and this smoothness is emphasised by the omission of any eaves or copings: the roof tiles finish flush with the gable ends. Articulation would have been provided by a large chimneystack, also of local rubble stone, adjacent to the main entrance (**1.18**). The south elevation demonstrates how White was now beginning to separate the ecclesiastical from the secular aspect of the house (**1.19**). The buttress and the single cusped window are the only intimations that this residence has any clerical connections. The eight-pane sashes are redolent of the old rectory, as well as being precursors of the revival of the Queen Anne style, while the stone relieving arches indicate White's awareness of the effects to be achieved by structural polychromy. The first-floor windows are mostly simple casements, in pairs or triplets, set close under the eaves, a feature that would become one of White's hallmarks. This would be adopted later by C.F.A. Voysey, who also seems to have heeded White's plea for prominent gutter 'brackets of iron, running as far down the wall as they are hung

1.18 The entrance elevation at St Ive rectory, showing the original chimneystack before it was dismantled.

out from it, with a twisted or otherwise ornamented, or even plain *stay*, to carry it.'[71]

The house accommodated the archdeacon of Bodmin and rector of St Ive, Reginald Hobhouse (another Oxford graduate and member of the Exeter Diocesan Architectural Society), his wife, Caroline, daughter of the 8th Baronet Salusbury-Trelawny, and their five children, who were all born there.[72] In 1861 domestic staff at the rectory consisted of a groom and his wife, a cook, two nursemaids and a housemaid. The service area was accommodated in a cross-wing at the western end of the house, with a single-storey extension (**1.20**). A yard separates this end of the house from detached stables, loose box and coach house, while the remains of sties and other farm buildings associated with the old parsonage perhaps imply that the archdeacon still maintained the glebe farm.

These two early designs demonstrate that, as the son of a clerical family, White was well aware of the ambiguous position of the parsonage house, being both ecclesiastical and yet, as a family home, also secular. White confronted this boldly, often, as at St Ive, placing the service wing in full view of the main entrance, as did Pugin in his own house at Ramsgate. This contrasts with William Butterfield's conventional plan for his 1845 parsonage at Coalpit Heath, Gloucestershire. These early years in Cornwall, where the local granite precluded anything but the simplest decoration, reinforced White's belief in the importance of massing and outline. But like all young architects, White needed commissions. A letter from his friend, the Rev. J.F. Kitson of Antony, acknowledged

1.19 The south elevation of St Ive rectory displays minimal ecclesiastical references. Red sandstone defines the tympana above the dining room sash windows.

1.20 The extended roofs of the service wing at St Ive form an almost sculptural composition.

that he was 'sorry to hear you have so little to do: I wish I could give you something to do here'.[73] (White's bank and solicitors' offices in Truro are considered in chapter 4.) Fortunately, it seems that White did not have to wait very long before an opportunity arose that would lead to his return to London.

2

From Notting Hill to the Cape

The Rev. Dr Samuel Edmund Walker, rector of St Columb Major since 1841, wished to increase his endowment for a separate Cornish bishopric, based at his White-designed rectory. On the death of his father in 1851 he invested his inherited fortune (reckoned to be £250,000) in speculative property developments, first in Gravesend, and then in west London. He decided to develop land at Notting Hill with, at its centre, a collegiate church with attached choir school in memory of his parents. He commissioned White to undertake the design, and chose a site, now on Talbot Road, on land purchased from the Portobello estate.

All Saints', Notting Hill

All Saints', Notting Hill, with its collegiate buildings, was White's first design in the capital, and was originally described by *The Ecclesiologist* as 'of great size and dignity'.[1] A copy of the 'large lithographed view, taken from the south-west' on which the commendation was based shows the church forming the south side of the choir school quadrangle, its four-bay nave and slightly lower chancel beneath steeply-pitched roofs, with a tall western steeple (**2.1**). The material appears to be ashlar under slated roofs: there was no mention of constructional colour. *The Ecclesiologist* was critical of the shallow roofs of the aisles and the smallness of the transepts, but considered the 'unusually lofty' tower to have 'great merit', and the associated buildings 'extensive … [with] a good, but simple, clock-tower.'[2] This accommodation was for ten 'foundation' choristers, who would be 'boarded, lodged and educated in vocal and instrumental music … free of expense.'[3] A further six boys were to receive a free education, both general and musical, and would dine with the choirmaster every Sunday and holy day. The choir would provide a full cathedral service daily, for which they would be required to 'attend the practices and rehearsals with strict punctuality'.

By the time of the fourteenth annual meeting of the Ecclesiological Society in June 1853, All Saints', measuring approximately 90ft x 60ft, was described as 'a church of large size and great cost, in which also the use of constructional colour will be exemplified.'[4] A report based on the working drawings noted that 'much internal constructive coloration

2.1 A lost perspective of White's original design for All Saints', Notting Hill, with its associated choir school. The only constructional colour would have been the red crested ridge tiles that became one of White's signature features.

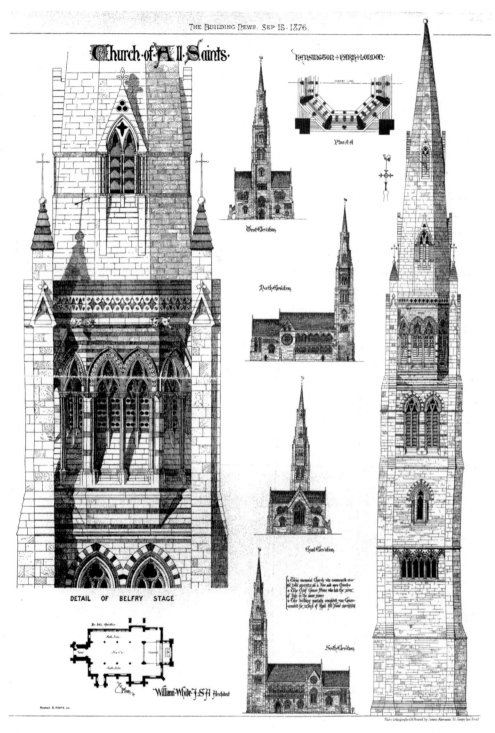

2.2 Although building began in 1852 and the church was consecrated when partially completed in 1861, *Building News* published this illustration of All Saints', Notting Hill, in 1876.

is intended to be used in the walls, and there will also be coloured bands in the tower, of red sandstone and Bath stone alternating.'[5] Eventually the design incorporated 'bands and arch-stones of coloured stone – red, grey, and buff – brought from Sudeley in Gloucestershire, Nailsea in Somerset, and St Columb in Cornwall' (**2.2**).[6] Although the three lower stages of the tower remain plain, the octagonal belfry stage is comprised of horizontal bands of different coloured stone with shafts of Devon and Cornish 'marble' in contrasting colours.

The question of constructional and applied colour was one of the compelling issues confronting nineteenth-century British architects. It developed from earlier European Romantic interest in the use of colour found in the eastern Mediterranean. In 1836 applied colour was of sufficient interest for the Institute of British Architects to establish a Polychrome Committee to examine traces of colour on the Elgin Marbles. The same year, the first coloured prints of Owen Jones's detailed drawings of the Alhambra palace, Granada, were published in London, the resulting volumes appearing in 1842-5. Jones was responsible for the decorative scheme for the Crystal Palace that became a *cause célèbre* in 1850. His proposals to paint the concave surfaces blue, the convex yellow, with red on the horizontal members and white on the verticals aroused intense criticism, but were approved by Prince Albert. In 1835 Pugin had constructed his first building, his own home, St Marie's Grange, Salisbury, of red brick with patterns of black brick headers and stone dressings, and employed similar polychrome patterning in the Bishop's House, Birmingham, five years later.

Being born and bred in Northamptonshire, White was accustomed to the traditional banding of the local stone that varies in colour from rich yellow to dark, chocolate brown. He later remarked that 'the diversity of tone, from brown to yellow … would not be safe or right to aim at by imitative means'.[7] And it would have been difficult for White to ignore Ruskin's espousal of the value of different coloured stones in his *The Seven Lamps of Architecture* of 1849. It was, perhaps, no coincidence that an early paper extolling the properties of polychromatic brickwork was read in 1847 to the Architectural Society of the Archdeaconry of Northampton (of which his mentor, Sir Henry Dryden, was a founding vice-president).[8] Although his client was sufficiently wealthy to build in stone, White could not have been unaffected by the polychromatic brickwork of Butterfield's All Saints', then rising in Margaret Street, Westminster. It is tempting to conjecture that the simple massiveness of White's original scheme was formulated in the granite fastness of Cornwall, but revised in the light of metropolitan influences after his move to London in 1851.

Internally White achieved a feeling of great spaciousness, due, in part, to the continuation of the nave arcades and clerestory windows across the transepts. Originally the lower part of the walls was lined with black, red and buff tiles and bricks, arranged 'to increase in lightness upwards'; while the height of the lining increased eastwards.[9] This banded polychromy, that reflected the growing interest in geology, was recommended

2.3 The plate tracery of the clerestory windows inlaid with turquoise, cerulean, ultramarine and chrysoprase mosaic, executed by Mr Steven of Pimlico.

by Ruskin in the first volume of *The Stones of Venice*, published in 1851, and adopted later by G.E. Street (see **2.4**).[10] The three pairs of clerestory windows each side of the nave were decorated with White's designs described as 'an arrangement of gold, red and blue circles, and triangles: on the inside of the church these are formed into flowers, and connected with green stems (**2.3**). Fortunately this mosaic work survived a World War II bomb that destroyed the south-east corner of the church and blew out all the glass. There is therefore no evidence remaining of the double-glazing that White later reported was effective in keeping out 'cold and noise'.[11]

Dr Walker was a naïve investor, advancing £66,000 to London builders, particularly to one D.A. Ramsay, on security of building leases that he himself granted. When Ramsay was declared bankrupt in February 1854, Walker's empire collapsed.[12] In March 1855 building work at All Saints' came to a halt, with £2,000 outstanding to the builder, Myers of Lambeth. Although it was roofed and glazed, the interior was undecorated and unfurnished and the spire and the great flying buttresses to the west side of the tower

44

were unbuilt (and remain so). The Rev. John Light, who was offered the incumbency by Dr Walker in 1859, eventually raised funds to pay off Myers and to complete the interior, reputedly under the supervision of his brother, a civil engineer. The church was consecrated on 9 April 1861, when it was described as 'a noble building … and of innovation on the ordinary run of Gothic revival', which, had it been completed according to White's plans 'would have more than rivalled its namesake in Margaret-street'.[13] Walker put his affairs in the hands of trustees and moved abroad, not returning until shortly before his death in 1869. In 1864 the painter Henry Holiday was commissioned by a Mr T.M. Kitchin to paint the east chancel wall with life-sized figures, the Nativity on one side of the altar, on the other the Annunciation, the latter reproduced by Charles Eastlake as the frontispiece to his *History of the Gothic Revival*.[14] White was not involved with Holiday's scheme, which was probably obliterated by the incumbent in 1932, who decided that the church was dingy and that 'the first necessity seemed to be a coat of whitewash!'[15] This, together with the later bomb damage, has left little evidence of the rich interior colouring that contributed to an overall cost of more than £20,000.

By comparison, just one quarter of that amount was spent on the erection of All Saints', Boyne Hill, Maidenhead, 1854-7, G.E. Street's first major church commission. Street had visited Italy in 1853 and published an account of his journey, *Brick and Marble in the Middle Ages*, in 1855, the year that construction began at Boyne Hill. Street's church (approximately 80ft x 45ft overall) is constructed of the local red brick, ornamented

2.4 All Saints', Boyne Hill, Maidenhead, 1854-7 by G.E. Street. The lower part of the chancel walls are a riot of stencilling and inlay of enamel and differently coloured marbles, as Ruskin recommended.

2.5 Henry Master White (1820-92), William's eldest brother, who first went to the Cape in 1848.

with horizontal bands of stone and narrow black bricks. Internally, the nave is of brick in bands and diaper pattern, while the upper part of the chancel is decorated with horizontal bands of green, yellow, red and buff vitreous tiles, alternating with alabaster, above stencilled patterning (**2.4**).

It is interesting to compare the inlaid decoration of All Saints', Notting Hill, and All Saints', Boyne Hill. White's design, although composed mostly of geometrical triangles and circles, is quite delicate and flowing; Street's is a more insistent, regular pattern of quatrefoils and circles, covering every inch of the east wall. White's constructional polychromy has been described as '(like his religion) … less aggressive, [and] more immediately engaging than … Street's'.[16] This seems to be a reflection of White's upbringing in a High Church, clerical family, where the quiet piety and reserve of John Keble would have been the accepted attitude to religion. Certainly William's eldest brother, Henry Master White, was remembered for his reserved manner. But Henry used his Oxford contacts and his various clerical positions to provide William with architectural commissions. The first of these was in South Africa.

South Africa

His education at Winchester and Oxford allowed Henry Master White to move in circles that were at the heart of the growing Tractarian movement (**2.5**). After his ordination in 1846, Henry remained at New College as a tutor. Together with the Rev. Henry Gordon Merriman of his college, he became a life member of the Oxford Architectural Society, whose president, the Rev. William Sewell, and vice-president, the Rev. William Heathcote, were among his Wykehamist friends. Sewell had established St Columba's College in 1843 to promote High Church principles in Ireland. Francis

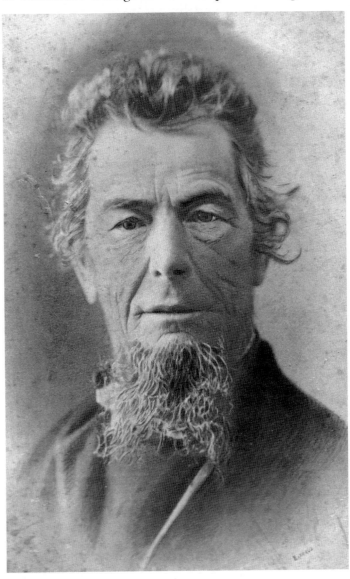

2.6 Nathaniel James Merriman (1809-82) appointed archdeacon of Grahamstown in 1848.

Gilbert White, William's brother, was at St Columba's in 1849, when William 'furnished him with plans' for new buildings at Holly Park, unfortunately never built.[17] Sewell returned to England, creating St Peter's College, Radley, in 1847. William Heathcote was cousin of the 5th baronet, patron of the living of Hursley, Hampshire, occupied from 1836 by John Keble. In 1848 Merriman's elder brother, Nathaniel, vicar of Street, Somerset, accepted a proposal to be archdeacon of Albany, based in Grahamstown, South Africa (**2.6**). This position was offered to him by Robert Gray, bishop of Cape Town, who was a patron of the Oxford Architectural Society (**2.7**).

In the spring of 1848 Bishop Gray wrote to his sister that 'God has richly comforted me on this day by a letter from Merriman informing me of Mr White, a Fellow and Tutor of New College, a first-class man, offering to come out for five years at his own expense. I was just wanting such a man ...'.[18] It seems that Henry chose to go to the Cape for his health, but where he could 'at the same time be useful in the Church.'[19] He duly accompanied archdeacon Merriman and his party and set sail from Gravesend in the *Gwalior* on 27 August 1848, arriving at the Cape in November. During the passage Henry began to learn Dutch and on arrival applied himself to 'Kaffir'.[20] He appears to have wasted no time in involving his brother William in proposals for buildings in the Cape Colony (**2.8**).[21] Bishop Gray had intended that Henry White should assist

2.7 Robert Gray (1809-72), bishop of Cape Town and founder of Bishops Diocesan College.

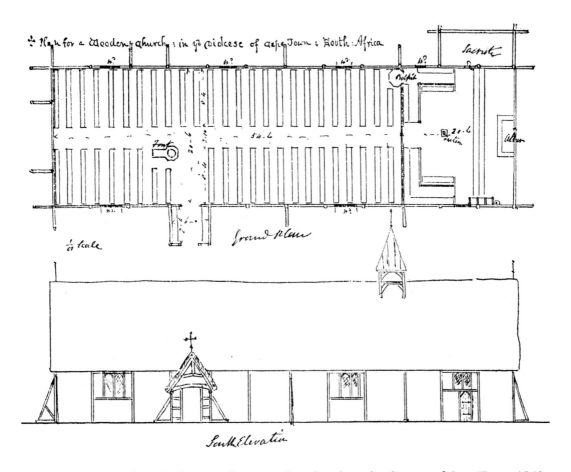

2.8 White's plan and south elevation for a wooden church in the diocese of Cape Town, 1849.

Merriman, and be the principal of a grammar school in Grahamstown, but delays in establishing a school there kept White in Cape Town. Gray took advantage of this to appoint Henry as acting principal of a collegiate school that he opened in March 1849 in unoccupied buildings adjacent to his residence at Protea, later known as Bishopscourt. He explained that 'We should wish our Institution to be somewhat similar to Radley, not taking children younger than 10, but keeping them perhaps till 17 or 18, or even longer … It is a disappointment to me not to secure White permanently, but I think he has set his heart on the East, on the score of health chiefly.'[22]

Bishops Diocesan College, Cape Town

In April 1849 Henry wrote to William explaining that,

> in the present house there cannot be much increase of numbers, & as more are
> likely to apply for admission, I think before long some new buildings must be

erected, or another house looked out. Now it seems to me that there are very great advantages in buildings erected for the purpose, & therefore I wish you to turn the matter over in your mind so as to be ready to send plans if I write for them – and particularly to see Radley so as to know their system, & the advantages of their internal arrangements. If you are at Oxford Sewell or Heathcote will give you the proper introduction; or Merriman will help you to get it. What I want is to have large bed rooms, with each bed parted off as it is at Radley, as that system allows of more privacy to each boy than anything short of separate bed rooms for each, and is more easily kept under perfect control than even separate rooms.[23]

The dormitory, with its emphasis on the rule of 'Sileatur in Dormitorio', was one of Radley's defining features. William Sewell announced in a sermon of 1853 that 'If silence, if privacy, and if separation cannot be maintained in your Dormitory, first I will close your Chapel, and then I will close the College.'[24] Sewell's regime provoked criticism from some of the old school who thought it 'calculated to make the boys *milk-sops*'.[25] However, others believed it was a system 'in many respects better suited for the sons of gentlemen who are wished to be brought up as gentlemen' believing that it would 'cure some of the worst evils of the old system'.[26] Henry White, having endured 'the roughness and brutality … of Winchester', obviously agreed.[27] In a letter home dated 9 August 1849, Henry remarked that 'There were two more boys come to the Collegiate School, so that we now have nine. I think it likely, though nothing is yet determined, that by Christmas another house may be procured for us! But we say nothing about it yet.'[28] However, there were many practical difficulties associated with the construction of a new school at the Cape, as Henry had made clear to William:

> In this country building is very expensive: there is but little building stone, (a short time ago none had been found near here); the country bricks are bad … Both

2.9   Derwent Coleridge (seated 2nd left), son of the poet, first principal of St Mark's College, Chelsea, established in 1841 as the National Society's first teacher training college.

masons & carpenters wages are high, especially those of the better sort of workmen … Good timber is dear, though deal may be got at about English prices and small fir trees which do very well for rafters for thatch grow in great numbers in this valley. I wish you would consider what style of building is likely to be cheapest in such a state of things.[29]

Although Henry wanted lofty rooms 'for the sake of coolness', he did 'not wish for any great ornament any where but should like to have the interior of the Chapel well arranged, and fitted.' Local thatch was pronounced 'excellent, being made of a hard kind of rush … [which] looks very well, & they say will last for 50 years.' He promised to enclose a rough sketch of his ideas for a building 'requisite for 40 or 50 boys, leaving space for subsequent additions. Just think over what wd. be the expense of doing it in the plainest way in England; & we may say double that for the Cape.'[30]

By September 1849 Henry was writing to his brother Francis Gilbert White, who was about to leave England to take up the post of vice-principal of St John's Theological College in Newfoundland. He explained that 'The Bishop has just purchased a house and a piece of ground, (about 50 acres) for a future College … Woodlands, as the estate just purchased is called, is about 5 miles out of Cape Town, and it is generally considered to be as healthy a situation as any in the District.'[31] The cost of the property, £1,100, was met by the well-known English philanthropist, Angela Burdett-Coutts, who had endowed the bishopric and paid for the bishop's residence, Bishopscourt.[32] Henry explained that 'Our new dormitory will easily admit of such an arrangement as that at Radley, and by enforcing strict silence there, we may secure to each boy entire freedom and privacy for his Morning and Evening Prayers.'[33]

In November, Henry was again writing to William about possible building materials and explaining the high insurance premiums for thatched roofs: 'I do not like slate, but we could get a ship load of blue Newcastle tiles.'[34] He was obviously consulting others besides William, for he added, ' I have sent to Mr Coleridge another ground plan, which I will send you, then I shall probably change my mind again. And I like two Quadrangles better than one, & the plan I sent him has but one.' In a later letter Henry expressed his pleasure that William was sending copies of the drawings to Mr Coleridge, 'a great helper & adviser to the Bishop & I should think very practical in arrangements of School Buildings.'[35] This was doubtless Derwent Coleridge, first principal of St Mark's College, Chelsea, and later incumbent of Hanwell, Middlesex (where William would design a new church for him) (2.9).

Besides aesthetics, there were practicalities, such as the scarcity of water: Henry proposed lead water tanks in the roof or of brick and slate underground to store rainwater, but admitted that he did not know if there was a spring close to the site for the new buildings at Woodlands. However, he expressed a desire, if possible, to have 'a Bath Room attached to each Dormitory, with Shower Baths etc.' As with any building, aspect was important and Henry needed to 'consult with people here as to the best fronts with respect to weather etc. & it must be remembered that the North is the sunny side. I do like even here to have the chance of some sun into a room; though the custom seems to prefer South windows.' Henry suggested a 'ball court against the School on the S: and I think a good space might be walled in there for the boys [sic] gardens, and play ground'. He believed that 'A great deal of the comfort and success will depend on the arrangements of the different parts, so that it deserves much thought.'[36]

Henry had put his mind to the fitting up of the chapel, where the seats would be of teak, the wood most used for interior work, to his own design. 'Though very plain they will be the best in the Colony at present; and will do, where real critics are scarce', he admitted. A lectern 'from Scole, Norfolk … is made by the design No.2 in *Instrumenta Ecclesiastica*', but stalls were more difficult: 'The Architectural Books generally have all the fine things wh. are out of ones power here: Nor is it easy to turn a perspective sketch into working drawings. I found considerable difficulties arise from want of fullness, even in Inst. Eccles. wh. is professedly to give simple things to work from.'[37]

William must have sent some preliminary plans, for Henry commented that

> Having two stories and not thatch, the whole style of the buildings must be grander more dignified than your sketch has made them and the Bishop thinks it will be necessary to have them so, near Cape Town. He likes your sketch, but that was almost his first remark … Another criticism was from another man (in which I quite agree) that the main gateway is not marked enough: It requires a tower or something else over it.[38]

In April 1851 Henry was writing to thank William for the 'plans of the college', although he admitted that 'It almost makes me sad to think how very far we are from having any thing of the sort for years to come.'[39] Henry agreed that English tiles should be used for floors and roofs; the latter he felt should be 'a good red', but he admitted that 'The exportation of cut stone is a question I cannot solve here: I have no notion of its weight. Stone is getting more accessible: it will do for wallings, as for Baldiu [sic] Church for instance, but does not cut well.' This was presumably the Table Mountain stone that he had earlier described as 'redder than the Blakesley pits'.[40] However, he was critical of 'Yr. South Elevation with Principal Entrance [which] seems to have too much blank wall' – and suggested some amendments, including south windows 'for air & coolness: the S.E. is Summer wind.'[41] The nagging question of cost was ever-present:

> I like the notion & the place of the covered play place. It wd. be very useful in wet weather but wd. it not be very expensive … the chance of getting an expensive building like the College finished is less than it seemed. I rather incline to have the cheapest building to enclose the required space, & leave it to posterity to rebuild it in stone, on the same ground plan. Study the construction etc. etc. of the Glass Exhibition house: Perhaps it would make the best & cheapest Schoolroom: How would it do to live under? & ??[sic] How does the roof do: can they make it opaque to keep out too much light and the Sun's heat.[42]

2.10 Drawing of Bishops College showing the chapel with dormitory above on the right, and the schoolroom on the left.

William's suggestion of a covered play area demonstrates his familiarity with the pioneering ideas of Fröbel and Pestalozzi that children learn through play. Although he was in the *avant-garde* of educational thinking, William was not prepared to accept iron as a legitimate material for architecture, because it lacked the 'massiveness' and the 'play of light and shadow' that were 'essential features of architecture'.[43] He must have been horrified at his brother's suggestion of a structure similar to the Crystal Palace. The plans Henry and William were discussing were presumably the earlier set referred to in a report in *The Ecclesiologist*, 1852:

> The designs for this college, which is that founded by the Bishop of Capetown, were entrusted to Mr W. White, who, in the first instance, prepared a very large and very satisfactory plan. It embraced a quadrangle, with chapel, hall, school-room, covered play-ground, cloister, and apartments for the officers and members and servants of the institution. We must say, the design was very admirable: the distinctive character of each part of the building was carefully preserved; and we are heartily sorry that the want of funds prevented the carrying out of the scheme. Unfortunately however the Bishop has been compelled to abandon the idea of building anything beyond the very cheapest and simplest possible structure, for the actual needs of the College. Accordingly Mr White has made a second design for two sides of a court,

of two long ranges of buildings, with plaister ornament and thatched roofs, without any pretence at architectural beauty: – but with good and suitable outline, and with all the actual requisites for the institution. We think he has achieved this task – a distasteful one under the circumstances of the case – very creditably. And we much hope that the college of Woodlands, even if built, in the first instance, with this unusual and excessive simplicity may so flourish that it may, ere long, be replaced by a more dignified architectural structure.[44]

2.11 At Bishops Diocesan College White designed the tall schoolroom lancets so that the top half would pivot open.

54

2.12 Entrance to the chapel, designed by White for Bishops Diocesan College with a dormitory above. The lower part of the shouldered chapel windows open inwards.

The next surviving letter from Henry to William is dated 5 November 1852 and is brief because 'We are in the midst of building: the contract is taken for all the Masons work – the windows are ordered in England: I hope very shortly to get all the carpenters work contracted for. Our foundation is in the sand the bricks being laid upon a base of Yorkshire Flagstone. The quality of Cape bricks is not very good: they are very porous and so will not do without plaster. I am going to send Mrs Gray a copy of the specifications etc. next Mail.'[45] Mrs Gray, the Bishop's wife, born Sophia Wharton-Myddleton of Grinkle Park, Easington, Yorkshire, had been an enthusiast of Gothic architecture for many years, as a volume of her drawings of architectural features executed 1836-47 testifies.[46] A friend of William Butterfield, she was a competent draughtsman who 'set to work to design churches for the colony – with a Victorian passion for correctness'.[47] (William White would later design a prayer desk and lectern for St Saviour's, the Grays' own parish church in Claremont, Cape Town, which had been designed by Sophia with help from William Butterfield.[48]) At this time the Grays were in England, where they encouraged their friends to subscribe to their colonial building projects, since there were few wealthy residents in the Cape. Angela Burdett-Coutts was a generous benefactor of the college, as was the SPCK.

Henry White obviously felt it prudent to keep Mrs Gray fully informed, and must also have hoped that she would notice that his building contract included slating (despite his earlier distaste) and that she 'would be in time to countermand' William's order for slates to be shipped to the Cape.[49] The confusion seems to have arisen as a result of the time taken for letters to be received, for Henry remarked that 'my slating was all but finished before your letter arrived' and concluded that 'when your slates come, I suppose we must sell them by auction, and get out of the bargain as well as we can.'[50] By June, he reported to his brother that he did not expect to make a profit on the sale, but hoped not to lose money, and he admitted later that tiles 'never would have done here: the South Easter would have stripped them off without fail.'[51]

The accommodation comprised a masters' common room, vice-principal's room and prefects' study, in a long block approximately 100ft x 12ft, with the chapel at the southern end, a dormitory and a master's room occupying the first floor. A 'short high wall' separated this block from the south facing schoolroom and lobby (approximately 55ft x 12ft), over which was a room used as a classroom and boys' library (**2.10**). Problems with the mail were also responsible for Henry's 'great disappointment about windows … [Because] one letter had not been written, & as there was no reference for the money, the order was not executed till they could hear from us again. It is possible they may bethink themselves of referring to the Bishop, & not delay us so long.'[52]

These must be the single lancets to the schoolroom, the top sections of which pivot to open, and the shouldered windows to the chapel with small lancets in the dormitory above (**2.11, 2.12**). The panes are divided not with lead, but with intersecting narrow bars of iron, making the windows very strong and cutting the brilliant sunlight. However,

2.13 Founder's Quad, Bishops Diocesan College. The original schoolroom on the extreme right has been extended to abut the chapel, masters' room, etc.

2.14 The narrow decorative band above the ground floor windows of the masters' and vice-principal's rooms at Bishops Diocesan College.

in Henry's last surviving letter to William, dated 20 June 1853, he explained that 'The New Buildings are now finished except the windows, & painting etc. and I am well pleased with them' (**2.13**).[53] There was, however, one deviation:

> the −x-x-x-x- work which you suggested in the plaster. Instead of being in the plaster I found that Mr Penketh [a local architect] had ordered it of Portland cement, to be fastened on by iron clamps. It has to my eye a somewhat hard appearance, but I had not quite the heart to forbid its being put up, after it was all made − and as it is the only bit of extra ornament we have got no one here will find fault with it unless I point out the error; & then they will not believe that simple scoring the plaster would have looked better (**2.14**).[54]

Apparently the buildings were not fully functional until 1854 because of the delay with the windows, and the chapel (used as such for seventeen years) was dark 'because the windows came out a foot shorter than those they ordered.'[55]

The correspondence between Henry and William White shows the degree of co-operation and confidence between them. William obviously learned to anticipate some of the many problems and acted accordingly: 'It was a good thought of yours sending the nails: they are very scarce here', Henry wrote.[56] Henry's difficulties are apparent in his comment that 'I often wish I had you at my elbow to advise and devise', but he concludes 'it does me good to be put to ones [sic] wits end to make out for the best.'[57] When it came to devising the curriculum, Henry needed no advice, modelling it, like that of his *alma mater*, on the Classics. However he was not blind to the sciences, being recalled by former pupils as taking scientific instruments on long walks with them. But he was also remembered as being 'reserved', a characteristic also ascribed to John Keble. It was his desire 'to provide such an education as may fit men to discharge their various duties in life, without forgetting that religion must be the pervading principle of the whole man'.[58]

St Bartholomew's, Grahamstown

Although Nathaniel Merriman and Henry White caused some offence amongst the expatriate population in the Cape by wearing cassocks, Bishop Gray reported that some people felt such dress 'appropriate to the offices of Archdeacon and Principal.'[59] Merriman's 'strict rubrical observances' challenged the strong Methodist presence in Grahamstown, so that Bishop Gray could report 'a great rise there, through his energy, zeal, self-denial, and power.'[60] Evidence of the growing influence of Merriman's Tractarian

2.15 St Bartholomew's church, Grahamstown, *c*.1870, showing White's original bell-cote and tall vane, replaced by a north-west tower in 1893.

Anglicanism was the decision to build a church on Settler's Hill, Grahamstown, where the Roman Catholics, Baptists and Presbyterians already had places of worship. This seems to have been instigated by Henry White in July 1849, when Merriman recorded in his journal that 'If in accordance with Mr. White's suggestions, I should commence building an additional church in Graham's Town, my earnest hope is that he may come here and act the part of incumbent to it'.[61] However, it was not until 3 December 1856 that William White exhibited his designs for the Grahamstown church at a committee meeting of the Ecclesiological Society. The site was not agreed upon until the following March and the land was not formally granted to the bishop of Grahamstown until 27 June 1857.[62]

White's design, described as 'unpretending' with moulded brick window arches with wooden transoms, was for a simple nave and chancel, a north-western porch and a south-eastern vestry. Although it was originally intended that the building should 'be wholly sent out' from England 'it being difficult to build properly on the spot', the cost of shipping all the materials from England to Port Elizabeth, and then carriage to Grahamstown, seems to have forced a reappraisal, and construction in the local Witteberg Quartzite was adopted.[63] It seems likely that the moulded brick dressings were imported, and the 'first of the timber' arrived on 13 April 1857, just eleven days after Merriman received White's plans.[64] Imported timber was needed for the framework of the wooden bell-cote at the western end of the steeply pitched dark slate roofs (2.15). White had used this form of construction at his church of St John, Hooe, Devon, in 1853.[65] *The Ecclesiologist* complained of White's design for the east window, where the 'interval between the lights and the strange-shaped opening above is too great'.[66] These lights, contained within a relieving arch outlined with brick voussoirs, were presumably designed to reduce the heat and glare while maintaining a traditional appearance (2.16).

The Rev. John Heavyside, priest in charge of the cathedral in Grahamstown (1833-61) reported that tenders for the building were opened on 30 April 1857.[67] The building committee had already spent about £1,000 on materials, freight and carriage, so rejected the tenders that came in at about £1,100, their own rough estimate being £790. Although it was later recorded that the church was built by soldiers, supervised by Heavyside and Merriman, at the laying of the foundation stone on 24 August 1857 the contractor was listed as a Mr Glass, and the superintending architect a Mr Stitt.[68] The contractor's men were obviously unskilled, for Heavyside records having 'twice shewed the workmen how to do the bevel work of string course', and two weeks later, 'Had to take a hammer and trowel in hand and make them pull out some work – part of the string course.'[69] The problems continued, with Heavyside instructing Mr Stitt 'to see to it as they were spoiling the Church.'[70] Merriman donated three-quarters of the total cost of £2,200 from the funds subscribed by his friends when he left England in 1848.[71]

The interior of St Bartholomew's was enriched by the High Church tastes and the wealth of Merriman's friends, many of whom were members of the Exeter Diocesan

2.16 St Bartholomew's, 1856–60, from the east. The local stone varies in colour from pale honey to dark blue-grey. Unfortunately, the decorative brickwork has been painted pale blue.

2.17 Undated photograph of the interior of St Bartholomew's shows an altar cloth that was surely designed by White.

Architectural Society. A 'Velvet Altar cloth worked by Ladies in England – friends of Archdn. Merriman' appears in his list of 'Special Gifts to the Church', and is possibly the one to be seen in an undated photograph (**2.17**).[72] The similarity of the embroidered motifs with White's painted patterns at Bishop's Court and at Humewood and Quy Hall (Chapters 5 and 6), is striking, with the implication that it is also to his design.[73] The red, black and cream encaustic tiles in the sanctuary were the gift of a Mrs Blagg, of St Albans, while a set of illuminated texts for the walls, also visible in the photograph, were given by the Rev. John Thynne, younger brother of the 3rd marquess of Bath, and rector of Street when Merriman had served as curate there. The nave windows are filled with quarries, the stained glass restricted to spots of colour in the tracery. St Bartholomew's was consecrated by the bishop of Grahamstown, Henry Cotterill, on 24 June 1860, although minor work continued as funds allowed. It was not until 4 April 1861 that it was agreed to 'board the ceiling of the Nave according to the Architect's specification', and a year later before a tender was accepted.[74]

St. Philip's, Fingo, Grahamstown

Merriman's missionary zeal had identified the need for a church in the black settlement of Fingo village on the north-eastern edge of Grahamstown. Unusually, the Mfengu inhabitants held the freehold of their land, and had adopted white customs. They assisted Britain in wars against the Xhosa in the 1840s and '50s.[75] At the same time as the grant of land for St Bartholomew's, two plots in Fingo were transferred to the bishop of Grahamstown 'for ecclesiastical purposes'. In 1860 *The Ecclesiologist* congratulated 'Mr. Bodley on his design ... of great vigour and promise ... in the simplest possible Pointed' for a church comprising

> a chancel, with round-ended apse, a vestry on its north side and an aisle on its south; a clerestoried nave with two aisles, and a western porch – ingeniously contrived so as to exclude the wind ... The internal arrangements are strictly correct ... The chancel proper stands below the tower, which is of massive and dignified proportions, and has a low square pyramidal capping. The aisles are very low, but the clerestory fully developed. The windows are plain, tall, chamfered lancets, but at the west end there are chamfered circles over couplets of trefoiled lancets. The arcades are of four arches rising from low cylindrical shafts. The spandrel spaces are relieved by low sexfoiled circles. Great character and a most excellent effect result from the good proportion of these simple details.[76]

Recent research by Alex Bremner has revealed that the commission appears to have been passed to White, whose design for 'a very simple Mission church for the Kaffirs' was exhibited at the Royal Academy in 1864.[77] The Rev. John Hardie, who had been curate to the Rev. George Cornish at Kenwyn, and who acted as principal of the Diocesan College, Cape Town, from April 1855 until May 1856 when Henry White was on leave in England, was appointed archdeacon of Kaffraria in 1857 and may well have advanced

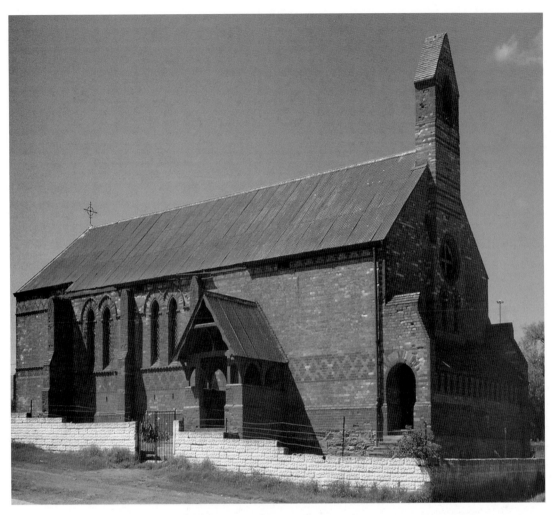

2.18 St Philip's, Fingo, Grahamstown,1862-7, has survived relatively unscathed.

White's name for this commission (**2.18**). It seems likely that the proposed 'massive' tower, the aisles and the rounded apse were abandoned on the grounds of cost. The canted apse, the long, unbroken roofline, western bell-cote and gabled porch are all reminiscent of White's 'cheap chapels' in Hatherden and Smannell of 1856 (see 4.17). However, the diapered brickwork under the eaves was not a feature found in his ecclesiastical work before St Mark's, Battersea Rise, of 1873, and was never repeated at stringcourse level as it is here. The extended chancel buttresses are typical of Bodley, while the west elevation appears to be a scaling down of Bodley's original intentions. White included a similar western narthex surmounted by a circular window beneath a tall bell-cote at Witham Friary, Somerset, in 1875 (**2.19**). White and Bodley were obviously close friends from their days in Scott's office, and had shared White's accommodation at 30a Wimpole Street

2.18 White's rebuilding of the west end of the church of St Mary and St John, Witham Friary, Somerset, 1875, shows a marked similarity to St Philip's.

from 1859 until 1861. It is quite likely, therefore, that there was a degree of co-operation between them and that, if White was called upon to produce a less expensive church, he retained aspects of Bodley's original design.

The corner-stone of St Philip's having been laid in 1864, the nave was in use for services in 1865. The parishioners of St Bartholomew's raised monies through sales of work, as well as offertories, towards the total cost of £1,580. When St Philip's was consecrated in 1867, £180 was still outstanding, but this was paid off by the donation of the whole of the St Bartholomew's Easter offering in the following year.[78]

Although both churches express Merriman's Tractarian sympathies, the differences in style between the sister churches of St Bartholomew's and St Philip's reflect the backgrounds of the parishioners they served. St Bartholomew's was designed for the mainly English settlers who had been encouraged to the area by the British Government in 1820 as a bulwark on the eastern border of Cape Province. Finding the farmland they were given unsuitable, they had migrated to Grahamstown where they could use their artisan skills in the development of the growing garrison. St Bartholomew's sturdy, modest exterior expresses the simplicity and reserve of John Keble. For the native residents of Fingo, who were probably originally refugees from Natal, Merriman needed a large, impressive, colourful church. With its unbroken expanse of roof, high windows and full-height buttresses, St Philip's not only reflects contemporary interest in early French Gothic architecture, but also epitomises the strength and grandeur of the Church of England. But typically White softens the imposing mass with a porch on the sunny elevation, its open timber framing and gabled roof providing a homely, welcoming entrance.

These commissions in South Africa brought White into contact with many of his brother's Oxford friends who were influential not only in the Church but also in the field of education. Schooling for all classes of society offered enormous opportunities for nineteenth-century architects. Based in London with its ever-growing rail links, William was well placed to undertake work throughout England.

3

Theory and Practice

In 1852 William White's practice address was 1 Seymour Chambers, Adelphi, the Adam brothers' classical Thames-side development just east of the present-day Charing Cross station.[1] By 1854 he had moved to 39 Great Marlborough Street, close to where Arthur Lazenby Liberty would later open his store; and the following year to 8 Argyll Place, between Regent Street and Great Marlborough Street, where he was a neighbour of Owen Jones.[2] Having become a member of the Ecclesiological Society in 1848, White was listed as a member of the Exeter Diocesan Architectural Society in 1853, and by 1857 also of the Worcester Diocesan Architectural Society.[3] Established in London, and with the benefit of H.M. White's membership of the Oxford Architectural Society, William now had the opportunity to promote himself amongst the most influential members of the secular and ecclesiastical elite. His determination to explain the theories that underpinned his designs was an effective form of publicity.

White's early writings

Some Victorian architects were great theorists, and White was of their number. A steady stream of letters and papers setting out his philosophy was published in the journals of these architectural societies, and later in the architectural press. His first known published letter, in response to Benjamin Webb's 1849 paper 'On the Draining and Drying of Churches' in *The Ecclesiologist*, called for the enunciation of the principles on which such work should be done.[4] White later emphasised his demand for 'definite principles and fixed rules to work upon, instead of every man having to work out for himself every point of fundamental principle'.[5] It was later argued that if an architect had to work out every problem from its first elements, he might design in his lifetime perhaps three buildings of moderate size.[6]

It was in his first published paper, 'On Some of the Principles of Design in Churches', read to the Exeter society on 8 May 1851, that White identified '*breadth*' as 'the first quality to be obtained in every building'.[7] Just two weeks later he reiterated his demand for 'treatment based … upon the principles of breadth and depth [rather] than of length

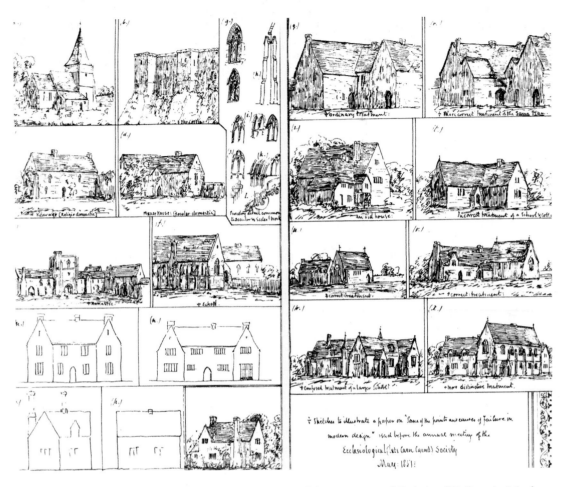

3.1 White's illustrations to his paper 'Upon Some of the Causes and Points of Failure in Modern Design', *The Ecclesiologist*, 12, 1851.

and height; and this not confined to the outline alone, but extending to the detail also' in a paper read at the twelfth anniversary meeting of the Ecclesiological Society.[8] With the help of twenty tiny sketches, White declared his belief that it was proportion and outline, not a reliance on details, which defined a building's purpose and character (**3.1**). Perhaps in an oblique reference to the recently published first volume of Ruskin's *The Stones of Venice*, White expressed his fear that 'it is detail that is snatched at by the multitude … and most specimens of "modern gothic" will abundantly prove this'.[9] Several of White's points, such as excessive copyism, and a proliferation of gables, were repeated by G.E. Street in his paper 'On the Revival of the Ancient Style of Domestic Architecture' two years later.[10]

White's passionate concern for colour can be glimpsed in that first letter in *The Ecclesiologist*, where he concludes with some words of advice regarding cast iron gutters.

He believed they should be painted 'a good deep red, or a good blue ... The usual stone colour or lead colour looks very poor when it is first painted, and when it has stood the weather for a few months, it looks wretched. Red or blue may appear (to many) rather staring at first, but a few weeks tone it down quite as much as is desirable.'[11] In a paper read in Exeter in 1852, White explained the emotional and moral associations provoked by various colours – 'red is suggestive of warmth ... Green is suggestive of coolness or repose: White, of cleanliness and purity: Black of penitence or sorrow'.[12] White's theory appears to be a response to Goethe's belief, expressed in his *Zur Farbenlehre*, 1810, translated into English by Charles Locke Eastlake in 1840, that 'particular colours excite particular states of feeling'.[13] Goethe formulated a theory of polarity, where the blue of shadows and distance balanced yellow and red, representing light and force. The subject obviously fascinated J.M.W. Turner, who lectured on the 'sentiments of color [sic]' in 1818 and expressed his interest in his painting *Light and Colour (Goethe's theory) – the Morning after the Deluge – Moses Writing the Book of Genesis*, 1843 (Tate Britain).[14]

In 1853 *The Ecclesiologist* published White's paper 'Modern Design: Neglect of the Science of Architecture', propounding the theory that medieval builders based the proportions of their churches on the equilateral triangle.[15] His future brother-in-law, the Rev. W.D. Morrice, had read his own paper 'Principles of Architectural Proportions' demonstrating that the basis of the finest medieval structures were the Masonic symbols, square, circle and equilateral triangle, to the Exeter Architectural Society in 1848.[16] Presumably, it was therefore a topic of discussion when White was a visitor at the rectory in Kenwyn. Although 'the several parts of a perfect building must be in certain relative proportions to each other', White admitted that in 'secular and domestic buildings we do not look for the same amount or kind of beauty, nor is the same exactness of proportion of equal importance, as in an Ecclesiastical [one]'.[17] In 1854 he repeated his demand for architects to be taught the principles of proportion in a long letter to *The Ecclesiologist*.[18] White insisted that 'if *perfect* harmony of proportion can be secured by rule, – by a rule which will *not* cramp his powers of conception, – why should not a man avail himself of it?'[19] White's methods were later praised for producing buildings with 'a most satisfactory appearance of harmony and decision.'[20]

The attention generated by White's writings, together with the generally favourable reviews of his buildings that appeared in *The Ecclesiologist*, helped to establish his position as one of the leading Gothic Revivalists. This resulted in a growing circle of patrons, many of them members of the architectural societies, who provided him with both conventional and unusual opportunities.

House of Mercy, Bussage

In 1827 Thomas Keble, younger brother of John, became vicar of Bisley, Gloucestershire. The parish, which included the hamlet of Bussage, was desperately poor, since the work of the hand weavers had been superseded by the great factories of the north of England.

3.2 The Rev. John Armstrong (1813-56), founder of the Church Penitentiary Association, and from 1854 bishop of Grahamstown, South Africa.

Thomas Keble, who supported his brother's High Church beliefs, and wrote four of the Tracts which gave the Tractarian Movement its name, introduced daily church services, raised money for parsonage houses so that resident clergy could minister to the poor, established schools and built and restored churches. On 21 November 1844, Thomas laid the foundation stone for a church at nearby Bussage, the cost of which was borne by a group of twenty young Oxford men.[21] Robert Suckling, a committed ecclesiologist, was appointed as perpetual curate there: he was a natural missionary, working in the school and Sunday school and at the Stroud workhouse, where he ministered to destitute prostitutes. Mrs Grace Anne Poole of Brownshill House, a widow and daughter of a wealthy clergyman, assisted him in this work. She became the supervisor of Kirby Cottage, Blackness, which Suckling established in January 1851 as a women's refuge.[22]

In 1844, when the Rev. George Cornish of Kenwyn was a vice-president, the Rev. John Armstrong, rector of St Paul's, Exeter, was a member of the Exeter Diocesan Architectural Society committee (**3.2**). Armstrong, vicar of Tidenham, Gloucestershire, from 1845, came to believe that the Church should help the many women driven by poverty to a life of prostitution. He believed that they could be saved by women of high moral character to whom he appealed 'to lose this life for the love of Christ – to spend and be spent in saving and guiding the lost sheep of your sex.'[23] His campaign led to the founding of the Church Penitentiary Association in 1852. By the time of Suckling's untimely death from typhoid at the end of 1851, Armstrong had received his bishop's permission to build a diocesan penitentiary for fallen women, which Suckling had persuaded him should be at Bussage, with Mrs Poole as the lady superintendent.

Although the Rev. George Cornish died in September 1849, it seems likely that as a result of earlier introductions to Thomas Keble and John Armstrong, William White was appointed in 1851 to design at Bussage what was called a house of mercy, because the local people did not understand the meaning of the word 'penitentiary'.[24] The Rev. E.N. Mangin, vicar of nearby Horsley, might also have been influential in White's appointment. H.M. White wrote to William, 'I am glad to hear you have made acquaintance with Mangin. He is a very good sort of man; we used to take long walks together.'[25] The house was 'to hold twenty-five inmates, besides matron, housekeeper, and rooms for '"sisters," who are not to be called so, for fear of giving offence: there will be a chapel.'[26] There were no architectural precedents for such an establishment, although Pugin had designed monastic buildings and Butterfield had built Anglican convents.

The layout of the original accommodation block at Bussage, with the chapel forming the head of a T-shape, appears not to indicate plans for a quadrangle, and the steeply sloping site would have made that both difficult and expensive. *The Ecclesiologist* of 1853 commented on 'A very simple but satisfactory design by Mr White', for a chapel with a range of buildings at right-angles to it.[27] Set on the steep west-facing bank of the Toadsmoor Valley remote from the settlements of both Brownshill and Bussage, now much altered and extended, it is possible only to see glimpses of White's original designs.[28] The accommodation in the original range still includes on the ground floor a large, beamed room with a tall, depressed arched stone fireplace, which may have been where instruction in needlework took place. Although there is no documentary proof that White visited the site, it would surely have accorded with his nature to provide from this simple building the superlative westerly view across the peaceful, wooded valley to help sooth the distressed women's troubled spirits.

Presumably the girls were treated much as they were at the house of mercy at Clewer, Windsor, which had been founded in 1849, and which by 1852 was run by an Anglican sisterhood, the Community of St John the Baptist.[29] At Clewer girls were taught needlework and laundry skills to prepare them for work in service. Undoubtedly much time at Bussage would have been spent in the chapel, a simple high-roofed nave with slightly lower chancel, constructed, like the other buildings, of the local golden rubblestone. The east end has now been turned into store rooms, but some of White's favoured diagonal boarding is visible, and in the roof space can be seen the stained glass in the two original east lancet windows, their rather stilted figures perhaps indicative of White's involvement with the design.

Perhaps because of Armstrong's departure in 1854 to take up his appointment as bishop of Grahamstown, South Africa, and his death there in May 1856, funds for the Bussage house of mercy were hard to obtain.[30] Mrs Poole and the penitents sold their needlework and were helped by Thomas Keble Jr, curate in his father's parish. But there were not funds to support a building programme such as Thomas Carter instituted at Clewer in 1854, with Henry Woodyer as his architect, nor G.E. Street's designs for the Rev. William Butler at Wantage a year later.[31]

St Michael's School, Wantage

Another 'special' school that White designed was for the training of pupil teachers. By the middle of the century elementary schools that received a good report from government inspectors could train pupil-teachers. Aged thirteen to eighteen, they were given ninety minutes of instruction by the head teacher each day, for which he was paid £5 for the first, £4 for the second and £3 for each additional pupil. The pupil-teachers were paid between £10 and £20 a year according to their age. They sat the Queen's Scholarship Examination at the age of eighteen and if successful were awarded a grant to attend a training college for two years.[32]

The foundation of such a training establishment was recorded by the Rev. William Butler, vicar of Wantage (later dean of Lincoln) in his diary on 4 October 1855, 'The Corner Stone of the new St Michael's Schools laid by Mrs Trevelyan the foundress.'[33] Butler had joined the Cambridge Camden Society in 1842 and four years later was appointed to Wantage (then in Berkshire, now Oxfordshire), where in 1849 he commissioned G.E. Street to design the vicarage. Mrs Trevelyan, whose husband, the Rev. Edward Trevelyan, curate of Stogumber, Somerset, was also a member of the society, had purchased the land for the school in 1853.[34] She had already founded a school at Littlemore, Oxford, to train young girls from the age of nine for domestic service. It was agreed that this earlier school would be moved to Wantage and be joined by a training school for pupil teachers, whom Butler needed for the village schools that he was creating in his parish.[35] Butler determined to produce 'mistresses of a more truly religious character than … I find from long experience, at present to be obtained.'[36]

The Ecclesiologist described White's 'building of considerable pretensions' as 'an institution for training domestic servants' (presumably because of the Littlemore connection), which would include 'a residence for the foundress as well as apartments for the superior, and accommodation for about thirty "students" (as they must, we suppose, be called.)'[37] The main range comprised a refectory, school-room and common room with dormitories above, accessed by an external staircase, as at Bishops Diocesan College. With no surviving plans, later much extended and now divided into apartments, it is difficult to discern the original layout, but a window with White's distinctive timber plate tracery perhaps lit the refectory (**3.3**). Further accommodation housed the superior, as well as a 'commodious dwelling' for the foundress, together with an oratory and common-room, as well as a dairy, laundry, washhouse, etc., all 'skilfully planned and

3.3 An example of White's typical wooden plate tracery at St Michael's, Wantage, 1855.

picturesquely grouped. The oratory, especially, is very nicely managed.' However, *The Ecclesiologist* could not praise White's three-light windows, and argued that the dormitory lights were 'merely square openings, and certainly have a mean effect in the drawings. The same may be said of some other windows in the building. We had almost forgotten to mention the material of the walls, which is brick — yellow, red, and black — arranged ornamentally.'

White was quick to point out that 'the whole is of Cirencester stone, with a few single bands, plinths, and alternate voussoirs of arches in red brick.'[38] He also mentioned that, with the exception of the oratory, the building was 'of the simplest and most inexpensive character' costing only £2,500. Perhaps the commodious dwelling for the foundress was funded, at least in part, by her, for it hardly appears simple and inexpensive. Projecting eastwards, parallel to the oratory (which was extended eastwards to the designs of A.B. Allin in 1888), it is 'entered by a distinct porch' – a moulded limestone arch set under a pyramidal tiled roof. The south elevation of the foundress's house boasts three bay windows (**3.4**). Internally, one bay is set beneath an arched arcade supported by a low, free-standing, polished marble pillar.[39]

Gable ends and dormers, some of them triangular, are often tile-hung, while the tiled roofs with their distinctive crested ridge tiles are punctured by several large battered stone stacks; and there are long, low windows tucked under the eaves – all features that would become typical of White's designs for secular buildings. Although indicative of their various functions, the high, buttressed oratory, the distinctive porch, the dignified residence and the institutional accommodation form a lively but sympathetic ensemble. White was correct in his belief that 'the grey of this stone ... comes out into admirable relief by contrast with the red' for this is a far gentler, more welcoming group of buildings than Street's of the same date, of plain limestone, at the Convent of St Mary the Virgin, Wantage.[40]

3.4   St Michael's, Wantage, 1855, from the south. Possibly the foundress's accommodation as internally it includes an arcade supported by a detached marble pillar with simply carved granite capital and base.

3.5 White's sketch, dated 10 November 1853, for Inner Lodge, later the chaplain's cottage, Arley Hall, Cheshire.

Arley Hall, Cheshire

Rowland Eyles Egerton-Warburton of Arley Hall (about four miles south of Lymm), Cheshire, was a member of both the Ecclesiological and Oxford Architectural Societies. A keen countryman and lover of vernacular architecture, he was an enthusiastic patron of several Gothic revival architects.[41] Having employed Anthony Salvin to design his private chapel in1845, in 1853 he turned to William White to design a cottage at Arley Green for his chaplain, the Rev. Charles Gutch.[42] White's rough sketch, dated 10 November 1853, shows a simple design with the low, broad windows he advocated (**3.5**). In 1850 White had written a letter to *The Ecclesiologist* pointing out that the window tax was based on a width of 4ft 9ins, although the height could be up to 11ft, thus favouring the classic style.[43] This 'very simple and inexpensive cottage' was constructed of the local soft red brick with simple diaper patterning in the gable ends and irregular single courses of blue brick as White had set out in his plans of January 1854 (**3.6**).[44] Unfortunately, White's other plans of the same date for a choir school attached to the chapel at Arley Hall and for a robust entrance lodge to the estate were never built. However, White designed a school on the estate at Great Budworth, and various buildings on the estate of Egerton-Warburton's relations at Rode Hall.

Heydour vicarage, Lincolnshire

White's increasing interest in structural polychromy can be seen in his design for rebuilding and extending the vicarage at Heydour (about six miles north-east of Grantham), Lincolnshire, of 1856 (**3.7**). This was for the Rev. Frederick Gordon Deedes, graduate of Wadham College, Oxford, who was probably known to H.M. White. Deedes, who was appointed to the living in that year, needed a home to reflect the status of his wife and cousin, Marianne, daughter of William Deedes, M.P. of Sandling Park, near Maidstone, Kent. The Architectural Society for the Diocese of Lincoln, praised the house as, 'an exceedingly picturesque erection; and by the admixture of brick with stone of which it is for the most part constructed, a little colour has been dispersed over its various façades, in a modest and judicious manner... [although] there is a little over exuberance of fancy in some of the details about its entrance'. However it had their 'entire approbation, and it has the advantage of at once bespeaking itself to be the clerical residence of the village.'[45] White was, of course, complying with Pugin's *True Principles* – that 'the external and internal appearance of an edifice should be illustrative of, and in accordance with, the purpose for which it is destined'.[46]

Heydour vicarage demonstrates White's restrained use of structural polychromy – confining it to a decorative treatment of the windows, linked in the limestone rubble walls by single courses of red bricks to provide that horizontalism which, as he argued, 'symbolizes repose'.[47] As at Wantage, White used alternate red brick voussoirs, emphasising the colour of the roof and the tile-hung gable ends (**3.8**).[48] Without plinths

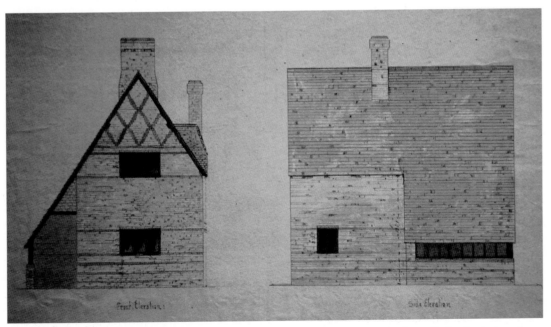

Front Elevation   Side Elevation

3.6 White's elevations for Inner Lodge, Arley Hall, 25 January 1854, show little deviation from his original concept.

3.7 Heydour vicarage, 1856–7, the entrance porch with wooden traceried window to staircase and hipped roof above low windows to the water closet.

or stringcourses, the flatness of the wall surface of the rear elevation emphasises the confident sculptural qualities of the entrance façade.

In White's parsonages the connection with the church is always expressed most prominently in the main entrance and the vicar's study, the two areas where the building interacted with the community. White often provided a separate door to access the study, a reflection of the stratification of society where it would have been thought inappropriate for poor parishioners to share the main entrance with the gentry.[49] Here, the entrance for parishioners led into a lobby, adjacent to which was a commodious room for 'stores' (3.9). The storeroom could not have been associated with the kitchen, which had its own pantry, larder and dairy, for access would have been problematical, but was presumably for storage of necessaries to donate to poor parishioners.[50]

The Ecclesiologist of 1857, obviously a less parochial organ than that of the local society, condemned White's design as 'not pleasing'.[51] This disparagement may have stemmed from the decorative treatment of the W.C., a prominent feature close to the entrance, and emphasising, perhaps, that the man of God is also flesh and blood like every other. It also remarked of Heydour that, 'We must always protest against the inadequate size of the "study." Here it is only 15ft 6in by 12ft.'[52] This may have been inevitable, as according to the specification the design was an enlargement and repair of the old vicarage. The Ecclesiological Society has been blamed for goading architects to provide larger studies

76

in their parsonage designs, and White 'in particular suffered rebuke' for small studies which were not suggestive of the learned priest with his extensive library.[53] As one of nine children, White seems to have been more concerned with providing modern conveniences for family life. There were day and night nurseries and a schoolroom at Heydour to cater for the needs of the five children of the family, as well as the usual domestic quarters.[54]

Pupils and assistants

Like most Victorian architects with busy practices, William must have spent many hours travelling by train to visit clients and sites. However, he kept only a small office as an obituary records that

> he relied upon himself alone to do the best he was capable of, trusting to his own common sense, and giving to the workmen the drawings of his own hand, that nothing of his intention might be lost for want of that intention being expressed as clearly as he could through the medium he employed.[55]

All White's assistants had successful careers and many, like White, had varied interests outside their profession. In the early years of his London practice, from 1852 until 1856, White's assistant was John Butler, who acted as clerk of works during the construction of All Saints', Notting Hill.[56] Butler attended the first meeting of the Society of Architectural

3.8 Heydour vicarage, the garden front showing the restrained polychromy and shadowless wall plane. A modern extension to the right.

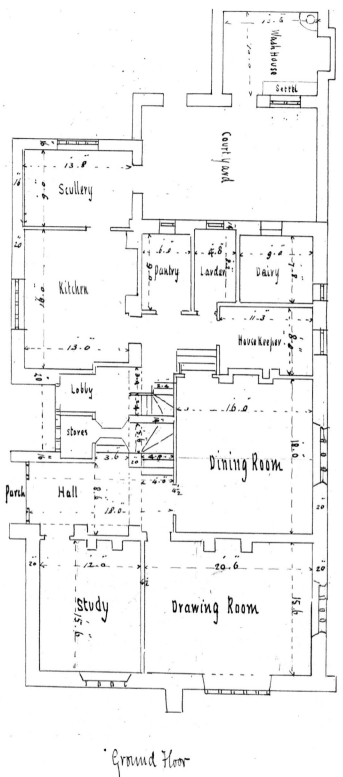

Wash House

Courtyard

Settle

Scullery

13.8

Kitchen

Pantry

Larder

Dairy

House Keeper

Lobby

stores

Dining Room

Porch

Hall

study

Drawing Room

'Ground Floor'

3.9 White's ground plan of Heydour vicarage shows the store room adjacent to the entrance for parishioners.

78

3.10 William Leiper (1839-1916) was in White's office *c.*1860-1, before becoming a successful architect in Glasgow.

Draughtsmen (that became the Architectural Association), and went on to become a fellow of the Royal Geographical Society and a member of the Society of Arts, the Japan Society and the Commons and Footpaths Preservation Society, as well as a councillor for the borough of Kensington, and surveyor to the Metropolitan Police.[57]

John Ford Gould, son of the borough surveyor of Barnstaple, Devon, was a pupil with White around 1860, before joining his father's practice. His vicarage at Yarnscombe, Devon, of 1867-8, demonstrates how closely he adopted many of White's characteristic features. His death in 1881, when he was in his early 40s, cut short a career that might well have enhanced White's reputation. Also in White's office for a short period around 1860/1 was William Leiper, who went on to establish a very successful practice in his native city of Glasgow (**3.10**). Having been articled there to Boucher and Cousland, Leiper travelled to London and was engaged with White and J.L. Pearson, 'both of whom he held in high esteem for their great abilities'.[58] Besides his wonderfully flamboyant carpet factory for Templeton's in Glasgow, Leiper designed many private houses where White's influence can be seen in notched timberwork, canted bays and welcoming timbered porches.

George Henry Birch was an 'improver' for two years with Sir Matthew Digby Wyatt before joining White about 1865.[59] He did not stay long before moving to Ewan Christian's practice. A keen historian and archaeologist, he became curator of the Sir John Soane Museum in 1894, a post he held until his death ten years later (**3.11**). Around 1867, White was assisted by Robert Medley Fulford, who had served his articles with

3.11   George Henry Birch (1842-1904), with White *c*.1865, became curator of the Sir John Soane's Museum in 1894. He is shown here in the dining room.

John Hayward of Exeter, a convinced Gothicist and architect to the Exeter Diocesan Architectural Society since its inception. Fulford did not remain long in London before returning to Devon, where he worked with Edward Ashworth, prior to establishing his own practice in Exeter, dealing mainly with church restorations.[60]

In 1880, White employed Stephen Powlson Rees as his assistant, a relationship that lasted for seven years.[61] Rees was later with T.G. Jackson for two years before joining H.M. Office of Works. In 1884 another assistant joined White's practice: Joseph Compton Hall, who had served his articles in Manchester.[62] Hall only stayed for a year before joining Paley and Austin in Lancaster. He was later responsible for rebuilding part of Dunham Massey for the 9th earl of Stamford, White's nephew. In November 1887 John Clark Stransom, who had been articled to William Ravenscroft of Reading, Berkshire, became White's assistant, perhaps in succession to Stephen Rees. In February 1889 Stransom left to join the Metropolitan Board of Works, and there is no record of any other assistants in White's office.

Besides his professional commitments, White found time to travel in Europe: he mentioned visiting Normandy, Picardy and Brittany in about 1850.[63] Closer to home, he was present at the inauguration of the Crystal Palace at Sydenham – perhaps as a guest of his neighbour, Owen Jones, who was responsible for the decoration of the Palace, first in Hyde Park and then at Sydenham. At the suggestion of friends, White published his impressions of the day: *The Palace, An Artistic Sketch of the 10th of June, 1854*.[64] Besides his pleasure in finding that the proportions fitted his theories, White noted Jones's decorative scheme, remarking particularly 'that in colouring it adds immensely to the effect to separate almost all colours from each other by white.'[65] Perhaps for the benefit of his sisters, White also remarked on the dresses worn, apologising for 'technical errors' such as the 'misapplication of terms when speaking of Flounces, Tucks, or Trimmings'. His interest was mainly in colour: 'A Net of black over a green Mantle, and black fringe, very good. Pink bonnets with green mantles, *frightful*.'[66]

White concluded his account by reporting that 'We left the grounds just in time to see the Sun setting brilliantly behind a golden bank of clouds'. It is tempting to conjecture that one of his companions may have been Ellen Floyer Cornish, whom he married a year later.

3.12 Robert Kestell Kestell-Cornish, brother of White's first wife and first Anglican bishop in Madagascar, with some of his family.

Marriage

The Cornish family can (confusingly) trace its roots in Devonshire back to the sixteenth century. In 1783 one James Cornish, collector of customs at Teignmouth, married Margaret Floyer, a descendant of Nicholas Wadham, who founded the eponymous Oxford college. Their youngest son, George, aide-de-camp to the governor-general of India, married an heiress, Sarah Kestell of Ottery St Mary. Their eldest son, George James, was a childhood friend of John Taylor Coleridge (nephew of the poet) before being sent away to school at Westminster (Coleridge went to Eton). Their friendship was renewed when they were both at Corpus Christi, Oxford, together with John Keble and Thomas Arnold. Cornish was described by Coleridge as reserved, modest, very affectionate and 'pure-hearted as a child'.[67] It appears that John Keble had hopes of an attachment to Cornish's younger sister, Cornelia, writing to her elder sister, Charlotte, in 1824 that 'I had rather a thousand times, if that were possible, wait all my life as I am doing, than be quite certain of any body else. ... Please distribute my love as you know I shd. wish, & leave a good slice for yourself'.[68] However, four years later Cornelia married the Rev. Henry Dudley Ryder, nephew of the 1st earl of Harrowby, thereby establishing links by marriage to the March-Phillipps family, Samuel Wilberforce and Henry Manning.

Aged only 25, George James Cornish married Harriet, daughter of Sir Robert Wilmot of Chaddesden, Derbyshire, and nine years later, in 1828, he was appointed to the valuable living of Kenwyn and Kea. The following year Cornish inherited Salcombe Hill, his parents' property on the outskirts of the fashionable Regency seaside resort of Sidmouth. Unfortunately his poor health precluded the advancement that was expected of him, and he was further undermined by the deaths of several of his children. His only surviving son, Robert Kestell Cornish, was a patron of William White in Devon and in Madagascar, where he was the first Anglican bishop (**3.12**). Cornish's daughters are shadowy figures: like so many nineteenth-century women they appear as footnotes to their husbands' titles and positions. The eldest, Harriet Sarah, died young. Esther Anne, born in 1822 and a god-daughter of John Keble, died in 1849. In 1848 she had married the Rev. William Morrice, who consistently commissioned work from William White. Cornelia Sarah united the Cornish and Keble families by marrying the Rev. Thomas Keble Jr of Bussage.

The third daughter, Ellen Floyer Cornish, was born in 1826. The Floyers, who were relatives by marriage of the Wilmot family, were also connected by marriage to the Bankes family of Kingston Lacy, Dorset, and through them to both the Acland family and to the earls of Falmouth. Ellen married William White on 7 June 1855 in the ancient church of St Mary and St Peter in the valley of the river Sid at Salcombe Regis, Devon. Since her father had died in September 1849, one of Ellen's maternal (Wilmot) relations officiated, while her younger sister Agatha, together with William's sister, Mary Martelli and his father, Francis Henry White, were witnesses. Ellen's signature is bold and sure, as she must have been to leave this particularly beautiful part of east Devon to set up home in London. In 1856 the couple moved from Great Marlborough Street to 8 Argyll Place, Regent Street, where their first child, Harriet, was born. In 1859 White moved his practice to 30a Wimpole Street, which would remain his professional address for the rest of his life and which he shared until 1861 with G.F. Bodley. At the time of the 1861 census the White family was living 'over the shop' and besides a second daughter, Ellen, of eight months, the household comprised a nurse and two young female servants born in Hampshire.[69]

Fellowship

Now well established in London, White enjoyed the company of other young avant-garde artists and designers. The Mediæval Society was formed in 1857 to collect and to promote the study of works of art of the Middle Ages. White was elected to the committee, together with Ruskin, Street, the Rossetti brothers, William Morris and others. The committee gave themselves the power 'to protest … against any attempt to destroy old works of art, either wantonly, or under pretence of restoration'.[70] The collection was to consist not only of casts of sculpture, rubbings of brasses, tracings of stained glass or frescoes, books and photographs, but also costumes, or copies of costumes, for the use of painters, and 'Specimens of Eastern textile fabrics, and of Ceramic Art.'[71] It was doubtless these specimens that reinforced White's interest in geometric pattern designs that he would use so effectively in his decorative schemes.

The Mediæval Society was short-lived, but many of its Pre-Raphaelite committee members went on to establish the Hogarth Club in 1858 as a forum for exhibiting work independently of the Royal Academy, and as a social meeting place with members and patrons who were not resident in the capital.[72] White was not listed as a member in 1859, so he presumably joined during 1860, when membership was increased to nearly 80.[73] Settling ultimately at 6 Waterloo Place, the club provided a London venue where artists, designers and architects could exhibit not only finished drawings and paintings, but also designs for buildings, stained glass and furniture, all categories in which White participated.

White was elected a fellow of the Institute of British Architects in 1859, at a time when only a small proportion of practising architects was prepared to accept its code of professional ethics.[74] He consistently demanded that architectural training should embrace science as well as art. His 1853 paper, 'Modern Design: Neglect of the Science of Architecture', pointed out that 'there is in Architecture a *science* as well as an art, – a science to be prosecuted, as well as an art to be practised'.[75] He therefore supported the introduction of examinations, not because he believed that art could be tested, 'but merely to ensure the acquirements of all those elements of construction and arrangements, without which the architect, whether true artist or not, must fail to satisfy the requirements of a civilised community.'[76]

White also recognised the 'individual isolation and seclusion' of many within the

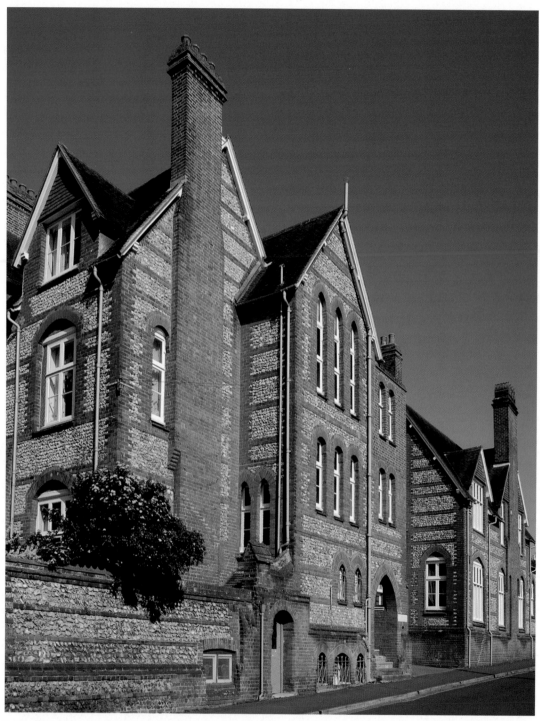

3.13 Entrance to Du Boulay's, Winchester, 1862–3, constructed of the local flint, with red brick chimneys, quoins and dressings. A modern extension has been added above the arched doorway to the master's house. The boys' accommodation to the right.

3.14   The garden elevation of Du Boulay's, showing the master's study on the right, drawing room with canted bay, and dining room to left.

profession. He perceived the benefits of discussion and mutual support, requesting in a letter of 1857,

> If any of your readers can tell me of the quiet nook to which they resort, in order to aid each other by friendly intercourse in searching for, and pointing out, practical defects and inconsistencies, or unintentional disobedience to principles to which they have upon calm deliberation subscribed; let them, for pity's sake, admit me to their number.[77]

Besides the fellowship offered by these artistic and professional groups, White soon reaped the benefits of membership of the extensive and influential Cornish family. In 1858 he was drawing up plans for the rebuilding of Sidmouth parish church, and the following year for the restoration of the chancel at nearby Sidbury church. In Algiers in 1860 Ellen's youngest sister, Alice Mead Cornish, married the Rev. James Thomas Houssemayne Du Boulay. Descendants of Huguenot immigrants and related by marriage to their compatriots the Cazenoves, the Du Boulays had settled in Walthamstow. Here in 1834 Archibald du Boulay, together with William Morris's father and other local gentry established Forest Proprietary Grammar School, where White would later design the chapel. A Wykehamist and former tutor of Exeter College, Oxford, the Rev. J.T.H. Du Boulay became housemaster at his *alma mater* in 1862.

Public schools

In England education for the middle classes had traditionally been provided by grammar schools, many of which had been established before the Reformation by the Church, craft guilds or groups of townspeople or merchants, or by individuals. Such schools were originally 'for teaching grammatically the learned languages' (Latin and Greek).[78] Many were restricted by their foundation deeds to employ only graduates from Oxford or Cambridge, and were also not permitted, until the 1840 Grammar School Act, to introduce new subjects. The master's stipend, too, was often defined and so, to ameliorate its falling monetary value, schools took in boarders and fee-paying pupils, as well as charging for everything except the basic curriculum, thus making a mockery of their status as 'free' schools. Some grammar schools that grew in this way during the eighteenth century became known as 'public schools', and were often notorious for their appalling conditions, bullying and indiscipline.

Reform was greatly stimulated by the appointment of Thomas Arnold as headmaster of Rugby School in 1828.[79] Arnold believed passionately in training his boys morally and religiously as well as intellectually; he advocated work as a sacred duty and demanded high standards of gentlemanly conduct. Arnold's staff and pupils spread his reforms into other schools, including the new public schools established for the rising numbers of middle-class parents anxious that their sons should acquire an education fitting them for the universities or for the higher echelons of government. The development of the railway system facilitated the establishment of these boarding schools in healthy rural situations, their extensive grounds redolent of the landed gentry. Many offered teaching in modern languages, mathematics and science and their alumni proved more successful in the new competitive entry to the Army, Navy and Civil Service than those from the ancient foundations, such as Winchester College. William of Wykeham's St Mary's College, Winchester, had been established in 1387 to educate 70 scholars, who would then enter New College, Oxford, Wykeham's other foundation.

Du Boulay's, Winchester College

In 1861 the government set up the Clarendon Commission to enquire into accusations of mismanagement of the endowments of seven long-established boarding schools – Eton, Winchester, Westminster, Charterhouse, Harrow, Rugby and Shrewsbury – together with two London day schools – St Paul's and Merchant Taylors'. Although the commissioners found the curriculum (based on the Classics) at Winchester very narrow, the teaching was very good. Marks were awarded for every lesson and piece of work, with progress through the school entirely dependent on the totals gained.[80]

Under the headship of the High-Church Rev. George Moberly, a competitive entry examination was introduced at Winchester College in 1857, resulting in a rise in the number of pupils so that boys had to be housed outside the college in boarding houses kept by assistant masters. Between 1859 and 1863 three such houses opened at the College, but Du Boulay's, designed by William White in 1862, was 'the first … tutor's house … built for the purpose' and was thus significant in the development of the physical environment of the college.[81] Although *The Ecclesiologist* reported that it had 'accommodation for eighty boarders', it appears that this was perhaps a misreading of 'thirty', for a photograph of the members of the house in 1864 shows 22 boys. A.F. Leach, who when he entered the school in September 1863 was the thirteenth member of Du Boulay's, reported that there were no more than 33 boys in the house in the period 1866-70.[82] It also seems unlikely that the house would have been built for 80, as it was apparently 'a piece of speculation on borrowed capital by an assistant master, the Rev. James Du Boulay, the headmaster not having been able to guarantee him any boarders at all.'[83]

Du Boulay's house is constructed of the local material, flint, in courses, interspersed with irregular bands of red brick. The entrance is on the imposing east elevation that straddles the crest of what was known as Southgate Hill (now Edgar Road), west of the college, its height emphasised by the fall of the road (**3.13**). White maintained a very flat wall plane – even the iron railings reflect his preference. The main entrance from the street to the master's residence is up a flight of steps under a pointed brick arch forming a porch, lit by three small lancet windows. The door itself is broad and iron-studded with long strap hinges set beneath a fanlight of White's typically pale stained glass with bright spots of colour. Inside the entrance hall diagonal boarding fills the underside of the pine staircase with its chamfered newels, lit by three tall windows at first-floor level and even larger ones on the second storey.

As in his designs for parsonage houses, White took advantage of the southerly aspect for the study, drawing and dining rooms of the master's accommodation, in a domestic style with tile-hanging to the gabled second-floor windows (**3.14**). All the sills are of angled bricks – a practical solution that also maintains the horizontal banding. The canted bay window of the drawing room, set between buttresses, overlooks the garden, where Leach reported that free time from 2pm until 3pm was 'generally spent … on small football in

3.15 Photograph by William Savage of Winchester, *c.*1870, shows the original configuration of the roof and the patterned brickwork at eaves level, now lost.

the garden … one half of which was devoted to us.'[84] A photograph of about 1870, shows the original configuration of the roof, with only two gabled dormers (**3.15**). The large, five-light, first-floor window had been extended downwards and given a small balcony by the time Leach's account was published in 1899, and house photographs show the present oriel window in place by 1923.[85] Leach also mentioned a 'fives court attached to the house' of which there is now no trace.

Savage's photograph reveals the limited extent of the original boys' accommodation to the west. Although the master's quarters have suffered few changes, many alterations and additions to the boys' lodgings have been made over the years, and no plans survive to show White's original design. Leach reported that in his day 'toys' – Winchester slang for desks (the Collegers had "scobs") – 'were in what is now the dining hall, and there were studies for the five seniors, and "toys" for two or three more in what is now the house library, then called the Study Room.'[86] The house library still exists on the north side of the house, while the present 'mugging hall' with very typical White braced ceiling beams, running along the street frontage to the north and east, may well have been the original dining hall. 'At Du Boulay's we never had occasion to complain of the food which was plentiful in quantity, excellent in quality, and well served', Leach reported.[87] Fagging in the house was almost non-existent, consisting only of waking the seniors in the morning, and in the afternoons running their baths after football.[88] No longer to be found is the feature that most impressed the young Leach, and which no doubt also appealed to William White, a 'great stone standing close by the house; a huge erratic boulder which had been dug up out of the foundations, and … was no doubt emblematic of the future greatness of the house.'[89]

Sanatorium, Winchester College

An outbreak of typhoid in 1874, resulting in the death of one of the pupils at the college, led to discussions of better medical facilities than could be provided in the college Sick House built in 1657. When it was decided in 1884 to build a sanatorium, the Rev. James Du Boulay would doubtless have championed White's appointment (Butterfield had resigned his connection with the college in 1882). The headmaster, the Rev. George Ridding, son of Charles Henry Ridding, formerly second master of the college and vicar of Andover, may also have favoured White for he had preached at the service to celebrate the re-opening of Selborne church after White's restoration of 1877-8.

White's design for the parallel isolation block and fever block is unlike any other in his œuvre (**3.16**). The southerly fever block has circular turrets under conical roofs at its south-eastern and south-western corners, whilst the northerly isolation block has similar turrets at its south-eastern and north-western corners. Unlike William Burges's Tower House of 1878, these towers did not contain staircases, but water closets and hand basins suitably removed from the main areas. The staircase to the two upper wards (one of six beds, one of four) of the fever block was in a projecting wing to the north (now demolished). Decoration is confined to moulded brick strings, one running over the narrow ground floor windows to form hood moulds, and to stone dressings above the ground floor windows of the turrets. Bricks set like billets under the eaves continue

3.16 Winchester College sanatorium (now the Art Department), 1884-6, of red brick under steep clay-tiled roofs; the buildings are raised above ground level on shallow arches.

round the towers to form a more obvious pattern. This leads the eye up to bold chimney stacks, those of the fever block being star-shaped in plan (**3.17**).

The isolation block had a central staircase and verandahs at both ground and first floor levels where beds could be pushed out for patients to enjoy fresh air and sunshine. Formed of Early English stone arches on squat pillars, the spandrels are decorated with moulded brick oculi. An adjacent administrative residence (now demolished) and a laundry (altered) completed White's design that won the highest award (silver medal) for 'School Sanatoria' at the 1884 Health Exhibition. Unfortunately the building suffered from the later distaste for Victorian architecture, being described as 'an unlovely thing … all too prominent' by one ex-warden of the college.[90]

3.17 Bold oversailing courses terminate the star-shaped stacks of the fever block, Winchester College sanatorium.

3.18 St Saviour's, Aberdeen Park, 1863-9, showing the patterned brickwork and heavy buttressing.

St Saviour's, Aberdeen Park, Islington

White's pleasure in brick construction is evident in a commission from another member of his wife's family — one where stone might have been expected. The Rev. William David Morrice (husband of Ellen's elder sister, Esther), with his brother John, had in 1850 inherited the Aberdeen Park estate from their uncle George Morrice of St Albans. It was a timely inheritance for the North London Railway from Fenchurch Street

3.19 Herringbone brickwork to the spandrels at St Saviour's is balanced by a cross set in a vesica piscis constructed of the same coloured bricks above the crossing arch.

had just opened and land in Highbury, already a wealthy suburb, was ripe for further development. The spiritual needs of the neighbourhood were served by Christ Church, Highbury Grove, an evangelical stronghold built in 1847-8. In 1863 W.D. Morrice, then vicar of Longbridge Deverill, Wiltshire, determined to build a new church in the centre of Aberdeen Park offering High Church services inspired by the Oxford Movement. The incumbent of Christ Church, Daniel Wilson Jr, argued that the forty houses on Morrice's land were insufficient to provide pastoral work for a minister.[91] Wilson and his patrons fought hard to prevent the erection of a new church that would be likely to appeal to fashionable, wealthy residents and thus diminish their pew rents, but the Ecclesiastical Commissioners ruled in favour of Morrice's proposal for a church where all the sittings would be free.

White's plan for St Saviour's is cruciform about an octagonal crossing tower with a short spire. The chancel is of three bays, the nave of only two-and-a-half, with squat transepts (**3.18**). The polychromy is restrained — red and buff Aylesbury bricks under a roof of 'Staffordshire strawberry coloured tiles'.[92] Extensive areas of plain brickwork, including the central tower under its tiled spire, allow the patterning of the upper parts of the walls to reinforce the extravagant height of this small building.[93] The subtlety of the small diaper pattern confined to the areas above the springing of the clerestory windows and in the gable ends is achieved by using buff bricks 'burnt of clay from the same locality as the red', so that there is 'an absence of that striped effect' and 'harsh and startling contrast of colour' which *The Builder* found 'often painfully conspicuous in modern work.'[94] The bricks are long and thin, laid with wide joints in 'Bruges bond'. This *The Builder* described as alternate courses of headers and stretchers, 'but the stretchers

3.20 White's design for the painted decoration to the sanctuary arch at St Saviour's, 1863-9, includes ears of corn; Christopher Dresser adopted a very similar motif in a design of 1874.

3.21 White putting into practice his theory, based on Goethe's, that the eye will find repose from the red brick in the cool blue-grey of the painted decoration at St Saviour's.

are placed, not over each other in their successive courses, but over each other in their alternate courses; whilst the headers come over each other in their bonding throughout. This in itself forms a sort of diaper pattern.' Fine limestone from the Ancaster quarries in Lincolnshire was used for the window tracery (mostly of a bold French plate design), capitals, corbels and crosses, but copings were of Bridgwater tiles, which maintain the overall soft, red outline of the building. Although described by John Betjeman as 'Great red church of my parents', St Saviour's demonstrates a development from the 'Splendidly mid-Victorian ... polychromatic brick' of Lyndhurst church towards a more subtle colouration, suitable for a quiet north London square.[95]

Internally, the decorative possibilities of brick have been fully realised: the arcades are of moulded red Staffordshire brick with buff brick pilasters, only their caps and some bases of carved limestone, the remaining dressings being of moulded brick. There are no notched edges to the arches and no horizontal banding: the red, black and buff bricks of the spandrels are used again, but more subtly, in a diaper pattern in the upper part of the clerestory walls, producing 'a "woven " effect, suggestive of tapestry'.[96] This patterning is repeated on the east wall of the nave, which opens through a high pointed arch to the crossing (**3.19**). The crossing tower, with its squinches of buff brick dressed with slender, red brick pilasters and patterned brickwork, has distinctly Moorish overtones, reflecting, perhaps, the influence of Owen Jones. The lantern is boarded and was originally decorated in blue with gold stars.[97]

The arch to the sanctuary is completely covered with painted decoration – including vertical bands of golden ears of corn (**3.20**). A complex central motif contains patterns that could have been inspired by Owen Jones's depiction of Egyptian and oriental sources, but they have been filtered through White's fertile imagination to emerge as a design completely his own. The wooden groining of the sanctuary is also painted and gilded, the central boss representing a star, its points of red, blue and golden light spreading down the wooden ribs. A report in *The Guardian* described the painting of 'An angel eight feet high' in 'each of the two easternmost compartments over the altar'.[98] The style of these two figures appears very much later than the 1869 *Guardian* report, so we must assume they have been over-painted.

In a radical move away from the geological banding of All Saints', Notting Hill, here the sanctuary walls are covered with a thin veil of stencilled pattern of stylised flowers, many set in lozenges, and chevrons, in a soft blue-grey highlighted with red and gold, through which the coloured brickwork is visible (**3.21**). This method of applying colour like fine lace over structural polychromy, seems to be unique to White.[99]

The Builder's criticism that the internal brickwork was too rough, was tempered by the knowledge that the walls would be 'diapered in colour, with the brickwork for a ground', though of different design, as the decorative painting that 'has been done ... on the east wall, on either side of the reredos'.[100]

Beneath Lavers and Barraud's rich stained glass east window, designed by Nathaniel

Westlake, White's reredos of three heavily crocketted gables is painted with chevrons and semi-circles of colour, each separated by white according to Owen Jones's theory.[101] It was described as being 'wonderfully lightened and harmonised by carving and colour': a central cross was 'boldly brought out by gold on a relieved surface', while 'shafts of serpentine marble' with carved capitals replaced the plain piers.[102] It originally contained three panels depicting the Agnus Dei, flanked by the two Saints John, painted 'in the process developed by Mr Gambier Parry' to White's cartoons.[103] All the painted decoration was executed by Mr H. Davies from White's designs.[104] The lace-like effect of the stencilled patterns softens the contrasting colours of the brick, while their geometric flower motifs link them not only to the encaustic floor tiles but also to the stained glass in the clerestory. At St Saviour's White invented a method of integrating the various elements of wood, brick, stone and stained glass.

In 1851 White had bemoaned the 'tardy pace' of the Gothic Revival in domestic architecture, due, he believed, to 'much too servile imitations of ancient models'.[105] *The Ecclesiologist* echoed his plea in 1856 when it looked forward 'to the successful solution of the problem of the application of the Pointed style to domestic buildings of all kinds – the mansion, the shop and the warehouse.'[106] It was unusual for an architect who had been praised by the Ecclesiological Society for his designs for churches, parsonages and schools to accept commissions for commercial buildings, and it reflects White's determination to prove the adaptability of Gothic.

4

The Versatility of Gothic

The rebuilding of the City of London after the Great Fire had set the tone for commercial buildings: the Classical style seemed to embody the seriousness and solidity of banks, insurance companies and trading organisations. Civic pride, as well as practical fire precautions, resulted in widened streets and planned development. Similar re-organisation and improvement occurred in agriculture where in the eighteenth century farm buildings were designed to implement new theories and systems. White's belief in the practical application of Gothic principles to all types of building resulted not only in commercial buildings, but in a model farmhouse and outbuildings to his designs. His first designs for a commercial building date from the early days of his Truro practice.

Bank and solicitors' offices, Truro

In the commercial centre of Truro, at the head of the mainly eighteenth-century Boscawen Street, the old Coinage Hall had held meetings of the Cornish Stannary Parliament until 1753. The coinage system that had for centuries controlled the tin trade was abolished in 1838, since when the Coinage Hall had been empty and redundant. With its demolition in May 1848 and a widening of the adjacent roads, the triangular site at the junction of Boscawen and Princes Street was acquired by the Cornish Bank, owned by the Tweedy and Williams families. As well as being chairman of the Cornwall Railway Company and secretary of the Royal Institution of Cornwall, William Mansell Tweedy was a member of the Exeter Diocesan Architectural Society and probably worshipped at Kenwyn, since he was buried there in 1859 and a memorial window erected in the church. It was no doubt through these latter connections that White was commissioned to design a new bank and solicitors' offices on this prestigious site. It was reported that the new building would have 'as handsome a character as would be consistent with the purpose for which it is designed.'[1]

White's bank, commanding the eastern end of Boscawen Street, is in the Perpendicular style with which he was no doubt conversant from his time in Squirhill's practice (**4.1**). However, it is set beneath three irregular, steeply pitched gables surmounted by chimneystacks with typical Cornish tapered caps. The main entrance is in the central bay

97

4.1 White's bank and solicitors' offices, 1848-9, of coursed rubble with granite dressings dominate the commercial centre of Truro.

that projects forward: its arched doors on either side hinge back on each other to reveal the porch. White's belief in the importance of horizontality is expressed by string-courses and drip-moulds, and by the band of carved decorative roundels below the central first-floor window. Above it an arched drip-mould to the attic window hints at the freer style of the flanking solicitors' offices, where some of the windows have pointed heads. All

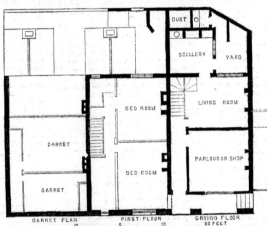

4.2 A row of shops at Audley, designed by White in 1855, includes an arched entrance that originally led to the stable yard and still gives access to the rear.

4.3 Flamboyant hinges on the main entrance door, Baldhu church, 1847–8, were noted in a report of the opening of the church.

are set flush with the wall plane, a feature that was typical of White. Also characteristic is his use of heavily corbelled exposed ceiling beams, and his employment of modern technology – the windows pivot and are operated by winding handles, as found in glasshouses of the time.

Shops, Audley, Staffordshire

Through his work for R.E. Egerton-Warburton at Arley Hall, White received commissions from his relatives by marriage, the Wilbrahams of Rode Hall. The Rev. Charles Philip Wilbraham, half-brother of Randle Wilbraham, was vicar of Audley, just over the county boundary in Staffordshire. He was probably instrumental in securing for White, in 1855, the commission to design a row of shops opposite his church. *The Ecclesiologist* praised the 'picturesque shop-cottages' with their striking 'arched tympana' above the windows, but was concerned at the narrow 'cloister' that provided a covered walkway at the front.[2] Although only 3ft 2ins wide because of the narrowness of the street, this would have provided shelter from the weather and was, *The Ecclesiologist* suggested, perhaps inspired by The Rows in Chester (**4.2**). Some changes to the design as built included the loss of a triangular dormer above the archway to the stable yard that would have expressed the falling ground level. This has resulted in a more regular rhythm of gables, windows and arches that White perhaps accepted, as he later admitted that 'it is impossible not to see a certain amount of beauty and dignity even in the monotonous repetition of the same form'.[3] The construction in the local brownish-red brick with some banding in black brick is considerably more subtle than was intended – perhaps a reflection of conservative local taste – but encaustic tiled paving in geometric patterns of buff, black, white, red, grey and cream brightened the shop entrances. A simple, but elegant, iron gate to the archway expresses White's concern with this medium.

Ironwork

Let us pause to examine White's interest in ironwork, which was no doubt ignited by Pugin's expositions in *True Principles* and examples of his designs executed by Hardman of Birmingham. In White's first building, the church at Baldhu, 'the beauty of the floriated

4.4 Stay to hold the drainpipe away from the wall at St Mary and St John, Witham Friary, Somerset, 1875-6. Similar stays can be seen at St Peter's, Linkenholt, Hampshire, 1869-71, and St Petroc's, Farringdon, Devon, 1870-1.

101

4.5 Altar rail at St Mary's, Andover, Hampshire, 1870-1, where the metal is drawn out into a spiral 'tendril'.

iron hinges' was admired (**4.3**).[4] Even the most utilitarian iron fixtures came under White's scrutiny. It was his practice to fix rainwater pipes with a simple twisted stay several inches from the face of the wall, not only to avoid a 'bend' over the plinth, but to allow 'the back of the pipe being easily painted' (**4.4**).[5]

During the course of several days wandering the courts of the 1862 Exhibition, where his own designs for the reredos of Claydon church, and some cheap plate for mission churches were displayed by Messrs Benham, White made notes on the treatment of ironwork.[6] When reporting at the Architectural Museum on 19 May 1863, he admitted that some of his comments 'may be thought rather hard, but it is with *iron* that we have to deal'.[7] White believed that cast-iron was suitable for 'screens, gratings, or panels formed by piercing', but was adamant in his condemnation of its use as sham wrought-iron.[8] He asserted that in wrought-work there should be 'a sufficiency of fine-drawn and finely-finished iron, standing in strong contrast to the more sturdy sections' to prove its handicraft (**4.5**).[9] White wanted to see more 'village smiths' producing work of which he believed 'with a little instruction, very many show themselves admirably fitted.'[10] Unfortunately records do not reveal who executed White's designs for iron. They range from the extravagant (**4.6**) to the minimalist (**4.7**).

4.6 White's altar rail at Holy Trinity, Elvington, North Yorkshire, 1874-7, contrasts angular, structural elements with sinuous curves.

White's concern with ironwork is evident in his presentation of a lengthy paper to the RIBA in 1865.[11] He admitted his long and 'active interest' in the subject and the difficulties 'of getting his intentions thoroughly or even correctly understood by the workman', often resulting in 'much personal application to the details of the work itself as it comes from beneath the workman's hammer' to achieve his aims (**4.8**).[12] Although he condemned cast-iron that masqueraded as handwork, White was no Luddite and realised that 'a vast population must have vast supplies at a reasonable cost' and that 'There is no drudgery so great … as in those branches of manufacture requiring large

4.7 Simple chancel rail at St Andrew's, Orwell, Cambridgeshire, 1880-3, shows the twisted decoration that White often employed.

4.8 White's churchyard gate at Mollington, Oxfordshire, 1855-6, is striking in its simplicity.

reproductions of one form … to which as yet machinery has not been extended. … Machinery is not only a necessity of the age we live in, but also one of its greatest blessings.'[13] Unlike William Morris, who, despite his Socialist principles, was never able to produce hand-crafted goods at prices affordable by the masses, White maintained that 'we want wares for the million' but not

> the poorest description of that which aspires to be of the highest order; but rather we want the best of its kind in everything, even in that which is of the lowest order of manufacture. For example; if iron or pewter spoons are wanted for our cottages, or for our kitchens, we do not require them to aim at the more ornate patterns employed in spoons of silver, or of gold … Simplicity is wedded for ever to utility.[14]

White's thoughts on iron extended to the 'sibling rivalry' between architecture and civil engineering.[15] Having admitted that to a certain extent they 'so run together and intertwine that it is difficult, if not impossible, exactly to define their point of contact or of separation', White determined that 'the real elements of the two are entirely distinct, the one consisting in the science and art of construction – the other in the science and art of composition and design'.[16] However, he admitted that the engineer could no more ignore composition and design than the architect could omit the principles of construction. White concluded that 'perhaps it would be well if each knew a little more of the other's branch than is sometimes evident at the present day.'[17]

Bank, St Columb Major, Cornwall

On 5 December 1856 the *Royal Cornwall Gazette* announced that the foundation stone of a new bank had been laid at St Columb Major, financed by Thomas Whitford. Around 35 people attended a dinner at the New Inn to celebrate 'the great improvement which the intended bank would afford in the appearance of the town', and the hope was expressed that every man engaged in the building would 'endeavour to excel'. Doubtless through the influence of the Rev. Dr Walker, William White had gained the commission and *The Ecclesiologist* praised his design as 'a creditable attempt to improve the architecture of our country towns.'[18] Unfortunately, the bank of Hawkey, Whitford, Collins, Carter & Co., which had branches in Falmouth and Padstow, failed in June 1866 and Bank House was sold for £1,500 in the following February to a Mr Geake of Liskeard.[19]

At Bank House White appears to have followed Ruskin's admonition to take advantage of 'every variety of hue … of natural stone', but true to Pugin's beliefs, he

4.9 The dark slate roof of Bank House, St Columb Major, 1856-7, is enlivened by White's favoured red crested ridge tiles, 'Wimpole Street' pattern, by Coulthursts of Bridgwater. The ground floor window on the right illuminates the banking hall.

4.10 The original entrance to the domestic quarters of Bank House was originally of two storeys with a sloping glazed roof from the eaves beneath the chimney

4.11 White's typically delicate stained glass behind castellated shutters at Bank House.

used only those to be found locally – fine-textured, light grey elvan, slatestone, limestone and pinkish porphyry – interspersed with irregular courses of granite and of soft red brick.[20] This exuberance is contained within a simple form of two parallel ranges, the rear one with a cross-gabled extension, allowing the various colours to maintain an unbroken emphasis. It is controlled by a sober, slated roof anchored to the gable ends with heavy stone copings (**4.9**). (The south gable end of the range fronting the road terminates in a small stone cross: perhaps an acknowledgement of the church opposite, and a belief that God and Mammon could exist side-by-side.) The colour is intensified around the pointed windows, with narrow voussoirs of red brick, dark slatestone and pale granite. This exterior vividness builds to a crescendo with encaustic tiles in the heads of the windows which identifies the banking hall . The interior of this room is equally sumptuous with encaustic tiles above the windows and surrounding the granite fireplace.

The extensive domestic quarters are entered from a side entrance that was originally a two-storey timber glazed porch (**4.10**). The remainder of the L-shaped building includes semi-basement kitchen offices, cellars and strong room, while the first- and ground floor rooms boast richly decorated fireplaces and, in the drawing room, an arcade of marble columns with granite caps and bases. Besides the vibrantly coloured stonework, Bank House has pale, almost feminine, stained glass. The ground floor windows are sashes, rather than White's usual casements, with the colour restricted to the heads (**4.11**). White's practical nature dictated that the occupants required maximum daylight, and his aesthetic sense determined that externally any stronger colouring would conflict with the wall material. Bank House is instructive, for we see here White's total vision and

4.12 Free-flowing grilles to the basement at Bank House are almost art nouveau in spirit.

control, encompassing constructive colouring both external and internal, joinery in the form of bookcases and cupboards, the boundary walls and gates and the wrought-iron grilles to the basement windows (**4.12**).[21]

Mawgan-in-Pydar, Cornwall

Much later in his career, in 1884, White was commissioned to restore the medieval parish church at Colan, less than four miles south-west of St Columb Major, Cornwall. One of the churchwardens involved was William Paget Hoblyn, who owned the extensive Fir Hill estate at Colan. A graduate of Queen's College, Oxford, and a justice of the peace, it appears that sometime before 1889 he commissioned White to improve one of his farmhouses, now known as Lower Denzell, about two miles north-west of St Columb, and to design model outbuildings nearby.[22] White added a cross-wing of two storeys with attics at the western end of the farmhouse; a central entrance doorway on the south, and a pent-roofed kitchen entrance further east. Beyond the limits of the garden on the east, a two-storey mill and single-storey associated buildings form a double-quadrangle with a separate stable block nearby. The material is coursed stone, the variations in colour from pale gold to dark grey giving a warm, speckled appearance under steeply sloping slate roofs. Although all are now private dwellings and have been altered and extended, the arrangement of thin pieces of stone like voussoirs round the heads of the windows (reminiscent of the church at Gerrans) and high relieving arches remain characteristic of White.

These commercial buildings all reflect the rise of the prosperous middle class in nineteenth-century England. But the bulk of White's architectural commissions, for churches, parsonage houses and schools, still sprang from the old hierarchy – the landed gentry and the established church. The Cornish family were influential in the West Country, but for generations Hampshire had been the heartland of the White family.

Hampshire

The Rev. Gilbert White was appointed vicar of Selborne in 1681. His grandson, also Gilbert, author of *A Natural History of Selborne*, was born and lived there as curate for more than 60 years, and is buried in the churchyard. William White's grandfather, youngest brother of the naturalist, was rector of Fyfield, near Andover, about 25 miles north-west of Selborne. His son, William's father, although incumbent of Pattishall, Northamptonshire, from 1843 until his death in 1864, appears often to have been resident at Abbots Ann, near Andover.[23] It is not surprising, therefore, that when Henry Master White returned home from the Cape in the summer of 1857 it was to the curacy of Andover. Here in November 1857 he brought his bride, Henrietta Alcock, who had been a worker in Bishop Gray's former parish of Stockton-on-Tees. Charles Henry Ridding, vicar of Andover since 1834, and formerly second master at Winchester College, was no doubt delighted to welcome another Wykehamist. Doubtless it was Ridding who, in 1856, identified the need for new churches in the countryside near Andover, and who was instrumental in securing endowments from the college. And it is likely that it was Henry Master White who ensured that William gained the commission.

Christ Church, Hatherden, and Christ Church, Smannell

The funds to build chapels for these 'most destitute hamlets' of Hatherden and Smannell, a few miles north of Andover, were very limited. As William White was to point out in a later lecture, this meant that it was impossible to impart 'the exact character of an old building of any definite style or period', his aim being to give each church 'a genuine character of its own'.[24] True to his principles, White constructed both Hatherden and Smannell churches of the local materials – flint and brick. In its unknapped state, the silvery whiteness of the flint contrasts strongly with irregular bands of red brick (necessary for structural stability) which is used also for dressings and voussoirs. Some of the voussoirs at Hatherden extend into the horizontal bands, giving the impression of bending (**4.13**). While at Smannell there are a few bricks above the west window that look as if they have 'escaped' into the flint wall (**4.14**).

White also took the opportunity of using the buildings as a test of the relative costs of

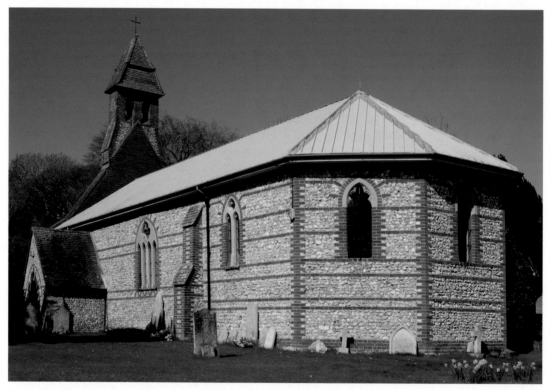

4.13 Christ Church, Hatherden, 1856-7, showing White's 'bent' voussoirs that extend into the horizontal brick banding.

110

4.14 Christ Church, Smannell, 1856-7, where some voussoirs in the west wall appear to have 'escaped' in a post-modernist fashion.

the 'simple-parallelogram and … the subdivided church'.[25] Based on his theory that the equilateral triangle was the basis of good proportion, White believed that the height of a building must be determined by its breadth.[26] He was pleased to discover that his church at Smannell, just 62ft long with a 22ft wide nave and 8ft wide lean-to aisle, designed to accommodate 200, would cost £648, while the single-cell church at Hatherden, 70ft long and 25ft wide, accommodating 160, would cost £700.

White designed apsidal chancels for both Christ Church, Hatherden (**4.15**), and Christ Church, Smannell (**4.16**). With a continuous roofline for economy, this was an ideal way to define the chancel, which was otherwise marked externally only by buttresses. Although condemned by Neale in 1844 as 'un-Anglican … un-natural …[and] not by any means well-looking without a long chancel', enthusiasm for continental Gothic had rendered

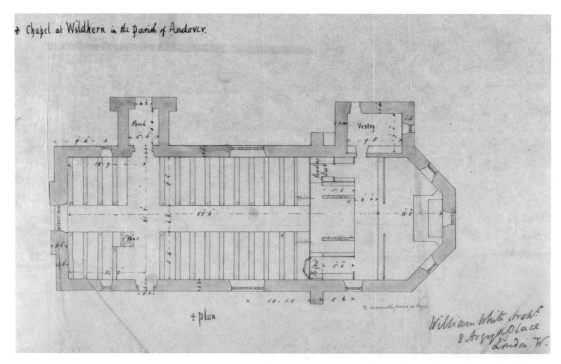

4.15 White's plan of Christ Church, Hatherden (Wildhern is a hamlet ½ mile to the east), 1856.

apses acceptable, and Street, for instance, used the form extensively.[27] Butterfield resisted such non-English forms, using an apse only once, at Rugby School. White soon moved away from eclectic sources, using the apsidal form mainly in poor, urban situations, such as St Mark's, Hanwell, Middlesex, and in his churches for Canon Erskine Clarke in the 1870s and '80s (see chapter 7).[28]

Both churches had clay-tiled roofs and tall brick and flint western belfries with pyramidal tiled caps (**4.17**), while the interiors were of buff and red brick, also in irregular bands.[29] The arcade to the north aisle of Christ Church, Smannell, is supported on slender brick piers that swell out without abaci (**4.18**).

Andover was within the parish of Abbots Ann, where the rector, the Hon. and Rev. Samuel Best, younger brother of the 2nd Baron Wynford, made applications to the ICBS for grants for these two new churches. White's determination to employ local materials and methods of construction did not meet the approval of the ICBS, who objected to his proposal for wooden windows. White argued that 'the extreme difficulty of obtaining stone in that District, – and hence also of there being any proper stone cutting masons in the neighbourhood', resulting in a high cost, precluded it.[30] He also pointed out that builders 'can work up materials to which they are accustomed, much more readily … than when other materials are forced upon them'. This awareness of the methods and

112

attitude of the workmen would later underpin the Arts and Crafts Movement. Despite White's claim that an insistence on stone 'would act as a great bar to the progress of proper architecture in rural districts if it were taken for granted that no deviation from precedent might be made to accommodate the construction of a Building to local circumstances', the Society was adamant that stone windows were a condition of their grant.[31] *The Ecclesiologist* endorsed the society's stance, remarking that 'Mr. White's fanlight wooden windows are anything but beautiful.'[32] In an effort to limit the cost, only the French-inspired, plate-traceried heads and mullions are of stone, the jambs are of brick, and all are flush with the wall surface.

Both external and internal structural polychromy in these small churches was restrained, no doubt due mainly to financial constraints. They also express White's belief that churches built at small cost should 'not be decked out in structural finery to which they are not entitled'.[33] White believed that this discipline was 'in one sense a school of art. It teaches us the best, the most natural, the most simple modes of construction, and fits us for the better use of our higher opportunities.'[34]

St Michael and All Angels', Lyndhurst

Such a 'higher opportunity' came to White as a direct result of these two 'cheap churches'. The Rev. John Compton wished to rebuild his dilapidated eighteenth-century

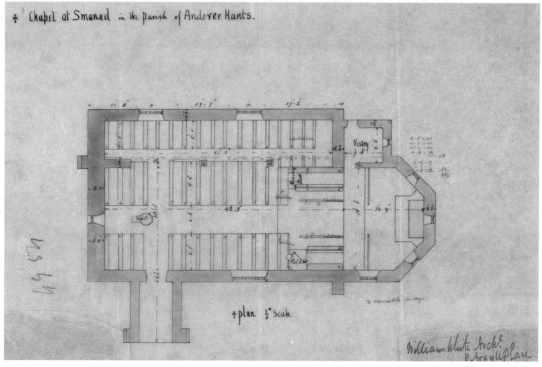

4.16 White's original plan of Christ Church, Smannell, with lean-to north aisle, 1856.

4.17 The belfry at Christ Church, Smannell, has been rebuilt lower, and with a single bell opening, rather than with the original pair. A large buttress on the south and the diagonal south-west buttress were added in 1893-4.

church at Lyndhurst in the New Forest, and asked his bishop to recommend an architect. Having just consecrated White's two little churches, Charles Sumner of Winchester replied that 'If I were about to build a church myself I should certainly apply to Mr. White, for taste, for solidity of workmanship, and for economy. In the latter particular he seems to me unrivalled.'[35] However, Compton appears to have invited other architects to submit their ideas also, for *The Builder* reported that 'Several designs were sent in and those of Mr W. White, London, adopted.'[36] Compton obviously envisaged a richly constructed and decorated church: White understood 'that there need be no stint in the ornamentation of the work which might be eventually carried out'.[37] However, significant modifications were obviously made, as White claimed £75 for a complete set of detail drawings that were not used.[38] A contract for the work was placed with J. & H. Hillary of Longparish for £5,830, although, as *The Builder* of 8 October 1859 reported, 'the tower and spire, porches, north aisle, several of the ornamental windows, and the whole of the carving will remain unfinished until the committee have funds.'

Set on rising ground, White's church of St Michael and All Angels, comprising a nave with north and south aisles, transepts and chancel, with overall dimensions of about 100ft x 50ft, commands the small country town of Lyndhurst (**4.19**). The tower, with its blind arcade and yellow brick spire ornamented with chevrons of red brick, was built in 1868-9, and at a height of more than 140ft is a prominent local landmark. The constructional colour is most prominent in the gabled north porch (**4.20**). Thin bands of red tile are again 'bent', as at Hatherden, to give the appearance of voussoirs. This practice was adopted by Lutyens in 1896 for the entrance to Gertrude Jekyll's house at Munstead Wood, Surrey (**4.21**).

A feature of Lyndhurst church is the four great triangular dormer windows that flood the nave with light.[39] In a printed circular to his parishioners dated 1 March 1859, the Rev. Compton referred to 'a very favourable opinion expressed by the first architect of the day, Mr Scott' to the main features of White's plans.[40] Scott was 'decidedly

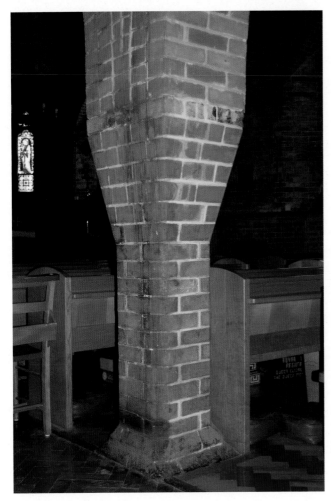

4.18 Christ Church, Smannell. Unornamented brick pier to original lean-to north aisle which was extended and separately gabled to White's design in 1893-4.

4.19 White charged the Rev. Compton of Lyndhurst three guineas for the preparation of the perspective and superintendence of the 'Drawing on Wood' used for this illustration.

favourable to the idea of gabled lights in the place of a continued clerestory they will I am sure look well both within and without and will give the church an individuality of character which it is not always easy to obtain'.[41] In fact, Scott had used similar triangular dormers in his dining hall of 1856 at Bradfield College, Berkshire. *The Ecclesiologist* noted the tracery in White's dormers, criticising the 'host of geometrical figures, very crudely combined, in the heads', which contains, in White's typical fashion, spots of rich colour in otherwise clear glass.[42] However, *The Ecclesiologist* praised the 'richly-moulded west door', which had been paid for by Jean Baptiste François de Châtelain, translator of the works of Shakespeare into French, who was a regular visitor to Lyndhurst. The west door had been the entrance used by royal dukes who resided at Queen's House, immediately west of the church. Although the last royal resident, the duke of Cambridge, had died in 1850, it was obviously thought fitting to decorate the archivolt with sculptures – of prophets and evangelists. Beneath wide brick voussoirs, the chamfering of the arch is overlaid with a broad band of stone cut into trefoils and decorated with rosettes, all flattened in White's preferred style (**4.22**).

Internally there is no sense of oppression from the rich colouring of the brick construction, for White has articulated the spatial volumes so that the church appears very much larger than its actual size. This is no doubt due to his careful regard for proportion – 'the effect likely to be produced by any certain relation of breadth to length in a building, or in its several bays or divisions.'[43] The red bricks of the arcade arches are laid to form notched edges; outlined with black bricks, these provide a strong contrast with the banded yellow and white brick spandrels. Each pier of the nave arcades is surrounded by eight slender slate columns. Although *The Ecclesiologist* referred rather disparagingly to these columns as a 'novelty', they were very necessary to spread the load on the brick piers.[44] They also contribute a lightness compared with, for instance, the heavy muscularity of Street's church of St James the Less, Pimlico, with its massive columns, and use of extensive notching, both internally and externally.

At Lyndhurst, the capitals of Bath stone were executed to White's designs. One of Compton's parishioners admitted that she would have to give up the idea of paying for a carving of 'the Vine and Fig', as there was insufficient room 'for them to be in proper relief, so I will have the pretty convolvulus band sent by the Architect' (**4.23**).[45] Having arranged for Thomas Earp to send a man down to carve a capital, White then informed the Rev. Compton that he would send another craftsman on the same terms. He instructed that 'When he goes there, Earp's cap should be boarded up – for I wish him to take his interpretation independently of Earp's – and then I shall be able to judge which carver of the two I should prefer for the other work eventually.'[46] White evidently chose the naturalistic style (which, 'of its kind', according to Eastlake, 'is excellent') of George Seale from Earp's Lambeth workshop.[47] Unfortunately there is no record of the craftsman responsible for the carving of the esoteric collection of portrait carvings of reformers and martyrs that form the corbels. Harry Hems of Exeter carved the great

4.20 The north entrance to St Michael and All Angels, Lyndhurst, 1858–69, where massive corner buttresses of red and yellow brick on huge red-brick plinths support the moulded arched doorway.

wooden angels holding musical instruments that decorate the roof.[48] These may have been part of White's original scheme, which had to be curtailed for lack of funds. A photograph, *c.*1880, shows the earlier configuration of the roof (**4.24**), but by 1893-4 the present hammer-beam roof was complete (**4.25**).

With its polychromatic brickwork and rich carving, St Michael's, Lyndhurst, shows the influence of John Ruskin's advocacy of continental Gothic. The Rev. Compton seems to have been keen to have a fashionable church, produced by the leading artists and designers of the day. He was certainly well-connected, as befitted the incumbent of a parish in the New Forest which, with its proximity to the royal retreat, Osborne House, on the Isle of Wight, had become a popular residential area for the aristocracy. His father was the M.P. for South Hampshire, his wife the daughter of Admiral Sir Charles Burrard, Bt, and his sister was married to Rear-Admiral Robert Aitchison, all of whom were generous benefactors of the church. Although White designed the choir stalls for the chancel and the seats for the south aisle, he appears to have had little say in some aspects of the interior decoration. However, he may well have suggested employing Morris, Marshall, Faulkner & Co. for stained glass, since both he and Morris were members of the Hogarth Club and on the committee of the Mediæval Society, and Morris had

4.21   White's 'bent' voussoirs adopted by Lutyens in the entrance to Munstead Wood, Godalming, 1896.

119

4.22 The arch to the great west door at Lyndhurst church where White has superimposed stone tracery over the moulding.

4.23 Capital in Lyndhurst church, carved by George Seale of Earp's atelier, to White's convolvulus design.

4.24 View, *c.*1880, of the interior of Lyndhurst church shows the original, simple treatment of the roof.

recently supplied glass for three churches designed by White's friend, Bodley. Despite that, it appears that Compton dealt directly with Edward Burne-Jones regarding the design for the seven lights, alternately broad and narrow, of the great east window in memory of Robert Aitchison, which *The Ecclesiologist* had condemned as 'thoroughly indefensible … a mere *capriccio*, … impure in style'.[49]

It seems that White was not consulted regarding John Hungerford Pollen's 'Tree of Jesse' decoration to the north and south sanctuary walls, nor about Leighton's fresco of the 'Wise and Foolish Virgins' on the east wall.[50] He later referred to Leighton's painting as 'a most magnificent failure' because, rather than a 'suggestive and symbolical treatment', the realistic depiction of Christ appears 'as it were, standing in the middle of the altar'.[51] When, in 1863, a monument was commissioned from G.E. Street for the north side of the sanctuary, there was no mention of referring the matter to White, who was now engaged with the construction of the new south aisle. (The gift of £400 from one Walter Williams had allowed the demolition of the old aisle and completion of the building to White's design.) Compton's only concern was that 'nothing must interfere with Leighton's picture'.[52] Compton must have consulted the artist, who replied that 'the <u>darker</u> stone of which you speak is the most likely to favour our fresco … [but] I should not wish to oppose any preferences of Mr Street's'.[53]

There are parallels here with Butterfield's All Saints', Margaret Street, where Beresford

Lyndhurst Church.

4.25 Postcard, post-1894–5, shows the present hammer-beam roof, surely designed by White, as it is very similar to his design for St Luke's Chapel at Brompton Hospital, 1891–2. It is first shown in a postcard of 1893–4.

Hope 'suggested several vital features of the architecture' and selected many of the craftsmen.[54] It is certainly not an easy position for an architect to defy a strong-minded patron who, in the case of Compton, had raised much of the funds on the basis of specific items of expenditure. However, Lyndhurst church is proof of White's position in the vanguard of modern architecture of the day, where his client wished to create an ensemble of work by the young men leading the Gothic Revival and Pre-Raphaelite art and design movements.

National Schools, Andover

It appears that Henry Master White was actively involved in all aspects of the parish of Andover. He was no doubt influential in obtaining the commission for William to design a school and master's house at Chute, five miles to the south-west, in 1858; and in 1860 he obtained a mortgage of £800 in order to spend £400 improving the vicarage house there, also to plans by William. He was presumably instrumental in the decision in 1859 to increase the size of the National Schools in Andover, to his brother's design. In 1854 William had designed a school at Great Budworth, Cheshire, which, with its separate rooms and entrances for boys and girls, pre-dated the demands of the Ecclesiological Society. Their *Instrumenta Ecclesiastica*, 2nd series, 1856, insisted on total separation of the sexes in schools and 'emphatically reminded … all persons connected with Schools … that very great moral evils may arise from neglect of these precautions.'[55] In his paper of 1851, 'Upon Some of the Causes and Points of Failure in Modern Design', White had set out his own criteria, emphasising that 'The schools should be the main object, the house and offices entirely subordinate both in size and detail.'[56]

The original Andover National School had been built in East Street in 1818, the cost of nearly £1,000 being paid by the Rev. William Stanley Goddard, who provided the site on part of his kitchen garden. Goddard had resigned as headmaster of Winchester College in 1809 and moved to Andover, his wife's home town.[57] White's plans, dated 19 March 1859, show a very thorough separation of the sexes. The range of buildings runs north-south, with the boys' school and playground at the north end and the girls' and infants' schools and playgrounds at the south, separated by houses and gardens for the teachers. The symmetrical, centrally-placed houses for the master and mistress each had a parlour facing the road, a pantry and a kitchen with scullery behind it facing north (**4.26**). On the first floor were three bedrooms, while an earth closet and coal shed stood in the north-east corner of each garden.

The whole building is of red brick, laid in English bond, with irregular horizontal bands of blue-grey bricks, those level with the springing of the pointed windows and at their bases being a double row with alternate yellow and red headers between. Despite the loss of the flèche above the girls' school and many of the battered chimneys with oversailing courses, this is still obviously a robust High Victorian building of the Butterfield genre (**4.27**). However, as the eye travels to the residences in the centre of the

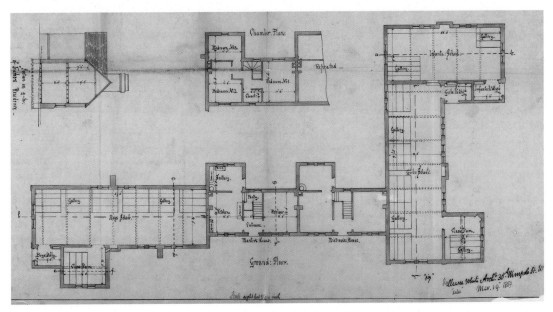

4.26 White's ground plan of Andover National Schools, 1859, showing the complete separation of boys and girls.

4.27 South-west corner of the girls' school, Andover, where White's wooden plate-traceried windows have been extended downwards, and the chimney has obviously been rebuilt.

main range facing the street, the roofline drops, the patterned brickwork simplifies, the windows become small, paired rectangles, the doors are boarded and plain (**4.28**). This, one feels, is the true, English, White, designing in a modest, unassuming style for comfort and tranquillity. A well and pump were placed between the two dwellings, each with their west-facing 'Flower-Garden' where the tired teachers could relax at the end of the day. Despite his High Church persuasion and his contacts with the Tractarian movement, White's schools are markedly less ecclesiastical and exude a lightness of spirit that is not to be found, for instance, in Street's school at Eastbury, Berkshire (**4.29**).[58]

In 1851 the government's Committee on Education had issued a *Memorandum respecting the organization of schools in parallel groups of benches and desks*, together with model plans showing desks arranged on one side of the schoolroom only.[59] Although neither the funds nor the staff existed for separate classrooms, this was an acknowledgement of the benefits of collective teaching. Previously children were divided into groups round the room and repeated their rote learning to monitors. It was intended that groups of desks could be separated by curtains to allow teaching by pupil-teachers under the overall superintendence of the headmaster, who could also, on occasion, give collective lessons to the whole school. The floor of the schoolroom rose in tiered steps (galleries), which allowed all children a clear view of the teacher, and he of them, while a separate classroom adjacent to the schoolroom could be used for older pupils. Although students were no longer required to leave their desks to recite their lessons to the teacher or to a monitor, space was still required at the front of each group for the pupil-teacher's blackboard and easel, 'or to draw the children from their desks, and to instruct them standing, for the sake of relief by a change of position.'[60]

White's detailed drawings for Andover School specified six desks 8ft 6ins long, a further six to be 1½ins higher, and six more to be 3ins higher, for the boys' and girls' schoolrooms. A note on the drawing of a lifting lid to the desks is marked '(in Girls School only)'. Perhaps White was aware of the noise implications if the boys were so provided! With backless benches attached, the desks were fixed in three parallel rows to plinths, so that each row was raised between three and five inches above the other. The detailed drawing for the galleried seating in the classroom adjacent to each schoolroom shows benches with backs, which was an improvement on the committee's belief that sufficient support was provided by leaning over the desks.[61] The infants' school with galleries at each end would have accommodated children from the age of three, who were often sent to school to allow mothers to work. Much of the infants' curriculum

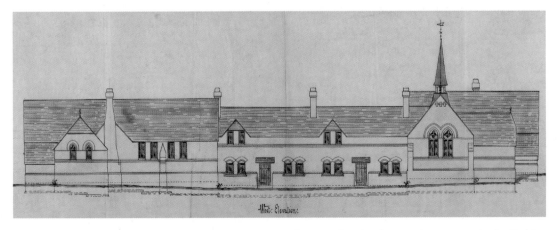

4.28 White's drawing of the west elevation, Andover schools, facing the street. As built, the porches are gabled, not the pent ones shown.

4.29 West elevation of G.E. Street's design for Eastbury school and schoolhouse, Berkshire, 1859, is a more overtly ecclesiastical design than White's at Andover.

involved noisy 'marching' and 'drilling'. The sound of these activities was screened by the girls' school from interfering with the boys' studies.

St Mary the Virgin, Selborne

The White family's proprietorial feeling for the village that is linked to their name is evident in a letter to William from his father in 1858, in which he reported that 'I have written to Mr Ball to ask if I can be admitted to the meeting which is to discuss Uncle White's Monument, and if I cannot whether he can manage to insist your name is amongst the Architects who may give sketches for the monument.'[62] The question of a memorial in Selborne to Gilbert White arose again in 1893, the centenary of his death. William White's opinion was that it should take the form of a drinking fountain in the village fed from the well-head nearby. He designed a stone fountain under a gabled roof surmounted by a cross. An oak seat on either side reinforced the inscriptions 'Welcome to the Weary' and 'Come ye to the Waters' that he proposed (**4.30**). Unfortunately, nothing more was heard of these plans. But perhaps it was inevitable that William White was chosen as the architect of various restorations and refurbishments of the village church in Selborne during the nineteenth century.

His first work at St Mary's for which documentary evidence survives was an extensive restoration completed in November 1877.[63] Besides rebuilding the north transept, the contractor, Dyer of Alton, replaced the rotten nave roof with one of king-post construction, while open benches on a wood-block floor took the place of the decayed pews.[64] In May 1874, Magdalen College, Oxford, as patron of the church, agreed to make a grant of £250 'payable in five years'; and in February 1877 ordered that 'a donation of £100 (payable in 4 years) be made towards carrying out the first part of the Restoration of Selborne Church.'[65] In 1883 the college gave their final subscription of £100, which was for the restoration of the south aisle of the church, again to White's plans and executed by Dyer. Most of the southern and eastern walls had to be taken down, each stone being numbered so that they could be rebuilt accurately. Jambs and cusps of two three-light

4.30 White's 1893 design for a memorial fountain in Selborne included a trough for dogs.

4.31 St Mary the Virgin, Selborne, where White restored the south aisle, 1882–3, and rebuilt the east wall of the chancel, 1886.

windows were found in the south wall, one of which White 'conjecturally restored' (in 1920 filled with stained glass depicting St Francis with birds as a memorial to Gilbert White), a lancet being substituted for the other (**4.31**).[66]

Gilbert White had described the east wall of the chancel as having two lancets 'of a moderate size'.[67] In 1793 his brother, the London bookseller and publisher, Benjamin White, had donated a sixteenth-century Flemish triptych but by 1877 this was affected by damp, so the incumbent, the Rev. Edward Russel Bernard, decided it needed a solid wall behind it. He raised subscriptions and obtained grants from the ICBS and the diocesan society.[68] The east wall was rebuilt with three short lancets, the glass being supplied by James Powell & Sons of Whitefriars. Powell's order books reveal that in April 1886 they had a tripartite client – C. Parsons (presumably a relative of the previous incumbent, the Rev. Frederick James Parsons), William White and the Rev. E.R. Bernard. The lancet triplet was in memory of the Rev. Parsons, the artist/craftsman was listed as Tate, and the subject was to be the Crucifixion with the Blessed Virgin Mary and St John 'from Lewes'. It was noted that 'Cartoons to be submitted to Mr White'.[69] Henry Holiday had designed windows for All Saints', Lewes, Sussex, and it is a mark of White's tight control that despite his eminence, Holiday's design was required to be submitted. By September 1886 the client appears as C. Parsons alone, the subject being described simply as 'The Crucifixion from Holiday's (Lewes) cartoons' on a grisaille ground, fixed by Tate.[70] The Rev. Bernard's widow later described altar rails 'of light iron and wood' (now in the south aisle), designed by 'Mr William White, of G. White's family, and we were very pleased with all his work.'[71]

These schools, parsonages and churches, both new and restorations, are typical of many of the commissions that comprised the bulk of a successful mid-nineteenth-century architect's practice. However, White was unusual in his brave attempt to break the bonds of precedent and utilise local materials and workmanship (that would later be a founding principle of the Arts and Crafts Movement) by employing wooden tracery at Hatherden and Smannell. His preference for local materials was not confined to small buildings constructed to low budgets; it can be seen also in the large, prestigious commissions that he gained.

5

Magnificent or Modest?

The publication of White's writings and the generally positive reviews of his designs by *The Ecclesiologist* strengthened his position as one of the leaders of the Gothic revival. Commissions from members of the Exeter Diocesan Architectural Society reflected his standing. In 1858 he designed 'a Pointed country house at Winscote, Devonshire' for barrister and later M.P., John Curzon Moore-Stevens. His drawings provoked 'an interesting discussion on the adaptation of Pointed features, and especially windows, to modern habits.'[1] The house, entered through an immense *porte-cochère* and arranged around a large, square, top-lit hall, was constructed of the local yellow brick with alternate voussoirs of darker brick to emphasise its pointed character. His client's father, the archdeacon of Exeter, had been a vice-president of the society with the Rev. George Cornish in 1844, and in 1853 again held this position, together with John Garratt Jr of Bishop's Court, Clyst St Mary, near Exeter.

Bishop's Court, Exeter

John Garratt's father, also John, a London tea and coffee merchant who had been lord mayor of the City in 1824-5, purchased Bishop's Court on his retirement in 1833. Originally the bishop's palace in the thirteenth century, the house had been rebuilt early in the nineteenth (**5.1**). By 1851 John Garratt Sr had moved to a smaller property in Clifton, Bristol, leaving his son to move into Bishop's Court. But it was not until his father's death in 1859 that John Garratt Jr, who had become a follower of the Oxford Movement while up at Christ Church, commissioned William White to remodel Bishop's Court. White's restoration, described by *The Ecclesiologist* as 'a happy opportunity well taken advantage of', included decorations and furnishings that recreated its past glory, but unfortunately no drawings or correspondence have survived.[2]

White's rugged, asymmetrical design was based on the existing north-south spine corridor, which he extended to the north to accommodate a new staircase. The stucco was stripped and a new main entrance via a glazed porch was provided in the angle of the library wing on the east elevation (**5.2**). As with his modest chapels in Hampshire, White

5.1   An estate map of 1833 gives a view of Bishop's Court as rebuilt by the 2nd Lord Graves, *c*.1803.

used local materials, here taking advantage of seven or eight varieties of local stone, including brown slate stone, reddish Heavitree sandstone, and creamy chalk stone from Beer.[3] They can be seen in buttresses, relieving arches and dressings to windows, including the oriel above the library, adjacent to the entrance. On the west (garden) elevation traces of the sixteenth-century house were preserved, while White superimposed flat Gothic arches supported by slender columns on to huge sash windows. He placed a tower at the north-west corner where one had been shown in a sketch by the Devon antiquarian, John Swete, in 1801. The ground-floor window here is decorated externally with portrait busts, as at Baldhu church, of the young Queen Victoria and Bishop Phillpotts, and internally with stencilled decoration (**5.3**).[4] To the south White grouped new domestic offices, with varied half-hipped gables, steep banded tiled roofs and extravagant chimneys, which contrast with the simple horizontal line of the parapet of the main range. Naturally the focus of the building was to be the chapel, which had previously been reduced to a

5.2 White retained the parapet to the earlier roof at Bishop's Court, to provide a strong horizontal balance to the large, buttressed central chimney. The porch, whose roof originally reached to the stone corbels visible on the library wall, has been dismantled by a former owner.

servants' hall, with a bedroom floor inserted. Protruding from the southern end of the main range of the entrance elevation, White asserted its purpose with massive buttresses below triple-lancet windows and surmounted it with a shingled bell-turret, topped with extravagant ironwork. The rich structural polychromy of the exterior of the house is matched, if not surpassed, by White's internal decoration that provides, in the words of the Grade I listing description: 'a serious mid-C19 architect's conception of domestic Gothic'.

What had been the billiard room was transformed by White into the entrance hall, separated from the spinal corridor by an arched arcade of polished black marble columns, their forms reflected by those to the windows. Here, as elsewhere in the house, White 'gothicised' the earlier cornices and ceiling decorations by picking out certain motifs and surrounding them with his own patterns. Above a wood-block floor and skirtings of buff, red and black tiles, the walls are painted a soft, buttery yellow and covered with stencilled decorations (5.4). This is a development from the simple 'geological' bands of colour that had been specified for All Saints', Notting Hill, while the dado border appears to reflect a knowledge of the Egyptian motifs recorded by Owen Jones, although the designs are distinctly White's own. In the west-facing reception rooms, decoration seems to have been confined to simple designs painted or stencilled on to the ceilings, and incorporating the earlier ceiling-roses.[5] In the library gilded whorls to the shutter hinges appear to be the only decoration and eminently suitable for this serious, masculine room. White's drawings illustrating the decoration of the dining room were shown in the Architectural Exhibition of 1863. Although supporting modern Gothic, the *Building News* reported that the scheme was 'uncompromisingly Mediæval', and therefore an inappropriate anachronism in the nineteenth century.[6] Since the inlaid patterns and painted ironwork to sideboards was the only decoration to survive, it is now impossible to judge White's design. However, since he always emphasised the importance of modern scientific improvements, it seems unlikely that White would have ignored them in such a prestigious project.

The climax of White's decorative treatment is in the chapel, which is reached by a corridor flanked by a nodding ogee-headed niche containing a white marble statue of St Gabriel, to whom it is dedicated. Although the stencilling of the corridor walls has been obliterated, above the doorway to the chapel are painted two angels, undoubtedly to White's design, which give an indication of the splendour within (**5.5**). The entrance

5.3 The wood-groined garden room at the base of the north-west tower of Bishop's Court has White's typical delicate stained glass, and stencilled wall decoration.

133

is beneath a wooden screen containing his characteristic geometric stained glass in pale colours, which supports a gallery accessible from the bedroom corridor above. Beyond is the lofty oratory where the walls are painted a creamy white, stencilled with red lines to represent masonry.[7] Stylised red flowers within whorled black tendrils are stencilled on to this grid, increasing in intensity at the east end, where stripes of colour interspersed with decorated roundels run below the windows. *The Guardian* reported that 'enough of the original work was discovered to serve as a good guide for the restoration of the windows and of the colouring of the walls.' The few surviving encaustic tiles were reproduced by William Godwin & Son of Lugwardine, Herefordshire, to form a richly patterned floor; and the altar was painted with geometric flowers and a central cross, all in red, blue and gold.[8] Together with a triptych depicting the Annunciation, Crucifixion and Nativity by N.H.J. Westlake, beneath the rich stained glass of the east windows by Lavers and Barraud, this results in a glorious, unified ensemble (**5.6**).

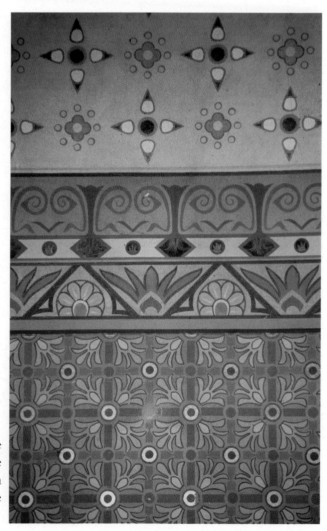

5.4 The stencilled decoration of the hall, where the intense pattern of the dado is separated from the more open design of the upper walls by a wide border of three horizontal bands.

5.5 The main corridor leads south to the chapel entrance, where the fresco shows angels playing musical instruments.

The Guardian report of the service for the re-dedication of the chapel confirms the close relationship between White and John Garratt. The offertory was devoted to funds for the erection of a church at Masbrough, Rotherham, where the curate was William's brother, Henry Master White. Henry ministered to 'upwards of 7,000' with no church, parsonage or schools in what was said to be 'the most destitute district within the diocese of York'.[9] Later, in 1870, John Garratt was a major subscriber to the rebuilding of the church in the nearby village of Farringdon, Devon, and no doubt ensured that William White was employed as architect. White obviously also designed the painted decoration to the brick and stone of the chancel there.

During the execution of his Bishop's Court design, White gave a lecture, 'A Plea for Polychromy', at the Architectural Museum, in London, in which he declared that colour was of equal importance to 'form, texture, or proportion'.[10] White pointed out that just as the beneficial effects of light and air were now becoming known, so colour was proving to affect the human body and psyche. He explained that a love of colour was one of the instinctive, unconscious influences that increased human happiness, as could be seen in the behaviour of young children. He maintained that this association with the pleasures of childhood is retained until old age, when the mind can be stimulated by coloured patterns. Twentieth-century clinical tests demonstrating that a dull environment turns the mind inwards for lack of external stimuli have proved White's argument.[11]

White's lecture continued with an exposition of the effects of different colours on the optic nerves: he maintained that the nerves 'are excited by the presence of red, soothed by the presence of green, and deadened or benumbed by the presence of blue.'[12] Psychological responses, such as that yellow-red produces an extreme excitement, noted by Goethe, were repeated in Viennese lectures on psychology published in 1845.[13] But

5.6 The rich colouring of stained glass, painted decoration and encaustic tiles reaches a crescendo at the east end of the chapel at Bishop's Court.

136

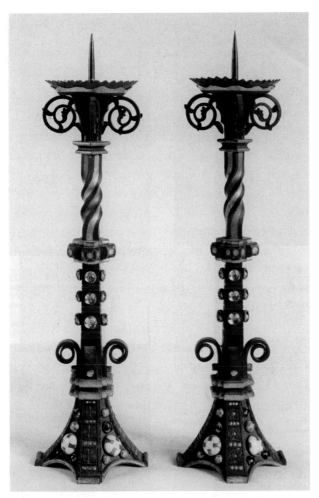

5.7 The jewelled copper candlesticks (now in the Fitzwilliam Museum, Cambridge), designed for the altar at Bishop's Court.

these ideas were then still very new – Hermann Helmholtz's *Physiological Optics* was published 1856-66, while in 1860 the Royal Society awarded the Rumford Medal to James Clerk-Maxwell for his paper 'Perception of Colour'. A year after White's lecture designer Christopher Dresser reiterated the same theory: 'yellow is of all colours the most allied to light, red is the most exciting, and blue is the most retiring.'[14]

White also explained that the optic nerves could be quickly excited in a dark or gloomy building by small applications of orange, yellow 'or, still better, gold'. Conversely, the eye could find repose in contemplation of a shady forest or in the cool, more distant blue of the sky or the sea – 'this most perfect combination of white with black, of light with darkness.'[15] For the chapel altar at Bishop's Court White designed candlesticks of copper, painted, gilded and ornamented with coloured glass 'jewels' (**5.7**). They were surrounded by tall, floor-standing, wrought iron holders, for two, seven and nine candles, their twisted stems gilded and painted with chevrons, diamonds and stylised flower patterns in grey-blue, red and gold. The flickering candlelight on the red and gold decoration would have quickly excited the optic nerve, according to White's beliefs, but the effect would have been tempered by the grey-blue colouring.

Bishop's Court furniture

A mirrored overmantel (still in place), a narrow, crocketted hall table (now in a private collection) and an oak hall stand (now at Knightshayes Court, Devon), together with a huge oak table were designed by White as an impressive entrance ensemble at Bishop's Court (**5.8**). The magnificent carved, mirrored oak sideboard, designed by White so that its decoration follows the line of the hall dado, is, as Clive Wainwright pointed out, 'far more successful than the totally painted pieces shown by Morris in 1862' (**5.9**).[16] A large oak mirror-backed sideboard and a buffet (now at Knightshayes Court), where colouring was confined to geometric inlay work and to decorative strap hinges, were intended for the dining room. A set of dining chairs, also designed by White for this room, could certainly not be criticised for being overtly medieval. They were very simple, with chamfered and notched legs, no stretchers, the original leather-upholstered backs bearing John Garratt's coloured and gilded monogram. They contrast with two oak open armchairs with ornate overscrolled arms and uprights, perhaps intended for the entrance hall. For the chapel, as well as the fittings, White designed a pair of oak rests with sloping tops and twisted and gilded iron supports, together with an oak *prie-dieu* and an oak lectern in the form of an eagle perched on a ball (now sadly missing). Clive Wainwright commented that the Bishop's Court's 'furniture belongs in the context of the splendidly polychromatic interiors … and represents an ensemble of international importance'.[17] Its sale and dispersal in 1994 is a terrible loss.

5.8 White's great oak table in the style of A.W.N. Pugin for the entrance hall at Bishop's Court. Present whereabouts unknown.

5.9 The mirrored sideboard in the hall at Bishop's Court, with decoration that reflects the stencilling of the walls.

It is surprising to find that the library bookcases at Bishop's Court are of the simplest design, and almost crude in their construction. This fits the pattern of John Garratt's expenditure: the exterior of the house was re-modelled, and an impressive entrance hall and staircase created. Money was spent on the chapel, but apart from the dining room, very little on the other reception rooms, or on the bedrooms. It seems entirely in keeping, then, that John Garratt would not have commissioned intricate and expensive furniture for his library. And White, too, might have recalled the Book Room of his mentor, Sir Henry Dryden, where the simple bookshelves, constructed by the estate carpenters, had cupboards beneath them where Dryden stored garden tools along with his medieval manuscripts![18]

White's designs for Bishop's Court obviously recognised its history as 'the favourite manor house of some twenty Bishops of Exeter.'[19] Where possible he retained vestiges of the earlier house, particularly some small rooms and a sixteenth-century fireplace west of the chapel. Neither did he sweep away the circular roof lights of the first-floor corridor and the ceiling decorations of the previous re-modelling. As with his parsonage houses, White did not hide the domestic quarters but abutted them boldly to the south wall of the chapel, their half-hipped striped roofs and varied casements close under the eaves forming a successful contrast with its buttressed grandeur. However, like most architects, the staples of White's practice were smaller buildings, at modest cost, where the human demands of family life or the spiritual requirements of a small congregation moulded the design. Constructed of local materials, these buildings have little of Bishop's Court's polychromatic impressiveness, but proclaim their Gothic credentials in a gentle, English manner.

Englishness

Northamptonshire, in the heart of England, is known for its long-established county families. The ancient manor house of Canons Ashby, home of the Dryden family since 1551, close to White's home at Blakesley and which he must have known well, is a picturesque agglomeration of different styles, in ironstone and brick. Also significant to White was the construction by Sir Henry Dryden (1818-99) at Canons Ashby of cottages, schools and farm buildings on his estate in an unassuming, vernacular style. These influences perhaps made White's voice more measured than many in the nineteenth-century debate on architectural style. White declared that he would not 'decline to treat a quasi-Classic house or church because a Gothic treatment of it would be incongruous and unsuitable'.[20] He believed that classical architecture was suited to the climate of Italy and Greece, but that the 'austere and changeable' weather of northern Europe favoured 'the especial characteristics of the Gothic style'. But he admitted that 'it is impossible not to see a certain amount of beauty and dignity even in the monotonous repetition of the same form, or in a long line of straight or curved cornice, such as is seen in Regent-street or Park-crescent.'[21] White's philosophy was 'to analyse the remains, to fathom the principles' of gothic in order to apply them to the 'purposes of modern requirement'.[22] He called for 'some sort of agreement amongst us as to principles of construction, and true treatment of available materials' to satisfy the needs of the age, 'whatever style may eventually prove to be the best fitted for our use.'[23]

A gradual waning of ecclesiological fervour paralleled a similar weakening of Pre-Raphaelite enthusiasm for the medieval. Dante Gabriel Rossetti and others involved with the firm of Morris, Marshall, Faulkner & Co. were influential in the development of the Aesthetic Movement. Massiveness was rejected in favour of delicacy, and primary colours gave way to soft, muted tones. Apart from oriental ceramics, foreign influences were discarded. Architects such as G.G. Scott Jr, Richard Norman Shaw and G.F. Bodley looked to English architecture, particularly that of Queen Anne in the early eighteenth century, for inspiration. White had links with this artistic circle through his membership of the Mediæval Society and the Hogarth Club. And it is tempting to believe that White's gentler, English style may have been an early influence on Bodley, a friend since their days together in Scott's office, and who shared White's office accommodation at 30a Wimpole Street from 1859 to 1861. Bodley's revised design for All Saints', Cambridge, of 1863, has been seen as setting 'the Gothic Revival on a new course, away from … foreign inspiration … and towards English models and ideals.'[24] Beaminster vicarage demonstrates that White was doing the same in the secular sphere four years earlier.

Beaminster vicarage, Dorset

In 1857 the Rev. Alfred Codd, for whom White had designed the rebuilt St Mary's Church, Hawridge (see 1.2), took up the incumbency of Beaminster, Dorset. Codd was a graduate of St. John's, Cambridge, and although he himself was not a member of the Cambridge Camden Society, his elder brother, Edward, had been one of its founders.[25] His introduction to White was probably through his wife, Emily Du Cane, whose family was related by marriage to the Prideaux-Brune family of Cornwall. White clearly established a close relationship with his client, later addressing him as 'My dear Codd'

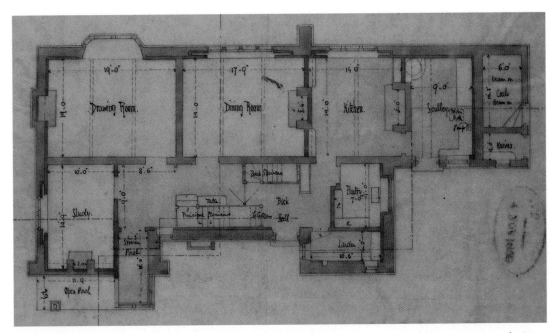

5.10 White's ground plan of Beaminster vicarage is typical of many of his parsonage designs, with the study close to the entrance and the main reception rooms taking advantage of the southerly aspect.

when writing with suggestions for the design of a memorial at Great Braxted, Essex, for his daughter, who died in 1881, and describing him as 'an old friend'.[26]

Despite its spectacular medieval church, Beaminster had been only a 'Chapelry annexed to the Vicarage of Netherbury' until 1846 and had no parsonage house.[27] By the end of October 1859 White's drawings for a new vicarage were complete, and a contract agreed with a local builder, John Chick, for £1,180, the ICBS contributing £400 and Queen Anne's Bounty £300.[28] The plan is typical of White: a generous L-shaped entrance hall to the north, an east-facing study, with the main reception rooms overlooking the south, garden front, while the domestic offices extend westwards (**5.10**). The Codd family obviously had a modest lifestyle: although they had four children under seven years of age, the 1861 census records them keeping only a housemaid and a nursemaid.[29] This lack of pretension is evident in the route parishioners would have taken from the back hall to the study, passing the doors to the dining and drawing rooms. The practicalities included a first-floor water closet (although no bathroom), and for warmth and security, sliding shutters to the study, dining room and kitchen, and folding ones for the drawing room. White specified the local limestone with only the lightest touch of constructional colour: a single course of red bricks running above the plate-traceried staircase window on the entrance façade (**5.11**).[30] Set flush in the rubble walls, this window confirms the ecclesiastical connection of the building. White achieved a subtle picturesque quality through the articulation of varied gables and windows and the timber porch. However, modifications and later alterations include a second plate-traceried window in place of

5.11 White's drawing of the north elevation of Beaminster vicarage, 1859, shows the single course of red bricks that emphasises the plate-traceried window.

5.12 The south-facing garden elevation of Beaminster vicarage,1859-61, with the tile-hung bay that anticipates the work of Arts and Crafts architects such as Ernest Newton, and also Lutyens.

the glazed gable end, a gabled, north-facing entrance porch in place of the 'Open Porch' opening to the east, and a two-storey canted bay to the study.

The south-facing garden elevation with its simple casements gives no indication of any ecclesiastical relationship. More colour is evident here, where the steeply sloping red-tiled roof is ruptured by a tile-hung bay running up from the ground to form a large dormer, a feature that would later be employed by Arts and Crafts architects (**5.12**). The first-floor window opens to allow an unobstructed vista across the valley to the magnificent tower of Beaminster church, which White was later to restore.

Elstead vicarage, Surrey

White's interpretation of a traditional English vernacular style can be seen most clearly in his parsonage house at Elstead, Surrey, of 1861-2. The commission presumably came through family connections: in 1849 his younger sister, Harriet, had married William Grey, brother of the 8th earl of Stamford. Grey's sister, Frances, was married to Joseph

Rhodes Charlesworth, the incumbent of Elstead since 1854. There was no parsonage house here, although one had been mentioned in the churchwardens' accounts in 1656; and the field south of the church was called the vicarage garden, which perhaps implied that the old cottage adjacent had been the curate's house.[31] White confirmed that the 'farm Cottage, Barn and Sheds on the Glebe … are so dilapidated and decayed' that they should be demolished 'and a parsonage house and offices built'.[32] The estimated cost of the house was £1,190, from which £40 was deducted for reuse of old materials.

White's plans, dated March 1861, provided a central hall and a service wing that extended to the north-west. Taking advantage of the warm southerly entrance elevation were the study, the bay-windowed drawing room, with east-facing dining room behind, and a 'parochial room' on the western corner (**5.13**). This was to be accessed from the kitchen entrance, and was presumably intended for various meetings, confirmation classes, etc. *The Ecclesiologist* remarked of this 'capital' scheme, 'A character is given externally by the arched doorways', these being the only ecclesiastical feature in an otherwise wholly domestic design.[33] The parochial room appears not to have been built, the study taking its place, with the main entrance placed under the small gable rather than to the left of it.

The material is local honey-coloured Bargate stone, so that as Gertrude Jekyll said

5.13 The gentle Englishness of White's Elstead vicarage, 1861–2. The porch has been substantially altered, and the house extended on the right-hand side.

144

of her own house at nearby Munstead Wood (designed by Lutyens in 1896 of the same material), it 'seems to grow naturally out of the ground.'[34] Jekyll noted and described an old Surrey cottage of Bargate stone with a brick relieving arch and brick framing of the windows.[35] At Elstead, White used similar details, but combined it with his own signature features: crested red ridge tiles and distinctive chamfering and notching to the stone mullions (**5.14**). Internally, the first-floor landing with its exposed arch-braces and collars also anticipates Lutyens, so that one wonders whether he knew this house, so close to his childhood home at Thursley. Roderick Gradidge credited Lutyens and Jekyll with popularising the 'Surrey style' in the 1890s, but thirty years earlier White had appreciated what it offered.[36]

Waddesdon rectory, Buckinghamshire

At Waddesdon White certified in 1868 that the 'old portions' of the rectory 'are quite decayed and the newer portions are ill constructed' and incapable of repair, and that rebuilding was required.[37] He incorporated some old materials (valued at £100), including the staircase, in his new rectory for the Rev. John Thomas Williams, on a site east of the old building. It was constructed in English bond in bricks of a special size, 10ins by 4 $\frac{7}{8}$ins by 2½ins (more usually 9 x 4½ x 2½), 'hard burned buff' with similar red ones for dressings.[38] These were doubtless the distinctive Woodham buffs, made just a mile away. The plan again gave the study, drawing and dining rooms the benefit of the southerly elevation, while the service areas formed an L-shape to the north-west. As at Beaminster, there was no dedicated entrance for parishioners to access the study.

There is very little indication at Waddesdon that this is the home of a clergyman. The porch with its barely pointed door and a cusped, two-light stone window to the entrance hall are the only ecclesiastical references (**5.15**). The tile-hung gable ends and the two-storey canted bay window in the centre of the garden front are reminiscent of Beaminster

5.15 Easterly entrance elevation of Waddesdon rectory, 1868–70, showing White's distinctive chimneypots. The windows either side of the study chimneystack do not appear on White's 1868 drawings.

vicarage (**5.16**). However, the asymmetry is more subtle and the sense of rhythm more regular in this later house. Most of the windows are taller, with shallow arches and dressings of red brick, which provide a strong contrast with the buff brick of the walls. The design and materials at Waddesdon demonstrate that White was anticipating the Queen Anne style of the 1870s.

Selborne Place, Littlehampton, Sussex

By the end of 1864 White and his wife Ellen had five young daughters. Perhaps it was obvious by then that Ellen's health was failing, for in December William drew up plans for three pairs of semi-detached houses overlooking the sea at Littlehampton.[39] Fronting a private, gated carriage drive, the houses were for the extended White family: no. 1 for his own household and no. 2 for Henry Master White and his family; no. 3 was for his sister, the widowed Mary Martelli and her children; it had an intercommunicating door with no. 4, home for his two unmarried sisters, Frances and Emily; while his younger brother, wealthy bachelor, John Edward White, was the occupant of nos 5 and 6. In March 1865 White negotiated a lease on the land that belonged to the Arundel estate of the duke of Norfolk.[40]

The three-storey houses are of local brown brick in Flemish bond, with irregular horizontal bands of red brick, under tiled roofs. They were constructed by Robert Bushby, a well-known local builder. Some of the windows are pointed and set under moulded brick hood-moulds, while others are set under tile-hung gables, some hipped in a Butterfieldian manner (**5.17**). The canted bay windows of the first-floor drawing rooms open on to verandahs supported by White's typical braced joinery. These were additions drawn up three weeks after the original designs, and were designed to overlook the south-facing gardens and open space that originally separated them from the sandy shore.[41] Like White's early parsonage houses, the entrances, on the north elevation, are set under plate-traceried stained glass windows to illuminate the staircase. And here, too, the service area is adjacent to the main entrance, screened by a brick wall, the upper part composed of terracotta honeycomb mouldings topped with crested ridge tiles.

Each house is separated from its neighbour by a cavity wall as, his niece recalled, 'Uncle William never grudged expense if it served some useful purpose and there was the money to spend. No one will deny the comfort of being cut off from the noises

5.16 The garden elevation of Waddesdon rectory. The first-floor window on the right is much larger than that shown on White's drawing and the gable above it is a later addition.

5.17 Selborne Place, Littlehampton, 1864-5. White's house for his own family on the right, and for his brother, the Rev. H.M. White on the left. The white hoods to the windows are unwelcome modern additions.

next door, especially if there were children about.'[42] Also for the children was a ground-floor playroom, opening into the garden. This was separated from the dining room by a wooden partition that could be folded back (**5.18**). Besides his signature stop-chamfering to joinery, typical door furniture and some pivoting windows, the houses were provided with wood-block flooring. White claimed that he invented this strong, comparatively noiseless system in the early 1850s.[43] His niece later reported that he 'refused to take out a patent, for he said that it was far too useful for anyone to be debarred from using it.'[44]

Presumably it was White's choice to name his little development Selborne Place. As his niece remarked, 'We had a right to the name … for we were Whites, and belonged to the same stock as that great and good man, Gilbert White'.[45] These houses demonstrate White's practicality and inventiveness, combined with a keen sense of place. Although the houses present in their entrance elevations a rather serious, Gothic aspect as befitted a clerical family, White's use of tile-hanging and shady verandahs on the garden elevations reflects their position in a popular Sussex seaside town.

Unfortunately, the sea air could not cure Ellen White, who died of consumption on 26 November 1866 at Weybridge, Surrey, home of her spinster sister Margaret. Her

148

grave in the churchyard of the parish church there is marked by a tombstone obviously designed by her husband (**5.19**).

Church of St Philip and St James, Maryfield, Antony, Cornwall

In 1847, after nine years of childless marriage, William Henry Pole Carew of Antony, Cornwall, celebrated the birth of his daughter, Geraldine. No doubt with the encouragement of the vicar of the parish, White's friend, the Rev. J.F. Kitson, he commissioned White to design a school house at Maryfield, to the south-east of his eighteenth-century home. There was also accommodation for a priest-in-charge, the first being the Rev. H.L. Jenner. In 1849 on 1 May, the feast of St Philip and St James, a son and heir was born and Pole Carew decided to build a church at Maryfield in thanksgiving. It was his intention that his son should lay the foundation stone when he came of age. However, in 1852 the Rev. Sudlow Garratt, younger brother of John

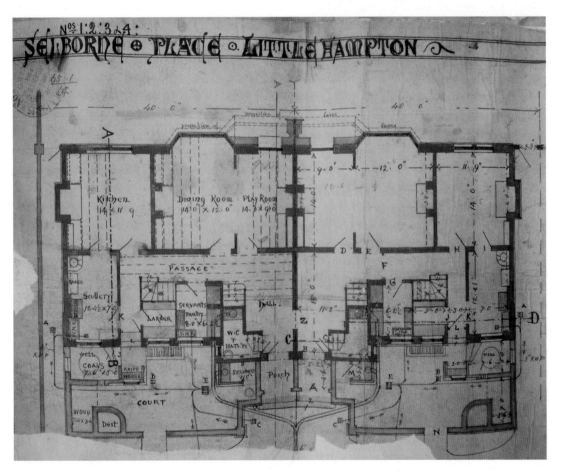

5.18 White's ground floor plan for the Selborne Place houses showing the playroom separated from the dining room by a folding screen. The drawing room and two bedrooms were on the first floor.

5.19 The grave of William's first wife, Ellen Floyer White, St James' churchyard, Weybridge, Surrey, 1866. White erected a similar tombstone over the grave of his eldest daughter, Harriet, in Hanwell churchyard ten years later.

Garratt of Bishop's Court, became the incumbent. After several years the Rev. Garratt suggested the immediate building of the church with the rent monies that he had not spent, and so the young Reginald Pole Carew laid the foundation stone on 18 January 1864.[46] William White's drawings of his design for the church were exhibited at the Architectural Exhibition in May 1866, when the 'proposed tower' was commented upon as 'the most important feature'.[47]

Although the body of Maryfield church is comparatively high, it still displays that marked contrast between the upright block of the western tower and the horizontal of the nave that Pevsner identified as a characteristic Cornish motif.[48] The plan consists of a nave with a lean-to north aisle, and a separately gabled chancel aisle that accommodates the organ and projects from a tall north transept where the Pole Carews had their seats. The building has an organic quality resulting from its construction of red sandstone rubble from Pole Carew's own quarry at Sheviock Wood further up the St Germans River, from whence it was brought down by barge.[49] Limestone dressings, sober slate roofs and a gabled south porch imply a conventional interior (**5.20**).

The intense patterning and colour found within the church recreates pre-Reformation polychromy. Arches are formed from alternate blocks of red and yellow sandstone; many of the walls, some plastered others of brick, are painted with geometric patterns, those in the chancel also having illustrations, to White's designs, of scenes from the life of Christ.[50] Above the chancel arch a painted scene of the Annunciation has Mary kneeling at a *prie-dieu* set in a courtyard, seemingly constructed of patterned tiles. Even in a pictorial scene of the Resurrection, White utilises geometric forms by placing the figure of Christ within an aureole composed of red and blue triangles. Although White's figures are stiff and medievalised, his abstract patterns here are a *tour de force*. They display a development from the purely geometric diapering of Bishop's Court into a freer, more open arrangement. The rich red of the brickwork, some of it over-painted, is balanced by the soft blues of the stylised flower motifs (**5.21**).

The body of the church was completed and licensed on 4 September 1866, the tower and spire that can be seen across the water from the crowded dockyards of Devonport being finished five years later. The lectern, font, choir stalls, reredos and ironwork all appear to have been designed by White.

Lyndon Lodge, Hanwell, Middlesex

From 1869 until 1881 White's address was listed in the *Post Office London Directory* as Lyndon Lodge, Hanwell as well as 30a Wimpole Street. Perhaps fearful for the health of his five daughters, he felt he should move out of London. Since 1864 the incumbent of Hanwell had been Derwent Coleridge, with whom White had corresponded when designing Bishops College in Cape Town. Although notorious for its huge lunatic asylum and London cemeteries, the old village north of the Great Western Railway retained its original tranquillity, while offering easy access to both Paddington and the West Country. Golden Manor Road, where Lyndon Lodge was situated, did not exist when the 1865 Ordnance Survey map of Hanwell was compiled, but the land must have been sold for

5.20 White's fine tracery in Decorated style at the church of St Philip and St James, Maryfield, near Antony, Cornwall, 1864-71.

5.21 White's stylised flower motifs on the chancel walls at Maryfield pre-figure many of the designs of Christopher Dresser.

development shortly afterwards. White mentioned designing a house for himself in his 'Descriptive Sketch of a Mansion at Humewood', a paper read at the RIBA on 4 January 1869.[51] The exact date of his plans for a family home is not known, but Kimberley of Banbury, who executed many of his commissions, was the contractor and was working on site between May 1868 and March 1869.[52]

Hanwell was popular with other professional men; White explained that his kitchen was on the ground floor, although his neighbour, 'also an architect, has built the kitchen down below.'[53] The aspect north and west from the rear of Lyndon Lodge, would have been across open fields, with the spire of the parish church rising above the winding banks of the River Brent. Lyndon Lodge was demolished and flats erected on the site in 1970. Apart from photographs of Golden Manor Lane showing the boundary fence with its distinctive notched upper edge, no records of the house survive, so there is little evidence of its appearance.[54] However, we know that it had three bay windows that Kimberley sent to site by rail on 14 October 1867.[55] Kimberley wrote in January 1868 that he was unable to procure any old tiles, and advised 'brushing over with Roman cement' so that the new ones would not be obtrusive. White's use of old materials no doubt reflects his desire that his home should fit into what was still an English village setting. We can perhaps assume that the plan and many of the details were similar to those employed in his parsonage designs: there were certainly shutters to the main rooms. The White family probably moved into the house in August 1868, before William departed for a holiday on the continent.[56]

By 25 January 1869 the joiners' work alone amounted to more than £300.[57] Relations between White and his builder were now less than cordial, in fact, positively hostile. The cause was not due to White's own house at Hanwell, or any other English project, but the execution of his most ambitious, but ultimately notorious, commission – the castle of Humewood in Ireland.

6

Two Great Houses

Humewood, Kiltegan, Co. Wicklow, Ireland

In stark contrast to the gentleness of his English commissions, White explained that he designed Humewood to 'incorporate the idea of the Scotch baronial hall with certain Irish peculiarities in the battlemented detail – exhibiting the fusion of the good old Scotch and Irish families of Hume and Dick'.[1] His client was William Wentworth Fitzwilliam Hume Dick, M.P. for Wicklow, son of William Hoare Hume of Humewood and Charlotte Anna Dick, whose father was one of the founders of the Bank of Ireland. Although the old house at Humewood, 45 miles south of Dublin, withstood a siege during the rebellion of 1798, Hume Dick's paternal grandfather had been shot by the rebels. Hume Dick commissioned White to design a new house which the architect referred to 'as an occasional resort in the summer recess, or the shooting season', at a cost not to exceed £15,000.[2] It is not known why Hume Dick chose William White although there is a tenuous connection between the Hoare family and the Du Boulays, through marriages to the Blennerhassett family. White visited Ireland in August 1866; his rough designs were approved by Hume Dick early the following year, and a tender prepared by Messrs Kimberley of Banbury for £13,560 was accepted in March 1867. On 11 April young James Kimberley, son of the builder, and a foreman set out for the site so that work could commence immediately.

White's plan was arranged around a long corridor running north-west to south-east. The entrance, through a *porte-cochère*, is at the south-east corner adjacent to the dining room, while the drawing room, library and suite of private rooms for the owner occupied the south-westerly elevation (**6.1**).[3] To improve the defensive strength of the house (for there was still political unrest), and to raise it above the damp ground, White designed a semi-basement service area. This extended to the north with covered passages to the stables and the laundry buildings. The latter were arranged in a logical progression: from the washing area, linen was hung in a drying room with a louvred tower under a pyramidal roof, before passing to ironing and folding rooms.

The castle is constructed in bold masses of granite rubble walling with granite

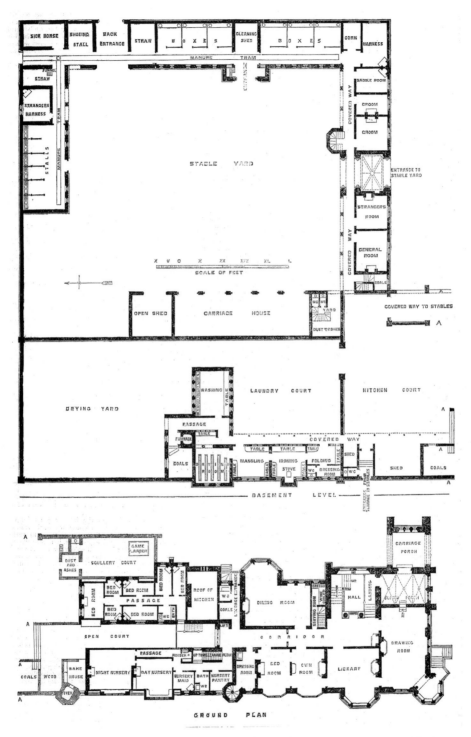

6.1 White's ground plan of Humewood, 1866-70, shows the extensive accommodation and large service and stable areas. *The Builder*, 8 August 1868.

6.2 Humewood from the south, the entrance under the *porte-cochère* on the extreme right.

dressings, rising to a mighty tower, the spiky outline of its roofs set against the rolling Wicklow mountains (**6.2**). White had intended to employ brick for the corbel-tables and in horizontal bands to stabilise the walls in order to limit costs and 'thinking also that the colour might tend to warm up the cold granite'.[4] On 30 March 1867, Albert Kimberley wrote to White telling him that two cases of clay from Humewood had not arrived; but by 4 April sample bricks were drying in the open air and as soon as they had been fired he would forward them. On 1 May, Kimberley was explaining that there was no limestone in the clay 'and when the bricks are made smaller they will be very much better.'[5] However, White described how Kimberley 'volunteered to use cut granite … so anxious was [he] … to make a good job of it.'[6] Experienced in the use of granite from his time in Cornwall, White pointed out that it demanded mouldings that are 'broad, bold, and massive'.[7] However, there was obviously some confusion over the use of bricks or stone, for Colthurst & Symons of Bridgwater demanded payment from Kimberley for the coping ridges and stringcourse bricks that were specially made for Humewood. Apparently White assured Kimberley that he would arrange to use them

156

in other projects.[8] The result is an absence of exterior colour, only patterns of light and shade cast by the weighty corbel-table to the tower, the crow-stepped gables, the buttresses and bays.

Unlike White's usual broad, low casements, the windows are tall and narrow, square-headed and, particularly on the south-west elevation, regularly arranged. In the main rooms the casements were designed to open inwards in European fashion, while the remainder opened outwards in English mode. The hinged fanlights above the transoms allowed ventilation even in wet weather, and the stained glass shields that decorate those in the main rooms were designed by White, he explained, to 'subdue the strong glare of light … without drawing down the blinds.'[9] All windows to the service areas were protected by substantial, but decorative, iron stanchions. There is more fine ironwork in decorative hinges, finials to flèches and in various gates to the gardens (**6.3**).

Internally, the colouring at Humewood is less extensive than that at Bishop's Court, as befits the concept of a defensive bastion.[10] The entrance is dramatic: under the vaulted

6.3 White's gate-posts and decorative iron gates at the southern end of the formal gardens, Humewood.

6.4 Designed to impress: the ascent from the entrance to the main corridor at Humewood.

6.5 The main corridor, looking towards the entrance hall. The star-shaped decorations to the ceiling bosses are similar to the one in the sanctuary at St Saviour's, Aberdeen Park (3.20).

6.6 Kimberley's superb joinery at Humewood, here the drawing room door where the black bog oak pins contrast with the pale sycamore mouldings.

porte-cochère an arched doorway is offset under bas-reliefs of the arms of Hume and Dick. A small vestibule leads to the staircase hall, with its notched newel posts, aptly described by Mark Girouard as 'totem poles'.[11] Illuminated by tall plate-traceried windows of armorial glass, the ascent to the reception rooms is dominated by two columns of black Irish marble of tremendous girth (**6.4**). These contrast with the pale stone of the arcades and the groined ceiling of the main corridor. A photograph of around 1875 shows the ribs of this groining painted a dark colour, the bosses surrounded with star-shaped patterns, while the panels between are decorated with painted geometric flowers (**6.5**).[12] Besides the stained glass, colour is provided by the intricate construction of the panelled doors – 'red deal framing, with oak panels and sycamore mouldings pinned on with black bog oak' (**6.6**).[13]

In the drawing room a wood-groined polygonal bay window, reminiscent of that at Bishop's Court, allows access to the garden. The exposed ceiling beams in this room are painted with a running pattern of narrow, cream-coloured triangles, rather like a backgammon board, interspersed with red and grey-blue stylised flowers (**6.7**). Between the beams the plaster is decorated with a stencilled design: some of the motifs are similar to those on an altar frontal for St Bartholomew's church, Grahamstown (2.17) and appear again at Quy Hall (6.16). The curvilinear pattern employed by White in the reredos at Aberdeen Park and used here in diagonal arcs or edging bands of contrasting soft reds and greys, can be found on Chinese porcelain. As at St Saviour's, Aberdeen Park, the painting was executed by Henry Davies.[14] This design at Humewood shows a move away from the stiff, regular, geometrical patterning of Bishop's Court. White appears to have succumbed to a certain degree of eclecticism, with motifs from oriental and Egyptian sources, together with Renaissance arabesques, which, combined with his own stylisations, results in a less satisfying composition.

White acknowledged that if Humewood had been a permanent residence 'it would have been on a far different scale', nevertheless it was 'furnished with every convenience', he wrote.[15] He also admitted that 'it has been worked up to a form very different to that which I, at first, sketched, by gradual and successive stages of idea on my own part, as well as of requirement on the part of the proprietor.'[16] No detail was overlooked. Besides magnificent marble fireplaces, wooden overmantels and library bookcases, there was a lift

6.7 Motifs in the altar cloth at St Bartholomew's, Grahamstown, can be seen in the drawing room ceiling at Humewood.

6.8 The design of the stables reflects the massing and outline of the main house that can be seen in the background.

to carry luggage and coals, while a tiny hatch in the still room allowed tea to be served in the garden. There were bathrooms and water closets for the servants as well as the family. An estimate of £109 for electric bells in both the house and the stables noted that the installation would require 'quite a mile of wire on account of there being so many long stretches and returns'.[17] In August 1868 Kimberley estimated £342 for a conservatory to be constructed of granite lined with brick and with oak framing, accessed from the billiard room. In November an estimate of £10 was submitted for an oak dinner trolley with boxwood wheels that was to run on tram rails to carry food up from the kitchen to the dining room.[18] In neat symmetry a 'manure tram' was to keep the stables clean! The extensive stable yard echoes the main range, with crow-stepped gables culminating in a massive clock tower above the groined entrance arch (**6.8**).

In December 1868, on learning that there was to be a new clerk of works, Kimberley resolved to employ a surveyor to handle all these variations to the contract.[19] By 18 January 1869 Albert Kimberley was expressing his concerns:

162

I have just received sketches of pillars and groining to the Servants Hall and also a pillar and groined arch in Tower for Cellar. You will remember when you were taking out the quantities you told me it was common vaulting ½ brick thick and only groined where it came in the way of doorways … I object to do it unless you allow the extra labour and materials for same.[20]

Relations between architect and contractor became increasingly tense with James Kimberley reporting to his father that the clerk of works had received instructions for extra work unbeknown to the firm.[21] In February 1869 Albert Kimberley suspended work, claiming that White refused to go into the variations to the contract.[22] However, work resumed in May, and by the 25th Kimberley claimed £2,000 for the completed work. He wrote again on 1 June, 'Surely your own judgement must tell you that I am entitled to a certificate [for £2,000]. It is now the ninth month since I had the last and there has been some thousands done since then.'[23]

While Humewood is an immensely satisfying composition and amply demonstrates White's 'ingenuity and vigour in design', it had a devastatingly negative effect on his subsequent career.[24] In June 1871 a case came before the Master of the Rolls brought by Kimberley, claiming £15,000 against Hume Dick and William White, as the cost of the building had risen to £25,000 which White refused to certify and Hume Dick refused to pay. Albert Kimberley claimed that his tender was based on White's initial sketches and that £6,000 of the tender sum was for lump sums based on White's rough estimate of quantities, which proved totally inadequate. It has to be asked, therefore, how such grave misunderstandings arose.

As the case dragged on it was revealed that Albert Kimberley had spent three days in White's office in March 1867 in order to prepare his tender. Kimberley claimed that neither then, nor when he signed the contract documents in June, having been ill with quinsy (inflammation of the throat), was he aware of Hume Dick's £15,000 ceiling, believing that all modifications and additions would be paid as 'extras'. Both Mr May and Mr E. Crutchloe (clerk) who worked in White's office, swore that Kimberley was well satisfied with the contract. Crutchloe prepared the specification, having been instructed by White to ensure that it agreed with the initial estimate and plans. White's clerk, Mr Frost who took the contract to Banbury for Kimberley to sign, denied that Kimberley was unable through illness to comprehend it. He recalled that Kimberley was satisfied, but had commented that there was no clause to cover strikes and that the penalties were excessive.[25] Kimberley was executing numerous contracts for White at this time, and the letter books reveal an easygoing style of working. For instance, during alterations to Drayton Parslow church he wrote to ask White whether timber was to be varnished 'As I have no specification to tell me'.[26] White obviously had a high regard for Kimberley's standard of workmanship, stating in his paper on Humewood that he had not seen 'a better piece of granite work, although I have lived in a granite country, or better joinery'.[27]

Reports of the court case reveal that Hume Dick's agent, Samuel Fenton, had noted various defects in Kimberley's work, including mortar made of clay and dirt instead of sharp sand and lime, poor work by the masons and frequent delay in provision of materials. However, the latter was not entirely the contractor's fault: in one letter to White his exasperation is evident – 'the Wexford people are shufflers, there is no business about them'.[28] On visiting Humewood on 20 June 1870, two days after Kimberley handed over the building, Fenton found several chimney flues full of bricks and rubbish, leaking walls, cracked soil pipes and poor woodwork.[29] These findings were substantiated by the report of J. W. Houghton, a Dublin architect and civil engineer, and by an affidavit of William Elliott, builder of Pimlico, who went to Humewood in August 1870 to complete the works. George William Chinnock, appointed clerk of works in August 1869, claimed that Kimberley's men ignored his instructions and that much of the building was not constructed in accordance with the plans and specification.

On 3 November 1871 the Master of the Rolls gave his judgement that an account should be made of the value of extra works executed under White's direction as well as work done under the contract 'though not included therein'; and an account of any omissions.[30] An inspection of the house was necessary, but when Kimberley and his surveyors visited early in 1872, Mr Fenton, the agent, who with his family occupied the house, refused them access.[31] Following an order from the Master of the Rolls, a second visit was successful and a judgement was finally given in favour of Kimberley. The Master of the Rolls ruled that

> there was evidence of an intention on the part of the architect to bind the builder
> by his incautious adoption of a contract not in accordance with his tender, and to
> gain credit to himself for the cheap performance of a considerable architectural
> work of great merit, which circumstance might induce him to cut down the claim
> of the plaintiff for extra work below what was equitable.[32]

Thomas Hayter Lewis, professor of architecture at University College, and Ewan Christian had both testified to White's honour and integrity, as well as his professional competence and the accuracy of his drawings for Humewood.[33] Unfortunately White had been 'rash enough to prepare quantities, involving several thousand pounds, merely by the aid of a rough sketch and his own imagination.'[34]

It was (and still is) not unusual for construction to run over budget – Robert Kerr's mansion, Bear Wood, Berkshire, 1865-70, for John Walter, proprietor of *The Times*, cost more than twice his original estimate. But White stated in his paper, read at the RIBA on 4 January 1869, that his design had been 'worked up to a form very different to that which I, at first, sketched', but that he had had to 'modify details … in order to meet the inexorable requirements of economy'.[35] Kimberley had informed him on 19 December 1868 that he would employ a surveyor to cost all the variations to the contract. Therefore when he was reading his paper, White must have already realised that the budget of

£15,000 would be greatly exceeded. As the instigator of the variations and as intermediary between client and builder, White must take the blame for not informing Kimberley of the £15,000 ceiling. It is likely that White's mental state was fragile. His wife had died of consumption on 25 November 1866, at just the time that he was working on the design for Humewood. Besides the emotional distress and his concerns for his five daughters, all under ten years old, White may also have been beset with financial problems. It appears that his late wife's marriage settlement ensured that on her death her money would be held in trust until her children married or reached their majority.[36]

It also appears from the letter books that Albert Kimberley was encouraged by his son, James, to seek recompense through the courts. The case was reported in detail by *The Architect*, which was highly critical of White. This bias is underscored by a letter from James Kimberley to the editor informing him of the date and time of the final judgement, 'thinking that you would like your reporter to be there', and explaining that 'I have not intimated this information to any of the other building papers.'[37] Kimberley was finally awarded almost all the monies owed to him, although he, like Hume Dick and White, did not escape criticism for 'rashness and want of caution'.[38]

The notoriety of the case should not be allowed to detract from the success of White's design. It embodies his belief that the equilateral triangle is the basis of successful proportion and demonstrates his espousal of innovations and modern appliances. At the end of White's paper describing Humewood, Robert Kerr, architect of Bear Wood and author of the influential *The Gentleman's House* (1864), admitted that he could not help admiring White's 'firm and muscular resolve … to make a thing crooked. … One cannot ask him to explain the principles on which he chooses to design; but there is a unity running through the whole which permits no doubt of his feeling perfectly satisfied in his own mind.'[39] Perhaps as a result of the endorsement of his peers, and before legal proceedings began, White had gained another country house commission – to restore Quy Hall, Cambridge.

Quy Hall, Stow-cum-Quy, Cambridgeshire

The small village of Stow-cum-Quy, in the flat fenlands less than five miles north-east of Cambridge, was an entirely agricultural community when Clement Francis purchased the late sixteenth-century Quy Hall in 1855. Francis was not only solicitor to the university, but also a partner of Gunning & Francis, solicitors, who dealt with the Quy enclosure award of 1839, so he knew the estate well.[40] The previous squire, James Martin, was affable and easy-going: he appeared unconcerned that alterations by his predecessors to provide impressive reception rooms had left some of the first-floor rooms with headroom of only 4ft 6ins.[41] The hall was of two storeys, with attics behind a crenellated parapet and with octagonal turrets at the east and west ends of the south elevation, the whole of which had been encased in stucco. A gallery had filled the original H-shape on the north. At first the Francis family remained at their

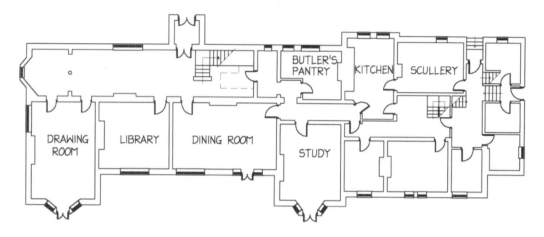

6.9 Ground plan of Quy Hall as rebuilt by White, 1869-73. The walls of the library and dining room abutting the entrance hall were retained from the old house, as was the butler's pantry and rooms above it, and the ancient beams from the dining room and library.

Emmanuel Street home in the city during the winter months, as the roads to Quy were often impassable, especially by bicycle, which became Clement's preferred method of travel.[42] In November and December 1868 William White examined and measured the old Quy Hall for Clement Francis, and in February 1869 he submitted a first set of drawings for a 'remodelling'.[43] Francis presumably would have known White through the Ecclesiological Society, of which he too was a long-standing member; and perhaps also because White was responsible for The How, a substantial polychromatic brick house being built for Gilbert John Ansley at St Ives, Huntingdonshire, only twelve miles away.[44]

There is no record of White's first proposals (for which he charged £31), but in April 1869 they were superseded by the scheme as built. The new schedule of work included demolition of most of the building, but with the materials, notably four old trusses which have now been dated as late fifteenth-century, being reused and some walls preserved, together with three doors and door-cases of around 1740.[45] The footprint of the main body of the house was retained, the gallery forming a staircase hall giving access to the three main reception rooms on the south (**6.9**). The adjacent offices, servants' hall, greenhouse with its furnace house and walled yard, all to the east, were replaced by extensive service quarters with varied gables, triangular dormers and a shingled bell-cote.

The Tudor brickwork, in horizontal bands comprising two courses of red brick and one of white, was replicated in the north elevation of the new service wing and for the ground storey of the main range, using English bond. For the first floor of the main accommodation and the south (garden) elevation of the service wing, White reversed the proportions, the change being marked by a decorative band. On the north (entrance) elevation he reproduced the curved Dutch gables of the old house. All the gables are diapered, while the tiled roofs are punctured by numerous brick chimneys, those rising from the west wall having star-shaped caps (like those he used later at the Winchester sanatorium) and are set on crow-stepped bases. The windows are tall and slender; French windows to the gardens from the main reception rooms have pine shutters and diminutive window seats, presumably for children. Both the canted two-storey bay windows are topped with decorative terracotta balustrades, a feature Lutyens adopted in 1905 for his office building for the Daneshill Brick Company, Basingstoke. The contract, dated 6 August 1869, with Bell & Sons of Cambridge was for £3,250, but eventually, with extras, totalled £4,535.[46]

This vividly polychromatic building reflects White's cognisance of place as well as the history of the house (**6.10**). The Dutch gables and bands of contrasting brick demonstrate the close links between the eastern counties of England and the Low Countries. White may also have been using colour more extensively here than elsewhere, since the flat landscape would have rendered absurd a composition relying on mass, such as Humewood. In confining himself to just two colours in an almost symmetrical composition of the main accommodation, White was reflecting, perhaps consciously, the solidity and permanence of his patron's professional employment. Clement Francis consolidated his estate with the acquisition of further land, and landscaped the park round the house. A carriage drive from the south passed over a delicate cast-iron bridge that he purchased from St John's College, before approaching the house from the north-

6.10 The south elevation of Quy Hall from the lake, the service area to the right. The original carriage drive approached from the left, sweeping round to the north, entrance front.

west. A formal garden, including a rectangular pond, lay to the south and south-east of the house, separated from the park by a ha-ha. White designed this 'Terrace Wall' in December 1870, as a series of low arches.[47]

Clement Francis was a generous employer – he recorded spending £210 on a workmen's feast when the house was finished on 28 January 1871.[48] Nor did he stint on the decoration and furnishing of his new home that amounted to £1,500. Besides his fee (£225) for design and supervision of the house, White made no charge for 'Selecting Furniture and designs for D[itt]o. (61 Drawgs.)'.[49] Furniture identified by Clive Wainwright as by White, appears to have been dispersed. An overmantel mirror, gilded and painted and obviously designed by White, was exhibited in 2008 (**6.11**). The mural decorations to the main rooms, previously assumed to be by Thomas Gambier Parry, can now be positively attributed to White. Clement Francis's papers include White's account for 'Details for mural and ceiling Decoration' amounting to £21 10s. The painting was executed by Henry Davies of 110 Bayham Street, Camden Town, who had assisted Parry with the ceiling of Ely Cathedral. It seems that Davies was also working on the decoration at Humewood, as his account of 30 October 1871 for staining and varnishing 'Drawing Room Lookinglass [sic] frame' and other items at Quy gives that address.[50]

6.11 White's design for an overmantel mirror for Quy Hall, exhibited by Paul Reeves in Sotheby's Best of British, *The Selling Exhibition*, March 2008.

6.12 White's decoration of the dining room at Quy Hall included painting and gilding of the eighteenth-century door and door-case retained from the old house.

White's designs cover the ceiling, walls and doors of the dining room (**6.12**). As at Bishop's Court, White divided the walls horizontally, but now at a higher level to form a frieze, as would become popular later in the decade. The stylised 'thistle' motif is similar to Christopher Dresser's 'opening leaf-bud', dependent not upon form 'but upon on arrangement of parts' (**6.13**).[51] Like Dresser, White was fascinated by the configuration of plants, which he examined under a microscope.[52] The ceiling panels are blue-grey to provide repose from the warm terracotta colour of the walls. Elaborate stylised flowers decorate the centre of each panel; leaves spring out on curved stems into the panels, giving a sense of movement to an otherwise static design (**6.14**). The eighteenth-century doorcases are decorated with diapers, triangles and flowers, while the door panels are painted with conventionalised flowers in gilded surrounds.

In the drawing room only decoration to the ceiling has survived, which includes a band of pattern forming an oval the length of the room (**6.15**).[53] Across the corners runs a stripe of undulating patterns, like a naïve representation of waves (**6.16**). These designs are all simpler and more homogenous than those at Humewood; White has tempered his earlier geometry with more plant-based forms and areas of plain colour. A very much simpler decorative scheme survives in the adjacent library.

It would seem that White also designed two of the borders for bedroom wallpapers, for they are very much in his style, and in a letter to his client certifying payment to Davies, he notes that 'The amount for the bordering paper, which I supplied, is not included'.[54] One border was very simple: black dots on a soft yellow background edged in black and topped with a narrow band of white and olive green, and was used above Morris's *Daisy* paper in blue. The other, a simplified 'star' pattern of red and olive on a cream background and banded with red and olive, was above *Daisy* paper with an off-white background. If White was designing borders, perhaps it can be assumed that he was responsible for the choice of wallpapers, many of which were from Morris, Marshall, Faulkner & Co., including *Trellis* and *Daisy*, two of their earliest designs, *Diaper* of 1868-1870 and *Spray* and *Venetian*, which were produced around1871.[55] One of the bedrooms was decorated with *Brazilian Birds*, a paper supplied by Cowtan & Mannooce, who may also have supplied the Chinoiserie style paper in another bedroom.[56] Quy Hall demonstrates that White favoured some of the most up-to-date designers, while using his own additions to maintain his stylistic authority.

Although Clement Francis had four sons as well as two daughters, the decoration at Quy Hall has a distinctly feminine bias. This may reflect White's situation at the time, living in a totally female environment with five young daughters, aged from fourteen to six, and two female servants.[57] It no doubt reinforced the gentle aspect of his nature evident in the close relationships he had with his sisters. Lucy had accompanied him to keep house in Truro; he was godfather to Harriet's only son, later the 9th earl of Stamford; and Mary (Martelli) took a keen interest in the

6.13 White's decorative motifs on the dining room walls are similar to Christopher Dresser's conventionalised drawings of a leaf bud.

6.14 The dining room ceiling decoration includes painting of the exposed beams with the same terracotta colour as the lower part of the walls.

6.15 In the drawing room ceiling at Quy Hall a wide band of decoration runs over the exposed beams.

upbringing of all his children. So it is not surprising that White espoused many aspects of the aesthetic movement of the 1870s and '80s. His three articles under the heading 'Aesthetical Sanitation', published in the *British Architect*, contained his observations of posture, breathing and movement that later became principles of the Alexander Technique. White disclosed that he and his family benefited from a system of gymnastics formulated by Colonel Ling of the Swedish army – these exercises were later popularised by the Modernist movement in the 1920s. He advocated non-restrictive clothing for both sexes, noting pithily that a 'waspish figure, unlike a waspish disposition, is considered a thing of beauty and a joy for ever'.[58] White drew attention to pointed and high-heeled shoes that threw the body out of balance, so contributing to a diminution of female beauty and grace. His concerns for the welfare of young women included a condemnation of the imposition in many girls' schools of 'silence or of very quiet talking', which he believed destroyed 'cheerfulness of spirit and conversational power'[59] Although White's designs for the painted decorations, and possibly his choice of wallpapers, show this lighter, feminine sensibility, his furniture never lost a masculine, Gothic aesthetic.

Although reporting of the Humewood case began in mid-1871, White's relationship with Clement Francis, which had always been formal, appears to have been unaffected, and in 1878 he was commissioned to restore the church at Stow-cum-Quy, largely at Francis's expense. However, new commissions in 1871 numbered just four, only 20 per cent of the annual number ten years previously. Evidently confidence in White had been

6.16 Decoration of the corners of the drawing room ceiling includes motifs also seen at Humewood (6.7).

173

badly shaken. Apart from the new vicarage for St Mary Abbots, Kensington (1876-7), and the bishop's palace at Wakefield (1890) for the first bishop, William Walsham How, there is no record of his designing another large house. However, he continued to receive commissions for schools, boarding houses, parsonage houses, and churches, both new and restorations. One client with whom he enjoyed a long, friendly and fruitful relationship was Canon John Erskine Clarke, rector of the extensive parish of Battersea.

7

The Rev. John Erskine Clarke of Battersea

John Erskine Clarke (1827-1920) was a man of enormous energy. In 1872 he was appointed by the patron, Earl Spencer, to the parish of St Mary, Battersea. A graduate of Wadham College, Oxford, Clarke had already written, *inter alia*, *Children at Church*, and was editor of the *Parish Magazine* (1859-95), *Chatterbox*, a children's periodical (1867-1902), and *Church Bells* (1871-95). He was the eldest son of William Fairlie Clarke, of Cossipore, Calcutta, the site of a huge East India Company ordnance factory. His mother, Arabella Anne, was the daughter of John Cheap, a member of the Bengal Civil Service in Calcutta.[1] Clarke grew up in Edinburgh, before going up to Oxford in 1846, graduating in 1850 and being ordained two years later. As vicar of St Michael's, Derby, from 1856 to 1866, he determined to build a new church to serve the increasing population of his parish. Doubtless through his friendship with a fellow local incumbent, the Rev. Melville Horne Scott, he commissioned Scott's brother, George Gilbert, to design the new St Andrew's church. Probably due to misunderstandings, the budget overran, the builder went bankrupt ,and Clarke felt compelled to take over the unfinished church and help to repay the debt.[2]

Several potential candidates had declined Earl Spencer's invitation to the incumbency of Battersea following the death of the rector in 1871. However, for his part Clarke wanted another working-class parish and having visited Battersea at the beginning of January 1872 to assess its needs, he accepted the position and was instituted on 2 February (**7.1**).

St Mark's, Battersea Rise

Battersea had been a small riverside village until the early years of the nineteenth century, but, as at Derby, the building of the railways had resulted in a huge increase in population. To accommodate this growing community Clarke announced in July 1873 that he had 'a scheme afloat' for a new church on Battersea Rise, in the area south of the old village and close to Clapham Junction station.[3] An infant school had been built there in 1866, largely through the generosity of the stockbroker Philip Cazenove, on a site that had been given by Earl Spencer, and in 1868 a temporary iron church had been

7.1 The Rev. John Erskine Clarke (1827-1920), rector of Battersea, 1872-1909.

erected adjacent to it.[4] Philip Cazenove's mother was a member of the Houssemayne Du Boulay family, and therefore connected to the family of White's first wife. Clarke, too, may have known the Cornish family, for in 1786 the Rev. G.J. Cornish's aunt, Charlotte, had married Sir John Shore, Governor-General of India (1792-7). J.T. Houssmayne Du Boulay declared that since that event, which 'had a far-reaching effect upon the fortunes of the family', the younger members 'naturally turned their thoughts to India' and many lived and worked there in various capacities.[5] Clarke was obviously keen to employ the revived Gothic style but wanted to avoid a repetition of his problems with Scott. White's connection with the Cornish family and his reputation for innovative design at modest cost may have been instrumental in his gaining this commission.

White's plans for a church consisting of an aisled nave, transepts and apsidal chancel to be built of concrete faced with brick, were initially rejected by the ICBS committee of architects (**7.2**). On behalf of the committee, White's old friend, G.E. Street, recommended the employment of a clerk of works for the careful supervision of the concrete construction. He also advised that the bonding courses should be of three courses of brick and that all exposed timber in the bell tower should be of oak. But his most wounding comment was that the church seemed 'to be too ambitious in its general

176

SECTION OF WALLING.

SEPARATE BRICKS

PLAN OF BRICK PIERS.

PLAN

SCALE OF FEET

"A BRICK AND CONCRETE CHURCH"
—S MARK'S BATTERSEA RISE S.W.
WILLIAM WHITE F.S.A.
ARCHITECT

LONGITUDINAL SECTION LOOKING NORTH

7.2 White's perspective and plan of St Mark's, Battersea Rise. The distinctive tower makes a bold statement on the brow of the hill.

scheme for the small sum which is to be expended upon it.'[6] White rejected any criticism of 'superficial display', arguing that apart from the 'arcaded apse and Crypt below' his design was 'massive in its parts' and 'simple in its arrangements and details.' He also defended the use of concrete: 'if it is to be condemned at all it ought to be condemned upon its own demerits and not as an unworthy means of bringing pretentiousness of design within reach.'[7] He was emphatic that if the walls would not stand with one course of brick bonding, as he had specified, they would not stand with three, and the cost would make it uneconomical to use concrete at all. White admitted that his estimate of £4,800 was 'somewhat below the average', but pointed out that 'it would be a serious matter for regret if cases most needing assistance should be deprived of a grant only because an expensively built Church meets with more favour than one in which studious regard is paid to cost.' White explained to the secretary of the ICBS that the precedent for his construction was some 'ancient Roman walls still in existence' of concrete with 4ins brick facings and no bonding courses. He also drew attention to the approval granted by the district surveyor and the Metropolitan Board of Works 'who have examined the specimens of the construction, and have licensed its use for this Church'.[8]

White's case was supported by Philip Cazenove's son, Arthur, rector of Reigate, Surrey, who informed the ICBS that the Surrey Church Association and the Diocesan Society were happy to make a grant of £500 to the church if a clerk of works was employed.[9] The Rev. Cazenove later reported that he and his father had 'inspected the walls and have no doubt that you [the ICBS] will be satisfied.'[10] Eventually the committee of architects grudgingly admitted that 'the works have been very carefully executed' and that a grant of £300 would be authorised. However, this was not to be considered 'as a precedent of their approval of the use of brick and concrete together, as this mode of construction unless extraordinary care and constant supervision be exercised, is not in their opinion as safe as it should be.'[11] White explained the construction in some detail, including problems with the swelling of the concrete, in a paper read to the Architectural Association.[12] He also defended his decision to divide the clerestory into equal bays, even though they do not line up with the arcades beneath.[13] He felt that 'greater breadth and repose' was achieved than 'by a mere vertical correspondence of parts'.[14]

St Mark's occupies a prominent position on the crest of Battersea Rise, and was described as 'A Country Church' when White's work was profiled by the *British Architect* in 1881.[15] It is surprising, therefore, to find that he employed a high polygonal apse in the French style as advocated in Street's 'On the Proper Characteristics of a Town Church'.[16] It seems likely that the apsidal form was favoured by Clarke, since many of the churches that White designed for him in Battersea, as well as the country church of Elvington, North Yorkshire, of which he was patron (and where he is buried) take that form. The apse with the descending windows of the ambulatory is one of the most striking features of St Mark's. White utilised the eastwards fall of the land to construct extensive vestries and classrooms under the chancel, although his original plan for the brick groining to be supported by a single pillar resulted in collapse during construction. Unfortunately, the large square brick pillars that were substituted restrict the useable space.

The facing of the concrete walls of St Mark's is of Kentish stock bricks, with buttresses and dressings of red bricks from Slough, the moulded bricks being supplied by Locke & Sons of Aylesbury. The height of the church is accentuated by a band of red brick diaper pattern under the eaves and across the gable ends. The same pattern decorates the second and third stages of the jaunty south-western tower under an oak-shingled broach spire. The corbel table below the large louvres of the bell stage was added 'to give greater height'. [17]Diaper patterning also adorns the western vestibule, whose red-brick arched doorway dies into the wall of the church, which is battered back to allow easier access – turning a functional necessity into a decorative feature. Unfortunately this feature has recently disappeared when a link corridor to the new parish room was constructed.

Internally, the apse provided an impressive focus for services. The incumbent reported that the 'effect of the choir ascending from the subterranean regions was of very great interest'. [18] They would then have processed round the ambulatory, its brick arches supported on columns of moulded Aylesbury brick with stone capitals and bases, under stained glass windows by Lavers, Barraud & Westlake (**7.3**). The Bath stone capitals were

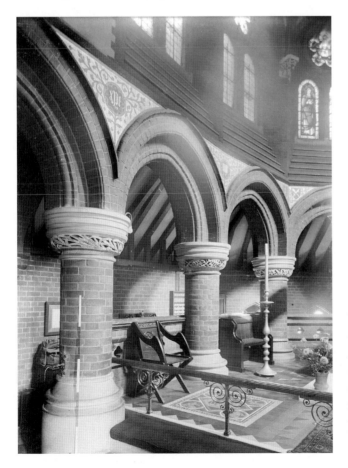

7.3 The carved capitals of the columns of the ambulatory at St Mark's include one of wheat; three ears of wheat feature in the Cheape coat of arms of Erskine Clarke's mother's family. The original mural paintings in the spandrels were of angels playing musical instruments.

carved by Harry Hems of Exeter in a conventionalised style, very different from Earp's naturalistic carvings at Lyndhurst. Red brick is used for dressings throughout the church, but White was obliged to sacrifice his brick pillars of the arcades for stronger Pennant stone. Further colour is provided by red and black floor tiles to the passages, those in the chancel enriched by panels of mosaic tesserae and marble depicting Old Testament subjects executed by Minton to designs by Clayton & Bell, as at St Andrew's, Derby.[19] Simple open benches, set on White's wood-block flooring, accommodated 600 people. The church was consecrated on 30 September 1874; the cost was later reported as £6,500.[20] This no doubt included various items of decoration, such as the carving of the capitals, the mural painting, etc. that were undertaken as funds became available. In 1887 a parish hall, also designed by White, was built on the north side of the church.[21]

St Peter's, Plough Road

In 1874 at the northern end of Plough Lane (now Plough Road), close to Clapham Junction, Clarke bought Captain Burney's house and garden to serve as the nucleus for a new district, St Peter's, within his parish. On this site he erected a school-church seating 300 people, to White's design, at the expense of George Cubitt, M.P. for West Surrey, eldest son of the builder, Thomas Cubitt.[22] (George's younger brother, the Rev. Charles Cubitt, was curate of Great Bourton, Oxfordshire, who had contributed £500 towards the building of a vicarage there to White's design in 1868-9.) The area was solidly working class, most of the inhabitants being employed by the London & South-West and the London Brighton & South Coast railways. Thanks to an anonymous donation of £5,000 (from George Cubitt), it was not long before White was drawing up plans for a permanent church to serve this community. On an awkwardly shaped site, White's church was almost as broad as it was long and had an unusual apsidal west end that accommodated the font. The church was constructed by Carters of Holloway, with W.H. Williams as clerk of works, in cream brick with red brick and Bath stone dressings in an Early English style (**7.4**). It was enriched with Minton encaustic tiles and a pulpit and font, to White's designs, carved by Harry Hems, the total cost amounting to about £10,000.[23] The laying of the top stone of the spire by the vicar, the Rev. John Toone, accompanied by White, Mr Carter, Mr Williams 'and a few others' took place on 24 April 1876, and the church was consecrated on 29 June.[24] Sadly the church was severely damaged by fire in 1970 and was later demolished, apart from the tower, which survived until structural problems prompted its demolition in 1994.

National Schools, Green Lane and Mortuary Chapel, St Mary's

No doubt Clarke was also responsible for White's enlargement of the National Schools in Green Lane in 1875 where the work was undertaken by Thomas Gregory, and with W.H. Williams again the clerk of works. The additions, costing about £2,000, included two large classrooms on the ground floor and 'a large room, 100ft by 24ft, built over

7.4 The crow-stepped gable of a later extension to White's original school-church, and St Peter's church, Battersea, 1875-6, with its massive south-eastern tower.

the old schools, with cloak-rooms and lavatories'.[25] This upper room was later licensed for worship while the parish church was closed for restoration in 1878-9.[26] The whole building is now converted to housing. White also designed in 1874-5 a mortuary chapel in the churchyard of the parish church of St Mary. It was required for corpses dredged from the river and as a sanitary place for laying-out the dead of families who lived in single-room accommodation, but appears to have been built rather smaller than White's original intentions, and was later demolished.[27]

St Matthew's, Gowrie Road

In 1876 Canon Clarke (he had been appointed an honorary canon of Winchester the previous year) again turned to White, this time to design a daughter church, St Matthew's in Gowrie Road, off Lavender Hill, to be served by curates from St Mary's. The site, in the east of the parish, was a gift from a Mr J. Westwood and the builder W.H. Williams of Clapham.[28] White's design, in brick, incorporated a nave lit by twelve gabled clerestory

7.5 The apsidal east end of St Michael's, Battersea, 1880–3, with crow-stepped gables to north and south aisles. The gabled dormers to the chancel and the south aisle are just visible.

windows above wooden arcades, a chancel, low lean-to aisles, a south porch and western bell-cote. A wooden pulpit boasting a statue of the patron saint in a crocketted niche was executed by Harry Hems of Exeter, who also 'modelled the sgraffito panels' beneath the clerestory.[29] When a parish room, also designed by White, was built on the north side in 1882–3, it was reported that the entire cost of the church, £3,500, had been supplied by Canon Clarke.[30] In the 1890s Clarke applied to make St Matthew's a separate parish, but the Ecclesiastical Commissioners ruled that it was a temporary building and would have to be completely reconstructed.[31] Instead it was decided to built a new church (St Barnabas') and by 1941 St Matthew's was closed, and shortly afterwards destroyed by bombing.

St Michael's, Cobham Close

In the first issue of the *Battersea Parish Magazine*, soon after his induction as vicar, Clarke recognised an 'urgent need for a School for young children, and for some place in which meetings for Worship can be held' and he hoped that 'an Iron Building will be put up in or near Chatham Road.'[32] In 1872 a plot of land was purchased by Philip Cazenove for £500, and by 8 August that year the first service in the temporary iron school was conducted by Clarke's hard-working curate, the Rev. H.B. Verdon, the Sunday School opening on 15 November. Clarke and Cazenove planned to build a permanent church, and negotiations to acquire more land began in 1878.[33] In 1873 Philip Cazenove had formally retired, though he remained the titular head of the stockbroking firm he had founded in 1854, and devoted himself to philanthropic works. There was 'scarcely a Church society in London, scarcely a hospital which needed help, scarcely a work of mercy of any kind, in the list of whose supporters his name is not to be read.'[34] The untimely deaths of the Rev. Verdon in October 1879 and Cazenove in January 1880, determined that the permanent church should be a memorial to both men. The Rev. Arthur Cazenove, Philip's son, wrote to Canon Clarke on 28 January 1880, 'At our family meeting today we have decided to offer you £500 for the completion of S. Michael's Church if you can see your way to setting about the work at once and getting it completed in reasonable time.'[35]

By 31 January 1880 William White was drawing up plans for St Michael's church and parochial room.[36] Although the church site was surrounded by housing on its east and west sides, White did not employ a high clerestoried design as in his previous Battersea churches. The aim was to build 'a really good church at a small cost', resulting in a design 'of the simplest construction'.[37] The north and south aisles are of almost equal widths, their crow-stepped gables set back from the polygonal apse on the east elevation and from the plain gable of the nave on the west (**7.5**). The material is stock brick with red-brick dressings and red and blue diapering under the eaves and in irregular bands across the gables. As funds were severely limited (the total cost was £4,500), White kept the slated roofs low, lighting the nave with tile-hung gabled dormers on each side, which introduce a domestic air to the building. This is countered by a timber bell-cote with shingled spirelet at the east end of the north aisle, and by the plate-traceried windows to the north elevation to Chatham Road. On this elevation a course of bricks under the eaves is set at an angle to form a notched pattern above the diapered patterning and the moulded brick hood moulds of the windows.

Internally, the breadth of the church is emphasised by the lightness of the brick arcades that are supported on rather spindly pillars of granolith, a mixture of crushed granite and cement. The floor is White's homely wood-block, providing a warm, quiet surface. The chancel and apsidal sanctuary are raised to allow an unobstructed view for all 700 seats and to allow for vestries in a crypt beneath. The darkness of the angular braced timber roof, with iron ties, focuses the gaze on to the painted boarded ceiling of the sanctuary. The original decoration (now over-painted) executed by Mr Clay to the 'designs and cartoons of Mr W. White', was of two tiers of angels, the upper one including St Michael killing the dragon. Below was 'a golden cross, crowned by two angels with a golden and jewelled crown, and the legend "I will give thee a crown of glory which fadeth not."'[38] The reredos appears to be to White's design, particularly the motifs decorating the cross

7.6 The reredos at St Michael's with its diapered gold background with spots of colour is similar to the stencilled patterning at Bishop's Court.

(**7.6**). Canon Clarke obviously took an interest in such details: White reported to him that Mr Keith had submitted proofs of the marble inlaying for the reredos. 'I think it is <u>excellent</u> – <u>quite</u> as good as that "opus" of Powells … and at a cost of about £52 instead of £125', White commented.[39] He advised that the marble should be left uncoloured, 'inlaying only the lines and shadows in colour, – and the foliage and background.' Canon Clarke was consulted regarding the six tiny windows in the apse, for which Mr Barraud, 'a parishioner and neighbour' had estimated five guineas each for stained glass angels that White considered 'very moderate for small figured windows.'[40]

At Christmas 1881 the west, 'Guardian Angel', window was erected in memory of Philip Cazenove by his grandchildren. Executed by Lavers & Barraud (as were the windows in the north wall, which were paid for by the Sunday School children), White's hand can perhaps be perceived in the slight stiffness of the figures.

St Mary le Park, Battersea Bridge Road

In 1885 a school building was erected on the south side of St Michael's, to the designs of a local architect, W. E. Wallis, White's plans for the school having been rejected by the Rev. J. Sheldon Barford, first vicar of the new parish.[41] However, White was busy with yet another scheme for Canon Clarke. This, Clarke's most ambitious, was for a new parish

7.7 A lost watercolour of White's initial scheme for St Mary le Park showing an imposing stone-built church with twin towers; the large parochial room is in the foreground.

7.8 A view of St Mary le Park from the south-east in 1883 showing the temporary gable where the south transept was designed to be built.

church, to be known as St Mary le Park, on a site on the corner of Albert Bridge Road and Park Road, close to the rapidly developing area around Battersea Park (**7.7**). White's design drawings for an imposing edifice, overall 180ft x 105ft, to seat 1500, were dated 17 March 1879.[42] Intended to be built in sections as funds became available, it comprised

7.9 The barely pointed brick arches and semi-circular apse gave a Byzantine flavour to the east end of St Mary le Park. The mosaics in the spandrels and on the floor were added in 1918.

a clerestoried nave with lean-to aisles, apsidal transepts, chancel and south chancel aisle, and symmetrical towers to south and north, the latter being flanked by a large gabled chapter room. Such a room, originally scheduled to be the first portion built, is an indication that perhaps Clarke hoped this church would be the seat of a new diocese in south London (Battersea having been transferred in 1877 from the see of Winchester to that of Rochester).

On 10 March 1880 White submitted a plan for the chancel and chancel aisle to be built first, which the Commissioners approved. The design was altered in 1881 to reduce the cost: brick with stone bands replaced the original stone; the southern tower was abandoned and the height was reduced overall resulting in the five lancet windows of the apse being two-thirds of their original height.[43] The patron, Earl Spencer, and George Cubitt, M.P. (who had given £1,000) were members of the committee that about 1881 were trying to raise the £4,000 required for the second section of the church.[44] The apsidal chancel and south chancel aisle, with temporary annexes to the west and north, was dedicated on 5 May 1883, having cost £4,350, complete with furniture and fittings, the contractor being Macey & Sons (**7.8**).[45] Internally, the sanctuary was flooded with light from the five tall, deeply-splayed lancets. The windowless ambulatory below was formed by four stone pillars with carved capitals (so similar to those at St Mark's that they must, surely, have been executed by Harry Hems) supporting the moulded brick arches and vault (**7.9**).

By 1895 Clarke realised that White's original design had been 'on too dignified a scale' and that even with White's reduced plans he would require assistance from the ICBS.[46] Grants and subscriptions allowed three bays of the nave and north aisle to be built in 1896, terminating in a slate-clad 'temporary lobby' to the west and a 'temporary passage' to the south. Fund-raising efforts in 1898, spearheaded by a donation of £500 by George Cubitt, now Lord Ashcombe, resulted in the erection of a north vestry and the installation of heating apparatus by 1901.[47] Further appeals in 1901 and 1902 culminated in the completion of the vestries and north transept by the architect John S. Quilter, White having died in January 1900. Unfortunately the church remained incomplete and was eventually demolished in 1967.

St Luke's, Ramsden Road

In 1874 Canon Clarke had purchased a site on Thurleigh Road, part of the grounds of Old Park House, on which he re-erected the iron church, now dedicated to St Luke, that had previously stood on the site of St Mark's, Battersea Rise. By 1882 the rapidly increasing congregation encouraged him to build a permanent church on the site. The following year Frederick William Hunt, who had designed St Anne's church and schools, Derby, in 1871, was appointed as architect for Clarke's new red brick, basilican St Luke's. We might speculate why White was not given this commission at a time when he had few projects in hand. Maybe the difficulties with fund-raising for St Mary le Park that

7.10 White's designs for the alabaster and marble pulpit executed by Farmer & Brindley, 1890, and the Derbyshire alabaster chancel screen, 1894, for St Luke's. The choir stalls and bishop's throne, executed in oak by Harry Hems, 1897, can be seen in the background.

led to the amended plans had caused tensions between White and some of Clarke's influential parishioners, or Clarke may have been persuaded that White should not have a monopoly in the parish. It seems more likely that White was unwell in 1882; significantly, his will was dated 8 June that year. The only known commission that he gained was in October, for the rebuilding of the church at Essendon, Hertfordshire.

Construction of St Luke's began in 1883, but it was not complete until 1889, the tower being built in 1892. And, in 1885, when a parish room was required for St Luke's, it was to White, not Hunt, that Clarke turned. White also designed the handsome marble and alabaster pulpit, the gift of Mr J.S. Jarvis in 1890, its round arches reflecting the Romanesque character of the church (**7.10**). Also by White is the alabaster chancel screen with pillars of marble from Italy, Turkey and Greece, installed in 1894. In 1896 White designed the canopied oak sedilia, 'bristling with crocketed pinnacles', executed by Harry Hems of Exeter, in memory of Robert Cooke and his sister, Mary, who had been benefactors of the church.[48] The following year, choir stalls and a bishop's throne 'of massive and crisply carved oak', all to White's designs, were dedicated by the bishop of Rochester.[49]

7.11   St Stephen's, Battersea, 1885-6, from the north-west, showing the western narthex and very low aisles.

St Stephen's, Kersley Street

In 1885 the indefatigable Canon Clarke resolved to establish a mission district and new church, St Stephen's, in a poor area around the junction of Battersea Park Road and Battersea Bridge Road, where it was anticipated that the population of 7,000 would quickly rise by 2,000-3,000. The bishop of Rochester's Ten Churches Fund promised £4,000 towards the cost of £5,400 to build a church to William White's plans.[50] With houses to the east and surrounded by roads on the other three sides, it is not surprising that there is an air of defensiveness in the windowless walls of the low, lean-to aisles and slender western buttresses of St Stephen's (**7.11**). Constructed of buff brick with red brick and stone dressings, the apsidal east end is raised to allow a vaulted vestry under the chancel. The tower, with splay-footed spire, has a clock face on each elevation, the hours indicated by pointed bricks. Unlike St Mark's, the clerestory windows are centred above the moulded brick arches of the arcades. Beneath the broad chancel arch, also of moulded-brick, modern alterations obscure the lower half of the stained glass in the east window that was described as 'from drawings by the architect of the church'. 'It represents the condemnation and martyrdom of St Stephen, with the Crucifixion and Ascension above'.[51]

St Philip's Mission Hall, Tennyson Street

White undertook other work in the parish of Battersea not commissioned directly by Canon Clarke. In August 1889, at the behest of the Rev. Patrick Watson, incumbent of Christ Church, Battersea Park Road, he prepared plans for eleven houses on unconsecrated ground to the south of the church.[52] Since the Rev. Watson was about to leave Christ Church, the Ecclesiastical Commissioners refused to consider the scheme, which was never executed. Five years later, across the tangle of railway tracks and close to the railway works, a 'small, domestic-looking building of red brick' was erected in

7.12 Holy Trinity, Elvington, of which the Rev. Clarke was patron, as rebuilt to White's designs, 1874-7. The upper stage of the rather heavy tower is reminiscent of St Mark's, Battersea Rise.

7.13 With its warm tiled roof and tall spire, White's original design for the church at Elvington, dated 15 December 1874, would have been a picturesque addition to a small country village.

Tennyson Road. This was St Philip's Mission Hall, designed by White, to serve St Philip's in nearby Queenstown Road.[53] The contract with J. Bloomer of Brentford, for about £580, was signed in August 1894 and the building completed by 18 February 1895.[54] It was demolished in the twentieth century.

Holy Trinity, Elvington, North Yorkshire

From 1877 until 1891 Clarke had been chaplain to the bishop of Rochester. In 1901 he became vicar of St Luke's, Battersea, and was also appointed an honorary chaplain to the Queen. In 1909, when over 80, Clarke resigned as rector of Battersea but retained his parish of St Luke's for another five years. He died on 3 February 1920 and was buried at Elvington, seven miles south-east of York. Through his mother's family of Cheape, he had been the patron of the living there and his younger brother, Alured James Clarke, had held the incumbency from 1865 until his death twenty years later. The medieval church of the Holy Trinity, Elvington, had been rebuilt in 1803, largely at the expense of the then rector, the Rev. A. Cheap.[55] It had an embattled west tower and tall, round-headed windows as an undated photograph in the church shows. In December 1874, Canon Clarke instructed William White to draw up plans for a new church, slightly to the south. A faculty was granted in February 1876 and in April J. Keswick & Sons of York contracted to build the church, in the local sandstone with a brick interior under a roof of Welsh slate, for £1,810, with a completion date of 25 February 1877.[56] The tall, banded tower over the north-west entrance, and the slate roof seem cold and inappropriate in this quiet rural setting, and one wonders if Canon Clarke had insisted on them (**7.12**). A year earlier, White's first design had a tower with a tall splay-footed spire, situated between the north-east vestry and the north aisle, and a traditional clay-tiled roof (**7.13**).

White's work, spanning 27 years, for John Erskine Clarke affords a rare glimpse of his relationship with a client. The correspondence between them regarding St Michael's, Battersea, reveals a decided familiarity, with White addressing letters to 'Dear Clarke' or 'My dear Clarke'.[57] There is even some irritation on White's side: 'You speak of the two little windows at the East end. I suppose you mean the three on either side?'[58] However, the stream of commissions from Clarke is indicative of a good working relationship. White must also have benefited from the publicity that Clarke provided through his editorship of *Church Bells*. In a report on the laying of the memorial stones to the Rev. Verdon and Philip Cazenove in St Michael's by the archbishop of Canterbury, it was stated that the choice of William White as the architect was based on his 'mastery of the principles of proportion and taste … directed to the practical problem how to build a really good church at a small cost.'[59] But as the demand for new churches diminished, White was increasingly involved with the restoration of old ones.

8

The Restoration Debate

Nineteenth-century interest in Gothic architecture led inevitably to the restoration of neglected and decayed medieval buildings. The restoration 'of mutilated architectural remains' was one of the main aims of the Cambridge Camden Society. Three approaches to restoration were defined in *The Ecclesiologist* of 1847 – Destructive, Conservative and Eclectic. Attention was drawn to the destructive attitude of medieval builders, who paid 'little or no regard ... to the conceptions of the original architect ... Each successive style rose only on the ashes of its predecessor'.[1] Contrasted with this was the conservative attitude of many contemporary architects who reproduced 'the exact details of every piece of ancient work' so that the restored church was a 'mere *facsimile*' of the original.[2] Eclectic restoration was considered to be the 'middle course' where, as circumstances dictated, the church was either restored or re-modelled (but invariably involving destruction of despised eighteenth-century features), and this was the approach advocated by the Ecclesiological Society.

However, in his The *Seven Lamps of Architecture* (1849) John Ruskin unhesitatingly condemned all restoration:

> it is *impossible*, as impossible as to raise the dead, to restore anything that has ever been great or beautiful in architecture ... that spirit which is given only by the hand and eye of the workman, can never be recalled ... the spirit of the dead workman cannot be summoned up, and commanded to direct other hands, and other thoughts. ... Do not let us talk then of restoration. The thing is a Lie from beginning to end.[3]

In *A Plea for the Faithful Restoration of our Ancient Churches* (1850) George Gilbert Scott pointed out that the restoration of churches for the celebration of services was a necessary duty.[4] Publication of Scott's book was at the behest of members of the Northamptonshire Architectural and Archaeological Society (to whom it was first read as a paper in 1848) hoping to stem the 'torrent of Destructiveness, which under the title and in the garb of "Restoration," threatens to destroy the truthfulness and genuine

8.1 St Mildred's, Preston by Wingham, Kent, the south elevation showing the blocked aisle windows and White's triangular dormers, 1855-7. A similar pair of dormers lights the north side of the nave.

character of half of our ancient churches.'[5] Scott disagreed with the narrow focus of the ecclesiologists, advising that 'it is often preferable to retain reminiscences of the age of Elizabeth, of James, or of the martyred Charles, rather than to sweep away, as is now the fashion, everything which dates later than the Reformation.'[6] A course of action often ignored, not least by Scott. In a paper of May 1854, also read to the Northamptonshire Architectural and Archaeological Society, White's mentor, Sir Henry Dryden, spoke of attempting 'to check people's hashing and mutilating their churches', but pointed out that 'whether you or I agree with Mr. Ruskin or not, the public opinion is for using these old buildings for public worship'.[7]

For William White the restoration of churches was necessary to render them fit for the Tractarian services advocated by ecclesiologists, and to preserve their fabric as a visible link with the past and focus of present spirituality. Practicalities included a raised altar that was visible, as far as possible, throughout the church, as well as good acoustics, warmth, and comfortable seating. White's restoration of the church at Gerrans (p. 20-24) demonstrates that he agreed with Scott's regard for the character of a building, and the preservation of later features, although, like Scott, he usually despised evidence of the

8.2 Watercolour by H. Petrie, F.S.A., 1807, showing that the aisle windows at Preston had already been blocked and replaced by three gabled dormers.

previous century. White's later experience would reinforce Scott's view that the 'practical workman *detests restoration*, and will always destroy and renew rather than preserve and restore'.[8] Like Ruskin, White believed that a workman could only express the spirit of his own age, and he therefore railed against the re-working of ancient features. In 1865 he declared that

> one of the most dangerous and destructive elements in church restoration, [is] that infatuated desire for refined, clear, new finished sharp surface. It takes away all the associations of ancient work ... no tool, no scraper, no instrument whatever, ought to be used for the surface of old work, harder than a common clothes-brush.[9]

St Mildred's, Preston by Wingham, Kent

Typical of his many small-scale restorations is White's work at the church of St Mildred at Preston by Wingham, in 1856. *The Ecclesiologist* reported that White blocked the 'small, and mutilated, and inconvenient' windows of the aisles and lit the nave by the insertion of a pair of wide, triangular dormer windows on each side (**8.1**). This was described as 'extremely picturesque externally, and internally the light is abundant and very agreeably diffused – as if from a clerestory.'[10] Although it sounds an unusually radical restoration by White, a watercolour of 1807 by H. Petrie reveals that the aisle windows had already been blocked and replaced by dormers (**8.2**). White inserted lancet windows in the chancel, restored the tower, capping it with a pyramidal roof, and furnished the chancel with choir stalls and a simple wooden screen (that has not survived).[11]

On 22 November 1856 the ICBS received an application for funds for this work. On 10 February 1857 White wrote to request an alteration to the specification: instead of the usual boarded floor on joists under the benches he wanted 'wood blocks 9 x 4½ and 1½ in thick laid herring bone fashion in lime and hair upon a properly prepared bed.'[12] There was no objection to this proposal, but it was followed on 12 March by a sketch showing that longer blocks, 13½ x 4½ x 1½ins, were to be laid in a herringbone pattern on 4ins of concrete. In 1890 White claimed that 'not far from 40 years ago' he had 'first invented the flat wood-block paving', but the earliest documentary evidence is here at St Mildred's.[13] In October 1855 G.E. Street also varied a specification: for the restoration of St Mary the Virgin, Upton Scudamore, Wiltshire. It was agreed that instead of deal boards on joists the contractor should lay wood block paving on a concrete bed for an extra sum of £90 16s 10d.[14] However, unlike White's rectangular blocks laid in a herringbone pattern, these are heartwood blocks approximately 6¾ x 5½ x 1¾ins, laid in courses like bricks. White's system, which can be seen in many of his houses as well as churches, was still uncommon enough to provoke comment when used by G.F. Bodley in 1871. A report of the consecration of St John's, Tue Brook, Liverpool, noted that 'The floors are formed of blocks of oak – a novelty and a luxury which will be greatly appreciated in cold weather'.[15]

The incumbent of Preston was the Rev. Henry Lascelles Jenner, who had been the priest-in-charge at Maryfield, Cornwall, in 1848, and for whom White designed accommodation adjacent to the school house there. He then became a curate at St Columb Major when White rebuilt the rectory for the Rev. Dr Walker. Jenner had been on the committee of the Ecclesiological Society since 1851, and in 1856 he became the Society's secretary for music.[16] 'Because of 'our connection with its vicar', *The Ecclesiologist* took 'a special interest' in this church, making this an important commission. The 'simplicity and reality' of White's work, that preserved 'the old character of the building', avoiding 'a needless obliteration of ancient features', resulted in a conclusion that 'we have seldom seen a better restoration'.[17]

All Saints', Great Bourton, Oxfordshire

Many churches in the mid-nineteenth century were in a similar state as that of the thirteenth-century church of All Saints' at Great Bourton. For about 300 years this 'ancient chapel' had been 'desecrated and secularised', so those villagers prepared to walk almost 1½ miles worshipped in the north aisle of Cropredy Church, which became

8.3 Drawing by J.C. Buckler of Great Bourton 'Chapel now school', Oxfordshire, 1823.

known as the Bourton Aisle.[18] The chancel at Great Bourton was used as a school, the chancel arch filled in, and the remainder of the building converted to cottages (**8.3**). At some time it contained a grocer's shop, and the surrounding land was used as a garden, and later as allotments, the rent from which was used to purchase coal for the poor.[19] In 1854 the school vacated the building and the incumbent of Cropredy, the Rev. Augustus William Noel, had the chancel recognised for divine worship. His successor, the Rev. Philip Hoste, wrote of his Bourton parishioners that they 'are the lost sheep of the Parish – they have drifted away from the Church and must be reclaimed – the Parish Church … is quite insufficient to accommodate them'.[20]

White's restoration of the church in 1862-3 re-opened the chancel arch and inserted a three-bay arcade giving access to a new, gabled north aisle, with a chancel aisle and small vestry, together with a south porch (**8.4**). These additions were in 'the local red and grey sandstone' to blend with the old building, and incorporated various windows – simple lancets, traceried two-and three-light middle-pointed, and new and reused Perpendicular, complete with dripstones.[21] These elicited no comment from *The*

Ecclesiologist, which indicates, perhaps, a relaxation of its former rigidity in the face of the overwhelming volume of church building and restoration. The chancel was fitted for the proper celebration of services with sedilia and choir stalls. A new stone reredos with inlays of black, yellow and red triangles and circles, surely designed by White, was donated by the contractors, Kimberley & Hopcraft of Banbury.[22] Restored and extended, the church on its raised island site in the centre of the village regained its spiritual as well as its physical importance.[23]

All Saints, Newland, Gloucestershire

In later life White admitted that in 'some of my earlier work … I was not so scrupulous as I ought to have been in the restoration of the old work', but he also pointed out that in other cases 'the vicar and churchwardens have behind me gone and destroyed the work.'[24] As Scott had emphasised, a successful restoration could not be effected 'without the constant co-operation of the clergyman.'[25] Certainly White appears to have had little practical support from the Rev. George Rideout during the restoration of All Saints', Newland, in the Forest of Dean (**8.5**). In 1861 White prepared plans for the repair and restoration of this thirteenth-century church, often referred to as the 'Cathedral of the Forest', at an estimated cost of £2,750.[26] By re-arranging the interior with benches instead of pews, accommodation was to be provided for 585 people, of which 464 would

8.4 All Saints', Great Bourton, from the south-west, with White's new north aisle and south porch, 1862-3, but the original bell openings and west window preserved.

8.5 All Saints', Newland, Gloucestershire, restored by White, 1861-2, from the north-east. An eighteenth-century vestry was removed from the east side of the north chancel aisle.

occupy free seats, out of a population that totalled 2,990 in the 1851 census, most of whom were engaged in agriculture or the mining of iron or coal.[27]

Although partially repaired in 1852, by 1861 All Saints' was described as in a 'dilapidated state'.[28] White found that the floor sloped to the north and that the north wall needed to be rebuilt and supported by two buttresses, one at the west end and the other about the midpoint. The original thirteenth-century stone of the walls and piers was in good condition, but the later work had 'become pulverised and honey-combed', necessitating renewal.[29] The original stepped lancet windows in the north wall were reinserted, complete with their fine portrait label stops. White ordered that windows, doors 'and other dressed work as were capable of restoration, without entire renewal' were to be restored stone by stone.' His instructions were disregarded by the stonecutter working on the window in the south chantry chapel, who 'instead of restoring the traceried head … had worked a new one, on the ground that the old one was so irregularly cut that it was "more trouble than it was worth to reset it."'

Parts of the south aisle and south chancel aisle had to be rebuilt, but for White 'the most serious work was the rebuilding of the south pier of the chancel arch, which, together with the whole south side of the gable, had become dangerous from spreading to the south'. In a paper detailing his work read at the RIBA, White revealed that during the work it was found necessary, because of settlement, to rebuild three arches of the south arcade and two of the north arcade which separate the extraordinarily wide aisles from the nave. He described how during a site visit he was dismayed to find the workmen not only removing the colour wash from the stone, as instructed, but

> dressing down all the little inequalities of the chamfers and octagons of the pillars, caps and bases, – one of the very features giving them a character different from the later work, which appeared more regular and less rude. In answer to my remonstrances and denunciations for acting contrary to express orders, I was told they were at any rate 'erring on the right side.'

The eastern gable and part of the side walls of the chancel also had to be reconstructed, during which pieces of an earlier window sill were discovered. Despite the fineness of the six-light Perpendicular east window, White considered it past restoration and out of character with the rest of the building. His replacement, also of six lights, is filled with richly coloured Clayton & Bell glass. The wall below was decorated with encaustic tiles in a diaper pattern, now covered with curtains. A 'modern' vestry north-east of the chancel was removed to reveal 'a good and somewhat peculiar east window of Perpendicular Third-pointed date' in the north-chancel chapel. This had been founded to support a priest who would visit the scattered mines in the Forest of Dean. Unlike the east window, White restored it. The nave clerestory 'a very poor and bad one … [which] had arrived at a state of decay scarcely capable of sustaining its roof' was replaced with alternate single and three-light windows.

The roofs, where White had hoped to reuse the old oak timbers, were found to be so decayed that all had to be renewed, although he employed some of the old timber to construct a new pulpit. White described the line of the south aisle ridge as 'broken to a marvellous extent, like the contour of a distant range of hills', and the spread of the roof here, and elsewhere in the church, had carried 'the walls with them'. The roofs were once more covered with local stone slates, and the gable ends were decorated with stone crosses, that on the chancel replacing a chimney for the heating stove.

As an ecclesiologist, White delighted in 'the removal of incongruous and obtrusive fittings' and found it 'a pleasure to restore to its full meaning and dignity the ritual arrangement of the English Church'. Pews were replaced by open benches laid on a wood-block floor. 'Those in the aisles have been made removable by folding up, so as to leave the magnificently ample area as free as possible when not required for actual use', White explained. During his first visit to the church White discovered 'the table of the ancient high altar; it was laid down as a pavement slab'. Despite objections (he did not report from whom), White insisted on its being reinstated as the base for a new altar, and pointed out that its dimensions – 9ft 3ins x 2ft 3ins – were

> exactly the same geometrical proportion as is found in the length and breadth of several early churches, and of many early lancet windows, measuring from sill to spring. It was thought that this would be far too long for proper effect, but the new one framed after the old proportion is now acknowledged to be just suited to its position in so large a church.

The restoration included work to some fragments of brasses, 'originally coloured and gilt'. Fortunately, White 'dropped upon a boy just in time to save them from being cleaned and polished, but not in time to preserve their first condition.'[30] The principal memorial in the church is the large tomb chest of Sir John Joce and his wife. The tomb chest was 'traceried and canopied … the crockets and fynials [sic] … carved with spirit, but the greater portion had perished and dropped to pieces through damp.' White rejoiced to find that some panels which had been protected by their proximity to the jamb of the adjacent arch were in perfect condition and could be used 'to show the spirit and character of the work for the reproduction of the remainder. They were clean, bright and fresh as they came from the workman's hands.' Having given instructions for their removal and safe-keeping while funds were raised for the restoration of the monument, White was appalled by their subsequent treatment. The stonecutter had

> recut the surface of the effigies, to give them a freshness of finish, adding fingers and noses to the somewhat mutilated forms, leaving, indeed, the general form and outline as before, but scarce a particle of the original spirit. He also not only renewed the whole panelling of the tomb, but, so far as I could discover, made off with the old, excepting one poor fragment which he did not consider worth carriage, but from which I have taken the accompanying section, to contrast with the new section. The one is richly and cleanly undercut, the other is shallow and finished in a rough slovenly way, - perhaps in consequence of my former remonstrances as to the pillars, caps and bases of the nave.

White later revealed that a churchwarden – 'a man who was highly educated and of good position' – had employed the stonecutter to re-cut the canopied panels (**8.6**).[31]

The frustration of the architect who would later be blamed for this 'grievous damage' is obvious.[32] Should White be held responsible because of poor supervision, or is such a case typical where want of funds precluded a clerk of works so that the incumbent was left to fulfil that role? *The Ecclesiologist*, when reporting on White's reading of his paper described briefly his restoration of the Joce tomb: 'portions which had not fallen into decay had been reset in fresh panels, of Caen stone, in a manner as far as possible to retain their original characteristics.'[33] This provoked White to point out that this apparently referred to his 'lamentation over the ruthless destruction of the ancient character of a

8.6 At Newland the tomb of Sir John Joce and his wife was 'delicately but boldly cut in Caen stone', but contrary to White's instructions was re-cut by the workmen. White showed the old and new treatments of the stone in this illustration.

memorial'.[34] White complained of 'workmen charged, again and again, not to touch' old stones. He pointed out, in terms very similar to Ruskin's, that

> Imitation of old work may be tolerably faithful, but it is *not* old work … it is like the lifeless body; the spirit has taken its flight, and has left but the vague semblance of what it once was. And if haply any life-like spirit *is* infused into the re-production, it is not the spirit of the old, but the spirit of a new life; and whether worse or better than the original, it bears the impress of the mind, not of the ancient architect, or of the ancient mason, but of the modern.

It was typical of White's honesty that he wished to publicise his experience at

8.7 A small lancet in the south wall of the nave of St Peter's, Linkenholt, Hamphire, 1869-71, is decorated with fossilized sea urchins.

Newland by giving a paper at the RIBA for the purpose 'not only … of showing, for future reference, what is original and what is not', but so that all involved in restorations would 'learn more and more faithfully to discern and to preserve that which is good and valuable, and to adopt that method which shall best secure the great ends which we have at heart.' He was concerned that so few people were 'thoroughly and duly impressed with a sense of the responsibility which the touching of old work involves … [and] may be wanting a sufficient fear of injuring it by irreverent treatment.'

St Peter's, Linkenholt, Hampshire

Sometimes the features considered 'good and valuable' were remarkably few. High on the Hampshire Downs, at Linkenholt, north of Andover, was a medieval church, close to the manor house of Thomas Colson. Whether the church was 'so dilapidated that it was resolved to pull it down and erect a new one', or whether Colson emphasised its poor state of repair in order to remove it to a site that he donated further away from his home, we do not know.[35] Certainly this course of action was 'strongly recommended' by Samuel Wilberforce, bishop of Winchester, despite the additional cost of £100.[36] William White presumably concurred, for he prepared a plan for the new church on 5 November 1869. However, it was not until January 1871, after the advowson had been sold by the Colson family to the Rev. G.A. Festing, that an application for a grant towards the rebuilding was made to the ICBS.

It was intended to preserve, if possible, a portion of the west wall and window, and the south doorway of the old church. White's design for the new St Peter's incorporated the early thirteenth-century south doorway and window, as well as the Norman font from the previous church. The ancient window, now in the nave north wall, is emphasised not with coloured voussoirs, but with a band of fossilised sea urchins. There is similar decoration to a window on the south side (**8.7**) and to a window of the adjacent school, of the same date, also by White.[37] These fossils, known as 'shepherds' crowns', are found in the local chalk and are thought to bring good luck. Doubtless White viewed them in the same rational, scientific manner as his great-uncle described 'The fossil-shells' of Selborne.[38] The cool un-knapped flint is balanced by the warm colour of the tiled roof, and by a few irregular courses of red brick and tile (**8.8**). The western belfry originally had pronounced louvres that emphasised the splay-foot of the spire.[39]

Conservation: ICBS, RIBA and Society of Antiquaries

A growing appreciation of the architecture of all periods is evident in the records of the ICBS. Its committee of architects reported in June 1860 that

> There is a growing feeling of dissatisfaction at the want of due care for ancient remains and the Committee are anxious that in the performance of their duties in connection with the Incorporated Church Building Society they may not be subject to reproach for showing an indifference to the claims of ancient Buildings connected with momentous Historical events.[40]

8.8 St Peter's, Linkenholt, 1869-71, where the silvery unknapped flint defines White's simple design against the dark trees framing the site.

White was elected to this committee in December 1880, and in the following July was given responsibility for work carried out in the two dioceses of Gloucester and Bristol, and Salisbury.[41] His reports on proposed work to the parish churches of Bishops Cannings (1883) and Avebury (1884), both in Wiltshire, Milton Abbas, Dorset, (1888), Penderyn, Brecon (1894) and St Clement, Rhayader, Radnor (1898) survive.[42] At Milton Abbas he noted that the 'old seat ends are moulded and cut out of 2½ in. solid deal plank painted dirty white. There may not be much beauty in them, but they are particularly characteristic and ought on every account to be cleaned and retained'.[43] In 1889 White and four others of the committee visited St Michael's, Coventry, to inspect the restored tower.[44] Between 1890 and 1898 White regularly chaired the meetings of the committee, which considered, amongst other things, revisions to the Society's *Architectural Requirements and Suggestions*.[45] In May 1899 when revisions were still the subject of discussion, he submitted a drawing of a seat 'for Consideration'. Perhaps as a result of his work on the committee, White was chosen in 1893 as the assessor for the limited competition for the design of a new church at Westham, Weymouth. He chose the design submitted by G.H. Fellowes Prynne.[46]

In 1864, in response to a paper by G.G. Scott calling for a code of rules for restoring churches, the RIBA established its Conservation of Ancient Monuments and Remains Committee.[47] R.H. Carpenter suggested in 1875 that the Institute should create a national collection of drawings of unrestored churches, gathered from all restoring architects, and it was proposed that William White and others be invited to join the committee to assist with this.[48] However, Street and Butterfield objected to the trouble and expense involved in sending pre-restoration drawings to the Institute, and White's involvement with the work of the committee did not commence until November 1878 when, with Street and others, he inspected the roof of St Albans Cathedral.[49] Apart from attendance at meetings, there is no record of the extent of White's involvement with the work of the committee.

On 7 December 1863, perhaps as a result of his work at Newland, White was proposed as a fellow of the Society of Antiquaries, 'for his well known study of Architecture and knowledge of mediæval antiquities particularly in reference to color [sic]'.[50] The signatories to his application are indicative of the circles in which he moved. Those knowing him personally were Frederick Lygon, M.P. for Tewkesbury who succeeded as 6th earl of Beauchamp two years later; A.J. Beresford Hope, M.P. for Maidstone and president of the Ecclesiological Society; Joseph Clarke, a founder of the Architectural Museum and at various times diocesan architect of Canterbury, Rochester and St Albans; Thomas Hayter Lewis, professor at University College, London. Also in this category were John Loughborough Pearson, whose church of St Peter, Vauxhall, was nearing completion; Charles Faulkner, fellow and mathematical tutor of University College, Oxford, and business partner of William Morris; the Rev. John Sylvester Davies, incumbent of the new church of St Mark, Woolston, Southampton, designed by White and consecrated 14 November 1863; and Benjamin Ferrey, honorary architect to the diocese of Bath and Wells, consulting architect of the ICBS, who had published his *Recollections of A.N. Welby Pugin and his Father, Augustus Pugin*, in 1861.[51] White seems to have embraced both the high church, Tory, upholders of the *status quo*, and a member of the secular University College, as well as fellow architects involved with restorations. Although he had been a fellow of the Royal Institute of British Architects since 1859, White usually signed himself simply as 'Architect'. It is a measure of his pride in his fellowship that from the date of his election, 4 February 1864, he invariably appended his FSA.

White and the Society for the Protection of Ancient Buildings

In 1874 John Ruskin refused to accept the RIBA Royal Gold Medal. His reason was his perception of the destruction caused by architects in the restoration of ancient buildings in Britain and Europe.[52] In the same year William Morris joined Basil Champneys and others in a letter to *The Times* to remonstrate against the proposal to replace the Georgian tower of St John's, the parish church of Hampstead, with a Gothic one.[53] It was Street's restoration of the church of St John the Baptist, Burford, which finally provoked Morris to found the Society for the Protection of Ancient Buildings in March 1877.[54] Chris Miele has identified the Rev. Frederick Barlow Guy, who tutored Morris for his matriculation to Oxford, as an important influence who encouraged his interest in ancient buildings.[55] A fellow member of the Oxford Architectural Society with Henry Master White and William Grey, Guy 'had a passion for church architecture', and was instrumental in appointing William White as architect of the chapel for Forest School, Walthamstow, in 1857.[56] There were personal links, for in 1852 Guy had married Rebecca Gilderdale, daughter of the headmaster of Forest School, while in 1857 her sister Lucy married White's elder brother, Francis Gilbert White. William White and Frederick Guy enjoyed walking together in the Lake District, and White regularly attended Speech Days 'and watched the progress of the school with keen interest'.[57]

The principles of what Morris called the Anti-Scrape Society, 'a most laudable and honourable title', White declared later, included a plea to those dealings with buildings

> of all times and styles … to put protection in the place of restoration, to stave off decay by daily care, to prop a perilous wall or mend a leaky roof by such means as are obviously meant for support or covering and show no pretence of other art, and otherwise to resist all tampering with either the fabric or the ornament of the building as it stands; if it has become inconvenient for its present use, to raise another building rather than alter or enlarge the old one; in fine to treat our ancient buildings as monuments of a bygone art, created by bygone manners, that modern art cannot meddle with without destroying.[58]

However, G.G. Scott spoke for many older architects when he protested that, 'it will be useless to endeavour to persuade seriously thinking people that it is wrong "to restore churches from motives of religion." They were built from such motives, and must ever be treated with like aim.'[59]

This was the fundamental difference between Morris's society that saw churches as ancient monuments, repositories of history and aesthetics, and the ecclesiologists, for whom churches were 'living vessels of faith, emblems of fundamental Christian truths'.[60] It was articulated forcefully by G.E. Street during the discussion following J.J. Stevenson's paper, 'Architectural Restoration: its Principles and Practice', read at the RIBA on 28 May 1877. As a churchman, Street wanted to see churches 'used for the purpose of that religion', and he held 'that it is our duty … to take care that they are worthy of that use …That this can be done with entire consistency, while respecting every stone in them, and every old feature of artistic value'.[61] White contributed to the debate by highlighting,

8.9 White's design for the wall tiles in the chancel at Holy Innocents', Adisham, Kent, 1869-70, adds welcome colour to the panelled chancel.

from his own experience at Newland, the damage caused by builders and churchwardens working without the authority of a competent architect.[62]

In 1869-70 White restored the thirteenth-century church at Adisham, Kent, which he described in a paper to the Architectural Association.[53] He retained the step down from the nave to the lower level of the chancel, and pointed out the damage frequently caused by raising chancel floors above their original position. However, he did not shrink from decorating the chancel by painting the rafters and fixing wall tiles behind the choir stalls (**8.9**). White 'remonstrated against over-restoration, and urged the retention of ancient features … even if not of any special beauty.'[64]

He reiterated this point in his paper, '"Restoration" v. "Conservation"', read at the Architectural Association on 25 January 1878. Any ancient feature 'which might become, if handed down intact, the channel of association with the past, and a link in the history of art' should be venerated.[65] However, he demanded 'some general agreement of principle and of practice' to define which 'relics of the past ought to be, and what ought not to be "conserved," in respect of taste, of date, of construction, of character, of association'. Like most of his contemporaries, White had a poor opinion of eighteenth-century features, and had little hesitation in sweeping them away. However, when in 1875 he was working on the church at Witham Friary, where the round-headed windows had existed since the late-eighteenth century, he concluded that their restoration to their earlier proportions 'would involve more destruction of existing work than I felt justified in making'.[66]

White's advocacy of a selective process was, of course, in direct opposition to the SPAB's philosophy of comprehensive preservation. White believed that the 'real question was, however, not how far the claims of strict conservation might be defended or not, but how far they were practicable, and not merely theoretical'. He bitterly opposed the SPAB's suggestion that if a building could not be conserved so that it could serve its original purpose, a new one should be built adjacent. White believed that 'if old buildings were thus to become mere museums of antiquarianism, or of curiosity, all affection for them as the sacred repositories of art would very quickly die away.' They would become 'picturesque remains' that 'would inevitably be swept away, sooner or later, when they had ceased to serve any useful purpose.' Far better to choose restoration,

> done with the tenderest hand … carefully retaining every vestige that could safely be kept. In the restoration of old decayed or mutilated stone or wood work, let it be insisted on that the material should be pieced or repaired rather than renewed, and that some old crumbling scrap, – say, of an ancient door or window, – should be worked-in in the new work instead of completely obliterating all vestiges of the identity of the old building.[67]

Although disagreeing with its restoration philosophy, White appears to have been happy to co-operate with the SPAB. In February 1883, on learning that Essendon church, Hertfordshire, was to be restored by White, the SPAB approached him for further information. At their committee meeting on 22 February 1883, the secretary was instructed 'to thank Mr. White for his kindness in lending the Committee tracings of the Church and at the same time to say that the Society hopes that the interesting Tower so characteristic of Hertfordshire will be preserved.'[68] White's final paper on 'Church Restoration', published in the *Literary Churchman* in 1886, considered again what should be preserved.[69] He could not accept that a huge gallery, that 'darkens and disfigures the interior ... destroys the proportions ... [and] is inconvenient, obtrusive, and inharmonious', and which was erected 'not by sentiment, nor by architectural taste or propriety, but by the barest and most unmitigated utilitarianism', should be preserved. Nor could he condone the retention of dirty plaster, high pews, or a damp pavement 'laid as a make-shift by the village mason some fifty years ago on improved levels (devised of his own heart)'. White was equally critical of demands that architects should devise new forms 'more in accordance with the spirit of an enlightened age'. He believed that this was necessary for secular or commercial construction, but for religious buildings 'it is to Church principles alone that the Churchman can safely turn for guidance.'

White pondered whether a love and reverence for antiquity would be considered mere sentiment, 'fit only for the exercise of the female mind'. He believed sentiment was 'a powerful motive force in human nature'; that 'A man without sentiment lacks a fundamental part of humanity ...[and] will probably appreciate but little the difference between the effects produced by design and by execution; by the head and the heart, or merely by the hand.'[70] Stone that was scraped or re-cut was destroyed – 'its charm is gone, its character is changed ... It is past all rational hope of "Restoration," – and for ever.'

White was a sensitive restorer of churches, and his concerns over the scraping of stone at All Saints', Newland, long pre-dated Morris's 'Anti-Scrape' society. His antagonism to the SPAB stemmed from his strongly held belief in the functional integrity of every building, a view echoed today by English Heritage.[71] White was a realist, stating that

> If I should seem to be an opponent of the advocates of conservation, it is not that I object to the general principle or practice of conservation, but only to the exaggerated ideas of what is possible and what is prudent in the proposed retention of old work.[72]

This is the voice of an experienced architect who had been in practice for over thirty years. But his career was not yet over, nor his interests outside of architecture.

9

Later Life

A reduced, but steady, flow of commissions as a result of the economic downturn of the 1870s allowed White more time for travelling, writing and his other interests. He appears to have made regular visits to the Alps, where he enjoyed walking and climbing. On 3 May 1871 he registered his 'Improvements in Knapsacks and in the Mode of Suspending the same' with the Patent Office.[1] White's invention that he termed a 'porte knapsack', was a light frame that kept the knapsack clear of the wearer's back and distributed the weight over the shoulders and hips (**9.1**). This system, now known as the frame rucksack, was not developed further until the 1950s, long after White's patent had expired.

Doubtless White was using his invention when in 1872 he climbed the Jungfrau with the Hon. Albert Dudley Ryder, son of the 2nd Earl of Harrowby, and a relation by marriage of the Cornish family. This ascent qualified White for membership of the fashionable Alpine Club, to whose members he dedicated his composition, *The Alpine Queen, A Mountain Song*, 'set to music by Lalla'.[2] Three years later White published 'At the suggestion of friends', *The Tourist's Knapsack and its Contents*.[3] The list of items included a 'Prayer-book with hymns' as well as White's designs for a suit, travelling cap, slippers and writing case. Also recommended was a cane bath frame invented by White's younger brother, barrister and Assistant Endowed Schools Commissioner, John Edward White, over which could be spread a waterproof cape for bathing. The success of White's pamphlet for first-time walkers resulted in a second edition, *Knapsack Handbook; or, Pedestrian's Guide*, in 1883. It could be argued that White's lifestyle perhaps contributed to his longevity. Commenting on G.E. Street's sudden death in 1881 at the age of 57, Alfred Waterhouse remarked 'poor Street … [for] not knowing how to take a little leisure when he ought to have had it.'[4] But by the time White resigned his membership of the Alpine Club in 1885, Queen Victoria had expressed her disapproval of mountaineering and the Alps were reckoned 'to have been "done"'.[5]

The Queen's disapproval may have been shared with White's second wife. In September 1876 his eldest daughter, Harriet, had died at the age of 19, leaving White, a widower

212

THE ALPINE PORTE-KNAPSACK.
(As Patented by Mr. WM. WHITE, F.S.A.)
PRICE 30s.

PATENT PORTE-KNAPSACK

This Invention has received the approval of some eminently Practical and Scientific Men, including Members of the Alpine Club, of the Faculty, and of Her Majesty's Forces.

Those who have carried the Porte-Knapsack have declared they would on no account carry an ordinary Knapsack again.

The Inventor has received from the Inspector of the Schools of Anatomy a most satisfactory and gratifying Testimonial as to its bearings in a Medical point of view.

___

DESCRIPTION.

1. The Knapsack itself is like an ordinary Waterproof one, but is fitted with light stiffening canes, to allow of contraction in size, and of simplicity in the fastening of it.

2. The Porte-Knapsack has a very light cane frame, or Yoke, (y) to keep the bearing Webs in *tension*.

3. The whole of the weight, instead of dragging as usual from the *front* of the shoulders, is carried *upon* the shoulders of these tension webs (t), except what is distributed on to the back, by the back webs (b) resting gently against it.

4. The webs should be buckled just tight enough to keep the cane yoke (y), and the cross cane struts (c), at about the angle shown on sketch, when in use. If not tight enough the Knapsack will have a tendency to slip off, if too tight it will not fit pleasantly.

5. The proper adjustment is when it will just lodge on the shoulders and back, without the aid of the fastening straps (f), which are required to keep the load from jolting off, but which still allow perfect freedom from strain and leverage.

6. These fasteners, fitted with the usual hook and eye (h), should be buckled as short as they will go, without being tight enough to *press* against the front of the shoulder.

7. When not in use, the shoulder-yoke and the cane cross-struts may be kept folded close on to the back of the Knapsack, by passing these fasteners behind the tension webs and hooking them into each other.

8. The small neck-strap (n) should be tight enough only to keep the back of the cane yoke well off the neck of the wearer.

Maker, Wholesale and Retail,
CHARLES PRICE, 33 Great Marylebone Street, London, W.

9.1 White's knapsack designed to avoid 'all pressure upon the lungs and main arteries', patented in 1871.

213

9.2 White's design for the quarries at St Peter's, Bucknell, Oxfordshire, 1855-6, described by Martin Harrison as 'a very proto–Arts and Crafts treatment'.

since 1866, to care for his four younger daughters, aged between 11 and 15.[6] Besides this physical imperative, his reduced income may have been an incentive for White to find a wife with means. Nothing has come to light of his acquaintance and courtship of Jane Bateson Cooke. From the certificate of their marriage on 27 December 1877 at the parish church of St Mark, Notting Hill, we know that she was a spinster, 'of full age', residing at 178 Cornwall Road, and was the daughter of Charles Warren Cooke, a diamond merchant. The late Mr Cooke was described as of Clay Hill, Tottenham, in a later survey of White's life and work.[7] The second Mrs William White was later reported to have 'for a long time devoted herself to the help of governesses by the founding of a Home' that in September 1881 had 'lately removed to 9 St. Stephen's Square, W.'[8] She appears to have had a particular interest in young people, suggesting to the London Diocesan Conference in 1883 that residential clubs should be established for students, clerks and other 'young men of the educated class'.[9] It is tempting to speculate that Jane Cooke might not have been a lady of means, but perhaps was formerly a governess or housekeeper to the family.

Early in 1879 Jane gave birth to William's only son, William Edward Bradden Holt; daughters Gertrude and Helena followed in 1880 and 1881. Jane seems to have had social ambitions, giving each of her three children four Christian names, including Holt.[10] (The

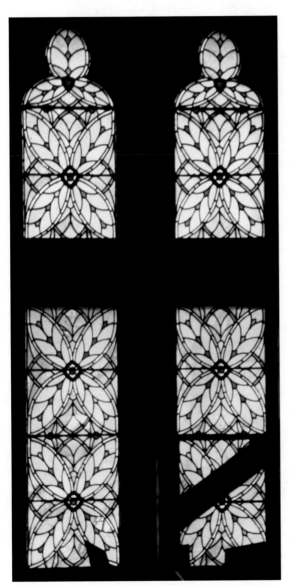

9.3 White's glass in the staircase window at Barton Hill, Marlborough College, 1863. The spidery leading lines and small points of colour are characteristic of White's secular designs in this medium.

9.4 The west window of St John the Baptist, Leusdon, Devon, designed and executed by White, 1879, demonstrates his theory of colour – warm reds and pinks are balanced by cool blues. The rather stiff figures and the tartar-like helmets of the soldiers are found in many of White's designs for windows and frescoes.

9.5 White's series of stained glass windows at Brighstone, Isle of White, 1881, begin with Christ carrying the Cross. They were commissioned by the incumbent, the Rev. W.E. Heygate, a friend of John Keble.

Holt-Whites were cousins who had inherited the estate of heiress Ann Holt, William White's great-grandmother).[11] It is easy to suppose that there may have been tensions between Jane and her elder stepdaughters. At the time of the 1881 census Ellen and Margaret, aged 20 and 19 and both described as students, were at home at Lyndon Lodge. Also there were William, aged 2, Gertrude, one, and one-month old Helena, yet their mother was absent.[12]

Stained glass

However, William must have been delighted to have a son and heir at last. No doubt in thanksgiving, he designed and executed in 1880 a three-light stained glass window, depicting the Nativity, Resurrection and Ascension, for the apse of St Mark's, Notting Hill. White's typical geometric patterning filled the base and heads of the lights, as well as the quatrefoils in the tracery.[13] *Church Bells* reported in June 1880 that the window 'reproduces with good effect the quiet tone and colouring of the medieval glass. It is artistic in execution and devotional in feeling, and the blending of the colour is singularly happy.' Unfortunately when St Mark's was closed in 1971, prior to demolition, the glass was disposed of by the Church Commissioners and cannot now be traced.

White had always taken a close interest in stained glass, designing the quarries at St Peter's, Bucknell, Oxfordshire, in 1856 (**9.2**) and memorial windows at Brimpton, Berkshire in 1859 and 1861, amongst others. In 1868 J.C. Powell called on William White to discuss the glass for St Mary's, Bletchley, then being restored by White. White thought the figures in the medallions were too crowded and demanded that haloes should be added to all the figures.[14] White's distinctive stained glass can be seen in many of his secular commissions too. In his house for the bursar at Marlborough College, 1863, he developed the design he had used at Bank House (4.6) to provide light but privacy for the staircase that overlooked the carriage drive and the adjacent plot (**9.3**).

The windows in St Mark's, Notting Hill were not the first stained glass executed, as well as designed by White. The parish church of St John the Baptist, Leusdon, near Widecombe-in-the-Moor, Devon, had been built and largely financed by a wealthy widow, Charlotte Rosamund Larpent, in 1863. William's elder brother, Francis Gilbert White, became vicar of Leusdon in 1879, the same year that Mrs Larpent died. 'Upwards of one hundred of her friends and fellow parishioners' decided to install a stained glass window in her memory, which was designed and executed by William White at a cost of 'a little over £120'.[15] White's pictorial panels of Christ's baptism, John preaching before Herod, Herod feasting and John's beheading are set between areas of geometrically patterned glass, which also fills the cinquefoils above, and is probably similar to his design for St Mark's Notting Hill (**9.4**). White set plain glass in the exterior of the new tracery, to form double-glazing. This not only kept out the cold, as he pointed out when referring to All Saints', Notting Hill, but protected the stained work from the heavy wind and rain that sweeps across the moor.

9.6 Engraving from a photograph taken by a Mr Abraham Kingdon of the consecration of White's St Laurence's Cathedral, Antananarivo, Madagascar in 1889.

A similar scene of the Baptism of Christ, together with John preaching, and his head being carried on a salver, can be seen in White's 1897 design for a three-light window in the south aisle of St Mary's church, Brighstone, Isle of Wight.[16] This was a memorial to Ann Margaret Judkins, daughter of the incumbent Canon William Edward Heygate. Canon Heygate, who as a young man had been curate at Gerrans, had commissioned in 1881 a series of stained glass designs from White for St Mary's. For the three easternmost lancets in the north wall of the chancel White created the carrying of the cross (**9.5**), the Crucifixion and the Descent, while the east window depicted the Resurrection and the east window of the south chapel the Ascension. 'They were all made by Pepper in London under the direction of W. White, Esq. Architect, F.S.A., and the greatest pains used in the selection of the glass', reported Heygate.[17] The designs are simplified, with plain blocks of colour forming the backgrounds, and the figures bursting through the decorative edging. Despite being the most expensive at £85 (the lancets cost £17 10s each, the Resurrection £78), the Ascension is the least successful, with a doll-like figure of Christ in a fringed stole suspended in a blue mandorla.[18] Heygate's Parish Record makes no mention of White visiting the Isle of Wight. Nor is there evidence that he ever travelled outside Europe, although, once more, he had commissions further afield.

St Laurence's Cathedral, Antananarivo, Madagascar

In 1864 the Church of England had established a mission on the island of Madagascar, and ten years later White's brother-in-law, Robert Kestell Cornish (3.12), was consecrated bishop. There was competition for converts from other Christians, such as the Jesuits and the Norwegian Lutherans, who had built permanent places of worship. Cornish returned to England in 1879 to raise £5,000 'for a good permanent church to be erected at Antananarivo', which he felt was necessary 'for the further development of our work … in order that the Malagasy may really see our worship in the fullest power of which it is capable.'[19] White's plans for what by the time of its consecration on 10 August 1889 had become the cathedral of St Laurence have not survived, but fortunately the building has. Raised on a terrace 25ft 'above the sacred plain of Andohalo', its bold simplicity reflects the struggle to convert the population to Anglican Christianity (**9.6**).[20] At approximately 125ft long and 54ft 6ins it is roughly the same size as St Michael, Lyndhurst, but very different in spirit. Here the great windowless apse rears up defensively between apsidal

9.7 View of St Laurence's Cathedral from the south-east. Leaded lights of pale green glass in deeply splayed windows filter the strong sunlight.

9.8   White's simple, sculptural design for benches for St Mary's, Andover, Hampshire, 1870-1. Variations on this form can be found in many of the churches where he worked.

transepts, completed later, with tiny quatrefoiled windows in their upper stages (**9.7**). It was reported that the bishop had raised the entire cost of about £8,000 himself, mainly from 'friends in England, but nearly £1,000 from friends in Australia and New Zealand'.[21] The Societies for the Propagation of the Gospel and the Promotion of Christian Knowledge each contributed £1,000.

Financial constraints precluded any but the simplest decoration – a corbel table under the eaves of the ashlar walls. Simple arched arcades separate the lean-to aisles from the nave, which is filled with open-backed benches. The importance of baptism can be gauged from the enormous stone font with pyramidal wooden cover that occupies the apsidal north-western baptistery. White's wrought-iron chancel screen stands before sixteen steep steps to the altar, its mystery emphasised by the darkness of the windowless sanctuary. Bishop Cornish was pleased with the cathedral's 'great massiveness', and praised 'the perfection of its acoustics.'[22]

Church furniture

White's concern with physical fitness and correct posture was reflected in his designs for church seating – a topic of concern to all parishioners. Many of the benches designed by White are sculptural in their simple massiveness. Typical are those in St Mary's, Andover (**9.8**). In his paper, 'Church Seats', he pointed out that sloping backs to seats were 'pre-eminently uncomfortable … except to those whose backs have become bent to the

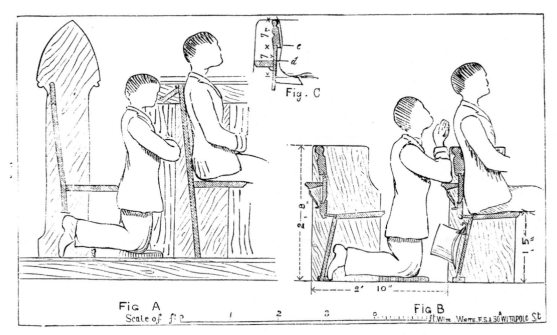

9.9 White's illustration to his paper 'Church Seats', in which he advocated his own design, Fig. B.

required extent'.[23] White believed that everyone 'should be taught from their earliest childhood to sit well back in the seat of a properly formed chair'. However, a high or sloping back to a seat would prevent this, as he showed in his diagram Fig. C. His solution, Fig. B (**9.9**), was designed to support the back, although the design was not 'in strict accord with the rigid architectural lines of the mediæval benches' (Fig. A) reproduced in many churches. White disclosed that he had persuaded a supplier to manufacture a Windsor-type chair, the "Shrewsbury", with a wooden seat (since rush seats tended 'to harbour unpleasant companions') to his design. White wrote to the secretary of the RIBA, William H. White, enclosing a copy of his paper, which, he remarked waspishly, 'I would specially commend to your notice in case of any future alteration in the seats of the Lecture Hall, which at present contribute to anything but the mental repose so needful for the ready reception of scientific information, or the relief of the backs of those who may be supposed to have done a hard day's work.'[24]

White was equally concerned with the correct height of the lectern, pointing out that 'I have myself from time to time been in the habit of reading the Lessons, and from all sorts of lecterns.'[25] Although White's height is unknown, he protested that 'it is rarely high enough … for the reader to see his book without bending his head down, to the very great detriment of his voice and the distress of his hearers.'[26] He advocated a gabled double lectern 'nearly of the height of the reader', perhaps not such an impractical suggestion at a time when many incumbents spent a lifetime in a single parish. White's pulpits invariably have a book-board that can be raised or lowered to suit the speaker's height, and choir stalls often have book-boards set quite high on decorative iron supports.

St Paul's, Rondebosch, South Africa

The first vice-principal of Bishops College, Cape Town, under the leadership of Henry Master White, was the Rev. J. Hopkins Badnall. He had been Robert Gray's curate in Stockton, and accompanied Gray to the Cape on his appointment as bishop of Cape Town. Badnall left the college in 1855, but in 1869 he returned as archdeacon of Cape Town and rector of Rondebosch, on the east side of Devil's Peak, to the south of the city. The original church of St Paul, designed in 1834 by Major C. Michell, the Surveyor-General, became the chancel when the church was enlarged in 1848-50, possibly to designs by the bishop's wife, Sophy Gray. Plans for extending the chancel were abandoned in 1866 on the grounds of cost. However, Badnall was forced by ill health to return to England in 1876, where he raised £250 towards a new chancel.[27] It is likely that he discussed his plans with William White, for by 5 April 1880 White was producing working details of his proposals.[28]

White's design included north and south transepts, a new chancel and an equally large gabled chapel to the south. To the north of the chancel a short organ aisle supported a

9.10 White's new east end for St Paul's, Rondebosch, South Africa, 1880-4, in stone with slate roofs.

223

lean-to vestry on its eastern side (**9.10**). Compared with his earlier work in Grahamstown, a more refined design was possible, since the complex tracery of the windows and the floriated crosses for the gable ends could now be produced locally. White's detailed designs for the choir stalls (the gift of Mrs Badnall) were executed by craftsmen trained at the so-called Kaffir College established in 1858 at Bishopscourt by Bishop Gray, which moved two years later to Zonnebloem, north of Rondebosch.[29] These 'Zon' craftsmen, as they were known, also produced the reredos, doubtless to White's design, given by the Rev. and Mrs Badnall in 1883 in memory of their daughter, Blanche Elizabeth.[30]

It is interesting to compare White's chancel for St Paul's, Rondebosch, with his contemporary design for the church of St Michael, Battersea (Chap. 7). What is immediately obvious, even allowing for the high price of materials in the Cape, is the difference in cost: the construction of St Michael's amounted to £4,500, St Paul's £8,500. The great wave of church-building in England was coming to an end, but missionary zeal in and for the colonies perhaps made subscriptions easier to raise for projects in the Cape. St Michael's is a cheap church for a poor community; Rondebosch was developing as a middle-class area that could take advantage of skilled local labour at low rates. However, true to his Puginian principles, White did not indulge in unnecessary decoration at Rondebosch, any more than he was able to in Battersea; in each location he relied on simple mass, pleasing proportions, sound materials and restrained embellishments.

9.11 White's design for St Alban's Cathedral, Pretoria, 1888-90. It was intended to begin by building part of the north aisle which would serve as the chancel, the existing small church acting as the nave.

St Alban's Cathedral, Pretoria, South Africa

With the British annexation of the Transvaal in 1877, the Church of England determined to establish an Anglican bishopric in Pretoria, the capital of the former Boer republic. In 1878 the position was offered to Henry Bousfield, who had earlier commissioned White's work for his parish church in Andover, Hampshire. Despite the siege of Pretoria and the defeat of the British in the Transvaal in 1881, leading to the departure of many English residents, Bousfield continued to organise his diocese and establish schools.[31] He determined to extend the simple church of St Alban to make it more worthy of its cathedral status, and when in England for the 3rd Lambeth Conference in the summer of 1888 he commissioned White to draw up plans.[32]

With its apsidal sanctuary flanked by the apses of north and south chancel aisles, and a western narthex, this can be seen as a development of White's design for St Mary le Park. Despite its size (180ft x 80ft overall), it lacks the stately grandeur of the earlier design. A plethora of buttresses with pyramidal caps rising above the lean-to aisles conflict with the triple lancets of the clerestory (**9.11**). The main material was intended to be 'an indifferent local red brick, specially made, of thinner and longer make than usual'.[33] The details were to be manufactured locally using 35 special brick moulds sent out from England. The scarcity, and consequent expense, of local stone meant that it would be reserved for the pillars of the arcades. A lofty spire was intended for the squat central tower 'when some of the proceeds of the neighbouring gold fields and diamond diggings shall have fallen into the hands of a few faithful and earnest Churchmen.'[34]

Although Bousfield laid the foundation stone on 27 March 1890 in the presence of Paul Kruger, president of the Republic, and other worthies, sufficient funds were available for only part of the north aisle to be commenced. It had been decided to delay construction until more money was to hand, but the imminent arrival of a pipe organ, the gift of a Mr Struben, forced Bousfield's hand.[35] However, it seems that the constant political and social difficulties in the Republic, culminating in the Boer War, 1899-1902, caused the whole scheme to founder, not to be resuscitated until 1905 under Herbert Baker. The foundation stone for White's design was destroyed in a fire in 1956.[36]

Bishopsgarth, Wakefield, Yorkshire

In 1888, after nine years ministering in the East End of London, William Walsham How was appointed the first bishop of Wakefield. A committee of ladies of the new diocese raised more than £10,000 for a residence, but no suitable house could be found close enough to the city centre.[37] A building committee was formed and, despite the presence of a coal seam beneath it, a site was chosen, approved and purchased for £1,500 at Westfield Grove, and plans and specifications obtained from William White.[38] Bishop How perhaps knew of White's three boarding houses at Shrewsbury School, his *alma mater*, and must have been aware of his vicarage for St Matthias, Bethnal Green. The unpretentious new bishop approved of White's plans, although many local critics who

9.12 The low brick entrance porch under the tower at Bishopsgarth, Wakefield, 1890-3, was originally sheltered by a glazed porch.

wanted a more imposing palace for their bishop considered them too modest.[39] In fact, with an overall footprint of 160ft x 88ft, it was one of White's largest new buildings.

Entered through a groined brick entrance porch (**9.12**), the building is constructed of red bricks 'thinner and longer than usual, with special mouldings, the windows having stone sills and brick mullions', and the roof of Welsh slate relieved by crested red ridge tiles.[40] White's plan involved a low, almost claustrophobic entrance that opened into a spacious, galleried, top-lit central hall that allowed light to spill into the heart of the house (a strategy often employed by Lutyens). The drawing room and library, separated by a room for the chaplain, significantly placed between two buttresses, occupied the south side of the ground floor, while the chapel and a large dining hall to accommodate the 'candidates for holy orders' faced east, with the domestic offices stretching northwards (**9.13**). Besides family accommodation, including day and night nurseries, the upper two floors provided separate bedrooms for ten trainee priests, an examination hall over the

226

chapel and a studio at the top of the entrance tower. There would have been no areas of contemplative gloom in this residence – the many windows are tall with elegant narrow brick mullions. Bishopsgarth has been a training centre for West Yorkshire Police since 1945, and alterations have obscured much of White's original intentions, but the varied gables, many slate-hung, are distinctive, as are the arch-braced gallery and staircase and an oak settle in the hall.

Arnos Grove, Southgate

On 20 August 1898 William White led a party of about twenty members of the Architectural Association (of which he had been a member since 1867) to look at the work he had carried out at Arnos Grove, a mansion in Southgate, Middlesex, which has since given its name to the locality.[41] Originally a sixteenth-century house, it had been rebuilt early in the eighteenth century and altered by Sir Robert Taylor in 1788. It was bought by the brewer Isaac Walker in 1777 and inherited by Mr Vyell Edward Walker, a renowned cricketer and one of the founders of the Middlesex Cricket Club, in 1889. As it was reported to be the first house in Southgate to have electricity (1896) and until that date did not have a single bathroom, perhaps we can assume that it was about this time that White became involved with improvements to the house.[42] How White gained the commission is not known. The contractor, Gregory of Clapham, generously provided the AA visitors with tea at the Cherry Tree Inn after their visit![43]

South Elevation

William White 71st Arcßt

9.13 White's south elevation of Bishopsgarth, Wakefield, its ecclesiastical connections indicated by gabled buttresses either side of the chaplain's room.

9.14 The west elevation of the house called Arnos Grove, Southgate, London, from which the area took its name. White added the cupola and inserted ironwork to support the wall above the semicircular bay, c.1896.

White pointed out that the old slated roof had been formed 'in five ridges with gutters between' that were a constant source of leaks. He had therefore covered them with a flat leaded roof, but left the slates on the outer slopes (**9.14**). He had also designed a small staircase to the roof, 'terminating in a cupola, which serves also for the house bell', that could also be used as an alarm 'the rope being accessible from each landing.'[44] Although approached by a flight of steps, the original entrance had no porch: White added a portico of brick and stone, 'without any pretence to strict architectural precedent, or direct imitation of existing treatment to be found in the house.' By now he had obviously overcome his earlier opposition to concealed ironwork, for he used it to support the sagging wall above the semicircular bay, which was reputed to have been added to the drawing room by Sir Robert Taylor.[45] White resisted the addiction of some nineteenth-century architects to black mortar, ordering the pointing of the house where there were bricks of 'red, plum, grey, and yellow' to be done 'in a very subdued tone … In order to avoid an unnecessary appearance of newness'.[46]

White led his group into the double-height entrance hall decorated in 1723 by the Flemish artist, Gerard Lanscroon. His painting, the *Apotheosis of Caesar*, on the ceiling had been cleaned but the plaster beneath one of the beams had become detached. White was careful to avoid damaging the mural, instructing a joiner to tie the plaster back to the beam with copper wire, using 'clamps formed of 25 pierced halfpennies', that can still be seen today. However, he admitted that his 'ruthless treatment of the old handsome oak staircase may perhaps be criticised.' He took three steps out of the upper flight and raised

9.15 White added large fluted and carved newel posts to stabilise the original staircase balustrade at Arnos Grove.

229

9.16 St Dionis' vicarage, Parsons Green, London, 1898-9. The study and dining room were to the left and right, respectively, of the central entrance, with the drawing room on the first floor above the study.

the lower flight by the same amount to increase the height of the doors to the dining room and library, and to allow for the insertion of a 'dinner staircase, and a dinner lift from the basement'. As the balustrade was weak, White added some balusters and carved newels (**9.15**), deepened the handrail and in what he feared 'may perhaps be regarded as an insult to the original design', he added 'a carved fascia to the whole of the landing'.[47]

Although White had previously expressed little regard for eighteenth-century work, he refused to wilfully destroy what he considered the 'very shaky and shabby construction, warped and insecurely fixed' of many of the walls of rooms and passages. This 'thin square framing in very large panels' he ordered to be 'subdivided and the framing strengthened and enriched with mouldings planted on.' Similarly, in the dining room of Taylor's extension to the house, he 'coffered the ceiling ... dividing it into nine panels by enriched ribs, with corbels and pilasters beneath'.[48] This curious decoration composed of two tiers of Ionic pilasters has puzzled later commentators.[49]

St Dionis' vicarage, Parsons Green, Fulham

White's last known commission was for a modest parsonage house in the developing area west of Chelsea. A small proportion of the proceeds of the sale of Wren's St Dionis Backchurch in the City of London had been reserved to build a parsonage to serve the new church on Parsons Green designed by Ewan Christian, 1883-5.[50] Plans to buy a local property and sell the land were rejected by the Ecclesiastical Commissioners, but it was not until the Rev. William Samuel Carter became the incumbent in 1898 that a scheme to build was implemented. For the previous two years Carter had lived in the White-designed vicarage for St Matthias, Bethnal Green, so it is not surprising that he turned to White for plans for a parsonage adjacent to St Dionis' church.[51] In July 1898 Carter requested the Ecclesiastical Commissioners to pass the plans 'as expeditiously as possible, as I wish to have the Roof on by the Winter.'[52] The Commissioners insisted on a fourth bedroom on the first floor, which White accomplished by increasing the length of the central bay and inserting a gabled window and a chimneystack above the front door.[53] Approval was granted and the foundation stone was laid on 3 October by the Rev. Sinclair, who had been the first incumbent of the parish.[54]

On 4 August 1898 Dove Bros of Islington agreed a contract price of £2,300 for the building, in stock brick with red-brick dressings under a clay tile roof (**9.16**), and began work the next day.[55] The centrally placed arched entrance of moulded brick is only slightly pointed, with a stained glass fanlight with characteristic spots of rich colour. A more egalitarian attitude to parishioners removed the need for a separate entrance to access the vicar's study, and there appears never to have been a 'green baize door' to divide the servants' areas from the family space, nor a separate service staircase. Water closets were included on the ground floor in both the family and service areas, while the first floor bathroom has pivoting windows, and there is a separate W.C. As at Wakefield, the windows are tall rather than broad, with slim panelled shutters, and set below shallow internal arches. However, White had not completely abandoned the pointed arch, which can be seen at either end of a service passageway at the rear of the house. The Rev. Carter and his family moved into the new vicarage on 22 June 1899, seven months to the day before William White died.

Epilogue

Until the end of his life White continued to play an active part in the affairs of the Architectural Association, of which he had been president in 1868-9. He reported on a visit that he led in August 1899 to Grim's Dyke, W.S. Gilbert's house, extended by Richard Norman Shaw, commenting approvingly that 'Some of the work is very simple, without any effect of baldness.'[1] For the *Architectural Association Notes* White wrote an obituary of Sir Arthur Blomfield, who died suddenly on 30 October 1899. White concluded that Blomfield 'stood deservedly high as one of the promoters and followers of the great Gothic revival – one who happily never discovered its unfitness for modern use.'[2] This might appear to be a condemnation of White's own predilections, but his designs express his development of Gothic to reflect 'modern requirements'.[3]

In January 1900, the architectural writer, T. Francis Bumpus sent the proofs of his review of All Saints', Notting Hill, which was to appear in an architectural journal, to William White to review. 'The courteous letter accompanying the return of the proofs … must have been the last penned by that distinguished architect' for it arrived on the morning of 22 January 1900.[4] On that day, at 24 Gayton Road, Hampstead, the home of a Mrs Longhurst, William White died of heart failure caused by influenza. His daughter, Margaret, recorded that he 'passed away very peacefully … He was working up to the end'. She assured Mr Bumpus that 'your very kind letter and the very appreciative notice of his work, which he read aloud to me, did much to make his last two days happier.'[5] White's sister, Mary Martelli (who lived nearby in Prince Arthur Road), was present and it was she who registered the death. Two days later, Margaret White, who was living with her aunt, purchased a grave plot in Hampstead Cemetery.[6] White was buried there on 26 January, and on 1 March his grave was marked by a temporary wooden cross that still remains. It bears the date of his burial, but no name.

The lack of a durable monument to White in Hampstead Cemetery is a sad reflection of his financial situation and what seems to have been the unhappy state of his second marriage. White's business affairs had been in difficulties for some time. In 1868, two years after the death of his first wife, he had mortgaged his seaside home, 1 Selborne Place, Littlehampton, jointly to his younger brother, John Edward White, the Rev. John Smith Gilderdale and the Rev. Frederick Barlow Guy.[7] By 1882 he was investigating the possibility of raising some money from his first wife's marriage settlement, but his

The 'temporary' wooden cross that marks William White's grave in Hampstead Cemetery. Besides the sacred monogram, IHS, it gives the date of White's burial and the words 'Christo et in pace', but no name.

brother, John Edward White, one of the trustees, had been advised that such a course would be illegal.[8] His home, Lyndon Lodge in Hanwell, appears to have been let from this date, at one time to the Irish Yeats family.[9] In 1884 White had a mortgage on another property, 7 Brunswick Gardens, Kensington.

From 1890 until 1899, 30a Wimpole Street (on which he had taken a lease in 1870) still appears as White's business address, the living accommodation being occupied at the time of the 1891 census by a professor of zoology at London University and his wife. By March 1893 Lyndon Lodge had been sold for £1,775, and a surveyor valued 30a Wimpole Street at £1,000 and 7 Brunswick Gardens at £2,160.[10] White, at this time a tenant at 2 Little York Street Mews, believed that he could sell 1 Selborne Place for £1,000. On the basis of these valuations, White's nephew, the 9th earl of Stamford (son of his sister, Harriet, and the Rev. William Grey), agreed to advance him £2,500 to settle all mortgages. White's letter of thanks, dated 18 May 1893, expressing his 'sense of the great kindness and assistance which you have given me', indicates the extent of his difficulties – 'it gives me material help in my struggle for life.'[11] Even allowing for family bias, Mary Martelli's judgement that Jane White would have spent her husband's money 'long ago had she had her way …leaving the children penniless' is a telling one.[12]

At the time of his death, White's leases on 30a Wimpole Street and 1 Selborne Place, Littlehampton, as well as his freehold property, 7 Brunswick Gardens, all remained unsold. By November 1900 the earl of Stamford and Charles Martelli, White's nephews and surviving executors, claimed probate of White's last will, dated 1 January 1896, together with two codicils, and the contents of an earlier will of 8 June 1882. Jane White contested the probate on behalf of her two daughters, who had not yet reached their majority, and her son, claiming that the intentions of the 1882 will were not valid.[13] This earlier will referred to the trust fund drawn up the day before White's marriage to Ellen Floyer Cornish, by which at White's decease all the monies held in the trust were to be divided equally between Ellen's surviving children. On 27 September 1895 at White's behest, Charles Martelli had cut out this part of the will 'under the erroneous belief' that the terms of the original settlement would ensure that the funds were distributed as intended.

Although she made no demand on her own behalf, Jane White and her children claimed that White had revoked his will of 1882 and that under the terms of the later wills, on the death of his widow, all his property was to be divided equally between all the surviving children. White's indefatigable sister, Mary Martelli, gave her evidence to the court that her brother believed that his first family were provided for by the 1855 marriage settlement. Giving judgement on 15 December 1900, Sir Francis Jeune ruled that White's intention had been expressed in the will of 1882, and as it had not been expressly revoked by the later will, the settlement funds should be distributed as it directed. The costs of the case were to come out of the estate, which was valued at just £4,244 17s 10d.[14]

By a codicil dated 5 May 1896, White left his office furniture ('used by me at any office or place where I shall be practising my profession of an Architect'), together with books, plans, drawings, account books, letters and professional papers, George Ribbon, silver and plate equally amongst the four surviving daughters of his first marriage – Ellen

Frances, Margaret Kestell, Susan Amy and Katherine Mary White.[15] The George Ribbon, a gift from White's godfather, was given to their cousin, the earl of Stamford and is now displayed at Dunham Massey, Cheshire. Susan, a 'Scholar and Student of St Hugh's Hall, Oxford', was teaching at Oxford High School in 1893, before becoming headmistress of Bishop Auckland High School and eventually principal of Auckland School, Bexhill.[16] Ellen and Katherine both attended Miss Slater's establishment at Upton Park where they trained for missionary work in South Africa, while Margaret appears to have been a companion to her aunt, Mary Martelli.[17] William Holt-White (as he styled himself) became a writer, chiefly of science fiction. He married but had no children. Like her elder half-sisters, Helena also went to South Africa, as a nurse, where she married and had two sons. Her family were unaware of the existence of her sister, Gertrude, who, perhaps, died early in the twentieth century. Of White's personal and professional papers there appears now to be no trace.

Mark Girouard has said of William White that he 'spent much of his life balanced on the boundary between crankiness and brilliance' and that eventually 'he fell off on the wrong side, and a large proportion of his last years were wasted in trying to prove that Shakespeare was Bacon.'[18] Unfortunately other commentators have repeated this implication of lack of balance, or even insanity.[19]

Let us look at the Shakespeare/Bacon controversy. The Bacon Society was established in London in December 1885 and began publishing a journal the following year.[20] It was reported that Thomas Gaisford, dean of Christ Church, Oxford, had credited Bacon with most of the plays attributed to Shakespeare and the debate spread to France, Germany and the United States.[21] William White's contribution, 'Francis (Bacon), Lord High Chancellor of England', an analysis of Bacon's life and character, appeared posthumously in the 1900 volume of *Baconiana*, together with a letter from White regarding Bacon's cipher writing.[22] The theory that Bacon wrote the works of Shakespeare, either alone or with others, is still the subject of lively debate in the twenty-first century. William White cannot be denigrated for his part in the argument in the nineteenth, nor were his last years wasted, as he was producing satisfying and interesting buildings to the end.

Apart from his contribution to *Baconiana* and his paper on the Galilee (narthex) of Durham Cathedral, most of White's writing during the last ten years of his life consisted of letters, none of them displaying anything other than sound judgement and commonsense. In 1891 the (failed) Parliamentary Bill for compulsory registration of architects provoked a debate in *The Times*. White submitted a measured contribution to the issue. He did not want 'to quarrel with Mr Norman Shaw for his high view of art', but he believed it was clearly necessary 'to ensure the acquirements [sic] of all those elements of construction and arrangements, without which the architect, whether true artist or not, must fail to satisfy the requirements of a civilised community.' Besides genius, White believed an architect needed 'a large capacity for ingenuity, a fund of general information, and a considerable amount of what Vitruvius calls "Ratiocination."'[23]

White's continuing love of music is evident in his efforts to improve congregational singing through the Church Congregational Music Association that held its first annual meeting in February 1890.[24] White demanded 'the best vehicle for words, not for musical display. We want simple and harmonious principle, free from eclecticism.'[25] He likened services which could only be sung by an 'elaborately trained choir', such as those led by Benjamin Webb at St Andrew's, Wells Street, to the eclecticism of so much church architecture, with its mixture of styles, 'ostentatious ornamentation and 'loud' colour decoration.' The CCMA aimed to select and publish music 'within the compass of almost all ordinary voices' at a price 'within the reach even of the poor who know how to read.'[26]

Although there is no evidence that White supported organised socialism (or had any particular political allegiance) he often expressed his beliefs in social justice. He chided the Peabody Trust for limiting occupancy of their properties to those earning a minimum wage of at least twenty-three shillings a week, rather than favouring those on lower incomes; and pleaded for tenants to be provided with light and air and more generous accommodation, kept in good repair.[27] He drew attention to the necessity of strongly enforced sanitary legislation to protect tenants, and pointed out that tradesmen 'are deserving of consideration and fair treatment equally with ourselves'.[28]

The debate on vivisection in the latter part of the nineteenth century provoked letters from White to *Church Bells*. An animal lover (he wrote a poem entitled *Un Chat Fidèle*), White pointed out the 'enormous, indeed the stupendous, benefits', not only for humans but for animals also, arising from medical research that included vivisection.[29] However, he believed that such experiments had to be undertaken responsibly, and be properly authorised. He attacked the hypocrisy of armchair critics who denounced research on animals, yet expected medical research to find a cure for diseases such as malaria.[30]

White's obituaries mentioned the output of his practice: 'more than 250 churches … over eighty parsonages, and about a hundred schools …[as well as] hospitals, business premises, and a large number of houses of all dimensions'.[31] Despite many years of research, including investigations in the uncatalogued archive of Messrs Kimberley of Banbury that revealed several previously unknown White commissions, almost a hundred of the churches remain unidentified, as do nearly half the parsonages and schools. They were described as 'characterised by much robustness and certain well-marked skill in grouping and outline of mass.'[32] In 1890 *The Times* styled White, together with Charles Barry, Ewan Christian and Alfred Waterhouse, as one of the 'eminent architects' who appeared as witnesses in 1885 in support of J.L.Pearson's scheme for the restoration of Westminster Hall. [33] White's long life militated against his reputation, as his work was 'inevitably … considered out of date', although one obituary admitted that 'looking at some comparatively recent designs of his, we think they contain much of real character and value.'[34] Although White was defined as a 'firm adherent of the Gothic revival', it was pointed out that he was 'one of the ablest exponents of the application of its principles to modern buildings', and that his talent was 'inventive and ingenious'.[35] White's position as a 'proto-Arts and Crafts' architect is confirmed by the view that he 'gave to forms, mouldings, and ornament a distinctive character, in harmony not only with the nature of the material, but also with the methods and tools employed by the craftsmen.'[36]

Attention was drawn to White's many papers and his contributions ('in a quaint and characteristic manner') to debates, and his 'exceptional practical knowledge and experience'.[37] *The Builder* admitted that 'it was not unusual for us to receive an original and trenchant letter' from White, 'in which he often hit the nail on the head'.[38] However, the writer claimed that at meetings he 'spoke badly and did not do himself justice', although 'there was always a kernel of solid matter in his remarks.'[39]

White was described as 'a sincere friend to his artistic brethren', 'warmly enthusiastic in his work', 'a worthy man … and an architect of high repute.'[40] One of his pupils (perhaps Robert Medley Fulford) recorded that 'As I was for about six months in his office, I should like to bear testimony to his great zeal for his profession, and his sterling worth. He was so <u>thorough</u> in everything, and of a deeply religious character.'[41] Despite all vicissitudes, it is that enthusiasm for nature, for life and particularly for architecture that is so evident in White's work. His buildings embody his belief that,

> there is no branch of Art so comprehensive, or which does so continually come before us, and has the power so forcibly, or so often, of intruding itself (so to say) upon the notice, as Architecture. Whether it be good or bad, the Architecture cannot be hid. It meets us in our every day walk; in our going out and coming in it is almost always with us in some shape or other. No one can escape.[42]

Abbreviations

A	*The Architect*
AAN	*Architectural Association Notes*
AASRP	*Associated Architectural Societies Reports & Papers*
AH	*Architectural History*, Journal of the SAHGB
AHA	Arley Hall Archives
BA	*British Architect*
BAL	British Architectural Library, V & A
BCA	Bishops College Archive, Cape Town
BerksRO	Berkshire Record Office
BLA	Bedfordshire & Luton Archives & Records Service
BL	British Library
BN	*Building News*
Bod	Bodleian Library, Oxford
BoE	Nikolaus Pevsner et al., *The Buildings of England* series
BRO	Buckinghamshire Record Office
B	*The Builder*
CamRO	Cambridge Record Office
CB	*Church Builder*
CBells	*Church Bells*
CCB	Cathedral & Church Buildings Library, London
CDCA	Canterbury, Dean & Chapter Archives
CEAJ	*Civil Engineer & Architect's Journal*
CERC	Church of England Record Centre
CCA	Cheshire & Chester Archives & Local Studies
CL	Cory Library for Historical Research, Rhodes University, Grahamstown, South Africa
CL	*Country Life*
CRO	Cornwall Record Office
CumRO	Cumbria Record Office
CUL	Cambridge University Library
DerbRO	Derbyshire Record Office
DMA	Dunham Massey Archive, John Rylands Library, Manchester
DRO	Devon Record Office
DHC	Dorset History Centre
Eastlake	C.L. Eastlake, *A History of the Gothic Revival*, 1872
EC	Ecclesiastical Commissioners' files, C of E Record Centre
EDR	Ely Diocesan Records, Cambridge University Library
E	*The Ecclesiologist*
FRC	Family Record Centre, London
G	*The Guardian*
GBC	Gordon Barnes' Collection, Cathedral & Church Buildings Library

GM	*Gentleman's Magazine*
GRO	Gloucestershire Record Office
HRO	Hampshire Record Office
HertsRO	Hertfordshire Record Office
ICBS	Incorporated Church Building Society files, Lambeth Palace Library
ILN	*Illustrated London News*
KA	Uncatalogued archive of Messrs Kimberley of Banbury, Oxford RO
KCA	Keble College Archive, Oxford
LeicsRO	Leicestershire Record Office
LRO	Lincolnshire Record Office
LPL	Lambeth Palace Library
MCA	Magdalen College Archive, Oxford
MF	*Mission Field*
NMR	National Monuments Record, Swindon
NkRO	Norfolk Record Office
NRO	Northamptonshire Record Office
ORO	Oxford Record Office
OSPSGA	*Oxford Society for Promoting the Study of Gothic Architecture*
QAB	Queen Anne's Bounty files, CERC
RA	Rotherham Archives
RCG	*Royal Cornwall Gazette*
RIBAJ	*RIBA Journal*
TRIBA	*Transactions of the RIBA*
RIC	Royal Institution of Cornwall
RU	Rhodes University, Grahamstown, South Africa
ShA	Sheffield Archives
SAO	Southampton Archive Office
SomsRO	Somerset Record Office
SP	stereoscopic photographs of some of White's commissions, private collection
SPG	*Society for the Propagation of the Gospel*, Rhodes House Library, University of Oxford
SRO	Suffolk Record Office
T	*The Times*
TEDAS	*Transactions of the Exeter Diocesan Architectural Society*
TNA	The National Archives, Kew
UCTL	University of Cape Town Library
V&A	Victoria & Albert Museum
VCH	*Victoria County History*
WarRO	Warwickshire Record Office
WRO	Wiltshire & Swindon Record Office
WSRO	West Sussex Record Office
WYAS	West Yorkshire Archive Service

Endnotes

Introduction

1. William White, 'A Plea for Polychromy', *BN*, 18.1.1861, p. 55.
2. Letter, *B*, 18.7.1857, p. 402. White was a member of the Working Committee and donated three guineas to the Pugin Travelling Fund, Benjamin Ferrey, *Recollections of A.N. Welby Pugin and his Father, Augustus Pugin* (London, 1861), p. 473.
3. *CEAJ*, 38, 1868, pp. 4-5.
4. Charles L. Eastlake, *A History of the Gothic Revival* (London, 1872), p. 292.
5. Letter, 'Heating Apparatus', *CBells*, 24.3.1883, p. 310. Unfortunately, all the glass was destroyed by bombing in the Second World War but White's double-glazing at Leusdon, Devon, survives.
6. *G*, 6.9.1854, p. 695.
7. *E*, 19, 1858, p. 414.
8. *BN*, 7.2.1890, p. 224; Miss H.M. White, *Cameos* (1960), p. 9, BCA file 4, White 1.
9. White, 'Ironwork: Its Legitimate Uses and Proper Treatment', *TRIBA*, 16, 1865-6, p.17.
10. White, *The Palace, An Artistic Sketch of the 10th of June 1854* (London, 1855), p. 24.
11. *BN*, 28.5.1880, p. 624.
12. White, *TRIBA*, 16, 1865-6, p. 20.
13. Ibid., p. 30.
14. Peter Ferriday, 'The Oxford Museum', *AR*, 132, 1962, p. 412.
15. *CEAJ*, 31, 1868, p. 2.
16. Ibid.
17. Ibid., p. 3.
18. Ibid.
19. Ibid.
20. White, 'Architectural Uniformity and its Claims', *BN*, 17.2.1860, p. 132.
21. Ibid., p. 134. A view shared by Le Corbusier, who praised the uniformity of the Crystal Palace, *AR*, 81, 1937, p. 72.
22. 'On Some of the Principles of Design in Churches', read 8.5.1851, published in *TEDAS*, 4, 1853, pp. 177-8.
23. 'Modern Design. On Windows', *E*, 17, 1856, p. 328.

Chapter 1. Early Years

1. Vols 1781-4, British Library, Add.MSS. 43814-7; vols 1785 and 1788, Bodleian Library, Bod.MSS.Eng. misc.b.33, c.154. His sons also kept detailed diaries.
2. F.H. White to the Rev. H. Grey, 22.1.[?1849], DMA EGR 4/6/1/1/17.
3. 'A Journal kept at Maidford by SW, 1818', Bodleian Library, Bod. MSS.Eng.misc.c.198. The laconic entry for 4 May reads 'A Wedding – Emma and Harriet [his daughters] went to Blakesley.'
4. DMA EGR 5/2/6/13.
5. Nicholas Carlisle, *A Concise Description of the Endowed Grammar Schools in England and Wales* (London, 1818), 2, p. 201.
6. Ibid.
7. Miss H. Mary White, MSS 'Down the Ages', n.d., BCA file 4, White 1. Although no mention is made of the girls' education, letters reveal that they travelled to Northampton for singing and drawing lessons, DMA EGR 5/2/4/16.
8. F.H. White to the Rev. H. Grey, 22.1.[?1849], DMA EGR 4/6/1/1/17; NRO GI/265; LeicsRO DG11/930.

9. Lyndon F. Cave, 'A Dictionary of Architects & Surveyors who Practised in Leamington Spa 1800-c.1840', typewritten notes, n.d., WarRO B.LEA.CAV(P).

10. Charles Squirhill was 'a purveyor of the feeblest sort of early nineteenth-century Gothic', according to Howard Colvin, *A Biographical Dictionary of British Architects 1600-1840* (London, 1995), p. 914. White was living with the family 'over the shop' at E[a]ton Villa, letter from his sister, Harriet White, 6.9.1841, DMA EGR 5/2/4/13.

11. Lyndon Cave, *Royal Leamington Spa* (Chichester, 1988), p. 138.

12. *B*, 31.10.1885, p. 623.

13. Bodleian Library, BOD. MSS.Eng.misc.c.198, Fri. 9 Oct.1818; c.157, Tues. 20 Jun. 1820.

14. Miss H. Mary White, *Cameos from Childhood* (1961), BCA file 4, White 1.

15. Letter, 27 Nov., KCA John Keble's correspondence, 68.

16. Thomas Henry Watson, obituary of White, *RIBAJ*, 7, 1900, p. 145.

17. *Personal and Professional Recollections by the late Sir George Gilbert Scott, R.A.*, (G. Stamp, ed.) (Stamford, 1995), pp. 88-9. 'Elevation of the Cathedral Church of St Chad, Birmingham. By A.W. Pugin. London. 1840', *Dublin Review*, May 1841, the first part of *On the Present State of Ecclesiastical Architecture in England*, published 1843.

18. In *History of the Protestant Reformation*, first issued as letters 1824-7, and *Rural Rides*, (London, 1830), *see* Phoebe Stanton, 'The Sources of Pugin's *Contrasts*', in John Summerson (ed.), *Concerning Architecture* (London, 1968), pp. 134-6.

19. *Contrasts*, (1836) 2nd ed. (1841) (reprinted Reading, 2003), p. 43.

20. *True Principles* (1841) (reprinted Reading, 2003), p. 1. Some of Pugin's most telling illustrations appeared for the first time in the second edition of *Contrasts*, 1841.

21. James F. White, *The Cambridge Movement* (Cambridge, 1962), p. 42.

22. *Oxford Architectural Society Report January 1848 to July 1849*, p. 34.

23. Miss H. Mary White, MSS 'Down the Ages', n.d., BCA file 4, White 1.

24. *Cambridge Camden Society, Laws*, (1839), 1841 edition reprinted in Christopher Webster (ed.), *'temples … worthy of His presence'*… (Reading, 2003), p. 47.

25. Geoffrey K. Brandwood, 'A Camdenian Roll-Call' in Christopher Webster & John Elliott (eds) *'A Church as it Should be', The Cambridge Camden Society and its Influence* (Stamford 2000), pp. 365-452.

26. David B. Brownlee, 'The First High Victorians: British Architectural Theory in the 1840s', *Architectura* (Munich, 1985), pp. 33-46.

27. Meeting, 12.11.1845, *Proceedings of the OSPSGA*, 1845, p. 24.

28. 'Victorian Office Practice and Victorian Architecture: The Case of Sir Gilbert Scott', in Peter Lukehart (ed.), *The Artist's Workshop, Studies in the History of Art*, 38 (Washington, 1993), p. 163.

29. Baldhu church, 'Form of Enquiry', 18.9.1848, describes White as 'late of Craven Street, London', ECE/7/1/17863.

30. White's younger sister, Lucy Ann White, was at the same address at the time of the 1851 census.

31. 'Family Records and Reminiscences written down by Robert K. Kestell Cornish, Bishop, A.D. 1906, aetat 83', private collection.

32. *RCG*, 21.7.1848.

33. Ibid.

34. Letter from the Rev. W. Haslam, 31.7.1848, LPL ICBS 3905.

35. *RCG*, 4.5.1849, p. 5.

36. Ibid; letter, 29.3.1849, ICBS 3905.

37. Letter, 13.4.1849, ICBS 3833.

38. *E*, 10, 1850, pp. 246-7.

39. Clive Wainwright, 'Ardent Simplicity', *CL*, 18.10.1990, p. 151.

40. Grant of land, 14.5.1849, CRO DDP 97/2/45/1.

41. Reported in *E*, 12, 1851, p. 296. The foundation stone records the principal benefactors as the earl

and countess of Falmouth, William Daubuz of Killion, John Davies Gilbert of Trelissick, G.J. Cornish and his curate, John Hardie.

42. *E*, 7, 1847, p. 1. The curriculum believed to be appropriate in the mid-nineteenth century for the poor was the '3 Rs', together with sewing for girls.

43. Ibid., pp. 2-3.

44. Henry E. Kendall Jr, *Designs for Schools and School Houses Parochial and National* (London, 1847), preface.

45. Joseph Clarke, architect to the diocesan boards of education of Canterbury, Rochester, and Oxford, *Schools and School Houses* (London, 1852), introduction.

46. White, 'Modern Design. On Windows', *E*, 17, 1856, p. 330.

47. *T*, 3.3.1845, p. 7.

48. Edward Whitley, *Journal of the Royal Institution of Cornwall*, 7:1, 1881, p. 57.

49. Plans and specification dated 1849 reported by Charles Henderson, *St Columb Major, Church & Parish, Cornwall* (1930), p. 16.

50. Ibid. The author quoted from the specification, to which were attached plans, which at that time were preserved in the diocesan registry, Truro, but none seems to have survived.

51. *E*, 12, 1851, pp. 69, 234.

52. Ibid., p. 69.

53. Register no. W.63-1979; currently in store.

54. Letter from 'A Churchman', *G*, 6.9.1854, p. 689.

55. Nikolaus Pevsner, 'Foreword' in Alan Savidge, *The Parsonage in England* (London, 1964), pp. xiii-xv.

56. Timothy Brittain-Catlin, *The English Parsonage in the Early Nineteenth Century* (Reading, 2008).

57. Friday, 28 Sept. 'Tobacco Leaves gathered, & cut green by R. Smith; then dried & prove to be excellent Tobacco; with a fine flavour like ye Havannah Segars', Henry White Diary, 1781, British Library, Add.MSS.43814.

58. R.H. Clutterbuck, *Notes on the Parishes of Fyfield, Kimpton, Penton Mewsey, Weyhill & Wherewell* (Salisbury, 1898), pp. 28, 38-9.

59. White's parsonage house at Landkey, Devon, 1866, has a commodious storeroom adjacent to the study.

60. Francis Goodwin, *Domestic Architecture* (London, 1833), design no. 5, parsonage house.

61. Ibid., design no. 6, rectory house.

62. *Rules & Proceedings OSPSGA,* Oct. 1849 – Dec. 1850, p. 40.

63. A. Welby Pugin, *True Principles*, (1841) (Reading, 2003), p. 63.

64. *E*, 12, 1851, p. 152.

65. Ibid., p. 69.

66. Paper A.B. referred to in affidavit of William White, 6.2.1850, CRO D/R uncatalogued diocesan records, Ruan Lanihorne.

67. Ibid., document E.F., specification.

68. Brittain-Catlin, pp. 156-8.

69. Document E.F., specification, CRO D/R uncatalogued diocesan records, Ruan Lanihorne. Described as 'a small folly' in the estate agents' details of 2008.

70. *E*, 12, 1851, p. 310.

71. White, 'On the Draining and Drying of Churches', *E*, 11, 1850, p. 155.

72. 1861 census return, FRC RG9/1527 St Ive. Their youngest daughter, Emily, became notorious for her support for Boer women and children held in 'concentration camps' in South Africa in 1900.

73. 4.4.1851, KCA John Keble's correspondence, 68.

Chapter 2. From Notting Hill to the Cape
1. *E*, 13, 1852, p. 299.

2. Ibid.

3. Rules and regulations supplied by Dr James Pech, organist and choir-master, G, 6.9.1854, p. 695.

4. E, 14, 1853, p. 273.

5. Ibid., p. 212.

6. B, 13.10.1855, p. 486.

7. White, 'Architectural Uniformity and its Claims', BN, 17.2.1860, p.134.

8. Rev. Thomas James, 'On the Use of Brick in Ecclesiastical Architecture', 4th Report of the Architectural Society of the Archdeaconry of Northampton, 1847, pp. 25-37.

9. B, 13.10.1855, p. 486.

10. See Michael Hall, 'G.F. Bodley and the Response to Ruskin in Ecclesiastical Architecture in the 1850s', in Rebecca Daniels & Geoff Brandwood (eds), Ruskin & Architecture (Reading, 2003), pp. 252-9.

11. CBells, 24.3.1883, p. 310.

12. F.H.W. Sheppard (gen. ed.), Survey of London, 37, Northern Kensington (London, 1973), p. 232.

13. BN, 12.4.1861, p. 301.

14. Henry Holiday, Reminiscences of my Life (London, c.1914), p. 116.

15. Rev. J.H.C. Twisaday, Thirty Years at All Saints, Notting Hill, London, W.11 (1964), p. 5, LMA P84/ALL/14.

16. Jonathan N. Mané, 'Polychromatic Elements in High Victorian Church Architecture' (MA dissertation, Courtauld Institute, London), 1974, p. 33.

17. Letter from Harriet White to William Grey, 3.2.1849, DMA EGR 4/8/6/31.

18. Letter to his sister, Anne Williamson, H.L. Farrer, Life of Robert Gray, (London, 1876), p. 183.

19. Letter from F.H. White, 22.1. [?]1849, DMA EGR 4/6/1/1/17.

20. Letter from Harriet White to William Grey, 3.2.1849, DMA EGR 4/8/6/31.

21. Pen drawings by William White, dated 3.12.1849, plan, elevations, sections and details, Lot 288, B. Weinreb Ltd., Catalogue 14, The Gothic of Gothick, 1966.

22. Letter to Dr Williamson, 11.1.1849, Farrer, p. 210.

23. H.M. White to W. White, 27.4.1849, BCA file 4, White 1.

24. Published in Sermons to Radley Boys and quoted in M.T. Cherniavsky and A.E. Money, Looking at Radley (Radley College, 1981), p. 30.

25. Review of Preface to the Sixth Edition of 'Tom Brown's School-Days', GM, 205, 1858, p. 73.

26. Ibid.

27. Ibid.

28. Miss H.M. White, MSS notes, BCA file 4, White 1.

29. H.M. to W. White, 27.4.1849, BCA file 4, White 1.

30. Ibid.

31. Letter, 6.9.1849 reprinted in South African Church Magazine, Oct. 1852, pp. 311-17. John Gardener, Bishops 150, A History of the Diocesan College, Rondebosch (Cape Town, 1997), p. 220.

32. Gardener, p. 220; Oxford DNB.

33. South African Church Magazine, Oct. 1852, p. 317.

34. H.M. to W. White, 28.11.1849, BCA file 4, White 1.

35. H.M. to W. White, 29.4.1851, BCA file 4, White 1.

36. H.M. to W. White, 28.11.1849, BCA file 4, White 1. The fives court was finally demolished in 1921.

37. Ibid.

38. Ibid. William of Wykeham's New College, Oxford, H.M. White's alma mater, was the first Oxford college to have a gate tower, BoE: Oxfordshire (Harmondsworth, 1974), p. 168.

39. H.M. White to W. White, 29.4.1851, BCA file 4, White 1.

40. H.M. White to W. White, 28.11.1849, BCA file 4, White1.

41. H.M. White to W. White, 29.4.1851, BCA file 4, White 1.

42. Ibid.

43. Discussion on 'Iron and Mild Steel as Building Materials', *BN*, 28.5.1880, p. 624.

44. *E*, 13, 1852, p. 301.

45. H.M. to W. White, 5.11.1852, BCA file 4, White 1.

46. Referred to by R.R. Langham-Carter, 'Architect and Builder, South Africa's First Woman Architect', *Architect and Builder*, [South Africa], March 1967, p. 15.

47. Peter Hinchcliffe, *The Anglican Church in South Africa* (London, 1963), p. 36.

48. R.R. Langham-Carter Papers, UCTL A1.1, 'Anglican Churches', Butterfield supervised the making of the worked stone and woodwork in England and chose the fittings; Miss H.M. White, 'Some Memorials of the Ven. Archdeacon H.M. White', *St Saviour's Parish Magazine*, September 1941, p. 2, BCA file 4, White 1.

49. H.M. to W. White, 19.3.1853, BCA file 4, White 1.

50. Ibid.

51. H.M. to W. White, 20.6.1853, BCA file 4, White 1.

52. H.M. to W. White, 19.3.1853, BCA file 4, White 1.

53. H.M. to W. White, 20.6.1853.

54. Ibid.

55. H.E. Morris, 1887, quoted by Gardener, p. 65.

56. H.M. to W. White, 20.6.1853, BCA file 4, White 1.

57. Ibid.

58. *South African Church Magazine*, Oct. 1852, p. 312.

59. Letter to Dr Williamson, 31.8.1849, Farrer, p. 247.

60. Farrer, p. 248.

61. D.H. Varley & H.M. Matthew (eds) *Cape Journals of Archdeacon N.J. Merriman 1848-1855* (Cape Town, 1957), p. 59.

62. St Bartholomew's Vestry Book, Vestry Minutes, p. 1, CL PR 3514(a).

63. *E*, 8, 1857, pp. 65, 185; identification by Prof. J.S. Marsh, Dept. of Geology, Rhodes University, Grahamstown, who states that to ship stone to Grahamstown would have been akin to 'taking coals to Newcastle', e-mail, 5.10.2005. On 16 March 1857 the building committee discussed a request for remission of import duty on materials costing £716 imported from England, which may have included timber that arrived on 13 April, *Heavyside Diary*, pp. 67, 77, CL MS 16 606.

64. *Heavyside Diary*, pp. 72, 77, CL MS 16 606.

65. Drawing, DRO Plymstock: Hooe parish records, 724/64. In 1893-4 this was replaced by a stone bell-cote to designs of 'Mr Sedding', possibly E.H. Sedding (1863-1921), J.D.'s nephew..

66. *E*, 18, 1857, p. 65.

67. *Heavyside Diary*, p. 82, CL MS 16 606.

68. R.D. Crozier, *Saint Bartholomew's Grahamstown 1860-1985* (Grahamstown, 1985), p. 6; cutting from *Anglo-African*, 7, No. 215, attached to *Heavyside Diary*, p. 117, CL MS 16 606.

69. 20.10.1857 and 5.11.1857, *Heavyside Diary*, pp. 129, 133, CL MS 16 606.

70. 29.1.1858, *Heavyside Diary*, p. 160, CL MS 16 606.

71. Varley & Matthew, ix.

72. St Bartholomew's Vestry Book, Vestry Minutes, p. 2, CL PR 3514(a); photograph, undated, CL PIC 3280/1, which must be post-1890 when the stained glass in the east window was given by the Merriman family.

73. Unfortunately, the whereabouts of this frontal is now unknown.

74. St Bartholomew's Vestry Book, Vestry Minutes, pp. 9-10, CL PR 3514 (a).

75. Emily O'Meara, *Grahamstown Reflected* (Grahamstown, 1995), p. 86.

76. *E*, 21, 1860, p. 113.

77. G. Alex Bremner, 'Out of Africa: G.F. Bodley, William White, and the Anglican Mission Church of St Philip, Grahamstown, 1857-67', *AH*, 51, 2008, pp. 185-210; *E*, 25, 1864, p. 151.

78. Crozier, p. 7.

Chapter 3. Theory and Practice
1. White exhibited a picture of St Peter's Mancroft church, Norwich, at the RA in 1852, Algernon Graves, *The Royal Academy of Arts, Complete Dictionary of Contributors ...* (London, 1906), p. 257.
2. *Post Office London Directory*; Owen Jones lived at no. 9.
3. *TEDAS*, 5, 1856; *Christian Memorials ... designed by Professional Members of the Worcester Diocesan Architectural Society*, review in *E*, 18, 1857, pp. 134-5.
4. Webb, *E*, 9, 1849, pp. 354-7; White, *E*, 11, 1850, pp. 153-5.
5. 'Upon Some of the Causes and Points of Failure in Modern Design', *E*, 12, 1851, p. 306.
6. H.S. Goodhart-Rendel, 'How Architecture is Made', *The Architect and Building News*, 29.3.1946, p. 198.
7. *TEDAS*, 4, 1853, p. 178.
8. 'Upon Some of the Causes and Points of Failure in Modern Design', read 22.5.1851, *E*, 12, 1851, p. 313.
9. Ibid., p. 306.
10. *E*, 14, 1853, pp. 70-80.
11. *E*, 11, 1850, p. 155.
12. 'Symbolism, its Practical Benefits and Uses', read 25.7.1852, *TEDAS*, 4, 1853, p. 315.
13. J.W. von Goethe, *Theory of Colours*, translated from the German with notes by C.L. Eastlake (1840) (1970), p. 305, par. 762. Goethe considered this his most important book.
14. Turner, lecture V, 1818, *see* John Gage, *Colour in Turner, Poetry and Truth* (London, 1969), p. 207.
15. *E*, 14, 1853, pp. 313-30. Others had published similar theories, *see* letter from W.P. Griffith, *B*, 22.10.1853, pp. 653-4, and White's reply, *B*, 5.11.1853, p. 683.
16. *E*, 9, 1849, p. 60.
17. *E*, 14, 1853, pp. 320, 322.
18. *E*, 15, 1854, pp. 291-7.
19. Ibid., p. 295.
20. Goodhart-Rendel, 1946, p. 199.
21. M.D. Lambert, *Saint Michael and All Angels Bussage 1846-1986* (Stroud, 1986), p. 6.
22. Ibid., p. 13.
23. John Armstrong, *An Appeal for the Formation of a Christian Penitentiary* (London, 1849), p. 12.
24. O.W. Jones, *Isaac Williams and his Circle* (London, 1971), p. 118.
25. Letter, 19.4.1851, BCA file 4, White 1. Robert Kestell Cornish married Dorothy Fountaine Addison, younger sister of the Rev. Mangin's wife.
26. Isaac Williams, *Short Memoir of the Revd Robert Alfred Suckling*, 3rd ed. (London, 1853), p. 183.
27. *E*, 14, 1853, p. 214.
28. T.T. Carter claimed that 'The new buildings at Bussage ... erected on the site of the old cottage' were planned in part by the Rev. John Armstrong, *see Memoir of John Armstrong D.D.* (Oxford, 1857), p. 244.
29. John Elliott and John Pritchard (eds), *Henry Woodyer Gentleman Architect* (Reading, 2002), p. 142.
30. Letter from Armstrong to Mrs Poole, 7.11.1853, ' a set of robes ... [will] stir up my spirit, when in remote South African stations I robe myself in vestments made in a place which is endeared to me so much'; Armstrong was buried in the rochet made by the Bussage penitents, Carter (1857), p. 256.
31. Butler had founded an Anglican order of nuns, the Community of St Mary the Virgin, at Wantage. After the death of Mrs Poole in 1898, the house at Bussage was eventually handed over to the Wantage Sisters, who maintained it until 1947 as a home where girls aged 14-18 were taught laundry skills, Lambert, pp. 20-1.
32. Initially, the training was designed to last for three years, but so many students left after only one year that the courses were redesigned, S.J. Curtis & M.E.A. Boultwood, *An Introductory History of English Education Since 1800* (Foxton, 1960), p. 62.

33. Dean Butler's diaries, 1853-7, p. 201, BerksRO D/P 143/28/2.

34. Sister Jane Monica, C.S.M.V., *The Story of S. Michael's House*, 1982, p. 1.

35. Agnes Gibbons and E.C. Davey, *Wantage Past and Present* (London, 1901), pp. 138-9.

36. A.J. Butler (ed.), *Life and Letters of William John Butler* (London, 1897), p. 147.

37. *E*, 17, 1856, p. 75.

38. Letter from 8 Argyll Place, 11.3.1856, in *E*, 17, 1856, pp. 158-9.

39. Similar pillars exist in White's boarding houses at Shrewsbury School.

40. *E*, 17, 1856, p. 159; John Elliott & John Pritchard (eds), *George Edmund Street: a Victorian Architect in Berkshire* (Reading, 1998), pp. 119-20.

41. Michael Hall, 'Building Without Sham', *CL*, 4.4.1991, pp. 92-5.

42. Obituary, *G*, 7.10.1896, p. 1512, reveals that 'Mr Gutch had so outlived his contemporaries' that few realised 'how much we in the Church of England owe him.'

43. *E*, 11, 1850, pp. 212-13.

44. *E*, 15, 1854, p. 287. Although much altered and extended, White's intentions can still be seen.

45. *AASRP*, 4, 1857-8, p. xiv.

46. Pugin (1841) (2003), p. 42.

47. White, 'On Some of the Principles of Design in Churches', *TEDAS*, 4, 1853, p. 177.

48. Although the specification lists 'best Newcastle or Burton red plain tiles', Christopher Dalton reported that until 1977 it had a roof of 'original Collyweston stone slates', 'Parsons' Pleasures', *CL*, 16.4.1987, p. 152. It has recently been re-roofed with red tiles.

49. At Coopersale vicarage, Essex, 1856, White provided an ingenious double door, presumably to keep out the wind in this exposed position overlooking the River Thames.

50. Drawings and specification, LRO MGA 379.

51. *E*, 18, 1857, p. 67.

52. Ibid.

53. B. Anthony Bax, *The English Parsonage* (London, 1964), p. 153.

54. 1861 census return, FRC RG9/2352, lists also a governess, cook, nurse, housemaid, laundry maid and nursery maid.

55. Thomas Henry Watson, *RIBAJ*, 7, 1900, p. 145.

56. *B*, 13.10.1855, p. 486.

57. Obituary, *RIBAJ*, 8, 1901, p. 101.

58. William Hunter McNab, *RIBAJ*, 23, 1916, p. 302.

59. *RIBA associates' nomination papers*, 5, p. 97.

60. On the death of his first wife, he was ordained priest, and the practice became Fulford, Tait and Harvey, *BoE: Devon* (Harmondsworth, 1991), p. 103.

61. *RIBA associates' nomination papers*, 13, p. 136.

62. Ibid., p. 149.

63. *BA*, 17.1.1890, p. 39. G.E. Street also visited northern France in 1850, but there is no record that they travelled together.

64. Published by Thomas Bosworth of Regent Street, 1855.

65. Ibid., p. 7.

66. Ibid., p. 27.

67. J.T. Coleridge, *A Memoir of the Rev. John Keble*, (Oxford, 1869), p. 29.

68. KCA John Keble's correspondence, fol. 143.

69. FRC RG 9/72, fol. 65.

70. *CEAJ*, 20, 1857, p. 283.

71. *Athenæum*, 15.8.1857, p. 1037.

72. Sheila Kirk, *Philip Webb* (Chichester, 2005), p. 18.

73. 'Artistic Members of the Hogarth Club, 1859', in W.M. Rossetti, *Ruskin: Rossetti: Pre-Raphaelitism, Papers 1854 to 1862* (London, 1899), p. 217; Deborah Cherry, 'The Hogarth Club: 1858-1861', *Burlington Magazine*, April 1980, p. 242; the British Library's copy of *Rules of the Hogarth Club and List of Membership*, 1860, can no longer be found.

74. RIBA Nomination Papers F, vol. 3 is unfortunately missing. Only 9% of those styling themselves 'architect' in the 1861 census were members, *see* Barrington Kaye, *The Development of the Architectural Profession in Britain: A Sociological Study* (London, 1961), p. 175.

75. *E*, 14, 1853, p. 314.

76. Letter, 'Architecture – A Profession or an Art?', *T*, 17.11.1891, p. 3.

77. 'Fraternities for the Development of Architecture', *B*, 27.6.1857, p. 361.

78. 1805 Lord Chancellor's ruling using Dr Johnson's definition, Curtis and Boultwood (1960), p. 15.

79. Arnold wrote to his friend the Rev. George Cornish, 'You have often wanted me to be master at Winchester, so I think you will be glad to hear that I am actually a candidate for Rugby.' Letter, 21, 30.11.1827, Arthur Stanley, *Life of Thomas Arnold D.D.* (1844) (London, 1901), p. 73.

80. *Quarterly Review*, July 1864, p. 190.

81. A.F. Leach, *A History of Winchester College* (London, 1899), p. 455.

82. *E*, 24, 1863, p. 131; photograph currently hanging in Du Boulay's; Leach, p. 489.

83. James Sabben-Clare, *Winchester College After 600 Years, 1382-1982* (Southampton, 1981), p. 16. He also reports that in 1866 the total number of boys in the college was 285.

84. Leach, p. 472.

85. Ibid., illustration facing p. 455.

86. Ibid., p. 477.

87. Ibid., p. 472. In houses where the master had a large family of his own, rations for the boys were often meagre.

88. Ibid., p. 462.

89. Ibid., p. 456.

90. Sabben-Clare, p. 24.

91. CERC EC file 21922, part 1.

92. *B*, 27.7.1867, pp. 549-50.

93. The internal dimensions are given as 100ft x 44ft x 52ft to the ridge of the nave roof, *B*, 20.10.1866, p. 781.

94. Ibid., p. 549.

95. John Betjeman, 'St Saviour's, Aberdeen Park', *Collected Poems* (London, 1970); *Guide to English Parish Churches* (1958) (London, 1993), p. 244.

96. Mané, 1974, p .34.

97. *G*, 17.3.1869, p. 295. The height (about 55ft from the floor) and lack of lighting, which is confined to near-ground level for the artists who now occupy the church, makes it difficult to discern.

98. *G*, 17.3.1869, p. 295.

99. White's design for similar stencilling at Christ Church, Smannell, Hampshire, accompanied his plans for extending the north aisle, 1893, HRO 21M65/336F/1.

100. *B*, 27.7.1867, p. 550; 20.10.1866, p. 781.

101. 'All the stained glass is by ... Lavers & Barraud', letter from the incumbent, the Rev. John Bicknell, to T. Francis Bumpus, 1881, GBC ISL/3/3a.

102. *G*, 17.3.1869, p. 295.

103. *B*, 27.7.1867, p. 550. This now contains mosaic panels, the central one of the Crucifixion by Sir Austen Henry Layard, the outer panels depicting the Virgin and St John of 1914.

104. *G*, 17.3.1869, p. 295.

105. 'Upon Some of the Causes and Points of Failure in Modern Design', *E*, 12, 1851, p. 307.

106. *E*, 17, 1856, p. 217.

Chapter 4. The Versatility of Gothic

1. 'New building for the Cornish Bank at Truro', *West Briton*, 5.5.1848, p. 2.
2. *E*, 16, 1855, pp. 190-1.
3. White, 'So-called Mediaeval v. So-called Classic', *B*, 14.2.1857, p. 90.
4. *RCG*, 21.7.1848.
5. *CBells*, 13.7.1888, p. 800.
6. *Official Catalogue of the International Exhibition of 1862*, Class 30, 5716.
7. White, 'The Wrought-iron Work of the Great Exhibition of 1862', *BN*, 22.5.1863, p. 390.
8. Ibid., p. 391.
9. Ibid., part 2, *BN*, 29.5.1863, p. 411.
10. Ibid., p. 412.
11. William White, 'Ironwork: its Legitimate Uses and Proper Treatment', *TRIBA*, 16, 1865-6, pp. 15-27.
12. Ibid., p. 15.
13. Ibid., p. 23.
14. Ibid.
15. *See* Andrew Saint, *Architect and Engineer, a Study in Sibling Rivalry* (New Haven, 2007).
16. *TRIBA*, 16, 1865-6, p. 19.
17. Ibid.
18. *E*, 18, 1857, p. 28.
19. Ivan Rabey, *The Book of St Columb and St Mawgan* (Buckingham, 1979), p. 80.
20. *The Seven Lamps of Architecture* (London, 1849), 2, XVIII.
21. Unfortunately the joinery has now disappeared, despite the building's listed status.
22. *Kelly's Directory of Devonshire and Cornwall*, 1906, p. 218. Hoblyn *v.* Hoblyn, Chancery Division, 1889, reported 'large sums' had been spent on the improvement of the estate.
23. Letters from Abbots Ann, 1849-58, DMA.
24. William White, 'Cheap Churches', *BN*, 11.3.1881, p. 258.
25. Ibid., p. 259.
26. White, 'Modern Design. Neglect of the Science of Architecture', *E*, 14, 1853, p. 315.
27. Cambridge Camden Society, *A Few Words to Church Builders*, 3rd ed., 1844, p.14; for example, Sts Philip & James, Oxford, 1859, and St James-the-less, Pimlico, 1860.
28. White rebuilt the church at Tangley, Hampshire, in 1872 with an apse because he believed that the old chancel arch with its opening of only 5ft 8ins was indicative of that form.
29. Alterations to the original belfry and porch at Christ Church, Smannell, were pointed out by John M. Bray, *Ecclesiology Today*, January 2001, p. 17. After a disastrous fire caused by a lightning strike in 1976, the roof at Christ Church, Hatherden, was replaced at a lower pitch.
30. Letter, 8.2.1856, ICBS 4953.
31. Ibid.
32. *E*, 17, 1856, p. 154.
33. *BN*, 11.3.1881, p. 260.
34. Ibid.
35. Letter, 28.11.1857, HRO 25M84/PW23.
36. *B*, 8.10.1859, p .669.
37. White to Compton, 24.10.1860, HRO 25M84/PW36.
38. Ibid.
39. White had used similar triangular dormers in his restoration of St Mildred's church, Preston, Kent, in 1856, and in the chapel at Forest School, Walthamstow, 1857.
40. Circular, HRO 25M84/PW22.

41. Transcription of letter from Mr Scott to Mr White, HRO 25M84/PW25.

42. *E*, 20, 1859, p. 288.

43. White, 'Systematic Proportion in Architecture', *CEAJ*, 31, 1868, p. 1.

44. White stated that he had used Telford's formula, amongst others, for calculating the load, and drew attention to the problems he had experienced with the construction during a discussion on a paper 'Remarks upon Failures in Construction', *TRIBA*, 17, 1866-7, pp. 187-9.

45. Letter from Ellen Dickson to the Rev. Compton, HRO 25M84/PW24.

46. Letter, 24.10.1859, HRO 25M84/PW37.

47. Charles L. Eastlake, *A History of the Gothic Revival* (London, 1872) p. 294; Earp's account, 17.12.1860, HRO 25M84/PW37/27.

48. Newspaper report, 24.2.1894, quoted in NADFAS Church Recorders' report.

49. *E*, 20, 1859, p. 288. In a letter to his mother, 26.4.1863, Frederic Leighton claimed that the window was 'executed at my desire from Jones' designs', Mrs Russell Barrington, *The Life, Letters and Work of Frederic Leighton* (London, 1906), p. 110.

50. Leighton was anxious to experiment with the 'spirit medium' used by Gambier Parry and was reported to have 'presented' his fresco to the church at Lyndhurst, Barrington, p. 104. Pollen wrote to the Rev. Compton about the decoration above the sedilia, 6.11. [18?], HRO 25M84/PW41.

51. *RIBAJ*, 17.4.1890, p. 289 in *RIBA Proceedings*, 6, 1890.

52. Rev. J. Compton to Edward Harland, 5.11.1863, HRO 65M84/PW50. The monument was to a benefactor of the church, Jonathan Hargreaves of Cuffnell, Lyndhurst, whose elder son married Alice Liddell, of Wonderland fame.

53. Frederic Leighton to the Rev. J. Compton, [1865], HRO 25M84/PW41.

54. Paul Thompson, 'All Sts', Margaret Street, reconsidered', *AH*, 8, 1965, p.75.

55. Cambridge Camden Society, *Instrumenta Ecclesiastica*, 2nd ser., 1856, 'School-Room and Master's House'.

56. *E*, 12, 1851, p. 311.

57. White's *Hampshire Directory*, 1878, and Arthur C. Bennett, *The Story of St Mary's Parish Church, Andover* (n.d.), p. 17.

58. West elevation, BerksRO D/EX 268/17.

59. Malcolm Seaborne, *The English School* (London, 1971), p. 207.

60. Ibid. p. 208.

61. Ibid.

62. 15.10.1858, DMA EGR 5/2/4/49. Perhaps the memorial was intended to mark the 65 years since Gilbert White's death in 1793.

63. *CBells*, 24.11.1877, p. 610. I have found no evidence that White was responsible for the rebuilding of the chancel arch in 1856, and English Heritage have been unable to provide any authentication for their assertion that it was to his design.

64. *Winchester Diocesan Calendar*, 1878, p. 88.

65. President Frederick Bulley's notebooks, MCA November 1872-October 1877, fols. 188, 471.

66. *Hampshire Chronicle*, 27.10.1883, p. 5. A three-light window is clearly shown in Grimm's 1776 view of the church.

67. *The Natural History & Antiquities of Selborne in the County of Southampton* (1813) (Henley-on-Thames, 1982), p. 10.

68. Unfortunately, ICBS file 8088 for Selborne is missing.

69. V&A AAD/1977/1 Powell Order Book, 1/07: 230, 8.4.1886.

70. Ibid., 1/60:004 21.9.1886.

71. The present altar rails are sixteenth-century. Letter from Mrs Bernard to the Rev. L. Sunderland, vicar of Selborne, 1939.

Chapter 5. Magnificent or Modest?

1. *E*, 19, 1858, p. 268. Construction must have been delayed as it was described as a 'new house' in *B*, 21.10.1865, pp. 746–7.
2. *E*, 24, 1863, p. 167. A number of White's drawings of Bishop's Court were shown at the Architectural Exhibition, 1863, *see BN*, 17.4.1863, p. 288.
3. Chris Brooks, 'Bishop's Court, Devon', *CL*, 15.2.1990, p. 55.
4. A thirteenth-century carved bishop's head was one of the stone fragments still preserved in the house in 1966, *see* N.W. Alcock, 'The medieval buildings of Bishop's Clyst', *Transactions of the Devonshire Association*, 98, 1966, Appendix B.
5. H.E. Smith, 'Decorative Painting in the Domestic Interior in England and Wales c.1850–1890' (Ph.D thesis, Courtauld Institute, London), points out that the ceiling decoration is on lining paper, whereas the wall decoration is directly on the plaster.
6. *BN*, 17.4.1863, p. 288.
7. The Rev. Edward L. Cutts noted that medieval church walls were often buff coloured and marked 'with single, double or treble lines of blood-red tint … [in] a pattern derived from masonry joints', *An Essay on Church Furniture and Decoration* (London, 1854), p. 15.
8. Made by Kimberley of Banbury to White's design at a cost of £8 5s, KA extras ledger, fol. 80.
9. *G*, 5.8.1863, p. 727.
10. *BN*, 18.1.1861, p. 50.
11. Frank H. Mahnke, *Color, Environment & Human Response* (New York, 1996), p. 23.
12. *BN*, 18.1.1861, p. 51.
13. Baron Ernst von Feuchtersleben, *The Principles of Medical Psychology*, translated by H. Evans Lloyd (rev. and ed. by B.G. Babingon, 1847, reprinted in *The Origins of Psychology, a Collection of Early Writings* (New York, 1977), 6, p. 98).
14. *Development of Ornamental Art in the International Exhibition* (1862) (New York, 1978), p. 20.
15. *BN*, 18.1.1861, p. 51.
16. 'Ardent Simplicity', *CL*, 18.10.1990, p.151.
17. Wainwright, *CL*, 18.10.1990, p. 154. The contents, including the furniture designed for the house by White, were auctioned in 1994.
18. National Trust, *Canons Ashby* (London, 2001), p. 15.
19. J.F. Chanter, 'Bishop's Court', *TEDAS*, 4, 1929, p. 87.
20. *BA*, 28.3.1884, p. 145.
21. *B*, 14.2.1857, p. 90.
22. *B*, 18.7.1857, p. 402.
23. *B*, 14.2.1857, p. 90.
24. Michael Hall, 'Ideas of Englishness in the later work of G.F. Bodley', Synopsis, 'Architecture and Englishness 1880–1914', SAHGB symposium, 2003.
25. Webster & Elliott, p. 382.
26. Letter, 31.10.1881, DorRO PE/BE/IN/10/6; letter (n.d. but *c*.1891), RIBA, box 33, folder 6, letter 6.
27. Letter from Alfred Codd dated 17.2.1859, EC File 436.
28. QAB file E1. The site plan shows White's proposed garden layout with formal flowerbeds, kitchen garden, orchard, 'Potting and Cucumber Garden', as well as stables.
29. 1861 census return, Beaminster, East Street.
30. The vicarage features in *Tess of the d'Urbervilles*. Thomas Hardy was trained as an architect and in 1863 won an RIBA Silver Medal for an essay entitled 'On the Application of Coloured Bricks and Terra Cotta to Modern Architecture', *Oxford DNB*, 2004.
31. H.E. Malden (ed.), *VCH, Surrey*, 3 (London, 1911), p. 608.
32. 16.3.1861, QAB File E. 63.
33. *E*, 23, 1862, p. 125.

34. Referring to Munstead Wood, near Godalming, less than five miles from Elstead, Gertrude Jekyll, *Home and Garden* (1900) (London, 1982), p. 32.
35. Gertrude Jekyll, *Old English Household Life* (1925) (London, 1975), p. 87.
36. Roderick Gradidge, *The Surrey Style* (Godalming, 1991), p. 8.
37. 22.5.1868, ORO ODP b.84.
38. Specification, ORO ODP b.84.
39. Block plan dated Dec.1864, plans and sections 3-10.1.1865, WSRO UD/LH/16/1 Selborne Place.
40. Papers of the 9th earl of Stamford, DMA Box 14/2.
41. Details of verandahs, 25.1.1865, WSRO UD/LH/16/1.
42. Miss H.M. White, *Cameos* (1960), p. 9, BCA file 4, White 1.
43. *BN*, 7.2.1890, p. 224.
44. Miss H.M. White (1960), p. 9.
45. Ibid., p. 2.
46. Letter from Miss G. Hext, 19.1.1864, Miss F. Julia Pole-Carew & Lieut. A.C.W. Bevan, *The Story of Maryfield*, n.d., not paginated.
47. *B*, 19.5.1866, p. 360.
48. *BoE: Cornwall* (Harmondsworth, 1951), p. 18.
49. Pole-Carew & Bevan.
50. This attribution is my own, based on the west window of Leusdon church, Devon, representing four scenes from the life of the Baptist, designed and executed by White, *CBells*, 17.1.1880, p. 106.
51. 'Descriptive Sketch of a Mansion at Humewood …', *TRIBA*, 19, 1868-9, pp. 78-88.
52. KA wages book and letter book no. 3, 1868-9.
53. *TRIBA*, 19, 1868-9, p. 87.
54. Sketch, KA contract book 1866-1871, fol. 297.
55. KA letter book No. 2, 1866-1868, fol. 443.
56. Letter to William from his sister, Harriet Grey, 1.8.1868, DMA EGR 5/2/4/55. There is no indication whether William would holiday alone or accompanied by his daughters.
57. KA letter book No. 3, 1868-9, fol. 350.

Chapter 6. Two Great Houses
1. White, 'Descriptive Sketch of a Mansion at Humewood, County Wicklow …', *TRIBA*, 19, 1868-9, p. 78.
2. Ibid., pp. 79, 84.
3. The layout was altered when, in 1873, Hume Dick employed James Brooks to design a ballroom in place of the nurseries, and to add a tall tower to the north to accommodate male servants.
4. *TRIBA*, 19, 1868-9, p. 79.
5. K.A, letter book no. 2, 1866-1868, fols 158, 169, 198.
6. *TRIBA*, 19, 1868-9, p. 79.
7. Ibid., p. 80.
8. K.A, letter book no. 3, 1868-9, fol. 252.
9. *TRIBA*, 19, 1868-9, p. 78.
10. 'Provision is made in various ways for defensive purposes, if necessary', *B*, 8.8.1868, p. 587.
11. Mark Girouard, *The Victorian Country House* (London, 1979), p. 261.
12. Hume (later Dick) family of Humewood archive, album of photographs, WRO 947/2182.
13. *TRIBA*, 19, 1868-9, p. 82.
14. Account with Clement Francis of Quy Hall, 1871, gives Davies' address as Humewood, Kiltegan, Co. Wicklow, CamRO R89/40.
15. *TRIBA*, 19, 1868-9, p. 79.

16. Ibid.
17. K.A, contract book 1866-1871, fols 205-7.
18. Ibid., fol. 439.
19. K.A, letter book No. 3, 1868-9, fol. 298.
20. Ibid., fol. 334.
21. K.A, letter book No. 3, 1868-9, fol. 416.
22. Letter to John Cox, surveyor, ibid., fol. 378.
23. K.A, letter book 1870, fol. 85.
24. Eastlake (1872), p. 292.
25. *A*, 17.6.1871, p. 322.
26. K.A, letter book 14 May 1864 − 15 October 1866, fol. 399.
27. *TRIBA*, 19, 1868-9, p. 79.
38. K.A, letter book no. 3, fol. 34.
29. *A*, 17.6.1871, p. 321.
30. *A*, 11.11.1871, p. 243.
31. *A*, 23.3.1872, p. 149.
32. *A*, 20.5.1876, p. 325.
33. *A*, 17.6.1871, p. 322.
34. *A*, 20.5.1876, p. 325.
35. *TRIBA*, 19, 1868-9, p. 79.
36. *Law Reports, Probate Division*, 1901, p. 46.
37. K.A, letter book No. 6, fol. 740.
38. *A*, 20.5.1876, p. 325.
39. *TRIBA*, 19, 1868-9, p. 86.
40. Peggy Day, 'Late Victorian Quy 1854-1897', draft, p. 2.
41. Peggy Day, *Life in Quy from the Beginning of Time to the Year 2000* (Quy, 2000), p. 28.
42. Christopher Jackson, *A Cambridge Bicentenary, The History of a Legal Practice 1789-1989* (Suffolk, 1989), p. 100.
43. White, memorandum to Clement Francis, 28.11.1871, Messrs. Mills & Reeve Francis archive, CamRO R89/40..
44. Gilbert John's uncle, Gilbert Ansley, was married to Mary Anne Martelli, sister of White's brother-in-law, Thomas Martelli.
45. William White, 'Estimate of Work in restoring and enlarging Quy Hall, July 1869', CamRO R89/40.
46. Memorandum of agreement, 6.8.1869; statement of costs and expenses, n.d., CamRO R89/40.
47. Drawing, 21.12.1870, CamRO R89/40.
48. Statement of costs and expenses, n.d., CamRO R89/40.
49 Memorandum, 28.11.1871, CamRO R89/40.
50. Another hand has inserted 'Humewood, Kiltegan, Co. Wicklow', CamRO R89/40.
51. Christopher Dresser, *The Art of Decorative Design* (London, 1862), p. 30.
52. Discussion following James Colling's paper, 'Art Foliage', *TRIBA*, 16, 1865-6, pp. 42-3.
53. A report on the condition of the interior in 2001 noted that beneath the paper of the drawing room walls, traces of blue paint might indicate part of an earlier decorative scheme.
54. White to Clement Francis, 4.10.1872, CamRO R89/40.
55. Invoice, 19.8.1872, CamRO R89/40.
56. Account for '18 p[iece]s Brazilian Birds on grey' 15.7.1872, CamRO R89/40. Cowtans were one of the leading artistic decorators, employed at Alnwick Castle and Cragside, *inter alia*.
57. 1871 census return, FRC RG10/1323, fol. 75.
58. *BA*, 22.7.1881, p. 363.
59. *BA*, 27.1.1882, p. 37.

Chapter 7. The Rev. John Erskine Clarke of Battersea

1. Memorial tablet, Holy Trinity, Elvington, North Yorkshire.
2. Information kindly supplied by Graham Fuller.
3. Letter from Clarke, 24.7.1873, ICBS 7658.
4. Anon., *History of St. Mark's Church 1873-1933* (1933) p. 9, Battersea Library.
5. James T. Houssemayne du Boulay, *Notes to Accompany a Pedigree of the Family of Cornyshe of Thurlestone in the County of Devon* (Winchester, 1903), p. 16.
6. G.E. Street's report, 27.10.1873, ICBS 7658.
7. White's reply to Street, 3.11.1873, ICBS 7658.
8. Letter, 12.11.1873, ICBS 7658.
9. Letter, 24.11.1873, ICBS 7658.
10. Letter, 16.2. [1874], ICBS 7658.
11. Resolution of Committee of Architects, 6.5.1874, ICBS 7658.
12. 'A Brick and Concrete Church, St. Mark's, Battersea-rise', *B*, 16.1.1875, pp. 48-50.
13. 'A Brick and Concrete Church, St Mark's, Battersea Rise', *A*, 16.1.1875, pp. 39-42.
14. Ibid.
15. *BA*, 16.9.1881, p. 464.
16. *E*, 11, 1850, pp. 227-33.
17. *B*, 16.1.1875, p. 49.
18. Ibid., p. 50.
19. *A*, 1.1.1875, p. 39.
20. *B*, 24.10.1874, p. 884.
21. *History of St. Mark's Church*, p. 17. Demolished 2006.
22. J.G. Taylor, *Our Lady of Batersey* (London, 1925), p. 294; printed sheet with background details in ICBS 7897; parish records, LMA P70/PET/78.
23. *B*, 22.7.1876, pp. 720-1.
24. *CBells*, 29.4.1876, p. 254. This, together with a report in *CB*, 1877, pp. 186-7, challenges the statement in *BoE: London 2: South*, p. 669, that the tower was added in 1911.
25. *B*, 20.11.1875, p. 1046.
26. Taylor, p. 298.
27. Plan and perspective, LMA DW/OP/70/5.
28. Basil Clarke & Gordon Barnes MSS, 'Demolished & Desecrated Churches of London', CCB.
29. *B*, 2.6.1877, p. 568.
30. Printed notice, 11.8.1882, minutes of committees and meetings, LMA P70/BAN/198.
31. Clarke & Barnes (n. 28).
32. Anon., *St Michael's Church, Wandsworth Common, Jubilee 1883-1933* (n.d. [1933]).
33. Letter, 2.4.1878, LMA P70/MIC/47/1.
34. Obituary, *G*, 28.1.1880.
35. LMA P70/MIC/47/9.
36. Plans A, B and C, LMA P70/MIC/056, and memo to Canon Clarke, LMA P70/MIC/48/1. White's account of 18.2.1882 intriguingly includes £8 10s for 'Special set of drawings (Jan.4/80) for gabled apse afterwards abandoned', LMA P70/MIC/48/10.
37. *CBells*, 4.6.1881, p. 427.
38. *B*, 17.11.1883, p. 671.
39. Letter, 24.6.1881, LMA P70/MIC/48/6.
40. Memo, 9.8.1881, LMA P70/MIC/48/9.
41. Anon., *St Michael's Church, Wandsworth Common, Jubilee 1883-1933* (n.d. [1933]).
42. Parish office, St Mary's, Battersea. White's working drawings for the chapter room area are dated

22.4.1879, and a design drawing for the reredos 16.11.1882.

43. *B*, 19.5.1883, p. 690.
44. Appeal for a new parish church, LMA P70/MRY/1.
45. EC 55267.
46. ICBS 9874.
47. Printed appeal, 1902, ICBS 9874.
48. *CBells*, 28.5.1897, p. 539.
49. Ibid.
50. Printed appeal, n.d., ICBS 9047.
51. *CBells*, 19.11.1886, p.1217.
52. EC 15137.
53. Clarke & Barnes.
54. EC 40160, Part 2.
55. Canon Basil Clarke's notebooks, XXIX, p. 18, CCC.
56. Borthwick Institute, UY, Fac.1876/4b-d; memorandum of agreement, PR ELV 23.
57. Letters, 24.6. and 27.7.1881, LMA P70/MIC/48/6-7.
58. Memo, 30.7.1881, LMA P70/MIC/48/8.
59. *CBells*, 4.6.1881, p. 427.

Chapter 8. The Restoration Debate

1. *E*, 7, 1847, p. 162, quoting from E.A. Freeman, *Principles of Church Restoration* (London, 1846).
2. Ibid.
3. *The Seven Lamps of Architecture*, vol. 6, pp. 18-19.
4. G.G. Scott, *A Plea for the Faithful Restoration of our Ancient Churches* (London, 1850), pp. 120-1.
5. Ibid., p. 2.
6. Ibid., p. 35.
7. Sir Henry Dryden, 'On Repairing and Refitting Old Churches', *AASRP*, 3, 1854-6, pp. 12-13.
8. Scott (1850), p. 33.
9. *E*, 26, 1865, p. 249.
10. *E*, 18, 1857, p. 323.
11. CDCA U3/245/5/B/8; ICBS 5056.
12. ICBS 5056.
13. *BN*, 7.2.1890, p. 224.
14. Addition A to specification, WRO PR/Upton Scudamore, St Mary the Virgin/1741/21. The woodblock paving at St James, Bierton, Bucks, also restored by Street in the 1850s, was not installed until 1926.
15. 'Consecration of the Church of St John the Baptist', supplement to the *Liverpool Daily Post*, 22.5.1871.
16. Geoffrey K. Brandwood in Webster & Elliott (eds) (2000), p. 408. In 1858 White designed the organ case for the church. Jenner was consecrated bishop of Dunedin, New Zealand, in 1866, but the diocese rejected him because of his High Church views.
17. *E*, 18, 1857, p. 323.
18. Application for diocesan grant, particulars of estimate, n.d., Bod. MS Top.Oxon.c.103, fol. 118; Irene Poulton, *All Saints Great Bourton* (1997), p. 1.
19. Poulton, p. 1.
20. Letter, 1.5.1862, ICBS 1938. In 1861 the Rev. Noel exchanged livings with the Rev. Hoste, moving to Stanhoe, Norfolk, where he immediately commissioned White to build a large rectory.
21. *E*, 24, 1863, p. 133.
22. *List of Subscribers*, ORO, Oxfordshire diocesan papers b.70, Wilberforce's scrapbook, fol. 228; White

certainly designed the cross that stands before it, KA extras, fol. 103.

23. This was reinforced by the addition in 1882 of White's magnificent bell tower forming a lychgate at the western entrance to the churchyard.

24. Discussion reported in *TRIBA*, 31, 1880-1, p. 189.

25. Scott (1850), p. 33.

26. ICBS 5832.

27. Ibid.

28. Ibid.

29. White, 'Notes on Newland Church, Gloucestershire, with Remarks on Church Restoration and Arrangements', read 30.11.1863, *TRIBA*, 14, 1863-4, pp. 29-40. To avoid constant footnoting, all further quotes in this section are from this paper, unless otherwise stated.

30. One is a unique brass, in relief, showing a medieval Forest of Dean miner, with hod and pick, and with a candlestick in his mouth.

31. White, 'Church Restoration', *The Literary Churchman*, 24.9.1886, p. 384.

32. *BoE: Gloucestershire: The Vale and the Forest of Dean* (Harmondsworth, 1976), p. 307.

33. *E*, 25, 1864, p. 43.

34. Ibid., p. 120.

35. Report of the consecration, *Marlborough Times*, 14.10.1871, HRO 109M70/P21.

36. Application for grant, 21.1.1871, ICBS 7222.

37. Previously 'assumed' to be by White, this is now proved by drawings in the records of the Education Dept, TNA ED21/6483.

38. Gilbert White, *The Natural History of Selborne* (London, 1789), Letter III.

39. *See Ecclesiology Today*, January 2001, p. 18.

40. Minutes of meeting 6.6.1860, ICBS MB39, pp.64-5.

41. Ibid., p. 165.

42. ICBS 8783, 8305 and 9227, respectively.

43. ICBS 9227.

44. ICBS MB39, p. 208; *CBells*, 18.10.1889, p. 1123.

45. ICBS MB39, p. 234.

46. *B*, 10.6.1893, p. 453.

47. *Papers read at the Royal Institute of British Architects*, 12, 1861-2, p. 82. Conservation of Ancient Monuments & Remains Committee, minutes 21.11.1864–11.2.1886, RIBA/Env, V&A. William White is not recorded in the minutes as a member until 4.12.1879 (p. 100), despite the report in *E*, 25, 1864, p. 39.

48. Meeting 8.12.1875, V&A CAMRC Minutes, p. 57. From 13.2.1861, White's name appears as a member of the RIBA Architectural Examination Committee, perhaps the source of the confusion.

49. V&A CAMRC Minutes, meeting 5.12.1876, p. 74; meeting 13.12.1878, p. 91. White's letters regarding the corbel-table at St Albans, *B*, 1.11.1879, p. 1218; 15.11.1879, p. 1273; 29.11.1879, p. 1327.

50. Society of Antiquaries, certificates of candidates for election, 8 January 1857-26 May 1870, fol. 233.

51. Ibid.; *Oxford DNB.*, 2004; Alison Felstead *et al*, *RIBA Directory of British Architects 1834-1900*; SAO *Hampshire Advertiser & County Newspaper*, 21.11.1863. Those having 'General knowledge' were listed as H.S. Ellacombe, John Henry Parker and Matt. A. Bloxam.

52. *See* John Harris, 'The Ruskin Gold Medal Controversy', *RIBAJ*, 70, 1963, pp. 165-7.

53. *T*, 8.8.1874, *see* Chris Miele, 'The Conservationist', in Linda Parry (ed.), *William Morris: Art and Kelmscott* (London, 1996), p. 74.

54. SPAB minute book, March 1877-8.

55. Chris Miele (ed.), *From William Morris: Building Conservation and the Arts and Crafts Cult of Authenticity, 1877-1939* (New Haven, 2005), pp. 37-8.

56. Ibid., p. 37; *E*, 18, 1857, p. 10.

57. Guy Deaton, *Schola Sylvestris* (Walthamstow, 1984), p. 69; *Forest School Magazine*, Lent 1900, p. 298.
58. *CBells*, 20.1.1893, p. 149. SPAB, *Notes on the Repair of Ancient Buildings*, 1903, appendix, 'The Principles of the Society for the Protection of Ancient Buildings as set forth upon its foundation in 1877', p. 74-5. At a meeting on 5.7.1877 Ruskin was unanimously elected a member of the SPAB committee, minute book, March 1877-8.
59. Sir George Gilbert Scott, *Personal and Professional Recollections* (1879) (1995), appendix C, p. 420.
60. Chris Miele, in Webster & Elliott (eds) (2000), p. 285.
61. *TRIBA*, 27, 1876-7, p. 262.
62. Ibid., p. 257.
63. *CB*, 1873, pp. 92-4.
64. Ibid., p. 93.
65. Reported *B*, 2.2.1878, p. 115.
66. Sketch of 1760 print, hanging in the church; *Somersetshire Archaeological & Natural History Society, Proceedings*, 24, 1878, p. 29.
67. *B*, 2.2.1878, p. 115.
68. SPAB, General Committee minutes, 27 May 1880-28 March 1883. The tower remains intact.
69. *Literary Churchman*, 24.9.1886, pp. 383-6.
70. Ibid., p. 386.
71. 'Ensuring that a historic building has a viable and, therefore, sustainable use is the key to keeping it in good repair', Richard Halsey, 'Historic Places of Worship', *Conservation Bulletin*, 46, 2004, p. 4.
72. *TRIBA*, 31, 1880-1, p. 188.

Chapter 9. Later Life
1. British Patent GB 1188. The patent would have expired after 14 years.
2. BL H.1778.x.(6.).
3. BL 10024.a.1.
4. Letter to Hamo Thorneycroft, 16.12.1881, Colin Cunningham & Prudence Waterhouse, *Alfred Waterhouse 1839-1905: Biography of a Practice* (Oxford, 1992), p. 140.
5. Fergus Fleming, *Killing Dragons, The Conquest of the Alps* (London, 2000), pp. 298, 319.
6. Burials in the parish of Hanwell, Middlesex, 1876, Ealing Local History Centre, X092/135 DRO/006/011-015.
7. *CBells*, 29.1.1892, p. 156.
8. *BA*, 16.9.1881, p. 466.
9. Letter from William White, *BA*, 1.6.1883, p. 269. White's interest in this scheme can be seen in the suggestion that such clubs should have a gymnasium and swimming bath.
10. Genealogy of Francis Henry White's family, DMA, 9th earl of Stamford's papers, box 11/29.
11. In 1901 Rashleigh Holt-White published *The Life and Letters of Gilbert White of Selborne*.
12. FRC RG11/1356, fol. 26.
13. Photo, n.d., LMA P84/MRK/207.
14. Powell order books, V&A AAD/1977/1/02:466, 4 Feb.
15. Inscription in reveal of the west window; *G*, 24.12.1879, p. 1804 and *CBells*, 17.1.1880, p. 106.
16. Illustrated in *BoE: Isle of Wight* (London, 2006), fig. 66.
17. *Brighstone Parish Record AD 1870*, 4.4.1881. William Morris Pepper had been a pupil of Clayton & Bell.
18. The Risen Christ at the centre of White's east window at All Saints', Hartley, Kent (1896), is very similar.
19. *G*, 3.9.1879, p. 1247. Subscribers were asked to send their contributions to the Rev. J.T. Houssemayne Du Boulay in Winchester.
20. *MF*, 36, 1891, p. 14.

21. *ILN*, 11.1.1890, p. 43.
22. *MF*, 36, 1891, pp. 14-15.
23. *CB*, 1884, p. 110.
24. March 1885, RIBA Library, WhW/Pam78, fols. 441-3.
25. *CBells*, 5.2.1881, p. 154.
26. Discussion on John P. Seddon's paper, 'Church Fittings', *TRIBA*, 6, 1890, p. 185.
27. P.A. Millard, *Centenary of the Parish of Rondebosch 1834-1934* (Cape Town, 1934).
28. 49 drawings, UCTL, Baker collection, BC 206.
29. 'Zon' craftsmen also executed the Rondebosch font, 1892, to White's design, UCTL, R.R. Langham-Carter papers, B. reference lists and notes.
30. Millard, p. 14. Unfortunately now gloss-painted. The central mosaic panel shows Christ in a mandorla, decorated with White's typical zig-zag patterns.
31. W.J. de Kock (editor-in-chief), *Dictionary of South African Biography* (Johannesburg, 1968), pp. 108-9.
32. Account, plan and perspective, *CB*, 1891, pp. 5-9.
33. Ibid., p. 6.
34. Ibid., p. 9.
35. *The Press*, Pretoria, South African Republic, 28.3.1890, p. 2.
36. B.F.L. Clarke, *Anglican Cathedrals Outside the British Isles* (London, 1958), p. 32.
37. J.W. Walker, *Wakefield, its History & People* (Wakefield, 1934), p. 279.
38. Ibid., pp. 153, 194.
39. *Oxford DNB*, 2004.
40. Ibid.
41. *AA Notes*, 13, 1898, p. 116.
42. Herbert W. Newby, *Old Southgate* (London, 1949), p. 75.
43. *AA Notes*, 13, 1898, p. 116.
44. Ibid., p. 117
45. This has been disputed on stylistic grounds, see Richard Garnier, 'Arno's Grove, Southgate', *Georgian Group Journal*, 8, 1998, pp. 122-34.
46. Ibid., p. 118.
47. Ibid.
48. Ibid.
49. See Garnier, 1998.
50. Meeting, 3.8.1882, EC file 62380, Part 1.
51. Letter from the Rev. Carter, 5.7.1898, EC 62380, part 3.
52. Ibid.
53. W2/4, Dove Bros collection, RIBA Drawings Collection
54. *Parsons Green, Fulham, Parish Magazine*, November 1898, p. xiv, in the vicarage.
55. Letter from the Rev.Carter, 5.11.1898, EC file 62380, part 3; *Parsons Green, Fulham, Parish Magazine*, Sept. 1898.

Epilogue
1. *AA Notes*, 14, 1899, p. 106.
2. Ibid., p. 164.
3. Mentioned in his first published writing (*E*, 11, 1850, p. 155) and repeated consistently throughout his career.
4. T. Francis Bumpus, *London Churches Ancient and Modern* (London, 1907), p. 330.
5. Ibid.
6. Plot J1, 108, 1st division, Hampstead cemetery records.
7. DMA papers of the 9th earl of Stamford, Box 14/2. John Smith Gilderdale was the son of Dr John

Gilderdale, headmaster of Forest School, Walthamstow.

8. Stamford and Another *v.* White, *Law Reports, Probate Division*, 1901, p. 48.
9. White is not listed at Hanwell in the *Post Office London Directory* after 1881; information from Mrs M. Gee of Hanwell.
10. Letter from J.G. Wilson, 5 North Bailey, Durham, 18.3.1893, DMA papers of the 9th earl of Stamford, box 14/2..
11. Letter from William White, 18.5.1893, DMA papers of the 9th earl of Stamford, box 14/2.
12. Letter to the earl of Stamford, 5.3.1901, DMA papers of the 9th earl of Stamford, box 14/3.
13. Stamford and Another *v.* White, *Law Reports, Probate Division*, 1901, pp. 46-51.
14. 'Death on or after 1st January, 1898', ref. 266, Principal Registry of the Family Division.
15. Ibid., ref. 267.
16. Records of Oxford High School; prospectus of Auckland School, DMA papers of the 9th earl of Stamford, box 14/3.
17. Letter from Ellen White, 13.6.1901; letter from Margaret White, 15.5.1901, DMA papers of the 9th earl of Stamford, Box 14/3.
18. *The Victorian Country House* (New Haven & London, 1979), p. 253.
19. Gavin Stamp & Colin Amery, *Victorian Buildings of London 1837-1887* (London, 1982), p. 84; Gavin Stamp & André Goulancourt, *The English House 1860-1914* (London, 1986), p. 56; Candida Lycett Green, *England, Travels Through An Unwrecked Landscape* (London, 1996), p. 132.
20. Vols. 1-196 (1999), Lawrence Library, Senate House, University of London.
21. *Baconiana*, n.s., 1, 1893, p. 146.
22. Ibid., n.s., 8, 1900, pp. 5-27, p. 51.
23. *T*, 17.11.1891, p. 3.
24. 'An earnest appeal for the personal co-operation and pecuniary support of all Churchmen was made by Mr. W. White, F.S.A.', *CBells*, 21.2.1890, p. 207.
25. *CBells*, 29.5.1891, p. 477.
26. Ibid.
27. Discussion on Prof. Kerr's paper 'On the Problem of Providing Dwellings for the Poor', *TRIBA*, 17, 1866-7, pp. 69-70. Although unable to attend the meeting, so keen was White to make his views known, that he forwarded his comments in writing.
28. *T*, 8.10.1880, p. 6; *BA*, 2.2.1883, p. 50.
29. *CBells*, 2.9.1898, p. 825.
30. Ibid., 11.8.1899, p. 778.
31. *BN*, 26.1.1900, p. 123.
32. *BA*, 2.2.1900, pp. 73-4.
33. *T*, 23.8.1890, p. 7. White's evidence to the Select Committee, *Reports from Committees*, 7, 1884-5, vol. 13, pp. 121-4.
34. *BA*, 2.21.1900, pp. 73-4.
35. *AA Notes*, 15, 1900, p. 20.
36. Letter from Martin Harrison, 1.2.2005; *RIBAJ*, 7, 1900, p. 145.
37. *BN*, 26.1.1900, p. 123; *B*, 27.1.1900, p. 91.
38. *B*, 27.1.1900, p. 91.
39. Ibid.
40. *AA Notes*, 15, 1900, p. 20; *B*, 3.2.1900, p. 104; *RIBAJ*, 7, 1900, p. 146.
41. *TEDAS*, 2, 1908, pp. 3-4.
42. White, 'Architecture and its Practical Benefits to Man', *AASRP*, 3, 1854-6, p. 46.

Catalogue of Works

1. 1847-8. St Michael, Baldhu, Cornwall. New church. *Incumbent:* Rev. William Haslam. *Mason:* W. Gerrish. *Carpenter:* W. Salmon. Stone. £2,160. *Stained glass:* Beer, Exeter. *Sculptured corbels:* W. Pearce Jr, Truro. Nave and chancel, gabled S aisle with entrance porch, NE tower with splay-footed spire. All fittings by White. Now converted to residential use, Tower House where pulpit is retained, and Porch House. Gabled lych-gate (demolished) but granite coffin rest set in ground. Gabled wellhead in churchyard.
Sources: ECE 7/1/17863. ICBS 3905. *RCG,* 21 & 28.7.1848. *E,* 9, 1849, p. 262.

2. 1847-8. School/chapel/vicarage, Maryfield, Cornwall. New building for William Henry Pole Carew (see no. 170). Stone. Schoolhouse with shingled spired bell-cote had screened area to serve as sanctuary on Sundays. Adjacent accommodation for the Rev. Henry Lascelles Jenner, priest-in-charge (see no. 55). Now Maryfield House.
1853. Extended to S, two storeys plus attics, with bays and granite dressings, for the Rev. Sudlow Garratt.
1860. Further extended to S and E, reputedly to accommodate the Rev. Garratt's family. Circular tower possibly not to White's design.
Source: Miss F. Julia Pole-Carew and Lieut. A.C.W. Bevan, *The Story of Maryfield* (n.d.).

3. 1848-9. Bank and Solicitors' Offices, Truro, Cornwall. New commercial premises for the Cornish Bank (owned by Tweedy, Williams & Co.) and for solicitors, on the site of the old Coinage Hall at the junction of Princes and Boscawen Streets. Stone. Two storeys plus attics and basement. Central bank building in Perpendicular style, with dripstones to windows, vaulted central porch with doors either side. Original staircase and exposed timbers to ceilings. Flanking solicitors' offices have some pointed windows. Now Pizza Express, Charlotte's Tea House and offices of Cornwall Rural Community Council.
Source: RIBAJ, 7, 1900, p. 145.

4. 1849. 'Plan for a wooden church in the Diocese of Cape Town, South Africa.' Plan, elevations, sections, details of windows, benches and font, dated 3.12.1849. Perhaps the same as 'the good modern church for the diocese of Cape Town', *E,* 10, 1850, p. 55. Nave and chancel, S porch, NE sacristy. No further documentary or physical evidence found.
Source: B. Weinreb Ltd, *Catalogue 14: The Gothic of Gothick,* 1966, Lot 288.

5. 1849. Plans for St Columba's College, Holly Park, Dublin, Ireland. Plans executed at the behest of William's elder brother, Francis Gilbert White, 'as the former ones are on much to [sic] grand a scale.' No further documentary or physical evidence found.
Source: Letter from Harriet White to William Grey, 3.2.1849, DMA EGR 4/8/6/31.

6. 1849-50. St Gerent, Gerrans, Cornwall. Rebuilding, apart from tower and spire. *Incumbent:* Rev. William David Longlands. *Mason:* W. Gerrish. *Carpenter:* W. Salmon. *Stained glass:* Powell. Stone. £1,090. Nave and chancel, N transept and gabled S aisle with porch, rebuilt using original materials as far as possible. Addition of vestry to NE. Font cover and rood screen removed, but White's altar rail and benches survive.
Sources: Plan, CRO P70/2/2-3. ICBS 3833. *E,* 10, 1850, p. 246. *RCG,* 4.5.1849, p. 5.

7. 1849-51. School, Kea, Cornwall. New National School. *Incumbent*: Rev. George James Cornish, father of White's first wife. Stone. Single-storey room with louvred flèche to ridge, and large N porch. Bargeboards probably a later addition and not to White's design. Now parish room with upper floor inserted.
Master's house built adjacent, 1852, similar, but not to White's design.
Sources: Plan of grant of land, CRO 97/2/46. *E*, 12, 1851, p. 296.

8. 1849-50. School, Probus, Cornwall. New school. *Incumbent*: Rev. Richard William Barnes. Stone. £300. Design of White's L-shaped schoolroom with two porches and small classroom shown on plans for extension by E.C. Farley, CRO SRP 63/2-6, 1870. Demolished.
Source: *E*, 10, 1850, p. 163.

9. 1849. 'A town pump house & lamp'. A design drawing, described as 'a pentagon on a heptagon', attached to those of no. 4. No further documentary or physical evidence found.
Source: B. Weinreb Ltd, *Catalogue 14, The Gothic of Gothick*, 1966, Lot 288.

10. 1849-51. Rectory, St Columb Major, Cornwall. Restoration/enlargement for Rev. Dr Samuel Edmund Walker (see no. 15). Stone. £7,000. Effectively a rebuild, using some old materials, largely on original foundations of moated house. Two storeys plus attics, intended as seat of new Cornish bishopric. Staircases, fireplaces, joinery, stained glass have survived. Now The Old Bishop's Palace.
Sources: *E*, 12, 1851, pp. 59, 69, 234-5. Print of White's drawing of 20.2.1851, *c*.1851, RIC TRURI:1000.339. C. Henderson, *St Columb Major, Church & Parish, Cornwall* (1930), pp. 8-18.
c.**1851.** Furniture for St Columb Rectory, Cornwall. Chair, oak with octagonal back inlaid with ebony, walnut and mahogany, V&A W.63-1979. Sideboard, oak with maple carving, gilded and ebonised details and applied matrix stones, exhibited Philadelphia Antiques Show, 2000, present whereabouts unknown.

11. 1849-53. Bishops Diocesan College, Woodlands, Cape Town, South Africa. New school instigated by Bishop Robert Gray. *Builder*: Mr Arnold. *Supervising architect*: Mr Penketh. Brick, plastered. £2,500. Much simplified version of White's original plans. Schoolroom, with library and classroom; chapel, masters' rooms and prefects' study with dormitory over, forming two sides of quadrangle. Now S corner of Founders Quad.
Sources: *E*, 13, 1852, pp. 283, 301; *E*, 14, 1853, p. 273. Letters from William's brother, the Rev. H.M. White (see nos 25, 88, 105, 145, 155), BCA. John Gardener, *Bishops 150* (1997).

12. 1850. St Martin, Herne, Kent. Restoration of choir stalls, sedilia, piscina, etc. *Source: CB,* 1892, p. 31.

13. 1850-1. School, Mevagissey, Cornwall. New National School. *Incumbent*: Rev. William John Alban. Stone. £260. Single-storey room with windows to E and S and large N porch. Much extended, now The Retreat.
Sources: Drawings, Oct. 1850, CERC. *E*, 12, 1851, p. 234. *RCG*, 4.7.1851, p. 6.

14. 1850-61. St Peter, Mithian, Cornwall. New church. *Incumbent*: Rev. Alfred Lord (see no. 97). *Builder*: Salmon, Truro. Stone. £1,087. White's 1850 plans revised and approved 1859.

Nave, chancel, transepts, W tower and spire, gabled S porch, NE lean-to vestry. Tower and spire demolished 1898. Tower rebuilt to another design 1928. Wood-block flooring, altar, children's bench and high-backed wooden sedilia (now in transept). Closed.
Sources: ICBS 4422. *E,* 12, 1851, pp. 240, 296. *RCG,* 4.7.1851, p. 6; 16.3.1860, p. 5. *CB,* 1862, p. 21. Tony Mansell, *Mithian in the Parishes of St Agnes and Perranzabuloe* (2003).

15. 1850-61. All Saints, Notting Hill, London. New church for the Rev. Dr Samuel Edmund Walker (see no. 10). *Builder*: Myers, Lambeth. *Mosaic work*: Steven, Pimlico. *Glass*: Lavers to White's design. *Clerk of works*: J. Butler. Stone. *c.* £25,000. Cloister and choir school planned on S side. Nave, with lean-to N and S aisles, chancel, short transepts, W tower with entrance under, gabled S porch. Double-glazed windows. Collapse of Dr Walker's investments in 1855 stopped work. Building finished by a civil engineer, but spire and W buttresses to tower not built. Loss of all glass and rebuilding of SE corner after bomb damage, 1940. Interior whitewashed, but inlaid work around clerestory windows survives.
Sources: E, 13, 1852, p. 299; 14, 1853, pp. 212, 273. *G,* 6.9.1854, p. 695. *B,* 13.10.1855, p. 486; 20.10.1855, p. 504. *BN* 12.4.1861, p. 301; 15.9.1876, p. 256. C.L. Eastlake, *A History of the Gothic Revival* (1872), p. 291.

16. 1850-1. Rectory, Ruan Lanihorne, Cornwall. New house. *Incumbent*: Rev. Henry Spencer Slight. Stone. Two storeys, L-shaped plan with generous entrance hall and main rooms to S. Stucco and non-structural timbering to S elevation and extensive additions to the N in Georgian style, but principal staircase and some fireplaces and internal shutters have survived. Now The Old Rectory.
Sources: Plans and specification, CRO D/R uncatalogued. *E,* 11, 1850, p. 417; 12, 1851, pp. 59, 69.

17. 1851. School, Blakesley, Northamptonshire. New school. Stone. It appears this was replaced in 1874 by the present brick Old School.
Source: E, 12, 1851, p. 297.

18. 1851-4. House of Mercy, Bussage, Gloucestershire. New buildings, including chapel, workroom and living accommodation. Stone. Extensive alterations and additions have left little of White's original work visible. Chapel has been extended to the W, and rooms constructed within the E end. Two original E lancets are visible in attic storage areas. Now Our Lady of Victory Trust and strictly private.
Sources: E, 14, 1853, pp. 117, 214. M.D. Lambert, *Saint Michael and All Angels Bussage 1846-1986* (1986).

19. 1851. St Keyne (Cuby), Kenwyn, Truro, Cornwall. Alterations and additions, including churchyard cross, in memory of the Rev. George Cornish.
Sources: E, 12, 1851, p. 75. Photographs of the cross, SP.
1854. Rebuilding of the Tregarvethen aisle (the local name for the N transept). *Incumbent*: Rev. E. Harold Browne. Stone. White's typical diagonal boarding can be seen in the ceiling.
Source: E, 15, 1854, p. 288.

20. 1851-77. Holy Saviour, Westbury Leigh, Wiltshire. New church instigated by the Rev. William David Morrice (see nos 111, 149). Stone. £4,000. Original site was on S side of the road, so White designed N porch and S vestry. Nave and chancel, S aisle, NE organ chapel and vestry, SW tower and provision for future N aisle. Now Westbury Leigh Community Hall.

1877. Nave and chancel built.

1888. Gabled S aisle built.

1890. SW tower completed as memorial to L.H. Phipps.
Sources: Appeals, lists of subscribers, WRO 1427/60. ICBS 9275. *E,* 12, 1851, p. 400. *CB,* 1888, p. 95.

21. 1852–4. Rectory, Lurgashall, W. Sussex. Restoration and enlargement. *Incumbent:* Rev. Septimus Fairles (see no. 346). *Builder:* Joseph Butler, Sussex. Stone. White probably added the two-storey E cross-wing, altered windows and created a new staircase. Now The Old Rectory.
Sources: Plan, private collection. *E,* 13, 1852, p. 438. *B,* 12.8.1854, p. 429.

22. 1852–4. Rectory, St Ive, Cornwall. New house, stables, etc. *Incumbent:* Rev. Reginald Hobhouse. Stone. Two storeys plus attics, L-shaped plan with main rooms to S. W cross-wing service area with slate hanging and sculptural roofs. Ingenious kitchen window with ventilators. Slate hung water tank above kitchen entrance added 1908. Stone drawing room bay and principal staircase collapsed; chimneystack adjacent to entrance demolished. Tiled skirtings, fireplaces, some shutters, and fitted cupboards to study have survived. Now The Chantry.
Sources: *E,* 13, 1852, p. 65. Detail drawings, private collection.

23. 1853–4. Chaplain's Cottage, Arley Hall, Cheshire. New dwelling on estate of Rowland Eyles Egerton Warburton (see nos. 35, 36, 40, 46). Polychrome brick. Brick and timber porch under catslide roof. Modern alterations and extensions. Now Red Lodge, Arley Green.
Source: Sketch and plans, AHA.

24. 1853. Designs for a row of private houses, Bayswater, London. Described as 'in the Pointed style'. No further documentary or physical evidence found.
Source: *E,* 14, 1853, p. 117.

25. 1853. Lectern and credence desk for St Saviour, Claremont, Cape Town, South Africa. Oak. Probably for the Rev. H.M. White, William's elder brother (see nos. 11, 88, 105, 145, 155). The desk has gouged quatrefoil decoration to the sides and a pattern of triangles and circles to the base strut. The bookboard of the lectern has an unusual decorative panel of arabesque design.
Source: *St Saviour's Parish Magazine,* September 1941, p. 2, BCA.

26. 1853. Design for parsonage, Dorchester, Oxfordshire. No further documentary or physical evidence found. Existing house designed by David Brandon, 1857.
Source: *E,* 14, 1853, p. 138.

27. 1853. School and master's house, Exning, Suffolk. New buildings. *Incumbent:* Rev. Percy James Croft (see no. 344). Stone. £650. Demolished or subsumed when existing school built in brick, 1876.
Source: *E,* 14, 1853, p. 214.

28. 1853. King Charles the Martyr, Falmouth, Cornwall. New N porch. *Incumbent:* Rev. William John Coope. Stone. Gabled, with diagonal buttresses.
Source: *E,* 14, 1853, p. 218.

29. 1853–4. Vicarage, Holy Trinity, Halstead, Essex. New parsonage. *Incumbent:* Rev. Duncan Fraser. *Builder:* J.W.C. Woollard, Long Melford, Suffolk. Polychrome brick. £1,145. Two storeys plus attics. Original plans amended to reduce slightly the service area and closets above. Glass slates specified for roofs over closets. Demolished.
Sources: Plans, QAB E118. EC 3026. *E*, 14, 1853, p. 436. *B*, 5.8.1854, p. 414. *RIBAJ*, 7, 1900, p. 146.

30. 1853–5. St John, Hooe, Plymouth, Devon. New church (proposed dedication, St Anne) initiated by Sir Frederic Rogers (see nos. 50, 80). Stone. £1,154. Nave and chancel, gabled S aisle with gabled porch. Corbels for original wooden bellcote visible on W wall, replaced by present stone bellcote, 1894–5, to the design of 'Mr Sedding', perhaps Edmund Harold Sedding (1863–1921), nephew of J.D. Sedding. Tiled flooring, font (marble top a later addition), pulpit, choir stalls, altar. E window damaged in WW2.
Sources: Plans, CRO 724/63–5. ICBS 4708. *E*, 15, 1854, p. 284.

31. 1853–5. Vicarage, Milton, near Sittingbourne, Kent. Alterations and enlargement. *Incumbent:* Rev. Charles Smart Caffin. £700. E cross-wing provided two new reception rooms with bedrooms over; enlargement of service area. New timbered entrance porch on S elevation. Demolished.
Sources: Plans, CDCA Dcb/DC/M15/1. *E*, 14, 1853, p. 436.

32. 1853–5. St Hilary, St Hilary, Cornwall. Rebuilding, apart from tower and splay-footed

spire. *Incumbent*: Rev. Thomas Pascoe. Stone. £2,370. Nave, chancel, gabled N and S aisles, gabled S porch, transepts forming crossing with eight tiny windows giving impression of a lantern. White's screen, pulpit, stalls, etc. painted in the C20 by members of the Newlyn School.
Sources: ICBS 4679. *E*, 15, 1854, p. 288; 16, 1855, pp. 393-6.

33. 1853. St Ia, St Ives, Cornwall. Rearrangement. *Incumbent*: Rev. David Edward Domville. *Builder*: John Lander and others. *Lectern*: Rattee & Kett. £580. Re-flooring, restoration of old benches and construction of children's and moveable benches.
Sources: Specification, letters, etc., CRO DDP 91/2/16/5-10. CamRO Rattee & Kett R100/09, fol.22. *E*, 14, 1853, p. 218.
1856. New NE vestry.
Source: Specification, CRO DDP 19/2/16/14.

34. 1853-4. St Andrew, West Tarring, W. Sussex. Restoration and additions. *Incumbent*: Rev. John Wood Warter. Flint with stone. More than £2,000. Work included new roofs to aisles and N porch, new flooring, seating, pulpit and reading desk, and construction of new vestry to S.
Sources: *CBells*, 3.5.1879, p. 253. *CB*, 1886, pp. 14-16. Canon Clarke's notebooks, VII, 4.

35. 1854. Arley Hall, Cheshire. Designs for additions to the chapel and a new choir school for Rowland Eyles Egerton-Warburton (see nos 23, 36, 40, 46). Polychrome brick. Proposed N chancel aisle to chapel. Attached to chapel at NW, a cloistered choristers' vestry and library, with attached living room, scullery, pantry, etc. and large brew house, with bedrooms above and 2nd floor garret bedrooms. Not built.
Source: Plans, AHA.

36. 1854. Arley Hall, Cheshire. Design for entrance lodge for Rowland Eyles Egerton-Warburton (see nos 23, 35, 40, 46). Polychrome brick. Proposed lodge over the bridge at Birch Brook. Heavily buttressed arched carriageway with living room and scullery adjacent and two bedrooms over. Not built.
Source: Plans, AHA.

37. 1854. St Peter's Almshouses, Brimpton, Berkshire. Boundary wall and arched gateway for Anne Frances, (dowager) countess of Falmouth. Polychrome brick and stone. Buttressed gabled arch with inscription and coat of arms under floriated cross.
Source: SP.

38. 1854. St Peter, Chatteris, Cambridgeshire. Designs for new vestry and organ chamber and reseating. *Incumbent*: Rev. Michael Augustus Gathercole. Proposed vestry to N of chancel to accommodate the organ, together with lowering of pews and removal of pew doors. Not executed.
Source: CUL EDR D3/5 FAC/Chatteris 1857.

39. 1854. School and schoolhouse, Cuminestown, Aberdeenshire. New school with 'very small lodging attached'. Stone. No further documentary or physical evidence found.
Source: *E*, 15, 1854, p. 287.

40. 1854–8. School and master's house, Great Budworth, Cheshire. New school and master's house for Rowland Eyles Egerton-Warburton (see nos. 23, 35, 36, 46). *Builder:* Fairhurst, Whitley. Polychrome brick. *c.*£1,000. S elevation with four traceried windows below gables. Separate entrances to N and S. Much altered and extended, but still functioning as the village primary school. Adjacent master's house with brick tympana above some windows and doors, and original hinges to doors. Now School House.
Sources: Correspondence and drawings, AHA. Drawings CCA SC1/71/1-4. *E,* 16, 1855, p. 315.

41. 1854–7. St Mary, Inverurie, Aberdeenshire. Additions. *Incumbent:* Rev. Alexander Harper. Stone. New chancel with cross-gabled N organ chamber and lean-to NE vestry. Sedilia, piscina, rails and tiled floor appear to be by White.
Source: E, 15, 1854, p. 285.

42. 1854–8. St Moren, Lamorran, Cornwall. Alterations and additions. *Incumbent:* Hon. and Rev. John Townsend Boscawen. Stone. N transept built to match that on the S. Roofs raised and windows altered. New granite arch to sanctuary, wooden screens to form new chancel at E end of nave, pulpit, choir stalls, altar rails, benches, tiled floor.
Source: E, 15, 1854, p. 359.
1858. Three-light stained glass W window by Lavers, scenes from the Life of Christ, cartoons drawn and painted under White's supervision.
Source: B, 23.1.1858, p. 60.

43. 1854–5. Vicarage, Lyminster, W. Sussex. New house. *Incumbent:* Rev. Charles Rous Drury. *Builder:* Messrs Bushby, Littlehampton. Flint, banded and dressed with red brick. *c.*£1,200. Two storeys plus attics. Original entrance on S (garden) elevation. Alterations and additions including large W wing. Now the Old Vicarage.
Sources: Plans and specification, private collection. *B,* 5.5.1855, p. 214.

44. 1854. School and house, Rode Heath, Cheshire. New school and dame's house for Randle Wilbraham of Rode Hall (see nos 45, 342). Brick. Single-storey school, much extended, now offices. Across the road, a pair of semi-detached cottages, of polychrome brick with hipped dormers, appear to be houses for the teachers.
Source: E, 15, 1854, p. 357.

45. *c.*1854. Estate cottages, Rode Heath, Cheshire, for Randle Wilbraham of Rode Hall (see nos 44, 342). Brick. Brook (now Mill) Cottage and nos 182 & 184 Congleton Road North, Scholar Green, identified by Stefan Muthesius as by White.
Source: Pevsner & Hubbard, *BoE: Cheshire,* pp. 322-3.

46. 1854. Warburton, Cheshire. Restoration of Warburton Cross for Randle Eyles Egerton-Warburton (see nos. 23, 35, 36, 40). Stone. Only the stepped base now remains.
Source: E, 15, 1854, p. 287.

47. 1855. Shops, Audley, Staffordshire. A terrace of three shop units, with two-storey accommodation above, with arcade forming covered walkway, arched carriage entrance and attached house. Polychrome brick. Now altered, one a shop, the rest dwellings.
Sources: E, 16, 1855, pp. 190-1. *B,* 11.8.1855, p. 378.

48. 1855-6. St Peter, Bucknell, Oxfordshire. Restoration of chancel. *Incumbent*: Rev. William Master, brother of White's mother (see no. 173). *Builder*: Messrs Coney. *Stained glass*: Lavers, to White's designs. Repair of walls, £270. Oak altar and credence. Distinctive quarries edged with coloured glass.
Sources: B, 7.6.1856, p. 313. Canon Clarke's MSS, 'Churches in the 19th Century', list of architects in Oxfordshire.

49. 1855-6. St Mary, Hawridge, Buckinghamshire. Rebuilding. *Incumbent*: Rev. Alfred Codd (see nos 89, 116, 294). *Builder*: James and Isaac Coney, St John's Wood, Middlesex. *Stained glass*: Lavers, depiction of the Crucifixion, donated by Misses Du Cane. Flint banded with brick. £418. Nave and chancel, louvred timber bellcote, gabled S porch. Brick splays to chancel windows, benches, pulpit, chancel screen, choir stalls, tiled flooring, wrought-iron altar rails. The 'simple fresco patterns on the plaster' reported in *The Guardian* have not survived. *Sources*: Contract, BRO PR 101/3/1. ICBS 4993. *G*, 26.11.1856, p. 900. *E*, 18, 1857, pp. 50, 63.

50. 1855. School and master's house, Hooe, Plymouth, Devon. New school and master's house. *Builder*: Messrs May, Devonport. Stone. £750. Single-storey gabled schoolroom running N from St John's church (no. 30), with gabled classroom projecting W at N end. Now church hall.
Two-storey master's house forms L-shape with school. Heavily buttressed central porch under steep pent roof. Later extension at E end and modern windows. Now Keble Cottage.
Sources: E, 16, 1855, pp. 50, 65. *B*, 21.4.1855, p. 189.

51. 1855-8. St Clement, Knowlton, Kent. Restoration at sole cost of Admiral D'Aeth. *Incumbent*: Rev. Charles John Hughes D'Aeth. Flint with stone dressings. New roofs to nave and chancel, stone bell-cote above W gable and most windows by White.
Sources: E, 16, 1855, p. 120. *B*, 7.4.1858, p. 166. Canon Clarke's notebooks, IX, 107.

52. 1855. St Mawnan, Mawnan, Cornwall. Restoration and re-ordering. *Incumbent*: Rev. William Rogers. Stone. Roofs restored. No evidence of White's proposed E window, nor his 'low screens' at E end of nave with new choir stalls, probably swept away in later restoration.
Source: E, 16, 1855, pp. 120, 193.

53. 1855-6. All Saints, Mollington, Oxfordshire. Restoration and enlargement. *Incumbent*: Rev. Thomas Henry Tait (see no. 106). *Joinery*: Bonham, Wardington. Stone. £413. New N aisle built on site of one demolished in 1786. Exterior repairs, re-roofing of porch. Aisle and tower windows of pale green quarries with stained glass to tracery. Quarries were 'ornamented by foliage patterns in outline which have been exceedingly well painted by the Misses Cowper [see no. 200] and Miss Harris of Wardington'. Removal of W gallery, raising and tiling of sanctuary floor, new seating, altar, font cover and base. Lectern, pulpit and prayer desk in oak by Bonhams to White's designs. Churchyard gate.
Sources: Bod. MS Top.Oxon.c.104. ICBS 4902. *Banbury Guardian,* 21.6.1855. *B*, 26.4.1856, p. 232. Canon Clarke's MSS 'Churches in the 19th century', list of architects in Oxfordshire.

54. 1855-7. St Felicitas, Phillack, Cornwall. Rebuilding, apart from tower. *Incumbent*: Rev. Frederick Hockin. Stone. £1,800. Nave, chancel, gabled N and S aisles, gabled S porch, gabled

S transept, cross-gabled NE vestry. New base to font, benches, painted chancel arch, wooden chancel screens, choir stalls, sedilia, altar.
Sources: ICBS 4946. Charles Thomas, *Phillack Church* (1960), reproduces two White watercolours of the old church.
1899. Tower screen with characteristic stained glass.
Source: Goodhart-Rendel Index, NMR.

55. 1855. St Mildred, Preston by Wingham, Kent. Restoration. *Incumbent:* Rev. Henry Lascelles Jenner (see no. 2). Flint and stone. £440. Repairs to tower, including new pyramidal roof, door, floors and glazing; new gabled N porch, and E and S windows to chancel. Large triangular dormers to nave replaced earlier small ones seen in 1807 watercolour, H. Petrie, ref. 285, Kent Archaeological Society. New benches on wood-block flooring, choir stalls, pulpit, wooden eagle lectern, font cover. White's simple wooden chancel screen (photos, 1952, NMR) has not survived.
Sources: Accounts, CDCA U3/245/5/B/8. ICBS 5056. *E*, 16, 1855, p. 50; 18, 1857, p. 323.
1858. Design for organ case.
Source: E, 19, 1858, pp. 63, 219.

56. *c.*1855. Penmellyn, Bank Street, St Columb Major, Cornwall. New house, reputedly for a medical doctor. Stone. Two storeys plus attics. Typically asymmetric with varied windows, including wooden plate tracery, triangular oriel and slate hung tympana. Original staircases and fireplaces survive.
Source: Roger Dixon & Stefan Muthesius, *Victorian Architecture* (1978), p. 49.

57. 1855–6. St George, Stowlangtoft, Suffolk. Restoration. *Incumbent:* Rev. Samuel Richards (whose wife was Ellen White's Wilmot aunt). *Builder:* Messrs Coney. £900. Work included repairs to tower and walls, new bell frame, new lectern and stone pulpit.
Source: Particulars of costs, SRO FL511/4/1.

58. 1855–6. St Michael's School, Wantage, (Berkshire) Oxfordshire. New school for Mrs Trevelyan. Stone with red brick bands. £2,500. House with pyramidal roofed entrance porch, chapel (extended E to designs of A.B. Allin, 1888), workroom and refectory with dormitory above. Later alterations and additions. Converted to dwellings *c.*1980.
Sources: Dean Butler's Diaries 1853-7, BerksRO D/P143/28/2. *E*, 16, 1855, p. 311; 17, 1856, pp. 63, 75, 158-9, 217. Canon Clarke's notebooks, XVI, 10-11.

59. 1856. St Michael, Axford, Wiltshire. Adaptation, after work had begun, of design by a local builder. Flint with bands and dressings of brick. £415. Nave and chancel under low roof. Gabled S porch. Lean-to NE vestry.
Source: E, 17, 1856, p. 154.

60. 1856-7. St Michael, Cadbury, Devon. Restoration. *Incumbent:* Rev. Frederick J. Coleridge. Rebuilding of N aisle and insertion of new windows, and of S wall and windows, new nave roof. Angel credence shelf appears to be by White, as does timbered lychgate.
Sources: Vestry Minutes, DRO 2540A/PV1. *E*, 18, 1857, pp. 50, 68.

61. 1856. Design for a lamp for a church in the diocese of Cape Town, South Africa. No further documentary or physical evidence found.
Source: E, 17, 1856, p. 135.

62. 1856-7. Vicarage, Coopersale, Essex. New house, stables, etc. *Incumbent:* Rev. Richard Fort. Polychrome brick with non-structural timber decoration to some dormers. Two storeys. Principal staircase, some fireplaces and sliding shutters, and ingenious double door to study to preclude draughts. Some later additions. Now The Old Rectory.
Source: E, 18, 1857, pp. 50, 67.

63. 1856-60. St Bartholomew, Grahamstown, South Africa. New church instigated by Archdeacon Nathaniel J. Merriman (see no. 140). *Builder:* Mr Glass. *Superintending Architect:* Mr Stitt. Stone with brick dressings. £2,200. Nave, chancel, NW gabled porch, and SE vestry. Original timber W bell-cote replaced by stone NW bell tower (not White's design), completed 1893. Benches, sedilia, stalls, font and cover.
Sources: Vestry Minutes, CL PR3514(a); Heavyside Diary, CL MS 16 606. *E*, 18, 1857, pp. 50, 65, 185.

64. 1856-8. St Mary & St Hugh, (Old) Harlow, Essex. Restoration of S transept. *Incumbent:* Rev. Charles Miller. Flint with stone. Subsumed in complete restoration of the church by Henry Woodyer, 1872-3.
Source: E, 18, 1857, p. 50.

65. 1856-7. Christ Church, Hatherden, Hampshire. New church instigated by the Hon. and Rev. Samuel Best (see no. 68). Builder: Messrs Hillary, Longparish. Flint with brick. £700. Single cell nave and apsidal chancel, tall W bell-cote, N porch (now blocked) and NE vestry. Matching gabled S porch added 1869. Roof, glass and interior destroyed by fire, 1976. New roof at lower pitch.
Sources: ICBS 4953 (Wildhern). *E*, 17, 1856, p. 154. *B*, 5.12.1857, p. 709. *BN* 4.12.1857, p. 1286.

66. 1856-7. Vicarage, Heydour, Lincolnshire. Rebuilding and enlargement. *Incumbent:* Rev. Gordon Frederick Deedes (see no. 194). Stone with irregular brick banding. Specification included reuse of some materials from original house. Three storeys. Pyramidal roof over WC above front entrance contrasts with very flat wall plane to garden elevation. Some modern additions, but staircase, doors, fireplaces, window ironmongery and gate piers survive. Now Heydour House.
Sources: Plans and specification, LRO MGA 379. *E*, 18, 1857, p. 67. *AASRP*, 4, 1857-8, p. xiv.

67. 1856-7. School and master's house, Ramsbury, Wiltshire. New school. Flint with irregular brick banding. Intended that boys' and girls' schoolrooms should be separated by the house. Only one schoolroom built, with windows under half-hipped dormers, and lean-to cloakroom. Later additions to rear. Now dwellings, The Nook and The Gallery.
Source: E, 18, 1857, p. 67.

68. 1856-7. Christ Church, Smannell, Hampshire. New church instigated by the Hon. and Rev. Samuel Best (see no. 65). *Builder:* Gue & Son, Andover. Flint with brick. £650. Single-cell nave and apsidal chancel, W bell-cote, SW porch, lean-to N aisle and NE vestry. Bell-cote has been lowered and now contains only one bell. Tile hanging to porch now extends down to crossbeam.

Sources: ICBS 4954. *E*, 17, 1856, p. 154. *B*, 5.12.1857, p. 709. *BN* 4.12.1857, p. 1286.

1893-4. Extension of N aisle with choir vestry and organ chamber under gabled roof. £385 paid by Mrs Earle, the lady squire. Repairs, including tie-rods to nave, buttress to S wall and at SW corner; tiling to floor and painted decoration to walls of sanctuary.

Source: Correspondence and drawing, HRO 21M65/336F/1.

69. 1856-7. Bank House, St Columb Major, Cornwall. New commercial premises and accommodation for Thomas Whitford. *Builder:* W. England. Polychrome stone. Two and three storeys, L-shape plan, central entrance to banking hall. Side entrance to living accommodation originally through two-storey conservatory. Decorative ironwork, garden walls and gate piers. Staircases, doors, shutters, stained glass, fireplaces, safes, survive, although fitted cupboards and bookcases have disappeared.

Sources: E, 18, 1857, p. 28. SP.

70. 1856-7. St John the Baptist, Forest School, Walthamstow, (Essex) London. New chapel in honour of the Rev. Dr John Gilderdale. *Stained glass:* Powell & Sons. Polychrome brick. Single-cell nave and chancel, S entrance.

Source: E, 18, 1857, p. 10.

1866-9. Addition of SW bell-cote and ventilator with shingled flèche, gabled SW porch and gas lighting.

Source: Guy Deaton, *Schola Sylvestris* (Forest School, 1984), p. 67.

1875-8. Enlargement of chancel with N and S lean-to aisles, extension of W end of nave, insertion of triangular dormer windows, instigated by the Rev. Frederick Barlow Guy. *Builder:* Ashby & Horner. *Stained glass:* Lavers & Barraud. *Carving:* four angels representing the seasons by Harry Hems to White's designs. Polychrome brick. £978. Loss of stained glass in WW2, later painting and gilding of angel statues.

Source: Forest School Magazine, Trinity 1876, pp. 265-7; Lent 1878, p. 197.

(White's brother, the Rev. Francis Gilbert White, and headmaster, the Rev. F.B. Guy, were married to the Rev. Dr Gilderdale's daughters, Lucy and Rebecca.)

71. 1856-61. St Bartholomew, Wigginton, Hertfordshire. Restoration, and addition of new N aisle. *Incumbent:* Rev. George Gaisford. Flint and stone. £400. Low aisle lit by three gabled dormers. Removal of W gallery. New SW window, S porch, stone pulpit, and chancel E window. Shingled bell-cote restored.

Sources: ICBS 5121. *E*, 19, 1858, pp. 416-7.

72. 1857. Design for Crimean Memorial Church, Constantinople, Turkey. Competition design in polychrome brick 'Especially Mentioned'. Not built.

Sources: E, 18, 1857, pp. 100-9. *CEAJ*, 20, 1857, p. 125.

73. 1857-8. Rectory, Little Baddow, Essex. New house. *Incumbent:* Rev. William Brice Ady (see no. 81). Polychrome brick. Two storeys plus attics of varying patterns of red and buff bricks,

some of great size. Tile-hanging above entrance porch, and tiles used edgeways to emphasise voussoirs to lancet windows. Now The Old Rectory.
Source: E, 19, 1858, p. 199.

74. 1857-8. St Petrock, Little Petherick, Cornwall. Rebuilding on old foundations. *Incumbent:* Sir Hugh Henry Molesworth (see no. 82). *Builder:* William Ball, Hackney. Stone. £460. Nave and chancel, gabled N aisle (extended W by one bay), W tower, gabled S porch, S chancel aisle. Three gateways to churchyard. Nave dormer windows, not by White, added later. Font cover. Complete restoration and re-ordering by Ninian Comper, 1908.
Sources: Volume of 'particulars respecting the rebuilding', CRO P185/2/30. *E*, 19, 1858, p. 416.

75. 1857. Designs for tombstones by members of the Worcester Diocesan Architectural Society. Two designs by White, one for a slate headstone.
Source: E, 18, 1857, pp. 134-5.

76. 1858. Vicarage, Boxgrove, W. Sussex. Rebuilding in brick and flint. *Incumbent:* Rev. William Burnett (see no. 77). Demolished, apart from gate piers.
Source: E, 19, 1858, p. 414.

77. 1858. St Mary the Virgin & St Blaise, Boxgrove, W. Sussex. Partial restoration of the priory church. *Incumbent:* Rev. William Burnett (see no. 76). Obliterated by Scott's later work.
Source: E, 26, 1865, p. 75.

78. 1858-9. St Michael, Bradden, Northamptonshire. Restoration. *Incumbent:* Rev. Cornelius Ives, cousin of White's mother (see no. 100). *Builder:* James Hinson. Stone. £1,064. Virtually a rebuild apart from W tower, nave arcades and C18 entrance door. Nave, lean-to N and S aisles, gabled S porch. Pulpit, lectern, font and cover, altar table, and glazing. Ingenious iron latch to N gate of churchyard.
Sources: Account, NRO Grant-Ives Collection, GI 433-4. *E*, 19, 1858, p. 198; 20, 1859, pp. 352, 422.

79. 1858. School and teacher's house, Chute, Wiltshire. New school and house. Flint with brick. £700. L-shaped single-storey boys' and girls' schools with separate porches. Later extensions to W. Now village hall.
Two-storey teacher's house attached at NE. Now Old School House, Chute Standen.
Sources: Plans, WRO 782/31. *E*, 19, 1858, pp. 268, 414.

80. 1858-62. Vicarage, Hooe, Plymouth, Devon. New house, stables, etc. *Incumbent:* Rev. Richard Lewis. Stone. Built to serve St John's (no. 30). Two storeys plus attics, L-shaped with slate-hanging reflecting exposed cliff-top site. Principal staircase, some shutters and fireplaces, and serving hatch have survived the Ministry of Defence. Inventive ladder stairs to hayloft in stables. Now St Anne's House.
Sources: Purchase of land, CRO 724/55. *E*, 19, 1858, pp. 198-9.

81. 1858. St Mary, Little Baddow, Essex. Reseating and repairs. *Incumbent:* Rev. William Brice Ady (see no. 73). Stone. £330. The S arcade had been removed previously and nave and aisle placed under one roof. White replaced two windows E of S porch with four-light square-headed one with reticulated tracery. Altar rail, small wooden pulpit, font with tall cover, benches. *Sources:* ICBS 5273. *E*, 19, 1858, p. 416.

82. 1858. School and master's house, Tregonna, Little Petherick, Cornwall. New school and house instigated by Sir Hugh Henry Molesworth (see no. 74), who carved the foundation stone. *Mason:* James Henwood, Wadebridge. *Carpenter:* William Ball, London. Stone. At cost of Mrs Mary Prideaux-Brune. Single schoolroom with floor of wooden blocks set in concrete, and three-bed house attached. Converted into two dwellings *c*.1910. Modern alterations and extensions, but tall, plate-traceried E window survives.
Sources: CRO P185/2/30. *RCG,* 12.2.1858, p. 5. *E*, 19, 1858, p. 414.

83. 1858-60. St Michael & All Angels, Lyndhurst, Hampshire. Rebuilding in phases to new design. *Incumbent:* Rev. John Compton. *Builder:* J. & M. Hillary, Longparish. *Carving:* Thomas Earp, £250. *Clerk of works:* Jesse Baker. Polychrome brick with stone dressings. *c.* £7,000. Nave, chancel, NE vestry, N transept, lean-to N aisle and NW gabled porch built first. Wood-block floor, choir stalls, benches (replaced in later re-ordering) and stained glass to tracery of triangular dormers
1862. S transept and lean-to S aisle. Benches with doors have not survived.
1869. Tower and spire.
*c.***1892.** Re-configuration of nave roof: simple arch-braces replaced with hammer-beams and carved wooden angels, perhaps to White's original (superseded) design as very similar to that at Brompton Hospital Chapel (no. 328).
Sources: HRO 239F/6-9, 25M84/PW18-55. ICBS 5267. *E*, 20, 1859, p. 288. *B*, 8.10.1859, p. 669. Eastlake (1872), pp. 292-4.

84. 1858. St Michael, Newquay, Cornwall. New church. *Incumbent:* Rev. Nicholas Ford Chudleigh. *Mason:* Farley, Truro. *Carpenter:* William Ball, London. Stone. £700. Nave, chancel, lean-to S aisle, W bell-cote, 'stencilled quarry windows at the East and West ends'.
Sources: *RCG,* 26.3.1858, p. 8; 17.9.1858, p. 5. *E*, 19, 1858, p. 197 (listed as S. Patrick, S. Columb Minor). *G,* 29.9.1858, p. 763.
1872. Enlargement. *Incumbent:* Rev. Richard Mildrew. Stone. £650. Extension of nave to W and construction of gabled N aisle.
Sources: ICBS 7500. Photograph, Canon Clarke's notebooks, XII, 74.
1881. Enlargement. *Incumbent:* Rev. Isaac Broad Eade. Gabled S aisle.
Sources: *BN* 4.3.1881, p. 250. Description of White's disused church after the building of the new St Michael's by Ninian Comper 1909-11, Goodhart-Rendel Index, NMR. Demolished.

85. 1858-61. St Giles & St Nicholas, Sidmouth, Devon. Rebuilding and enlargement. *Incumbent:* Rev. Hans Frederick Hamilton (see no. 121). *Builder:* Noah Miller; declared bankrupt and succeeded by Gosling for clerestory. *Clerk of works:* Place. Stone. *c.*£2,625. Demolition and rebuilding of (extended) chancel with aisles and NE vestry, new N and S transepts, new roof and clerestory to nave, rebuilding of N and S lean-to aisles with a gabled porch to each, new W window to tower. Choir stalls, pulpit and nave benches. White's wooden pulpit replaced 1866, but handrail remains. Marble shafts and capitals (not by White) added to nave arcades 1867. S chancel aisle extended, 1878, to plans by Hayward & Son.
Sources: DRO 1855A/PW 46, 74-6, 103-9; 1855A/PV3; 1855A/PZ 26-7; 4584Z-0/Z/1-2. ICBS 5352.

Peter Orlando Hutchinson, *A History of the Restoration of Sidmouth Parish Church* (1860). *E*, 20, 1859, pp. 132, 207; 28, 1867, pp. 310-12.

86. 1858. Thornton Lodge, Pope's Grove, Twickenham, (Middlesex) London. New house for Edward William Minster, publisher and editor. Polychrome brick. Two storeys. Now no. 95.
Sources: B, 7.8.1858, p. 542. *Kelly's Directory for Twickenham & Whitton*, 1860.

87. 1858-64. Winscott House, Winswell, Devon. New house for the Ven. John Curzon Moore-Stevens (see no. 157). *Builder*: Samuel Hooper, Hatherleigh. Stone with brick. More than £7,000. *Iron gates*: Tardrew, Bideford. Two storeys plus attics. The plan anticipated Humewood, with E entrance through a *porte-cochère* and entrance hall opening into a double-height staircase hall, here top-lit by a pyramidal capped lantern, and service wing to NW. Sashes to some ground floor windows. Demolished, but White's gate piers and garden gate at lodge survive.
Sources: E, 19, 1858, p. 268; 27, 1866, p. 244. *B,* 21.10.1865, pp. 746-7.

88. 1859-61. School and teachers' houses, East Street, Andover, Hampshire. New National Schools and residences, probably instigated by the Rev. H.M. White, curate (see nos 11, 25, 105, 145, 155). Polychrome brick. Boys' school to the N, separated from the girls' and infants' schools by W facing master's and mistress's houses. Loss of some chimneys and flèches and extensive additions to E and S, but boys' and girls' playground privies survive. Still a primary school.
Sources: Plans, HRO 20M65/6/6. *E,* 20, 1859, p. 211.

89. 1859-61. Vicarage, Beaminster, Dorset. New house, stables, etc. *Incumbent:* Rev. Alfred Codd (see nos 49, 116, 294). *Builder:* John Chick, Beaminster. £1,300. Stone with single course of brick. Two storeys plus attics. Tile-hung full height bay to garden elevation. Alterations to entrance elevation and additions, including bay added to E window of study and bedroom above, not to White's designs. Now The Old Vicarage. Stables demolished.
Sources: Plans and specification, QAB E1. EC 436. *E,* 21,1860, p. 326.

90. 1859. St Peter, Brimpton, Berkshire. Design of window in memory of the Rev. Edward Golding. *Stained glass:* Lavers & Barraud. Chancel S, two-lights depicting the Resurrection and Ascension above square panels of stylised flowers and leaves. Reinstated at building of new church 1869-72 (see nos 118, 159).
Sources: G, 14.9.1859, p. 788. *B,* 8.10.1859, p. 670.

91. 1859. St Andrew, Chilcomb, Hampshire. Reseating and repairs. *Incumbent:* Rev. Joseph Simmonds. Rubble flint with stone. S porch and W weather-boarded bell-cote. Altar rail, simple reading desk and benches.
Source: ICBS 5396, application but no plans or correspondence.

92. 1859-64. Bishop's Court, Clyst St Mary, Devon. Alterations and additions to house for John Garratt, Jr. *Stained glass:* Lavers & Barraud. *Triptych:* N.H.J. Westlake. *Tiles:* Godwin. Polychrome stone. Alterations to existing two-storey house, with new service wing to N. Extensive stencilled decoration to interior, typical pale stained glass, design of furniture. Chapel

fittings, including candelabra. Contents dispersed by sale, 1994. Glazed entrance porch dismantled.
Sources: E, 24, 1863, p. 167. *BN* 17.4.1863, p. 288. *G,* 5.8.1863, p. 727. KA extras, letter book 14.5.1864–15.10.1866.

93. 1859. St Matthew, Coldridge, Devon. Plans for reseating. *Incumbent:* Rev. Robert Kestell Cornish, brother of White's first wife (see nos1 185, 205, 275). Grant of funds cancelled 1864, so scheme presumably not implemented, although the choir stalls could be to White's design.
Source: ICBS 5468.

94. 1859–60. Vicarage, Great Maplestead, Essex. New house, stables, etc. *Incumbent:* Rev. Edgar Syritt Corrie (see nos 125, 316). *Builder:* Rayner & Runnacles. Polychrome brick. £1,312. Two storeys plus attics for the 'increasing family' of the incumbent. Top-lit staircase, window shutters and fireplaces survive. A modern extension to N. Now The Old Vicarage.
Sources: EC 4565. Building a/c, ERO D/P 83/3/3. *E,* 21, 1860, p. 115.

95. 1859. St James, Stoke Newington Road, Hackney, London. Reseating and decoration executed by J.W. Smith, Islington. £259. Polychrome decoration of interior of Sir Robert Smirke's church of 1821–4, together with reseating. Bombed in WW2 and later demolished.
Sources: B, 4.6.1859, p. 384; 24.9.1859, p. 640.

96. 1859. Trueloves, Ingatestone, Essex. New house, stables, and associated farm buildings for James Quick, a coffee planter. Polychrome brick. Two storeys plus attics. Jettied and braced three-storey porch on massive squat columns. Extensive alterations and modern additions. Stables have two-storey entrance gateway, single-storey wings round clerestoried central court. Single-storey dairy with roof supported on wooden piers on one side and gablets on each face. Now a Shaftesbury Society home.
Sources: E, 20, 1859, p. 211. E.E. Wilde, *Ingatestone & the Essex Great Road with Fryerning* (1913), p. 316, reports that it was a rebuilding. Copy of sale particulars, 1891, in the house.

97. 1859–64. Vicarage, Mithian, Cornwall. New house. *Incumbent:* Rev. Alfred Lord (see no. 14). *Builder:* W.W. Salmon. Stone. £1,000. Two storeys. Alterations, including exterior rendering, and extensive additions, but cusped staircase window, slate-roofed bays and principal staircase survive. Now The Old Vicarage.
Source: EC 4714.

98. 1859–60. School, North Kelsey, Lincolnshire. New school. *Incumbent:* Rev. William Frederick Chambers (see no. 112). Red and white brick. Photographs by Christopher Dalton show L-shaped building with battered chimney in the angle, large window rising through eaves to form half-hipped dormer, porch with long, low window, timberwork to gable end but no bellcote. Demolished.
Source: AASRP, 4, 1859–60, p. xxiv.

99. 1859. St Peter & St Giles, Sidbury, Devon. Restoration of the chancel for the Rev. Henry Fellowes. *Stained glass:* Lavers & Barraud. Walls pinned, opening of two Norman windows, new roof, flooring, choir stalls, pulpit, lectern. New three-light E window in memory of the

incumbent's son, the Rev. A. W. Dorset Fellowes of Nether Wallop, Hampshire, executed 'under the supervision of the architect'. All subsumed in later restorations.
Sources: Vestry Minutes, DRO 2096A/PV 5. *E,* 20, 1859, pp. 291-2. *G,* 7.9.1859, p. 766.

100. 1860-2. Rectory, Bradden, Northamptonshire. Rebuilding to new plan. *Incumbent:* Rev. Cornelius Ives, cousin of White's mother (see no. 78). Stone. Two storeys plus attics. Some twelve-pane sash windows perhaps from the previous house. Principal staircase and some shutters survive. Stables, dairy, etc. and garden walls, all with White's favourite crested ridge tiles. Now The Old Rectory.
Source: E, 21, 1860, p. 326.

101. 1860-1 St James, Bream, Gloucestershire. Enlargement. *Incumbent:* Rev. Cornelius Witherby (see no. 117). Stone. £1,440. Nave lengthened to W, new windows and higher roof, chancel extended to E and widened, new chancel arch, windows and higher roof, new gabled N aisle and arcade, NE vestry rebuilt, W octagonal bell tower demolished and replaced by new SW bell-cote. Altar rails and stained glass to E window appear to be to White's designs. Later alterations (not White) extended N aisle to E and moved S porch to W.
Sources: ICBS 5630. *G,* 1.5.1861, p. 410. Rev. E.F. Eales, *Notes 1896-1902.*

102. 1860-1. National Schools, Brimpton, Berkshire. Additions to school and house. *Builders:* Thomas Reynolds and John Rivers. Polychrome brick. £380. Existing infants' school extended to form boys' school with adjacent classroom, and girls' school at right-angles. House extended to provide sitting room with canted bay window and three bedrooms. House demolished, but girls' school survives as part of existing primary school.
Sources: Plans, BerksRO D/P26 28/2, 28/25; Vestry minutes, D/P26 8/2-3. SP.

103. 1860. Design for school, with chapel over, Buglawton, Cheshire. No further documentary or physical evidence found.
Source: E, 21, 1860, p. 325.

104. 1860-6. All Saints, (Low) Catton, E. Yorkshire. Chancel restoration for Mary and Lucy Gardiner, in memory of their brother, Henry, a former rector. *Stained glass:* Morris, Marshall, Faulkner & Co. Stone. Chancel roof raised, new windows with White's typical pale glazing, new N vestry, SW porch, pulpit, altar rail, choir stalls, wrought-iron painted and gilded candelabra. E window, Crucifixion, designed by E. Burne-Jones.
Source: E, 21, 1860, pp. 311, 328.

105. 1860-1. Vicarage, Chute, Wiltshire. Alterations and additions. *Incumbent:* Rev. Samuel Cosway. *Builder:* Annett. Brick. £400. Finance arranged by Rev. H.M. White of Andover (see nos 11, 25, 88, 145, 155). New lean-to study, butler's pantry, larder, dairy, with bedroom and garret over, and separate brewhouse. Additions later demolished.
Source: Plans, WRO D1/11/147.

106. 1860-1. St James, Claydon, Oxfordshire. Rebuilding, apart from tower and arcade. *Incumbent:* Rev. Thomas Henry Tait (see no. 53). *Builder:* Richard Wilson, Wardington. *Reredos:* Messrs Benham. Stone. £580. Nave and chancel, gabled N aisle, gabled S porch. Benches, font with cover, eagle lectern, chancel screen, choir stalls, sedilia, altar, reredos, now unfortunately painted over. Stone pulpit, with fine metal desk, has slate panels painted with stylised flowers, obviously to White's design.

Sources: Faculty, ORO ODP. c.748. Costs, Bod. MS. Top. Oxon. c.103, fol. 261. ICBS 5576. *E*, 22, 1861, pp. 60-1. *Official Catalogue of the International Exhibition of 1862*, Class XXX, [5716], 'reredos for Claydon Church, Oxon, with panels of enamelled slate'.

107. 1860. School, Hinton Charterhouse, Somerset. New 'mixed' and infants' school for Edward Talbot Day Foxcroft (formerly Jones). Stone. Delicate green and yellow stained glass in heads of large plate-traceried windows N and S of schoolroom, and ingenious stone fireplace with openings for convected warm air survive. Later alterations and additions. Now The Old School.

Sources: Correspondence, SomRO DD/RG 62. *E*, 21, 1860, p. 325.

108. 1860-1. School and mistress's house, Ingatestone, Essex. New school and house. Brick. Demolished.

Sources: Plans, ERO E/P 78/1. *E*, 21, 1860, p. 325.

109. 1860. Designs for cheap mission plate for Messrs Benham, London. Presumably that displayed in the Medieval Court of the Great Exhibition of 1862, see *Official Catalogue*, Class XXX [5716].

Source: E, 21, 1860, p. 200.

110. 1860-1. St George, Modbury, Devon. Restoration of sanctuary in memory of the Rev. Nutcombe Oxenham. *Stained glass:* Lavers & Barraud, five-light E window, 'subjects drawn by Mr Westlake, under Mr White's supervision'. Reredos (now in W baptistery) of inlaid geometric design, and eagle lectern appear to be to White's designs. Polychrome decoration of sanctuary has not survived.

Sources: E, 21, 1860, p. 181; 22, 1861, p. 285.

111. 1860. School, Monkton Deverill, Wiltshire. New school. *Incumbent:* Rev. William David Morrice, brother-in-law of White's first wife (see nos 20, 149). Stone. Single-storey, L-plan. Alterations, including loss of chimney, and additions. Now Old School.

Source: E, 21, 1860, p. 114.

112. 1860. All Hallows (St Nicholas), North Kelsey, Lincolnshire. Restoration and additions. *Incumbent:* Rev. William Frederick Chambers (see no. 98). Stone, some perhaps from demolished church of St Nicholas, South Kelsey, hence confusion over the dedication. New nave, gabled N aisle and NE vestry, parapet to tower. Benches, wrought iron decoration and desk to new wooden pulpit, delicate wrought-iron chancel screen, choir stalls.

Source: E, 21, 1860, p. 116.

113. *c.*1860. Sharow Lodge, Ripon, W. Yorkshire. Polychrome brick. A pair of two-storey semi-detached cottages with lean-to porches, half-hipped dormers, paired lancet windows under yellow and black brick voussoirs that indicate this date. Iron boundary railings and gates with ingenious latches.

112. 1860. All Hallows (St Nicholas), North Kelsey, Lincolnshire.

Source: 'Our Architects and their Works, no. 2, William White, F.S.A.', *BA*, 16.9.1881, pp. 464-5.

114. 1860. St Michael, Walton, Buckinghamshire. Restoration and additions to chancel (nave restored by G.G. Scott). *Incumbent:* Rev. George Wingate Pearse (see no. 115). *Stained glass:* Lavers & Barraud. *Font:* Kimberley, Banbury. Stone. New NE vestry. Recess created in chancel N wall to accommodate new Willis organ. New altar, altar rail, stone sedilia, oak choir stalls, pulpit, lectern and font. Decorative hinges to vestry door. E window repaired and 'glazed with stencilled quarries' that appear to be to White's design. All wooden fittings have been swept away. Now church of the Open University.
Sources: Faculty, BRO PR 217/6/2. *E,* 21, 1861, p. 61. *G,* 5.12.1860, p. 1058. KA extras.

115. 1860. Rectory, Walton, Buckinghamshire. Additions. *Incumbent:* Rev. George Wingate Pearse (see no. 114). Polychrome brick. New two-storey half-hipped entrance with wrought-

iron finial. Drawing room with bay window, and bedroom and dressing room above, and W service wing. Some 'internal polychromatic decoration' no longer visible. Now Walton Pre-Preparatory School & Nursery.
Sources: E, 21, 1861, p. 59. *G*, 5.12.1860, p. 1058.

116. 1861–3. St Mary, Beaminster, Dorset. Restoration and reseating. *Incumbent:* Rev. Alfred Codd (see nos 49, 89, 294). £2,160. New north porch and door. Repair of walls and windows. New roofs to nave and chancel. Incorporation into W end of S aisle of ancient Mort House, and reseating. Removal of galleries. Sedilia, screen, reredos.
Sources: Drawings, reports, DHC CW 9/11-12, CW 9/18-19. ICBS 5720. *CB*, 1863, p. 182.
1877–8. Restoration of tower. *Builder:* Charles Trask, Stoke-sub-Hamdon, *c*.£1,200. *Carving:* six statues for empty niches, Harry Hems, Exeter, £50. Stonework renewed. Pinnacles replaced and repaired.

117. 1861–2. School and master's house, Bream, Gloucestershire. New National Schools. *Incumbent:* Rev. Cornelius Witherby (see no. 101). Stone. £820. One mixed classroom and an infants' room. Adjoining to W, house with parlour, kitchen and scullery, and three bedrooms.
1872–3. Enlargement. Cross-wing to E providing boys' room. £425. Further additions and alterations (not to White's designs). Now Community Centre and Library.
Sources: Plan and correspondence, CERC. Rev. E.F. Eales, *Notes 1896-1902.*

118. 1861. St Peter, Brimpton, Berkshire. Design of window in memory of the Rev. Edward Cove. *Stained glass:* Lavers & Barraud. Although a brass plaque below the single lancet at the W end of the S aisle commemorates the Rev. Cove, the depiction of the Baptism of Christ does not appear to be a White design, and seems to have been cut down, perhaps at the rebuilding of the church, 1869-72 (see nos 90, 159).
Sources: B, 4.5.1861, p. 305. *G*, 1.5.1861, p. 410.

119. 1861. National Schools, Chacewater, Cornwall. Additions to school. Stone. NW wing added to 1848 school. Further extended by Silvanus Trevail, 1896. Still the village primary school.
Sources: Plan, CRO SRP13/2. *E*, 22, 1861, p. 236.

120. 1861. St John, Clanwilliam, South Africa. Font and cover. *Incumbent:* Rev. Thomas Browning, formerly tutor at Bishops Diocesan College. Octagonal Bath stone (now sadly painted white) on central stem surrounded by eight marble columns. Heavy pyramidal wooden cover with segments of diagonal boarding.
Source: KA plasterers.

121. 1861–3. St Nicholas, Combe St Nicholas, Somerset. Reseating and repairs. *Incumbent:* Rev. Hans Frederick Hamilton (see no. 85). Stone. £1,830. Extension of N and S aisles westwards, repair and repointing of walls, new nave roof and floor. Removal of W gallery, new benches, refixing of pulpit, new choir stalls, altar and rails. Unsigned, undated watercolour in the church shows proposed 1862 restoration, rejected as too costly, with hammerbeam roof decorated with wooden angels, heavily crocketted font cover and C15 rood screen in its original position.
Sources: Faculty plans, SomRO D/D/Cf 1862/1. ICBS 5894.

122. 1861. Rectory, Dartington, Devon. Restoration and extension. *Incumbent:* Rev. Richard Champernowne. Stone. Some re-modelling of the S (entrance) front and rebuilding of the E elevation with half-hipped roofs and dormers. Restoration of inner hall with arched doorways and gallery access to bedrooms. Altered 1928-9. Now The Old Postern, Schumacher College.
Source: E, 22, 1861, p. 284.

123. 1861-2. Vicarage, Elstead, Surrey. New house, stables, etc. *Incumbent:* Rev. Joseph Rhodes Charlesworth, whose wife was the sister of William Grey, White's brother-in-law. Stone. £1,280. Two storeys with typically varied gables and bays. Arch-braced landing anticipates Lutyens' design for Munstead Wood. Stables, walls and gateways of service area demolished. Now Bargate House.
Sources: Plans and specification, QAB E.63. *E*, 23, 1862, p. 125.

124. 1861-65. Christ Church, Freemantle, Southampton, Hampshire. New church. *Incumbent:* Rev. Abraham Sedgwick. Stone, with polychrome brick interior. £4,000. *Glass:* Baillie & Co., London. Nave with lean-to N and S aisles and gabled N and S transepts, gabled S porch, chancel with N and S aisles and NE vestry. Glass 'to be in large panes of rough plate, stencilled in simple ornamental patterns'.
Sources: ICBS 5618. *B*, 3.8.1861, p. 535. *E*, 23, 1862, pp. 123-4. *CB*, 1866, pp. 76-8.
1874-5. West tower and spire, £1,000.
Source: Centenary booklet 1865-1965, SAO PR/18/14/1-3.

125. 1861-2. St Giles, Great Maplestead, Essex. Enlargement and repairs. *Incumbent:* Rev. Edgar Syritt Corrie (see nos 94, 316). Flint and stone. £540. New lean-to N aisle and gabled transept, roof repairs. New benches, prayer desk, lectern and pulpit. Altar rail, painted wooden altar and wooden reredos with triptych of Crucifixion, Virgin Mary and St John, stained glass to three lancets of sanctuary, stencilled patterning to boarded sanctuary ceiling all appear to be by White.
Sources: Contract and specification, ERO D/P 83/6/1. ICBS 5779. *CB*, 1862, p. 62.

126. 1861-2. St Michael & All Angels, Great Torrington, Devon. Enlargement. *Incumbent:* Rev. Samuel Buckland. Stone. £1,700. *Stained glass:* Lavers & Barraud (Westlake). Removal of galleries and pews, new S porch and new windows throughout. Choir stalls, altar rail and nave benches. Three scenes from the Life of John the Baptist for the W window, the gift of the Rev. C. Palmer, designed by White. E window also appears to be by White, as does E gate to churchyard.
Sources: ICBS 5749. *E*, 22, 1861, p. 121. *BN*, 11.7.1862, p. 34. *CB*, 1863, p. 36. *TEDAS*, 2nd ser., 1, 1868, pp. 78, 191.

127. 1861-6. Holy Trinity, Little Woolstone, Buckinghamshire. Alterations and additions. *Incumbent:* Rev. Edward Hill (see no. 128). *Builder:* Kimberley, Banbury. *Stained glass:* design of E window by Frederick Preedy. Stone. £300. New chancel with fittings and NE vestry. Now Woolstone Community Centre.
Sources: ILN, 26.10.1861, p. 417. KA contract book 1866-71 and letter book no. 2 1866-68. BAL/V&A Preedy. Michael Kerney, *The Stained Glass of Frederick Preedy (1820-1898)* (2001), p. 101.

128. 1861. School and master's house, Little Woolstone, Buckinghamshire. New National School. *Incumbent:* Rev. Edward Hill (see no. 127). Polychrome brick. Two single-storey

schoolrooms in L-shape. Gabled brick bell-cote. Wood-block floor, iron and wood bench, and 'tortoise' stove survive. Attached two-storey master's residence. Modern additions and alterations. Now 19 Newport Road.
Source: E, 22, 1861, p. 59.

129. 1861-3. Preshute, Marlborough College, Wiltshire. Alterations and additions for the Rev. J. Franck Bright, housemaster. Brick. Extensive two- and three-storey additions to early C19 stone house to provide boarding accommodation. Modern alterations to interior.
Sources: Letter from White to Bursar Thomas, college archive. *VCH, Wiltshire,* 12, (1983), pp. 170-1.

130. 1861-2. Vicarage, Milcombe, Oxfordshire. New vicarage, stables, etc. *Incumbent:* Rev. Henry Charles Blagden. *Builder:* Kimberley & Hopcraft. Stone. £1,260. Two storeys plus attics provided seven bedrooms, and parochial room as well as a study. Rev. Blagden employed Kimberley in 1866 to build a new laundry adjacent without assistance from White. Modern alterations and additions. Now The Old Vicarage.
Sources: Correspondence, Bod. MS Top.Oxon.c.104, fols 43-8. EC 23964. KA contract book 1866-1871.

131. 1861-2. All Saints, Newland, Gloucestershire. Restoration. *Incumbent:* Rev. George Rideout. Stone. £2,500. Rebuilding of walls, new roofs to nave, aisles and chancel, new E window and clerestory, restoration of other windows. Demolition of vestry. Reseating on wood-block floor, choir stalls and lectern. Pulpit constructed from old oak from the roofs. New altar constructed from stone mensa previously laid in the floor. Massive stone lych-gate and shaft and base of churchyard cross probably by White.
Sources: ICBS 5832. *E*, 22, 1861, p. 236; 25, 1864, pp. 120-1, 264-6. *B*, 4.5.1861, p. 305. *G*, 1.5.1861, p. 410. *CB*, 1864, p. 37. White, 'Notes on Newland Church …', *TRIBA*, 14, 1863-4, pp. 29-44.

132. 1861-2. School and master's house, Oving, Buckinghamshire. New school. Brick. £280. L-shaped single-storey classroom and schoolroom with boys' and girls' entrances at E and W ends. Master's house not built. Insertion of floor and modern additions to N and W. Now The Old School.
Sources: Plans, BRO AR 39/65/43. *E*, 23,1862, p. 124.

133. 1861. St Mary, South Benfleet, Essex. Reseating and repairs. *Incumbent:* Rev. Thomas Julius Henderson. Stone. £110. Repair of S porch, lowering of nave floor, reseating, new E window, of which tracery glass only survived WW2.
Sources: ICBS 5876. *E*, 22, 1861, p. 285.

134. 1861-2. Rectory, Stanhoe, Norfolk. New rectory, stables, etc. *Incumbent:* Rev. Augustus William Noel. Flint and brick. £2,400. Some old bricks and tiles from the former farm buildings on site incorporated in this imposing two-storey plus attics house to Puginian 'pinwheel' plan. Study with dressing room (perhaps because no suitable vestry?). Staircases, fireplaces, cupboards, shutters and window ironmongery survive. Now The Old Rectory.
Sources: Plans and specification, NkRO DN/DPL 2/6/209. *E*, 22, 1861, p. 236.

135. 1861-3. St Mary the Virgin, Stockleigh Pomeroy, Devon. Restoration and repairs.
Incumbent: Rev. Robert Henry Fortescue. *Stained glass:* Lavers & Barraud. Stone. *c.*£1,300. Nave

134. 1861–2. Rectory, Stanhoe, Norfolk.

S wall, with new windows, and porch rebuilt, new roofs to nave and chancel. Tower parapet rebuilt, roughcast removed, new stringcourse and belfry windows. New floors and benches, incorporating old bench ends. Altar rails.
Source: E, 22, 1861, p. 285.

136. 1862. St Michael, Brixton Deverill, Wiltshire. Restoration and additions. *Incumbent:* Rev. Emmanuel Strickland. Stone. £300. Petition to reduce length of chancel contradicts report by *CB,* that it was doubled in length. New chancel roof, windows and fittings, including stone pulpit.
Sources: Faculty petition, WRO D1/61/4/22. *CB,* 1863, p. 74.

137. 1862–3. St Andrew, Caxton, Cambridgeshire. Restoration and reseating. *Incumbent:* Rev. Favill John Hopkins. Stone. £900. Rebuilding of lean-to S aisle and porch. New roofs and windows to nave, aisle and chancel. Arch between tower and nave opened. New floors and benches, incorporating old bench ends.
Sources: Plans and specification, CUL EDR D3/5 FAC/CAXTON 1862. ICBS 5896. *E*, 24, 1863, pp. 132–3. *CB,* 1863, p. 182.

138. 1862. St John, Coleford, Gloucestershire. Restoration of church of 1821. Demolished 1882, apart from tower of earlier church.
Source: CERC A124601.

139. 1862–3. National School, Cuddington, Buckinghamshire. New school. Polychrome brick. A single-storey mixed school, but with separate entrances for boys and girls, cross-gabled classroom, W bell-cote. Two-storey master's house at right-angles, linked to school by arched gateway. Modern alterations and additions, but still the village primary school.
Source: Plans, BRO AR 39/65/15.

140. 1862-7. St Philip, Fingo, Grahamstown, South Africa. Mission church instigated by Archdeacon Nathaniel J. Merriman (see no. 63). Polychrome brick. £1,580. Original plans commissioned from G.F. Bodley probably modified and adapted by White. Nave and apsidal chancel under continuous corrugated iron roof, lean-to S aisle, NW gabled porch, W bell-cote and lean-to narthex.
Sources: Letter, May 1862, SPG. *E*, 21, 1860, pp. 113; 25, 1864, p. 151. *Grahamstown Journal* 29.10.1866. R.D. Crozier, *Saint Bartholomew's Grahamstown 1860-1985* (1985), 7. G. Alex Bremner, 'Out of Africa: G.F. Bodley, William White, and the Anglican Mission Church of St Philip, Grahamstown, 1857-67', *AH*, 51, 2008, pp. 185-210.

141. 1862-3. All Saints, Great Bourton, Oxfordshire. Restoration and enlargement. *Incumbent:* Rev. Philip Hoste (see no. 203). *Builder:* Kimberley & Hopcraft, Banbury. Stone. £1,300. New N aisle, NE vestry and S porch. Choir stalls and pulpit with candelabra, oak font cover, sedilia, reredos with geometric inlaid decoration, painted metal altar cross.
Sources: ORO ODP. b.70, 'Wilberforce's Scrapbook', fol.228. ICBS 5938. KA letter book 1864-1866, and extras. *E*, 24, 1863, p. 133. Irene Poulton, *All Saints Great Bourton* (1977).
1882-3. Lych-gate with bell tower over for the Rev. Charles Cubitt in memory of his wife. Stone with timber bell tower under steep gabled roof. Wooden gates with decorative ironwork.

142. 1862-3. School and master's house, Great Maplestead, Essex. New school and house for Mrs Mary Gee of Earls Colne. Polychrome brick. £710. Schoolroom with cross-gabled classroom, attached to master's house by arch-braced covered passageway. Modern alterations and additions, but survives as village primary school.
Source: E, 23, 1862, pp. 124-5.

143. 1862-4. School and master's house, Heath & Reach, Bedfordshire. Mixed National School and classroom, but with separate entrances for girls and boys. Brick. Possibly a rebuilding or extension of the original 1846 school, as 'old window' is marked on S side of schoolroom and for kitchen and scullery of house. Designs for desks and benches similar to those for Andover (no. 88). Demolished 1992.
Source: Plans, BLA AD 3865 19/2-7.

144. 1862-3. Sick House, Marlborough College, Wiltshire. New infirmary. Polychrome brick. £1,900. Three storeys, the top floor designed as a reading room for junior boys with separate staircase. Loss of some chimneystacks and alteration of some windows. Now a boarding house.
Sources: Minutes of the council 1853-1873, minutes of general meetings 1845-93, college archive. *E*, 24, 1863, p. 131.

145. 1862-4. St John, Masbrough, Rotherham, W. Yorkshire. New church. *Curate:* Rev. H.M. White, William's brother (see nos 11, 25, 88, 105, 155). *Carving:* Kimberley, Banbury. Stone with brick. £3,700. The result of a competition (judged by the Ecclesiological Society), with one other entry. Clerestoried nave with lean-to N and S aisles each with gabled porch, hipped-roofed aisle W of N transept, chancel, lean-to NE vestry, SW gabled bell-cote. Benches on wood-block flooring, choir stalls, altar. Carved marble font with oak cover and oak alms box at a cost of £32.10.5, the gift of H.M. White. At the rededication of the chapel of Bishop's Court (no. 92), the offertory was devoted to the building of this church. Demolished 1976.

Sources: ICBS 5984. *E,* 23, 1862, pp. 178, 217; 24, 1863, p. 128; 26, 1865, pp. 50-1. *G,* 5.8.1863, p. 727. *AASRP,* 7, 1863-4, p. xcvi. *CB,* 1865, p. 88. KA letter book 1864-1866. Photos, 2032, 10019, RA.

146. 1862. St John, Sheep Lane, Potsgrove, Buckinghamshire. Apse added to existing school to form chapel. *Incumbent:* Rev. Norman Coles. *Glass:* Powell. Polychrome brick. Chapel area with two side windows of Powell's quarries, central window depicting St John, Minton tiled floor and plain fittings was screened off from schoolroom. No evidence of its survival.
Sources: Croydon's Weekly Standard 11.10.1862, BRO CRT 130 POT 2. *E,* 24, 1863, p. 130.

147. 1862-3. Du Boulay's, Winchester College, Edgar Road, Winchester, Hampshire. Boarding house for the Rev. James Thomas Houssemayne Du Boulay, brother-in-law of White's first wife. Flint and brick. First purpose-built boarding house outside the college precincts. Three storeys plus basement master's house with modern brick extension to street frontage and alterations to windows on garden elevation. Railings to basement, entrance door with stained glass above, staircase, fireplaces and shutters survive. Two- and three-storey boys' accommodation much altered and extended at various times.
Source: E, 24, 1863, p. 131.

148. 1862-63. St Mark, Woolston, Southampton, Hampshire. New church. *Incumbent:* Rev. John Silvester Davies. *Builder:* Bull, Southampton. Stone with polychrome brick interior. £2,500. Nave with lean-to N aisle, gabled N porch, N transept, NE vestry, chancel. 'Temporary' NW bell-cote (tower and spire never built). In C20 some interior brickwork painted white, and extension built adjacent to S porch.
Source: Centenary Booklet, SAO PR 27/39/1.
1866-7. Enlargement. *Incumbent:* Rev. Davies. *Builder:* W.H. Chapman. £980. S chancel aisle with apsidal E end intended to accommodate the organ, and S of that a cross-gabled choir vestry.
Sources: Minute book 1865, SAO PR 27/17. ICBS 6491. *CB,* 1867, p. 139.
1885-7. Enlargement. *Incumbent:* Rev. Geoffrey Hughes. *c.* £1,330. *Stained glass:* Morris, Marshall, Faulkner & Co. Gabled S aisle with SW porch and cross-gabled S transept. Organ moved to N transept. S chancel aisle seated and stained glass of Evangelists to designs of Burne-Jones in memory of Rev. Edward George Blomfield.
Source: Correspondence and minute book 1886, SAO PR 27/17

149. 1863-9. St Saviour, Aberdeen Park, Highbury, London. New church for the Rev. William David Morrice, brother-in-law of White's first wife (see nos 20, 111). *Builder:* Dove Bros, Islington. *Stained glass:* Lavers & Barraud. *Painted decoration:* Henry Davies. Polychrome brick. Nave with N and S lean-to aisles, SW gabled porch, N and S gabled transepts, chancel with N and S lean-to aisles to two westward bays, cross-gabled NE vestries, octagonal crossing tower and spire. All furniture and fittings by White, including reredos, design of decorative painting of lantern and part of chancel. Triptych of reredos no longer White's Agnus Dei flanked by two Sts John. Wrought-iron chancel railings and gates stolen, 1980s. Modern chimney to apex of N transept gable. Renovation by Dove Bros, 1984-6, included provision of aluminium gargoyles to tower and modern railings to churchyard. Now Florence Trust artists' studios. Wrought-iron arch to original entrance path survives amongst modern housing.
Sources: EC 21922. *G,* 17.10.1866, p. 1058; 17.3.1869, p. 295. *B,* 20.10.1866, pp. 360; 781-2; 27.7.1867, pp. 549-51. Drawings of N chancel wall, BAL Dove Y6/11.

150. 1863. Design for infant school, Buckingham. No further documentary or physical evidence found.
Source: E, 24, 1863, p. 131.

151. 1863. Altar table, Bishopscourt, Cape Town, South Africa. Design of oak table for the Bishop's residence. *Joiner:* Kimberley, Banbury. £2.9.9½. No evidence found of its survival.
Source: KA extras.

152. 1863-4. Rectory, Marchwood, Hampshire. Additions and improvements. *Incumbent:* Rev. John Durell Durell. *Builder:* Samuel, John & Walter Crook, Eling. Brick. £320. New service staircase and construction of attic bedrooms with dormer windows to Woodyer building. Extension of service area, new stables and carriage house. Stables demolished, service area altered. Now Dunclagh.
Source: Drawings, HRO 16M70/22/1-30.

153. 1863. Barton Hill, Marlborough College, Wiltshire. New house for the Rev. John Shearme Thomas, bursar. Brick. Thomas had to relinquish his role as housemaster on his marriage in 1863. Anticipating a time when housemasters might be married, White planned the house as the E side of a quadrangle, with dining hall to N and boys' studies on W and S, but only the house was built. Two storeys plus attics. Much altered and extended as boarding house, but timbered porch, shutters, fireplaces and stained glass window to staircase survive.
Source: Plans, college archive.

154. *c*.1863. Elmhurst, Marlborough College, Wiltshire. New boarding house. Brick. Adjacent and similar to, but more modest than Barton Hill. Much altered (including extensive tile-hanging) and extended, but still a boarding house.
Source: E, 24, 1863, p. 131.

155. 1863-4. Masbrough National Schools, Station Road, Masbrough, Rotherham, W. Yorkshire. New girls' and infants' schoolrooms and temporary boys' schoolroom probably instigated by the curate, William's brother, the Rev. H.M. White, (see nos 11, 25, 88, 105, 145). Brick. Extended to designs of C.C. Barras, 1887. Demolished 1960s.
Sources: 1864 report and accounts, ShA PR 32/65. Obituary, *RIBAJ*, 7, 1900, p. 146.

156. 1863-4. School and houses for master and mistress, Northchurch, Hertfordshire. New buildings for John Loxley of Norcott Court, site given by Earl Brownlow. School, flint with stone. Houses, polychrome brick. £1,650. A single-storey mixed schoolroom with SE classroom and separate entrances to E and W. Infants' schoolroom to N with N porch and NW classroom. Two-storey mistress's house to N with 'Club Room' at SW corner (upper storey of this room not built), and similar master's house to S. Loss of flèche from ridge, alterations and additions, but still the village primary school.
Sources: E, 26, 1865, p. 55. *BN*, 14.3.1873, pp. 300, 306-7.

157. 1863-5. St Peter, Peters Marland, Devon. Rebuilding, apart from tower. *Incumbent:* Ven. John Curzon Moore-Stevens of Winscott (no. 87). Stone. Nave and chancel, gabled N and S aisles, gabled S porch, NE lean-to vestry. Tiled flooring, font and cover, benches, choir stalls, altar

rail, altar table, screen to tower and stained glass tracery lights.
Sources: Drawings in church. *E*, 25, 1864, p. 248. *CB*, 1866, p. 40.

158. 1863–5. St Stephen, Reading, Berkshire. New church. *Incumbent:* Rev. Thomas Vincent Fosbery. *Builder:* Messrs Wheeler, Reading. *Carpenter:* James Matthews, Reading. Polychrome brick. £2,800. Nave, lean-to N aisle with gabled N porch, W bell-cote, chancel with N aisle and NE vestry. Gabled S aisle and S chancel aisle by C. Pemberton Leach added 1886, E clergy vestry added 1901. Demolished 1976.
Sources: BerksRO D/P 170/6/1; D/P 172/28/50. ICBS 6123. *E*, 25, 1864, p. 115. *BN*, 19.2.1864, p. 141. *CB*, 1865, p. 129. *Reading Mercury,* 13.2.1864; 18.3.1865.

159. 1864. St Peter, Brimpton, Berkshire. Design for alterations and enlargement. *Incumbent:* Rev. George Caffin. Not built. 1869–72 a completely new church built, designed by John Johnson.
Source: BerksRO Vestry Minutes 1861-1894, D/P 26/8/3.

160. 1864–81. St Lawrence, Broughton, Buckinghamshire. Restoration, in phases. *Incumbent:* Rev. John William Irving. *Lectern:* Harry Hems, Exeter. S porch rebuilt. New stonework to chancel windows. New choir stalls, altar rails and eagle lectern.
Source: CBells, 7.5.1881, p. 358.

161. 1864–6. School and master's house, Dolfor, (Montgomeryshire) Powys. Brick. Not more than £450. Schoolroom with classroom, separate porches and slate-covered bell-cote. Wooden tracery to windows, ironmongery to doors and iron gate. Three-bedroom house adjacent with modern windows and doors, now The Old School.
Source: E, 25, 1864, pp. 116, 247.

162. 1864–6. Holy Trinity, Drayton Parslow, Buckinghamshire. Enlargement, repair and reseating. *Incumbent:* Rev. Benjamin Spurrell. *Builder:* Kimberley, Banbury. Stone. £805. New nave roof, extension of chancel to E with new roof, E and SE windows. New flooring, benches, lectern, pulpit, choir stalls and sedilia. Carved stone reredos has not survived.
Sources: ICBS 6308. *CB,* 1866, p. 83. *E*, 28, 1867, p. 187. KA carpenter, plumbers etc., letter book 1864-6.

163. 1864–5. St John, Felbridge, Surrey. New church for Mr & Mrs George Gatty. Stone. Nave with lean-to N aisle, N and SW gabled porches and W bell-cote, chancel with gabled N chancel aisle. Benches and choir stalls survive re-ordering of 1972-4.
Sources: E, 25, 1864, p. 244. *CB*, 1865, p. 180. PCC, *Felbridge Parish and People* (1976), p. 11.

164. 1864–5. Vicarage, Felbridge, Surrey. New house. *Incumbent:* Rev. Edward Fellows. Stone. Demolished 1965.
Source: E, 25, 1864, p. 247.

165. 1864–6. St Martin, Fenny Stratford, Buckinghamshire. Enlargement. *Incumbent:* Rev. George W. Corker (see no. 202). Polychrome brick. £1,190. New nave (replacing S aisle of 1823), chancel, N chancel aisle to accommodate the organ and NE vestry, the C18 church forming a N aisle. Brick arcades, of herringbone and chevron patterns, some with stencilled over-painting.

Stained glass E window appears to be by White. C20 alterations, including extension of nave to W and new S aisle, new chancel fittings, extended vestries, and decoration of chancel ceiling. *Sources:* ICBS 6274. *CB,* 1866, p. 125. Edward Legg, *St Martin's Parish Church* (1986).

166. 1864–5. Vicarage, Finstock & Fawler, Oxfordshire. New house, stables, etc. *Incumbent:* Rev. Alfred Redifer. Stone. £1,300. Two storeys plus attics, with no ecclesiastical references. Characteristic bay windows and stained glass to inner entrance. Shutters, staircases, fireplaces and tiled floor to hall survive. Now The Old Vicarage.
Source: Diocesan grant, Bod. MS Top.Oxon.c.103, fols. 472-81.

167. 1864–9. All Saints, Gainsborough, Lincolnshire. Restoration. *Incumbent:* Rev. Jacob Clements. £500. Raising of chancel floor, new choir stalls, altar cloth and wall hangings to apse. Choir stalls survive.
Source: AASRP, 10, 1869-70, p. xiv.

168. 1864–6. Vicarage, Irton, (Cumberland) Cumbria. New house, stables, etc. *Incumbent:* Rev. Robert Gordon Calthrop (later took the name Collingwood) (see no. 233). *Builder:* John Thompson, Ravenglass. *Clerk of works:* Macklin. Stone. £1,700. Imposing two storeys plus attics. The 'waiting room for parishioners' commended by *The Ecclesiologist* retains its distinctive White stained glass and iron stanchions. Staircase, shutters and fireplaces survive, as do extensive outbuildings, walls, gates, etc.
Sources: EC 29798. *E,* 25, 1864, p. 117.

169. 1864–5. Nos 1–8, Selborne Place, Littlehampton, W. Sussex. Three pairs of semi-detached houses for White and his extended family, on land leased from the Duke of Norfolk. *Builder:* Robert Bushby, Littlehampton. Brick. Two storeys plus attics, with verandahs originally overlooking the sea. No. 1 for William White's family; no. 2 for the family of his brother, the Rev. Henry Master White; no. 3 for his widowed sister, Mary Martelli, and her children, designed to interconnect with no. 4 for his two spinster sisters, Frances & Emily White; nos 5 & 6 for his younger brother, John Edward White. No. 1 retains original honeycomb terracotta boundary walls and gate to original private access road, service area, stained glass, characteristic staircase joinery, wood-block flooring and door furniture. Nos 3-8 substantially altered and extended for business and residential use.
Sources: Plans, WSRO UD/LH/16/1. Miss H.M.White, *Cameos* (1960), BCA file 4, White 1. DMA papers of the 9th earl of Stamford, Box 14/2. Iris Jones & Daphne Stanford, *Littlehampton in Old Photographs* (1990), p. 41.

170. 1864–71. St Philip & St James, Maryfield, Antony, Cornwall. New church for William Henry Pole Carew (see no. 2). Stone. *Stained glass:* Clayton & Bell. Nave with lean-to N aisle, N transept, chancel with gabled N chancel aisle, W tower and spire. Extensive structural and applied polychromy to interior. All fittings to White's designs. Churchyard cross, walls and gates (woodwork renewed).
Sources: B, 19.5.1866, p. 360. Miss F. Julia Pole-Carew & Lieut A.C.W. Bevan, *The Story of Maryfield* (n.d.).

171. 1864. St Paul, Tupsley, Herefordshire. Design for limited competition. Design by Elmslie, Franey & Haddon of London, Malvern and Hereford chosen by Oxford Architectural

Society, the judges, but church built to design of another competitor, F.R. Kempson of Hereford. *Source: B,* 2.4.1864, p. 247.

172. 1865–90. All Saints, Bradford, Devon. Designs for restoration of chancel. *Incumbent:* Rev. John Carslake Duncan Yule.
Source: E, 26, 1865, p. 227.
1886. Restoration. *Incumbent:* Rev. Robert Lewis Bampfield. ICBS application reported that the chancel was still 'roofless'. In 1890 White refused to certify completion as 'A Resident layman so altered the work in the carrying out'.
Source: ICBS 9117.

173. 1865–6. National School, Bucknell, Oxfordshire. New school. *Incumbent:* Rev. William Master, brother of White's mother (see no. 48). Stone with brick dressings. Inscription near entrance 'WM / 65'. Extensively altered and extended, now Crossroads.
Source: KA letter book 1864–6.

174. 1865–70. St Mary, Cavendish, Suffolk. Restoration of the chancel. *Incumbent:* Rev. R. Godolphin Peter. *Builder:* Grimwood, Sudbury. *Carved reading desk:* Mr Cadge, Hartest. Flint with bands of clay tile. £770. N aisle extended to form lean-to N chancel aisle and vestry, repair of chancel roof. Reredos with temporary, painted zinc plates has disappeared, but Minton tiled floor, choir stalls, pulpit and reading desk survive.
Sources: E, 26, 1865, p. 56. SRO, *Bury & Norwich Post,* 19.10.1869.

175. 1865–7. St Michael, Cornwood, Devon. Restoration of chancel. *Incumbent:* Rev. Christopher Chadwick Bartholomew. Wooden altar with painted panels, alabaster reredos, extended to side walls, alabaster altar rail, wooden choir stalls and eagle lectern, tiled floor. Stained glass to three-light E window and four-light windows to S transept and to E end of S aisle all to White's designs.
Source: E, 26, 1865, p. 227.

176. 1865. St Andrew, Deal, Kent. Enlargement. *Incumbent:* Rev. Martin Edgar Benson. Stone. £850. Chancel extended to E, gabled N chancel aisle. Wooden chancel arch, choir stalls, altar rail. Choir stalls and sculptured reredos of three panels have not survived.
1866–7. Alterations and additions. *Incumbent:* Rev. Charles Shirley Woolmer. Demolition of old vestry and construction of gabled S chancel aisle, new NE vestry, £430.
Sources: CB, 1866, p. 83. *E,* 28, 1867, pp. 184–5. Gregory Holyoake, *Saint Andrew's Church Deal, The Boatmen's Church* (1984).

177. 1865–6. St Nicholas, Longparish, Hampshire. Alterations and additions. *Incumbent:* Rev. Henry Burnaby Greene. These 'Further embellishments' included a screen to the organ aisle and a metal cross with cresting added to the chancel screen, all swept away in a restoration of 1956. White's simple lychgate has survived.
Sources: E, 26, 1865, p. 227; 27, 1866, p. 251.

178. 1865–67. School, Loughton, Buckinghamshire. New school. Polychrome brick. Single-storey schoolroom with bell-turret to ridge, classroom and porch.

Source: E, 28, 1867, p. 186.

1892. Additional classroom at right-angles, with entrance and cloakroom. Now Old School House.
Source: Paul Woodfield & Milton Keynes Development Corporation, *A Guide to the Historic Buildings of Milton Keynes* (1986), p. 75.

179. 1865-6. Master's Lodge, Marlborough College, Marlborough, Wiltshire. New porch.
Builder: Hillier. Brick. Square, single-storey, buttressed, arches supported by columns with carved capitals, herringbone brickwork with open parapet.
Sources: E, 26, 1865, p. 227. Letters, college archives.

180. 1865. Designs for memorial brasses. No further documentary or physical evidence found.
Source: E, 26, 1865, p. 227.

181. *c*.1865. Rectory, Tarporley, Cheshire. Alterations and additions. *Incumbent:* Rev. James Hughes Cooper, rector 1865-88. Polychrome brick. Two-storey SE wing with bays and polygonal oriel, NE gabled oratory, alterations to windows and additions to W service wing. Gabled N porch is a modern replacement. Now The Old Rectory.
Source: BA, 16.9.1881, p. 465.

182. 1865-7. All Saints, Tilbrook, (Huntingdonshire) Bedfordshire. Restoration. *Incumbent:* Rev. Newton Barton Young. Stone. £1,400. Rebuilding of nave S wall and porch. New benches, chancel floor, choir stalls (incorporating some old fragments), pulpit of oak and wrought-iron, altar rails. Design of three-light stained glass E window, a gift of the duchess of Manchester.
Sources: G, 24.7.1867, p. 794. *AASRP*, 8, 1865-6, p. xxxv; 9, 1867-8, p. xlix.

183. 1866-8. St James & St John, Derwent, Derbyshire. New church. *Incumbent:* Rev. Francis Jourdain (see no. 330). Stone. £1,200. Nave with gabled S porch, N aisle, chancel with N chancel aisle and NE vestry. NW tower and spire added 1873. Body of church demolished 1944 prior to filling of Ladybower Reservoir. Tower blown up 1947.
Sources: Plans DerRO D2036 A/PI 10-17. ICBS 6519.

184. 1866-70. Humewood, Kiltegan, Co. Wicklow, Ireland. New house, stables, etc. for William Wentworth Fitzwilliam Dick, M.P. *Builder:* Albert Kimberley, Banbury. *Clerk of works:* Greenman (from 1867), George W. Chinnock of Bow (from August 1869). *Stained glass:* Lavers & Barraud. *Painted decoration:* Henry Davies to White's designs. Stone. £25,000. White's magnificent granite castle, two storeys with attics and semi-basement. Conversion of nurseries to ballroom, 1873, to design of James Brooks. Glazing, joinery, fireplaces, all to White's design. One original dining chair survives. Now in process of conversion to an hotel.
Sources: William White, 'Descriptive Sketch of a Mansion at Humewood, County Wicklow', *TRIBA*, 19, 1868-9, pp. 78-88. *B*, 8.8.1868, pp. 587-9. KA contract book 1866-71, letter books no. 2 1866-8, no. 3 1868-9, 1870, and no. 6. Album of photographs *c*.1875, WRO 947/2182.

185. 1866-7. Vicarage, Landkey, Devon. New house, stables, etc. *Incumbent:* Rev. Robert Kestell Cornish, brother of White's first wife (see nos 93, 205, 275). Stone with brick. £1,350.

Two storeys. A commodious storeroom opens off the study. Loss of service staircase and some modern alterations, but original door and window furniture, shutters and most fireplaces survive. A strange apsidal protuberance, with no internal or external access, has been constructed at the SW corner of the house. Now Glebe House.
Sources: Estimate, plans and specification, DRO Landkey faculty petitions.

186. 1866. Marlborough College, Marlborough, Wiltshire. Designs for additional buildings. Stone with brick. £4,800. Plans for a three-storey building to provide schoolrooms, classrooms and individual studies for eighteen boys and accommodation for a master. Not built.
Sources: Minutes of the council 1853-73, drawings, college archives.

187. 1866-7. Christ Church, Aldwarke Road, Parkgate, Rawmarsh, Rotherham, W. Yorkshire. New church. *Incumbent:* Rev. E. Wynne. Stone. £3,020. Nave, N aisle, NW bell-cote, S porch, chancel, N chancel aisle and NE vestry. Closed 1958 and later demolished.
Sources: ICBS 6575. Photo, 1914, ref. 3463, Rotherham Central Library.

188. 1866-7. St Mary, Salford, Bedfordshire. Restoration. *Incumbent:* Rev. Botelor Charnocke Smith. *Builder:* Kimberley, Banbury. Stone. £1,100. White's proposals to restore the roofs of the nave and S aisle to original pitch, and to restore and reopen S doors to nave and chancel not implemented. W brick tower removed and replaced, not by wooden bell-cote with broach spire as shown on drawings, but by curved timbers under gabled, shingled roof with central spirelet.

Restoration of gabled N porch, and roofs and windows of nave, S aisle and chancel, old benches, altar and pulpit. New wood floor to nave, Minton tiles to chancel, new choir stalls and altar rail. Pulpit removed 1916. Reredos and all but one choir stall removed 1971.
Sources: Report, estimate and drawings, BLA P77/2/0-1. *AASRP*, 9, 1867-8, p. xlix. KA contract book 1866-71, letter book no. 2 1866-8.

189. 1866. Tombstone. St James, Weybridge, Surrey. Marking grave of his first wife, Ellen Floyer White, who died 25 November 1866. Stone. Squat quatrefoil enclosing floriated cross inscribed 'let patience have her perfect work' and, verso, 'in christo et in pace'.
Source: Photograph, DMA EGR 5/2/8/12b.

190. 1867-8. St Mary, Bletchley, Buckinghamshire. Restoration. *Incumbent:* Rev. William Bennitt. *Builder:* Kimberley, Banbury. *Stained glass:* Powell, to designs of Henry Holiday. Stone. £1,690. Restoration of roofs and windows, tower, porch, arcades, pulpit and sedilia. New gargoyles to tower, windows to S elevation of nave and chancel, choir stalls, altar, reredos, altar rail, lectern and font. White instructed J.C. Powell to alter Holiday's design for the three-light S aisle E window, because he 'thought the figures in medallions too crowded, [and] would like nimbi introduced to all figures'. All fittings swept away in later re-orderings, but fine ironwork and brick wall with characteristic gate piers survives at S entrance to the churchyard.
Sources: Churchwardens' accounts, BRO PR 19/5/2. ICBS 6618. KA contract book 1866-71, letter book no. 2 1866-8, letter book no. 3 1868-9. Powell archives, V&A AAD/1977/1 order books 1/02:449, 1867; 1/02:466, 4.2.1868; cash book 1/55:017, March 1868.

191. 1867. Design of gate for Combe Court Lodge, Chiddingfold, near Godalming, Surrey. New oak gate and posts for George Henry Pinckard, director of Clerical, Medical & General Life Assurance Co. *Carpenter:* Kimberley, Banbury. £34. 7s. 9d.
Source: KA letter book No. 2 1866-8.

192. 1867-9. Lyndon Lodge, Golden Manor Road, Hanwell, (Middlesex) London. New house for White. *Builder:* Kimberley, Banbury. Windows in 'Own Room, Drawing Room, Dining Room' had shutters. Kimberley also supplied boundary fences and gates. Sold by White for £1,775 before March 1893. Later No. 29. Demolished in 1960s and replaced by block of flats.
Sources: KA contract book 1866-71, letter book no. 2 1866-8, letter book no. 3 1868-9. *TRIBA*, 19, 1868-9, p. 87. DMA papers of 9th earl of Stamford, box 14/2.

193. 1867-8. School and teacher's residence, Hanwell, Oxfordshire. Construction of school and alterations to cottage to form teacher's residence. *Incumbent:* Rev. Vincent Pearse, younger brother of the Rev. Thomas Pearse (see no. 270). *Builder:* Kimberley, Banbury. Stone. £290. Schoolroom with classroom and porch, but lacking its stone bell-cote, survives as The School House.
Sources: E, 28, 1867, p. 186. KA contract book 1866-71, letter book no. 3 1868-9.

194. 1867-8. St Michael, Heydour, Lincolnshire. Restoration. *Incumbent:* Rev. Gordon Frederick Deedes (see no. 66). Gate piers to S entrance to churchyard, outer gate to S porch, benches, font cover, stone pulpit with flowing ironwork to bookboard, lectern, chancel flooring,

choir stalls, altar, stencilled decoration to chancel walls. Reredos in memory of Marianne Deedes, the vicar's wife, who died 21.2.1867, has a diapered background similar to the wall decoration at Bishop's Court (no. 92).
Source: BoE: Lincolnshire (1989).

195. 1867. Rectory, Minchinhampton, Gloucestershire. Alterations. *Incumbent:* Rev. Edward Colnett Oldfield. All windows appear to be to White's design, also bays to rear, semi-circular porch to main entrance, and gate piers. Now Stuart Court.
Source: Plans and specification, GRO GDR/F4/1/Minchinhampton, too fragile to be accessed.

196. 1867-9. St Peter, Old Hurst, (Huntingdonshire) Cambridgeshire. Restoration. *Incumbent:* Rev. Charles Dashwood Goldie (see nos 197, 230). Stone. £280. Restoration of S wall, new lean-to N vestry, openings for two bells constructed in W gable, new continuous roof, the division between nave and chancel marked by a gabled wooden cross with a figure either side. New S door, benches, choir stalls and bowl for stem of ancient pillar piscina. The wooden figures from the roof are now preserved inside the church.
Source: ICBS 6778.

197. 1867-8. Vicarage, St Ives, (Huntingdonshire) Cambridgeshire. Enlargement. *Incumbent:* Rev. Charles Dashwood Goldie (see nos 196, 230). Stone. £930. Extensions to E, S and W to provide new drawing room, bays to study and dining room, entrance, private oratory, store room and pantry, with bedrooms and bathroom above. Demolished *c.*1964.
Sources: Plans, estimate and specification, CUL EDR/G3/39 MGA/99. Mid-C20 photograph, Norris Museum, St Ives PH/S.IVE/Chur.St/02.

198. 1867-8. St John the Baptist, St John, Cornwall. Restoration. *Incumbent:* Rev. John Lampen. Stone. Nave and chancel re-roofed, new choir stalls, pulpit and reredos. The latter has not survived. The three-light stained glass E window appears to be to White's design.
Source: E, 28, 1867, p. 187.

199. 1867-8. St James, Syresham, Northamptonshire. Restoration. *Incumbent:* Rev. Oswald Pattison Sargeant. *Builder:* Kimberley, Banbury. Restoration of walls, roofs and windows of nave, lean-to N and S aisles and chancel. Removal of tower parapet and construction of new spire in oak with oak shingles and gilded copper vane. New tiled flooring, choir stalls and altar rail. Painted decoration to chancel roof timbers appears to be to White's design.
Sources: KA contract book 1866-1871, letter book no. 2 1866-8, letter book no. 3 1868-9.

200. 1867-8. Aubrey Hall, Wardington, Oxfordshire. Additions to the home of the Misses Cooper (see no. 53). *Builder:* Kimberley, Banbury. Correspondence concerns installation of stone chimney-pieces, to White's designs, supplied by Bennetts of Birmingham. However bay windows, three-storey entrance porch, and skylight to staircase well with polychrome stencilled decoration (possibly executed by the lady owners), appear to be to White's designs.
Source: KA letter book no. 2 1866-8.

201. 1868-74. Holy Trinity, Barnstaple, Devon. Rebuilding, apart from nave N and S walls and tower. *Incumbent:* Rev. Christopher Haggard. *Stained glass:* Powell. Stone. £2,870. Aisleless

church of 1843-5 replaced by tall nave with lean-to N and S aisles, apsidal chancel with two cross-gabled aisles to N for organ and vestry, and two to S for seating. Stone chancel wall with brass decoration above and brass gates, brass altar rail, wooden choir stalls, stone pulpit and font.
Sources: DRO faculty petition; drawings 3053A/PW6. ICBS 6875.
1870. Memorial window in south aisle 'from a design of the architect'.
Source: B, 29.1.1870, p. 91.
1874. Design of stained glass windows of apse for J.P. Ffinch, executed by Powell. *c.*£264. N pair, Passion and Crucifixion; centre pair, Resurrection and Ascension; S pair, charge to St. Peter.
Source: Letter, DRO DD 35398A.

202. 1868-9. Vicarage, Fenny Stratford, Buckinghamshire. New house, stables, etc. *Incumbent:* Rev. George William Corker (see no. 165). *Builder:* Kimberley, Banbury. *Stained glass:* Lavers & Barraud. Polychrome brick. £1,830. Devon marble fireplaces with Minton tiles, windows 'similar to those for Golden Manor', and a large conservatory included in White's two-storey design. House extended for later incumbent. Demolished *c.*1957.
Sources: EC 10427/1. KA contract book 1866-71, letter book no. 3 1868-9.

203. 1868-9. Vicarage, Great Bourton, Oxfordshire. New house. *Incumbent:* Rev. Philip Hoste (see no. 141). *Builder:* Kimberley, Banbury. Stone. £800. Tiled hall floor, staircase, window ironmongery and some shutters and fireplaces survive. Originally a modest two-storey, three-bedroom house, it has been extended by two southerly wings. Now The Old Vicarage.
Sources: Correspondence, Bod. MS Top.Oxon.c.103, fols. 128-38. KA contract book 1866-71. A sheet referring to alterations and additions July 1874 by E.G. Bruton, architect of Oxford, KA box of unsorted documents.

204. 1868-9. Holy Trinity, Hinton-in-the-Hedges, Northamptonshire. Restoration. *Incumbent:* Rev. George Dewhurst Attwood. *Builder:* Kimberley, Banbury. Stone. Work included roofs, S porch, chancel windows, choir stalls, altar rail, lectern, benches, flooring and painted decoration to chancel roof.
Source: KA letter book no. 3 1868-9.

205. 1868-70. St Paul, Landkey, Devon. Restoration. *Incumbent:* Rev. Robert Kestell Cornish, brother of White's first wife (see nos 93, 185, 275). Stone. £600. Renewal of windows, new roof and arch to chancel, new benches, pulpit, lectern, screen, choir stalls, priest's door, sedilia, altar rail, altar, S chancel window and alterations to E window.
Sources: DRO faculty. ICBS 6998.

206. 1868-9. Marlborough College, Marlborough, Wiltshire. Design for additional house. Stone. £10,300. A large three-storey boarding house, including separate accommodation for a master and for a dame, with imposing carriage entrance under a tower. Not built.
Sources: Drawings and estimate, Minutes of the council 1853-1873, 25.11.1868, college archives.

207. 1868-9. Holy Trinity, North Ormesby, Middlesbrough, N. Yorkshire. New church. *Incumbent:* Rev. Vyvyan H. Moyle. *Builder:* A. King, N. Ormesby. *Clerk of works:* Job Sturdy. Polychrome brick. £2,050. Nave with lean-to N aisle, gabled N porch, chancel with N chancel aisle and NE vestry. Extended to design of Armfield & Bottomley, 1879.

1880-1. Addition of five-stage SW brick tower to White's design. Lady chapel and SW porch added in 1920s. Nave and chancel destroyed by fire 1977.
Sources: ICBS 6797. Gordon Barnes Collection, 'Churches Outside London', folder 'e'.

208. 1868-77. St Mary, Quainton, Buckinghamshire. Restoration. *Incumbent:* Rev. Thomas Chalk. *Builder* of first part (*c.* £400), Anthony & Son, Waddesdon. Stone. £2,600. Restoration of N and S arcades, clerestory, porch and NE vestry. New nave roof, benches, lectern, pulpit, chancel with choir stalls, piscina, sedilia, altar rail, altar, reredos.
Sources: ICBS 6860. Canon Clarke's MSS 'Churches in the Nineteenth Century', list of architects in Buckinghamshire. Laurie Cooper, *A Description of the Victorian Restoration of the Church by William White …* (1977).

209. 1868. St Nicholas, Ringwould, Kent. Restoration. *Incumbent:* Rev. Martin Edgar Benson. *Builder:* Messrs Denne, Walmer. *Fittings:* Kimberley, Banbury. Raising of nave roof to be continuous with that of chancel, insertion of new windows and chancel arch, exterior flint facing, restoration of N aisle roof, raising and tiling of floors. New font cover, lectern and oak reredos, painted and gilded to White's design, all by Kimberley, who may also have executed new benches, pulpit, choir stalls and altar. Reredos now in vestry.
Sources: CDCA U3/104/28/9. KA letter book no. 3 1868-9. *A Short History of Saint Nicholas, Ringwould* (n.d.).

210. 1868-?70. The How, St Ives, (Huntingdonshire) Cambridgeshire. New house, lodge, stables, etc. for Gilbert John Ansley. Polychrome brick. Corner stone dedication 30 June 1868 to John Henry Ansley, G.B. Ansley's father, who had died 1833. The family were related by marriage to White's sister, Mary Martelli. Large two storeys plus attics house, with varied gables, bays and prominent chimneys and bell-cote, overlooking the Ouse to the W of the town. Its exterior appears to have survived relatively unscathed.
Source: RIBAJ, 7, 1900, p. 146.

211. 1868-70. Rectory, Waddesdon, Buckinghamshire. New house, stables, etc. *Incumbent:* Rev. Thomas John Williams (see nos 266, 329). *Builders:* Crook and Goss, Aylesbury. Polychrome brick. £1,940. Old rectory on site further W demolished and some materials, e.g. principal staircase, incorporated in the new. Two additional windows to E elevation of study not shown on drawings. Some shutters, fireplaces, window and door ironmongery, tiled floors and stained glass survive. Modern extension to N. Now The Old Rectory.
Sources: Drawings, estimate and specification, ORO ODP.b.84. Carr & Gurney, *Waddesdon's Golden Years 1874-1925* (2004), p. 6.

212. 1868-82. St Petrock, West Anstey, Devon. Restoration. *Incumbent:* Rev. Robert Lewis Bampfield. *Builder:* John Cock, Jr. Stone. £2,456. Rebuilding of N wall, new roofs, windows, floors and benches (a few original benches restored), new chancel arch and additional arch at E end of N aisle, pulpit, lectern, chancel screen, choir stalls, altar and 5-panel wooden reredos painted to White's design.
Sources: Pre-restoration drawings by White in church. ICBS 8117. Canon Clarke's notebooks, XXVI, 47.

213. 1869-70. Holy Innocents, Adisham, Kent. Restoration. *Incumbent:* Rev. Henry Montagu Villiers. *Builder:* Messrs Denne, Walmer. *Stained glass:* Lavers, Barraud & Westlake. Flint with stone. £2,100. Restoration of gabled N porch, insertion of glazed wooden screen to form N vestry, vestry fittings and typical pale glazing, new flooring, benches, stem to font, pulpit, lectern. Chancel re-roofed with painted decoration to rafters, wall tiles, choir stalls, painted decoration to organ, altar rail with decorative ironwork, crocketted reredos. Rearrangement of 'all the old painted glass' under White's superintendence.
Sources: Drawings and specification for chancel, CDCA DCb/DC/A4/1. ICBS 6915. *BN,* 24.12.1869, p. 488. White, 'On Church Restoration', *CB,* 1873, pp. 92-4. Canon Clarke's notebooks, 1a, 170.

214. 1869-70. St Mary the Virgin, Eastry, Kent. Restoration. *Incumbent:* Rev. William Francis Shaw. *Builder:* Messrs Denne, Walmer. £672. New nave roof, restoration of walls. Penticed W porch between tower buttresses has White's distinctive ironwork and diagonal boarding. W door, chancel flooring, altar rail, stem and stairs to pulpit all appear to be to White's designs.
Sources: Denne's account, CDCA U3/275/6/B/12. Canon Clarke's notes, 'Church Restoration in the Nineteenth Century' Part 2 (1).

215. 1869. St Michael, Horsenden, Buckinghamshire. Alterations and additions. *Incumbent:* Rev. William Edwards Partridge. Flint with stone. Sanctuary extended eastwards, roof decorated with polychrome stencilled pattern of stylised flowers and geometric shapes. E wall decorated with encaustic and plain tiles in bold chevrons, choir stalls, sedilia, lectern, altar rail, tiled reredos with central panel low relief carving of Crucifixion in vesica framed with painted decoration, all appear to be to White's designs.
Source: Canon Clarke's notebooks, V, 111-12.

216. 1869-70. Rectory, Ickham, Kent. Enlargement and repairs. *Incumbent:* Rev. John Adolphus Wright (see no. 217). Brick. £740. New entrance porch and door, serving hatch and marble fireplace to dining room, bay window to study, dairy, larder, brew house, scullery, servants' bedrooms, repairs to stables and boundary fences. Porch and door survive, but other additions have been subsumed by later alterations. Now The Old Rectory.
Source: Drawings, estimate and specification, CDCA DCb/DC/I1/2.

217. 1869-70. St John the Evangelist, Ickham, Kent. Restoration. *Incumbent:* Rev. John Adolphus Wright (see no. 216). Re-pointing of chancel walls and provision of gutters and downpipes. It seems likely that the construction of the S porch and the splay-footed spire that in 1870 replaced a low spirelet, were part of White's commission.
Source: Estimate and specification, CDCA DCb/DC/I1/2.

218. 1869-71. St Peter, Linkenholt, Hampshire. Rebuilding, on a new site to new design. *Incumbent:* Rev. John Holmes Dixon. *Builder:* Messrs Hilary, Andover. *Stained glass:* E window, Clayton & Bell. Flint with brick and stone. £750. Nave with S porch and W timber bell-cote, chancel and lean-to NE vestry. S doorway, tub font and NE nave lancet survive from original C12 church that stood further N. White decorated the head of this window, and one to the SW, with fossil sea urchins found locally. Font cover, benches, pulpit, lectern, chancel screen and gates

and choir stalls all to White's design. Alterations to bell-cote have reduced the size of the original louvres.
Sources: ICBS 7222. Hants RO 109M70/PZ1 *Marlborough Times*, 4.10.1871.

219. 1869-73. Quy Hall, Stow-cum-Quy, Cambridge. Rebuilding for Clement Francis (see no. 274). *Builders:* Bell & Sons, Cambridge. *Painted decoration to White's designs:* Henry Davies. Polychrome brick. £4,535. Some roof timbers from the original house incorporated in two-storey design, largely to original footprint, with extended service wing to E. White's account shows charge of £21.10s. for 'Details of mural and ceiling Decoration' to three main rooms, previously presumed to be by Gambier Parry. White also listed 61 drawings for items of furniture. No records of dispersal of furniture can be found.
Source: Estimate, accounts, correspondence, Messrs Mills & Reeves Francis, CamRO R89/40.

220. 1869-70. St Mary, Wrawby, Lincolnshire. Reseating and repairs. *Incumbent:* Rev. John Rowland West. £530. Repairs to chancel roof and windows, choir stalls, altar rail, panelled reredos painted to White's design (surviving section now propped in S aisle), font cover. Pale glazing to N windows typical of White.
Source: ICBS 7027.

221. 1870-1. St Mary, Andover, Hampshire. Repairs, reseating and additions. *Incumbent:* Rev. Henry Brougham Bousfield (see no. 320). *Carving:* Harry Hems, Exeter. Flint with stone. Removal of W gallery and construction of new NE aisle to house the organ, construction of S entrance, formation of baptistery under W tower with alabaster font and crocketted cover. New benches for nave, alabaster pulpit, stone chancel screen, choir stalls, altar rail. Later reorderings have changed the position of the font, chancel screen and angel figures.
Sources: Plan and list of works proposed, HRO 21M65/11F/3; White's report on the stonework, HRO 60M67/PW45. *CBells,* 22.4.1887, p. 500.
1879. Construction of gabled S porch at the expense of Henry Pratt Moore and Sir Charles Pressly.
1887. 10 figures of angels by Harry Hems to White's designs erected on chancel screen at the expense of Miss E. Pressly in memory of her uncle, Henry Thompson.

222. 1870-1. School and master's house, Butlers Marston, Warwickshire. New school and master's house. Stone. Two-storey master's house with entrance porch. Attached gabled schoolroom, with pyramidal shingled timber bell-cote, and cross-gabled classroom with porch. Privies to S. Now The Old School House.
Source: Plans, WarRO CR962/31.

223. 1870-1. Holy Cross, Canterbury, Kent. Repairs. *Incumbent:* Rev. Francis Angel Smith. Flint with stone. £723. Repairs to tower so costly that proposed extension of S aisle for organ chamber not executed. Some characteristic pale pink and green quarries appear to be by White. Now the city's Guildhall.
Sources: ICBS 7114. Vestry book, CDCA U3/10/8/4.

224. 1870-1. Cotton Hall, Eton College, Eton, (Buckinghamshire) Berkshire. New boarding house for George Eden Marindin, Esq. *Builder:* Thomas Gregory, Clapham Junction.

Polychrome brick. £7,000. *Clerk of works:* Wooldridge. Three storeys provided accommodation for sixteen individual students' bedrooms, dame's sitting room and bedroom, and master's wing. Modern alterations and additions, particularly in service area, but many features survive, including stained glass to master's porch and screen in entrance hall, staircases, shutters, some fireplaces, and pierced wood dado panelling to boys' corridor.
Source: B, 29.7.1871, pp. 585-7.

225. 1870-1. St Petrock, Farringdon, Devon. Rebuilding. *Incumbent:* Rev. William Francis Gray. Stone. *Stained glass:* Hughes. An enlarged plan, comprising nave with lean-to N aisle and gabled SW porch, gabled N transept, narrower chancel with lean-to N aisle and vestry, small W tower with splay-footed shingled spire. Interior polychrome brick and stone with stencilled decoration. Tiled flooring, choir stalls, altar with painted stencilled patterns, pulpit, oak lectern with swivelling double desk, several small three-branch metal candle holders of sinuous stems and leaves.
Sources: DRO faculty petition with plans. *CBells,* 28.1.1871, p. 68.

226. *c.*1870. Trewan Hall, St Columb Major, Cornwall. Restoration and additions for Richard Henry Stackhouse Vyvyan. Stone. Probably included rebuilding of two-storey wing to form symmetrical U-shaped entrance façade, insertion of staircase window and other alterations to rear elevation.
Source: Charles Henderson, *St Columb Major, Church & Parish, Cornwall* (1930), p. 65.

227. 1870-1. Vicarage, St Margaret at Cliffe, Kent. New house. *Incumbent:* Rev. Ebenezer Curling Lucey. *Builder:* Messrs Denne, Walmer. Polychrome brick. £1,873. Two storeys. Modern alterations include loss of a chimney and addition of two canted bays to match one original, and two-storey extension to W. Now The Old Vicarage.
Source: EC 29513.

228. 1870-1. St Giles, Wigginton, Oxfordshire. Restoration. *Incumbent:* Rev. John Williams. *Builder:* George Anthony, Waddesdon. Stone. £680. Repairs to S aisle and re-roofing, repairs to chancel arch, removal of clerestory to chancel, lowering of walls and re-roofing, tiled floor, choir stalls and altar rail of wrought-iron.
Sources: Bod. MS Top.Oxon.c.104, fols. 471-83. F.D. Price, *The Church of St Giles, Wigginton* (1998).

229. 1871. School, Linkenholt, Hampshire. New school. Flint with brick. Adjacent to St Peter's church (no. 218). Single cell with pyramidal shingled timber bell-cote at W, SW gabled porch, half-hipped gabled S window decorated with fossilised sea urchins. Recent additions and conversion, now The Old School House.
Source: Drawings, TNA ED21/6483.

230. 1871-2. St John the Baptist, Woodhurst, (Huntingdonshire) Cambridgeshire. Restoration. *Incumbent:* Rev. Charles Dashwood Goldie (see nos. 196, 197). *Builders:* J. Saint, St Ives and Mr Bunting. Stone. £400. N wall rebuilt, new E window to gault brick chancel of 1848, roof to S aisle, S porch, choir stalls.
Sources: ICBS 7243. *B,* 1.6.1872, p. 430.

231. 1872. Vicarage, Figheldean, Wiltshire. New house, stables, etc. *Incumbent:* Rev. Henry Charles de St Croix. *Builder:* T. Gregory, Clapham Junction. Polychrome brick. Two storeys plus attics, L-shaped plan. Triangular oriel window as at Penmellyn (no. 56). Characteristic stained glass to porch and staircase, some fireplaces and principal staircase survive despite modern alterations and additions. Now Cleveland Lodge Care Home.

Source: B, 27.4.1872, p. 335.

232. 1872–3. St John the Baptist, Instow, Devon. Restoration. *Incumbent:* Rev. William Francis Dashwood Lang (see no. 335). Stone. £1,200. Buttresses to N and NW, restoration of S windows of transept and nave, new doors with stained glass to S porch, S door with sinuous curved hinges, stained glass to W screen, pulpit, lectern, font cover. Characteristic pale glazing with stained glass to tracery of W and N windows. Stained glass to three-light E window depicting Christ and John the Baptist, the Crucifixion, John baptising Christ, appears to be to White's design.
Sources: DRO faculty petition. Alison Grant & Others, *Instow, a History* (1999).

233. 1872. St Paul, Irton, (Cumberland) Cumbria. Additions. *Incumbent:* Rev. Robert Gordon Calthrop (who later took the name Collingwood) (see no. 168). *Mason:* Eugene Mayell, London. *Joiner:* Joseph Huddart, Santon Bridge. Pebble-dash with stone. Chancel extended eastwards with gabled N chancel aisle for organ and vestry. Hammer-beam roof to sanctuary. Characteristic stylised plant forms to stained glass in vestry. Nave dado panelling with quatrefoil piercings, and benches typical of White's work. Seven-light brass altar candlestick on triangular foot and decorative metal screen to tower also appear to be to his designs.

Sources: Irton & Drigg Parish Magazine, December 1872, CumRO YPR 13/52. *Cumberland Pacquet* 14.1.1873, p. 3.

234. 1872–4. St John the Baptist, Alma Street, Stockton-on-Tees, Co. Durham. New church. *Incumbent:* Rev. Thomas William McCririck. Polychrome brick. £3,400. Nave with lean-to N and S aisles, W narthex and bell-cote, gabled S porch, apsidal chancel and N and S transepts, NE apsidal vestry. Demolished 1985.

Source: ICBS 7415.

235. 1872–6. St Thomas of Canterbury, Tangley, Hampshire. Rebuilding. *Incumbent:* Rev. Charles Henry Everett. Flint, banded with edge-on red tiles, and stone. £610. Rebuilt mainly on original foundations. Nave with gabled S porch, apsidal chancel. New N chancel aisle. Tiled

flooring, benches, choir stalls, desk (to serve as pulpit and lectern) survive.

Sources: Plans and correspondence, HRO 21M65/395F/1. ICBS 7367 (mistakenly labelled St John the Baptist).

1897–8. W tower and spire. Stone with oak-shingled splay-footed spire. £800. Window replaced

N door to nave. All at sole expense of Henry Merceron, local landowner and churchwarden. *Source:* Drawing and correspondence, HRO 21M65/395F/2.

236. 1872-3. St Calixtus, West Down, Devon. Restoration and reseating. *Incumbent:* Rev. William Chorley Loveband. Stone. Re-roofing, including N transept where an unusual type of arch-braced, clasped-collar-purlin rafter roof was discovered beneath the plaster, new doorway to S porch, new windows to S wall of S transept, SW and N of nave, N wall of N chancel aisle (converted from former vestry), and E window of chancel. Nave benches, lectern, chancel screen, decoration of Commandment boards and painted wooden reredos appear to be to White's designs. *Sources:* DRO faculty petition. *TEDAS,* ser. 3rd ser., 31, 1878, pp. 79-80.

237. 1873-6. St Mark, Battersea Rise, Battersea, London. New church. *Incumbent:* Rev. John Erskine Clarke (see nos 242-4, 250, 261, 276, 281, 308-9, 325). *Builder:* Thomas Gregory, Clapham Junction. *Clerk of works:* W.H. Williams. *Stained glass and murals:* Lavers, Barraud & Westlake. *Carving:* Harry Hems, Exeter. *Marble pavement:* designed by Clayton & Bell, executed by Minton. *Stone font:* Faulkner, Exeter. Polychrome brick and concrete. £6,500. Nave with lean-to N and S aisles, gabled S porch, W narthex and NW half-hipped porch, SW tower with shingled splay-footed spire, hipped-roofed N and S transepts, canted apsidal chancel with pent-roofed ambulatory over brick-vaulted crypt vestries. Innovative construction of concrete within brick casing. Altar, reredos and benches removed, but all other fittings original. Additions 2006-7 have unfortunately obliterated the NW entrance.
Sources: ICBS 7658. *B,* 24.10.1874, p. 884. William White, 'A Brick and Concrete Church', *A,* 16.1.1875, pp. 39-43, *BN,* 15.1.1875, pp 77-8; 22.1.1875, pp. 105-6; 1.12.1876, p. 559. *CBells,* 3.10.1874, p. 518.
1887. Parish hall to N. Polychrome brick. Lower hipped porch to E echoed the apse of the church. Modern extensions. Demolished 2006.
Source: Anon., *History of St Mark's Church 1873-1933* (1933), p. 17.

238. 1873-94. St John the Evangelist, Brigg, Lincolnshire. Alterations and additions. *Incumbent:* Rev. William John Wylie. Removal of front four rows of pews to allow new choir stalls on raised flooring.
Sources: Lincoln, Rutland & Stamford Mercury, 13.6.1873, p. 5; 17.10.1873, p. 4. Canon Clarke's notebooks, XVII, 35.
1882. Alterations and improvements. *Incumbent:* Rev. Philip Henry Brierley. *Builder:* J. Parker, Brigg. New chancel screen, new steps to altar and tiled flooring.
Source: Lincoln, Rutland & Stamford Mercury, 15.12.1882.
1893-4. New W window to commemorate the Rev. Brierley. Three-lights, panels depicting the two Marys at the tomb, the Risen Christ in a *vesica piscis* above two Roman soldiers, and Christ with two disciples on the Road to Emmaus, with geometric patterns above and below.
Source: Parish Magazine no. 20, August 1894, quoted by Frank Henthorn, *A History of 19th Century Brigg* (1987), p. 126.

239. 1873-5. St Laurence & All Saints, Eastwood, Essex. Reseating. *Incumbent:* Rev. Arthur John Spencer. £180. Relocation of font, organ and stove, new benches to nave, pulpit and choir stalls.
Sources: Faculty petition, ERO D/CF 12/2. ICBS 7596.

240. 1873–5. St Peter & St Paul, West Wittering, W. Sussex. Reseating and repairs. *Incumbent:* Rev. William Underwood (see no. 347). Stone. £1,135. Re-roofing of nave and chancel, restoration of NW porch, S wall of S chancel aisle and all windows except two NW chancel. New benches, new choir stalls incorporating some C16 remnants, pulpit and conical font cover. *Source:* ICBS 7637.

241. 1874–6. St Cecilia, Adstock, Buckinghamshire. Reseating and repairs. *Incumbent:* Rev. James Niven. Stone. £1,010. Proposed NE vestry not built. Restoration of roofs, gabled S porch, and walls and windows of sanctuary. New benches, pulpit, lectern, choir stalls and wrought-iron three-light candelabra with sinuous stems and leaves.
Sources: Plan, BRO PR 2/3/4. ICBS 7784.

242. 1874(?)–5. St Mary, Battersea, London. New mortuary chapel in the parish churchyard. *Incumbent:* Rev. John Erskine Clarke (see nos 237, 243–4, 250, 261, 276, 281, 308–9, 325). Intended to accommodate corpses pulled from the river and those from overcrowded local dwellings. Photo in St Mary's parish room shows that as built it was smaller than White's surviving plans. Demolished post-1945.
Sources: Sketch and plans, LMA DW/OP/70/5. B, 21.11.1874, p. 964, refers to plan 'by the architect of the Rev. Erskine Clarke'.

243. 1874. St Peter, Plough Road, Battersea, London. New school/chapel. *Incumbent:* Rev. John Erskine Clarke (see nos 237, 242, 244, 250, 261, 276, 281, 308–9, 325). At sole cost of George Cubitt M.P. Extended S *c.*1879, with crow-stepped gables, probably to White's design, it became the church hall.
Sources: LMA P70/PET/78. *B*, 29.8.1874, p. 738.

244. 1874–7. Holy Trinity, Elvington, N. Yorkshire. Rebuilding for the Rev. John Erskine Clarke (see nos 237, 242–3, 250, 261, 276, 281, 308–9, 325). *Incumbent:* Rev. Alured James Clarke, his brother. *Builder:* J. Keswick & Sons, York. *Carving:* Cole, York. Stone. £1,810. White's drawing dated 15.12.1874 in the church shows proposed N elevation: nave with N aisle and chancel with polygonal apse, all under one roof, NE lean-to vestry, NW gabled timber porch, N tower with tall splay-footed spire. Drawings for faculty dated 15.12.1875 show lean-to N aisle, cross-gabled NE vestry and entrance under short NW tower with small splay-footed spire. As built, to N of site of previous church, nave and polygonal chancel with continuous roof, lean-to N aisle, large cross-gabled NE vestry, entrance under tall NW tower with short, splay-footed shingled spire. Benches, pulpit, metalwork lectern, choir stalls, altar rail, characteristic pale glazing. Boundary wall of brick and iron with iron gate.
Sources: Borthwick Institute, drawings and citation, FAC 1876/4a–d; contract, PR ELV 23. Canon Clarke's notebooks, XXIX, 18-19.

245. 1874–83. Holy Cross, Hoggeston, Buckinghamshire. Restoration and additions. *Incumbent:* Rev. Charles Henry Hole. *Builder:* George Hipwell Green, Wellingborough. Stone. £1,410. Execution delayed for lack of funds. Chancel rebuilt and extended eastwards with new window; small saddle-backed NW tower replaced with shingled tower with splay-footed spire, but other 1874 plans for rebuilding of aisles and addition of NE organ aisle and vestry not executed. New roofs throughout, repairs to N porch, walls and arcades. New benches, pulpit,

choir stalls, altar and rail, painted and gilded metal lectern and three-light candelabra, boundary walls and gates.
Sources: Drawings 1874, and alternative scheme of 1878, minutes, accounts and correspondence, parish box. Canon Clarke's notebooks, XV, 19.

246. 1874. St John the Divine, Sharow, W. Yorkshire. Enlargement. *Incumbent:* Rev. Edward Gray. Stone. Removal of W gallery, new chancel with lean-to S chancel aisle and lean-to N organ aisle. Original E window re-erected. New choir stalls.
Sources: BA, 16.9.1881, p. 465. Anon., *St. John's Church, Sharow, Historical Notes* (n.d.).

247. 1874-6. St Michael, Thorpe-le-Soken, Essex. Restoration and enlargement. *Incumbent:* Rev. Abraham Henry Rumboll. *Builder:* Henry Everett & Sons, Colchester. *Chancel floor tiles:* William Godwin, Lugwardine. Stone. £3,560. Rebuilding of S and E walls and S arcade, with addition of new NE vestry, restoration and re-facing of N wall and porch, restoration of roofs, new chancel arch, new windows throughout. New benches and seats for children, glazed wooden screen to tower, notice boards to porch, font cover, pulpit, lectern, chancel screen, choir stalls, sedilia, altar rail, altar, reredos (installed in the C20 to White's design but lacking his stencilled decorative scheme). Stained glass to three-light E window appears to be to White's design.
Sources: Drawings, ERO D/P 8/7/2. ICBS 7844.

248. 1874-5. Our Lady, Upton Pyne, Devon. Restoration and additions. *Incumbent:* Hon. and Rev. Francis Godolphin Pelham. *Builder:* Berry, Crediton. *Clerk of works:* J. Jerman. Stone. £1,920. Removal of plaster from exterior walls, re-roofing of nave, S aisle and chancel and restoration of gabled S porch and N arcade arches. Repairs to parapet and new pinnacles to tower. Construction of NE organ aisle and vestry and arched opening to SE to accommodate new pulpit. Removal of gallery and pews, new flooring, font and cover, wooden eagle lectern, choir stalls and altar rail. Incised patterning in the rendered walls implies a painted decorative scheme, not executed.
Sources: Woolmer's Exeter & Plymouth Gazette, 2.4.1875. Sir John Stratford Northcote, *Notes on the Parish Church of Upton Pyne* (n.d. [c.1890]).

249. 1875. Green Lane Parochial Schools, Battersea, London. Enlargement. *Builder:* Thomas Gregory, Clapham Junction. *Clerk of works:* W.H. Williams. Brick with stone. £2,000. A large room above the original girls' and infants' schools, and two classrooms to ground floor. Now Windsor Court, Vicarage Crescent.
Source: B, 20.11.1875, p. 1046.

250. 1875-6. St Peter, Plough Road, Battersea, London. New church. *Incumbent:* Rev. John Erskine Clarke (see nos 237, 242-4, 261, 276, 281, 308-9, 325). *Builder:* Carter, Holloway. *Clerk of works:* W.H. Williams. *Carving:* Harry Hems, Exeter. Polychrome brick. £10,000. To fit the awkward site, broad nave with lean-to N and S aisles, gabled SW porch, canted apsidal W end forming baptistery, shallow chancel with N choir aisle, S choir vestry, vestry, SE tower with banded brick and stone spire, further entrance porch in SE angle. Church demolished 1970 following a fire, tower and spire followed in 1994. Church hall (no. 243) survives.
Sources: ICBS 7897. *CBells,* 29.4.1876, p. 254; 8.7.1876, pp. 374-5. *B,* 22.7.1876, pp. 720-1. *CB,* 1877, p. 187.

251. 1875. St Mary the Virgin, Brighstone, Isle of Wight. Design of eagle lectern presented by Mrs Way, wife of churchwarden T. Way of Limerstone. Oak, made in London. £14.16s. Desk, supported by bird of ferocious appearance standing on an orb, swivels on an octagonal stem (brass candlesticks added 1904).
Source: William Edward Heygate [incumbent], 'Brighstone Parish Record AD 1870', June 1875.

252. 1875-6. St Michael & All Angels, Clyst Honiton, Devon. Enlargement. *Incumbent:* Rev. Henry Bawden Bullocke. Stone. £1,200. New S choir aisle, rebuilding of chancel, repairs to other walls, new roofs and windows except E and W of N aisle. New glazed wooden screen to tower, benches, pulpit, choir stalls and sedilia.
Source: ICBS 7893.

253. 1875. St Michael, Dinham Road, Exeter, Devon. Design of scheme of banners, wires, etc. to improve the acoustics. *Incumbent:* Rev. Joseph Theophilus Toye. No evidence that it was implemented.
Source: Drawings and letter, DRO 2931A/PW9-11, 2931A add2/PW15.

254. 1875. Vicarage, St Andrew's, Halstead, Essex. New parsonage. *Incumbent:* Rev. David Ingles. Brick. Two and three storeys with crested ridge tiles, tile hanging to some gable ends and to two-storey rear bay. Demolished 1975, some materials used in construction of modern vicarage.
Sources: RIBAJ, 7, 1900, p. 146. Doreen Potts, *Halstead's Heritage* (1989), p. 76.

255. 1875. St Mary the Virgin, Hawkwell, Essex. Restoration and reseating. *Incumbent:* Rev. James Augustus Montagu. Stone. £400-£500. Restoration of walls, gabled S porch and timber spire, new roof to chancel, new windows and N vestry. Removal of W gallery and pews, raising and re-tiling of chancel floor, reseating throughout. Vestry and fittings removed in re-ordering and construction of new N aisle 1995-6.
Source: Citation, ERO D/CF 14/6.

256. 1875. Rectory, Langdon Hills, Essex. New house, stables, etc. *Incumbent:* Rev. Eusebius Digby Cleaver (see no. 264). Polychrome brick. Two-storey house with projecting SW apsidal drawing room and prominent porch to N. Fine principal staircase with plate-traceried stained glass window, fireplaces, shutters to main ground-floor windows. Modern additions to E service area. Now The Old Rectory.
Source: BA, 16.9.1881, p. 465.

257. 1875. Little Woolpits House, location unknown. Fireplace details. No further documentary or physical evidence found.
Source: Drawings with those for restoration of church at Thorpe-le-Soken (no. 247), ERO D/P 8/7/2.

258. 1875-83. St Botolph, Slapton, Northamptonshire. Restoration and reseating. *Incumbent:* Rev. Philip Lockton. Stone. £864. Rebuilding of W tower with new foundations, removal of clerestory, new roofs and floors to nave and chancel. New benches, choir stalls, altar

rail, restoration of windows with characteristic pale glazing and spots of colour to tracery lights.
Sources: ICBS 8087. *AASRP,* 14, 1877-8, p. xli. D.R. Mumford, *St. Botolph's Church, Slapton* (1993).

259. 1875-6. St Mary & St John, Witham Friary, Somerset. Restoration and enlargement. *Incumbent:* Rev. Alexander D'Arblay Burney. Stone. £1,570. Demolition of 1828 W tower and gallery, removal of external plaster and pointing of walls, construction of additional W bay to nave with stone vault, W narthex forming entrance porch and vestry, bell-gable with circular window, restoration of nave roof and construction of twelve flying buttresses. New tiled flooring, benches, lectern, choir stalls, and notice board. Restoration of original font found in foundations of tower.
Sources: Faculty plans, SomRO D/D/Cf 1875/8. ICBS 7875. *CBells,* 30.9.1876, p. 519. White's description of his restoration, *Somersetshire Archæological & Natural History Society's Proceedings,* 24, 1878, pp. 25-32.

260. 1876-8. Cottage Hospital, Junction Road, Andover, Hampshire. New hospital. *Builder:* Annett & Sons. Polychrome brick. £1,490. Two storeys with diapered brickwork beneath the eaves and crested tiles to ridges and boundary walls. Extended 1906, demolished 1990s.
Sources: B, 4.3.1876, p. 225. *BA,* 16.9.1881, p. 464 (illustration). HRO 21M65/K1/2, *Winchester Diocesan Calendar* 1885. *The Hospital,* 29.6.1907, p. 352.

261. 1876-7. St Matthew, Gowrie Road, Battersea, London. New church. *Incumbent:* Rev. John Erskine Clarke (see nos 237, 242-4, 250, 276, 281, 308-9, 325). *Builder:* W.H. Williams, Clapham. *Carving and sgraffito panels:* Harry Hems, Exeter. Brick. £3,500. Nave and chancel under continuous roof, gabled clerestory, lean-to N and S aisles with wooden arcades, gabled S porch. In 1894 declared a temporary building by Ecclesiastical Commissioners and not suitable as a parish church. Closed 1941, demolished 1960s.
Sources: EC 52601. *B,* 2.6.1877, p. 568. Chas H. Drew, *The Story of St Matthew's* (1937).
1882-3. Parochial Room adjoining. *Builder:* William Ellis, Lavender Hill. £458. Demolished 1960s.
Sources: Minutes of committees, LMA P70/BAN/198; contract, P70/BAN/201/2. *B,* 30.9.1882, p. 447.

262. 1876. Tombstone, St Mary, Hanwell (Middlesex), London. Marking the grave of White's eldest child, Harriet Elizabeth White, buried 11 September, aged 19. Stone. Squat trefoil enclosing floriated cross, identical to that of her mother (no. 189).

263. 1876-80. Vicarage, St Mary Abbots, Kensington, London. New house, stables, boundary walls, etc. *Incumbent:* Hon. and Rev. Edward Carr Glyn. *Builder* (of stables and probably of the house): Thomas Gregory, Clapham Junction. Brick. £6,200. A large two-storey plus attics house with crow-stepped gables to N and W, a copper-covered spirelet over the top-lit staircase, large 'Prayer Room' to NE and semi-basement service areas. Demolished *c.* 1965.
Sources: Copy of drawings and photograph, church archive. EC 2179. *B,* 29.1.1876, p. 110. *BN,* 3.8.1877, p. 100.

264. 1876-7. St Mary the Virgin & All Saints, Langdon Hills, Essex. New church. *Incumbent:* Rev. Eusebius Cleaver (see no. 256). Stone. Nave with lean-to N aisle, gabled S porch, chancel, cross-gabled N organ aisle, NE vestry. Interior plastered, but brick splays to windows.

Tiled flooring, benches, wooden pulpit, chancel-rail, choir stalls and altar rail, stone sedilia and credence.
Source: BA, 16.9.1881, p. 465.

265. 1876–80. St Mary, Longstock, Hampshire. Rebuilding. *Incumbent:* Rev. William Ball Drewe. *Stained glass:* Mayer, Munich. Flint with tile bands, and stone. £2,600. Nave with gabled S porch, chancel, separately gabled N aisle and NE vestry/organ chamber, NW tower with splay-footed shingled spire with prominent wooden louvres. Built mainly on the old foundations. Wood-block flooring with tiles to chancel, wooden benches, lectern and pulpit with attached wrought-iron and gilded double candle holder, two gilded and painted *coronae luces.* Carved wooden chancel screen, choir stalls with detachable processional candleholders, carved wooden angels to chancel corbels. Chancel at cost of Lady Barker-Mill.
Sources: Plans and correspondence, HRO 21M65/236F/1. ICBS 8254.

266. 1876–87. St Mary Magdalene, Upper Winchendon, Buckinghamshire. Restoration. *Incumbent:* Rev. Thomas John Williams (see nos 211, 329). Stone. £1,277. Work delayed for lack of funds. Roofs and walls repaired, gabled S porch reconstructed, N door re-opened. New wood-block flooring under new benches, choir stalls, glazing to E window of N aisle. No evidence of proposed wooden cross reaching to the roof above the altar, or of reredos below with painted panels of the Virgin and St John 'for which the figures have already been drawn by the architect.'
Sources: ICBS 9139. *CBells,* 23.9.1887, p. 1029. C. Oscar Moreton, *Waddesdon and Over Winchendon …* (1929), p. 123.

267. 1877–80. St Mark, Hanwell, (Middlesex) London. New church. *Incumbent:* Rev. Derwent Coleridge. *Builder:* Thomas Gregory, Clapham Junction. Polychrome brick. £3,600. Nave with lean-to N and S aisles, gabled N porch, N and S transepts, apsidal chancel, SE gabled vestry; planned SW tower and spire not built. Wood-block flooring, tiling in chancel, pulpit, choir stalls, sedilia. Stone reredos with mosaic panels, in memory of Sir Alexander Young Spearman, possibly to White's design. Two stained glass windows, to his own designs, presented by White, one in memory of his daughter, Harriet Elizabeth; the other the first of a series of the twelve apostles. Declared redundant 1980. Windows vandalised before conversion into flats *c.*1985.
Sources: ICBS 8269. *CB,* 1879, pp. 78-81. *Middlesex County Times,* 24.11.1877; 1.2.1879; 3.5.1879; 13.12.1879; 3.1.1880. *CBells,* 5.6.1880, p. 435. Photos, T301, Ealing Local Studies Library.

268. 1877. St John the Evangelist, adjacent to Norfolk Wharf, Littlehampton, W. Sussex. *Builder:* Robert Bushby, Littlehampton. Wood framing, covered, inside and out, with lath and plaster. £648. Commissioned by local committee of parishioners, amongst whom were White's younger brother, J.E. White, and his sister, Mary Martelli, and her daughters, who objected to ritualistic practices of the Rev. Charles Rumball (see no. 319), of St Mary's parish church. St John's a temporary church 'for the performance of the services of the Established Church of England in a plain and simple manner'. Nave and N aisle, pulpit, prayer desk, chancel seat and altar rails.
1880. New S aisle and SE porch. £200.
A youth theatre by1950. Demolished 1967.

Sources: Minute book 1877-84, WSRO Par 126/12/1. *BN,* 11.3.1881, p. 260. H.J.F. Thompson, *Little Hampton Long Ago* (n.d.), pp. 95-6.

269. 1877-8. St Mary the Virgin, Selborne, Hampshire. Restoration. *Incumbent:* Rev. Edward Russel Bernard. *Builder:* Messrs Dyer, Alton. £1,300. New nave roof, rebuilding of N transept and reconstruction of N windows. Some old benches restored, new benches on wood-block flooring, old encaustic tiles laid at E end of S aisle.
Sources: Winchester Diocesan Calender, 1878, pp. 88-9. *CBells,* 24.11.1877, p. 610.

1882-3. Restoration of S aisle and porch. *Builder:* Messrs Dyer, Alton. £960. *Warming apparatus:* Messrs Haden, Trowbridge. Demolition and rebuilding of aisle E and S walls, restoration of windows, new roof. Reconstruction of three-light SE window and lancet immediately E of porch, and insertion of single lancet in place of similar three-light S window.
Sources: Hampshire Chronicle, 27.10.1883. *CBells,* 10.11.1883, p. 972.

1886. Rebuilding of E wall of chancel with new windows. *Stained glass:* Powell, in memory of the Rev. Frederick James Parsons, Crucifixion with Mary and St John, 'from Holiday's Lewes cartoons … to be submitted to Mr White'. New altar rails of wrought-iron and wood, now in the s aisle.
Sources: V&A Powell archive AAD/1977/1 order book 1/07:230, 8.4.1886; cash book 1/60:004, 21.9.1886. Gilbert White's House, Selborne, letter to the Rev. L. Sunderland from Mrs Bernard, 1939.

270. 1878. All Saints, Fittleton, Wiltshire. Restoration and reseating. *Incumbent:* Rev. Thomas Pearse, elder brother of the Rev. Vincent Pearse (see no. 193). £400. Repair and restoration of N pier, removal of plaster from internal walls of nave, N and S aisles and re-colouring. New wood-block flooring and benches.
Sources: Drawings and faculty, WRO D1/61/29/10. Canon Clarke's notebooks II, 154.

271. 1878. All Saints' School, Norfolk Square, Paddington, London. Alterations. *c.*£330. No further documentary or physical evidence found.
Source: B, 19.1.1878, p. 74.

272. 1878-82. Rigg's Hall, Shrewsbury School, Shrewsbury, Shropshire. New boarding house for 42 boys for the Rev. George Thomas Hall, brother of the Rev. E.G. Hall (see nos 297, 327). *Builder:* Oliver Jones, Shrewsbury. *Clerk of works:* George Smith. Polychrome brick. £11,000. Two parallel ranges of two and three storeys with cross range to form U-shape, similar to Churchill's Hall (no. 273). Circulating hot air heating and ventilation was commented on. Wooden plate tracery to staircase windows, characteristic wooden principal staircase and shallow arched alcoves to housemaster's accommodation have survived numerous alterations and additions.
Sources: B, 10.9.1881, pp. 330-5. *Eddowes's Shrewsbury Journal & Salopian Journal,* 2.8.1882, p. 5.

273. 1878-82. Churchill's Hall, Shrewsbury School, Shrewsbury, Shropshire. New boarding house for 42 boys for the Rev. Charles John Scott Churchill. *Builder:* Oliver Jones, Shrewsbury. *Clerk of works:* George Smith. Polychrome brick. £11,000. Two parallel ranges of two and three storeys with cross range to form U-shape. Circulating hot air heating and ventilation was commented on. Plan similar but not identical to Rigg's Hall (no. 272). Stone tracery with stained glass to staircase windows, wooden principal staircase, free-standing pillar between two

kitchen windows in housemaster's accommodation have survived numerous alterations and additions.

Sources: B, 10.9.1881, pp. 330-5. *Eddowes's Shrewsbury Journal & Salopian Journal,* 2.8.1882, p. 5.

274. 1878-80. St Mary, Stow-cum-Quy, Cambridge. Restoration. *Incumbent:* Rev. Edward Ventris. *Builder:* Foster, Bedford. *Altar:* Rattee & Kett, Cambridge. Flint with stone. £4,000. Largely at the expense of Clement Francis (see no. 219). Removal of lime render, repair of walls and windows and raising of roofs, removal of embattled brick parapet and timber upper stage of tower and replacement with plain stage of flint and stone, new N and S porches, new window openings. Removal of plaster from interior walls and re-plastering, new floors and benches, new wood and glazed screen to W tower vestry, wrought-iron three-branch candelabra fixed to seats, wooden eagle lectern, choir stalls, five-branch wrought-iron candelabrum on tripod base, stone reredos painted and gilded with characteristic geometric design. Wooden altar with stop chamfers and notching, but also with sinuous carved details reflecting those on the bench ends. *Sources:* Faculty petition, specification and correspondence, CUL EDR D3/5 FAC/Stow-cum-Quy 1879. *Cambridge Chronicle,* 27.11.1880, pp. 7-8; 4.12.1880, p. 8. *B*, 4.12.1880, p. 681. *BN,* 3.12.1880, p. 659. *CBells,* 4.12.1880, p. 3. Drawings of altar, CamRO R100/09, Rattee & Kett, 'Portfolio of drawings of fonts & covers', 680A & B.

275. 1879-89. St Lawrence's Cathedral, Antananarivo, Madagascar. New cathedral. First Anglican bishop, Robert Kestell Cornish, brother of White's first wife (see nos 93, 185, 205). Stone. £9,000. Impressively sited on a terrace and approached by a flight of steps. Nave with N and S lean-to aisles, gabled S porch, N and S transepts terminating in canted apsidal towers,

chancel with canted apse, SW polygonal baptistery. Characteristic glazing in pale greens and browns to lancet windows. Steep flight of steps to sanctuary, where boarded roof has stencilled patterns and pierced border. Open-backed wooden benches, pulpit, reading desk and conical cover to tall octagonal stone font.
Sources: G, 3.9.1879, p. 1247. *CBells,* 6.9.1879, p. 471. *Mission Field,* 1889, pp. 439-40; 1891, pp. 14-15. *ILN,* 11.1.1890, p. 43. B.F.L. Clarke, *Anglican Cathedrals Outside the British Isles* (1958), p. 48.

276. 1879-1902. St Mary le Park, Parkgate Road, Battersea, London. New church. *Incumbent:* Rev. John Erskine Clarke (see nos 237, 242-4, 250, 261, 281, 308-9, 325). *Builders:* Macey & Sons (1881-3); W. Johnson & Co. (1900-2). Brick with stone. £11,000. White's original plans for an impressive apsidal church of stone with twin towers and large chapter room perhaps intended as seat of new S London diocese. Scarcity of funds forced revised, less ambitious, plans in brick with stone bands, to be built in phases. Brass eagle lectern, wooden benches, pulpit and choir stalls.
Sources: B, 10.5.1879, p. 528; 19.5.1883, p. 690. Appeals, correspondence, etc., LMA P70/MRY/1. Plans, TNA WORK 16/9/1. ICBS 9874.
1881-3 Chancel with ambulatory and chancel S aisle.
1895-6 Three bays of nave and N aisle.
1900-2 NE vestries and N transept with bell tower. Architect J.S. Quilter may have altered White's plans.
Demolished 1967.

277. 1879-80. St Leonard, Bengeo, Hertfordshire. Restoration. *Incumbent:* Rev. George Ruthven Thornton. *Builder:* Ekins. £150. Making good of roof timbers and floors, renewal of some glazing, removal of external and internal plastering and of W gallery. Further restoration in 1883 by J.T. Micklethwaite.
Source: White's report, HertsRO D/P17/6/8.

278. 1879. St Nicholas, Kemerton, Worcestershire. Restoration of the tower by Disney L. Thorp in memory of his brother, Archdeacon Thomas Thorp. Stone. £520. Stained glass comprising triangles and spots of colour to tracery of central S window of nave appears to be by White, as does the lych-gate.
Sources: Canon Clarke's 'Church Restorations in the 19th Century', 2 (1); notebooks, XX, 32-3.

279. 1879. St John the Baptist, Leusdon, Devon. Design and execution of W window in memory of Charlotte Rosamond Larpent, the founder of the church, by 'upward of one hundred of her friends and fellow parishioners'. *Incumbent:* Rev. Francis Gilbert White, William's elder brother. *c.*£120. Four-lights, rectangular figurative panels depicting the Baptism of Christ, John preaching before Herod, Herod and Salome feasting, John's execution, with geometric patterns above and below and in tracery above. Plain glass retained on exterior to form double-glazing. The S door and the wooden font cover appear to be to White's designs also.
Sources: G, 24.12.1879, p. 1804. *CBells,* 17.1.1880, p. 106.

280. Pre-1881. Temporary church, Park Road, Brighton, E. Sussex. Brick, with wooden clerestory but stone pillars to arcades. £2,000. No documentary or physical evidence found.

Source: William White, 'Cheap Churches', *BN* 11.3.1881, p. 260.

281. 1880–3. St Michael, Cobham Close, Battersea, London. New church. *Incumbent:* Rev. John Erskine Clarke (see nos 237, 242–4, 250, 261, 276, 308–9, 325). *Builder:* J.D. Hodson. *Stained glass:* Lavers & Barraud. *Carving:* Harry Hems, Exeter, 10 gns. *Mosaic panels to reredos:* Mr Keith, £52. Polychrome brick. £4,500. A memorial to Philip Cazenove, who purchased the site, and the Rev. H.B. Verdon, curate. Nave, with gabled dormers, N and S aisles with crow-stepped gables, timber bell-cote, W narthex, S entrance through adjacent school, 1887–9, by W.E. Wallis. Polygonal apse with vestry crypt. Wood-block flooring, timber roof with iron ties, pale glazing, benches, font and cover, pulpit with angel carvings by Harry Hems, choir stalls, inlaid marble and gilded reredos to White's design.
Sources: Plans, correspondence, etc., LMA P70/MIC/47/10-12, P70/MIC/48/1-10, P70/MIC/49/3, P70/MIC/056. *BA,* 16.9.1881, p. 464. *B,* 8.10.1881, p. 470. *CBells,* 4.6.1881, p. 427.
1883. Decoration to ceiling of apse by Mr Clay to White's designs and cartoons. Now overpainted.
Source: B, 17.11.1883, p. 671.

282. Pre-1881. Residence, Copt Hewick, W. Yorkshire. No further documentary or physical evidence found.
Source: 'Our Architects and their Works, no. 2, Wm. White, F.S.A.', *BA,* 16.9.1881, p. 465.

283. Pre-1881. Haileybury, Hertfordshire. 'School work'. No further documentary or physical evidence found.
Source: 'Our Architects and their Works, no. 2, Wm. White, F.S.A.', *BA,* 16.9.1881, p. 465.

284. Pre-1881. Houses, Hanwell, (Middlesex) London. Described as 'in English Gothic'. No further documentary or physical evidence found.
Source: 'Our Architects and their Works, no. 2, Wm. White, F.S.A.' *BA,* 16.9.1881, p. 465.

285. 1880. St Mark, St Mark's Road, Kensington, London. Design and execution of E window. *Incumbent:* Rev. Edward K. Kendall. Three-lights depicting the Nativity, Resurrection and Ascension. Possibly in gratitude for the birth of White's only son, William, born 1879, following White's marriage here in 1877, to Jane Bateson Cooke. Demolished 1971.
Sources: G, 16.6.1880, p. 788. *CBells,* 19.6.1880, p. 462.

286. Pre-1881. Parochial Room, St Mary Abbots, Kensington, London. Shown adjacent to the vicarage (no. 263) on Ordnance Survey map, 1894–6, reproduced in *Survey of London,* 37, p. 43. Demolished.
Source: 'Our Architects and their Works, no. 2, Wm. White, F.S.A.', *BA,* 16.9.1881, p. 465.

287. Pre-1881. The Manor House, Marshalls, near Edgware, (Middlesex) London. No further documentary or physical evidence found.
Source: 'Our Architects and their Works, no. 2, Wm. White, F.S.A.', *BA,* 16.9.1881, p. 465.

288. 1880–3. St Andrew, Orwell, Cambridgeshire. Restoration. *Incumbent:* Rev. Henry Carr Archdale Tayler. *Builder:* Samuel Foster, Kempstone, Bedfordshire. *Tiles:* Godwin. Stone. £865.

Renewal of decayed chancel roof including coats of arms recorded in MSS at Wimpole Hall, and insertion of iron ties. Removal of external plaster and renewal of decayed portions of walls, including vestry, NW pier of chancel arch, S aisle, clerestory and porch. Renewal of decayed windows and reglazing, including discovery of two C14 windows in porch. Figures of crucified Christ and St John discovered above the wall plate placed at E end of S aisle. Tiled chancel floor, new altar and altar rails.
Sources: Report, estimate, etc., CamRO P127/6/2; P72/1/10. *CBells,* 6.10.1883, pp. 864-5. Canon Clarke's notebooks, VI, 102.

289. 1880-84. St Paul, Rondebosch, Cape Town, South Africa. New chancel with aisles and vestry. *Incumbent:* Rev. John Hopkins Badnall, formerly vice-principal of Bishops Diocesan College (no. 11). Stone. £8,500. Extension and widening of E bays of N and S lean-to aisles to form transepts, chancel with gabled N organ aisle and lean-to NE vestry, and gabled S chancel aisle. Altar and rails, credence and aumbry (accessible from both sanctuary and vestry), tiled flooring. Vestry extended *c.* 1933 and screen altered.
Sources: Drawings, UCTL, Baker collection, BC206. P.A. Millard, *Centenary of the Parish of Rondebosch 1834-1934* (1934).
1883. Choir stalls and reredos, commissioned by the Badnall family, executed by 'Zon', the Kaffir College, Zonnebloem, Cape Town.
Sources:: UCTL, R.R. Langham-Carter papers, reference lists and notes.
1892. Alabaster font with scenes from the life of Christ in relief, and wooden cover. Erected in memory of Maria Deane Anderson by her husband.
Sources: UCTL, R.R. Langham-Carter papers, reference lists and notes.

290. Pre-1881. Rugby, Warwickshire. 'School work'. No further documentary or physical evidence found.
Sources: 'Our Architects and Their Work, No. 2, Wm. White, F.S.A.', *BA,* 16.9.1881, p. 465. Also included in list of 'Scholastic houses and buildings', obituary, *RIBAJ,* 7, 1900, p. 146.

291. Pre-1881. Training College, Salisbury, Wiltshire. Additions. No further documentary or physical evidence found.
Sources: 'Our Architects and Their Work, No. 2, Wm. White, F.S.A.', *BA,* 16.9.1881, p. 465. Described as 'new wing to training college' in obituary, *RIBAJ,* 7, 1900, p. 146.

292. 1881-94. St Matthias' vicarage, Bethnal Green Road, Bethnal Green, London. New house. *Incumbent:* Rev. Francis William Briggs. *Builder:* Gregory & Co., Clapham Junction. Brick. £2,475. Long delays caused by lack of funds. Several revisions. Two storeys plus attics, crow-steps to main gables of entrance and rear elevations. Demolished 1960s.
Sources: Drawings and specification, Guildhall Library MSS.19224/494. EC 19995.

293. 1881. St Mary the Virgin, Brighstone, Isle of Wight. Design of stained glass windows for the Rev. William Edward Heygate (see no. 348). *Stained glass:* Pepper, London. £242. 10s. Three E lancets in chancel N wall, Carrying the Cross, Crucifixion and Descent; chancel E window, the Resurrection; S aisle E window, the Ascension.
Source: W.E. Heygate, *Brighstone Parish Record AD 1870,* April 1881.
1896-7. Stained glass window to E of S entrance in memory of Canon Heygate's daughter,

Anna Margaret, wife of the Rev. E. Judkins, (born St John the Baptist's Day (24 June) 1856, died 3.2.1896). Three-light window depicts St John preaching, his head being carried on a dish, and the Baptism of Christ, the composition of the latter very similar to that at Leusdon (no. 279). Design of pictorial panels and geometric patterning much bolder and simpler than the earlier work, and better for it.
Source: Sketch dated 10.2.1897, HRO 21M65/508F/3.

294. 1881–2. All Saints, Great Braxted, Essex. Design of memorial for Cecilia Mary (born 30.5.1854, died 29.9.1881), daughter of the Rev. Alfred Codd (see nos 49, 89, 116) and his wife, Emily (Du Cane). *Stonework and ironwork*: Harry Hems, Exeter. Marble cross on granite steps, decorative iron railings.
Source: Correspondence, DHC PE/BE/IN/10/6.

295. 1882–4. St Mary the Virgin, Essendon, Hertfordshire. Rebuilding, apart from the tower. *Incumbent:* Rev. Frederick T. Hetling. *Builder:* Gibbons & Co., Buntingford. *Carving:* Harry Hems, Exeter, £120. Flint with stone. £4,000. Nave with gabled N and S aisles, gabled N and S porches, chancel with N and S chancel aisles, sanctuary and SE vestry. Flint and stone in chequer pattern between windows and to gable ends. W door to tower and internal screen. Wooden benches, pulpit, lectern, choir stalls, altar. Stone angel to font by Harry Hems now adjacent. E end rebuilt 1917 following Zeppelin damage.
Sources: Faculty and plans, HertsRO D/P37/6/1-2. ICBS 8776.

296. 1883. All Saints Memorial Church, Alexandra Road, King William's Town, South Africa. Design of stained glass for J.J. Irvine in memory of Amy Douglas Irvine. Resurrection for three-light traceried E window. Church survives but present location of glass unknown.
Sources: BN, 1.6.1883, 767. *Kaffrarian Watchman*, 6.4.1883, 2–3.

297. 1883–5. St Silas, Penton Street, Pentonville, London. Enlargement. *Incumbent:* Rev. Edward Grainger Hall (see no. 327), brother of G.T. Hall (see no. 272). Stone. £784. New shallow chancel with arch, stalls, chancel screen, sedilia and credence added to S.S. Teulon's church of 1860.
Source: ICBS 8895.

298. 1883–4. St George, Ramsgate, Kent. Reseating and additions. *Incumbent:* Rev. Charles Edward Shirley Woolmer. Brick. £1,500. Extension of NE and SE single-storey brick vestries to form rectangle, not polygon, as White had originally planned, with castellated parapet to match existing. New wooden benches to nave, choir stalls, pulpit, brass altar rail, carved and painted stone reredos.
Sources: Faculty, CDCA DCb/EF Ramsgate St George 2. Canon Clarke's notebooks, IX, 104.

299. 1884. St Andrew, Beddingham, E. Sussex. Rebuilding of S aisle. *Incumbent:* Rev. William Parry Crawley. Flint with stone. Lean-to aisle with gabled porch, characteristic braces replicated in N aisle, together with typical pale glazing. E window of chancel, chancel S door, choir stalls, altar rail and lectern all obviously by White, as are bookboards, one under E window of N aisle and another in tower vestry.
Source: Canon Clarke's notebooks, II, 78.

300. 1884-5. St Colan, Colan, Devon. Restoration. *Incumbent:* Rev. John James Murley. Stone. £900. Repair of walls and roofs, new wooden gate to S porch. Wooden screen to S vestry, new benches on wood-block flooring, tiled floor to chancel, choir stalls, altar rails and altar, brass eagle lectern in memory of two daughters of Rev. John Creser, hanging oil lamps, characteristic pale glazing to N window. Lychgate at S entrance to churchyard with typical iron railings and crested ridge tiles to attached shed, probably by White also.
Sources: ICBS 8907. *CB,* 1884, p. 79.

301. 1884(?). Lower Denzell, Mawgan-in-Pydar, Cornwall. Alterations to house and construction of farm buildings for the Hoblyn estate. Stone. William Paget Hoblyn of Fir Hill was landowner and churchwarden of Colan (see no. 300). Hoblyn *v.* Hoblyn, Chancery Division, 1889, reveals that 'large sums' had been spent on improving the estate. Farmhouse has characteristic bay windows, arched entrance door with decorative hinges, porch to side entrance. Farm buildings now converted to dwellings, The Mill, The Stables, The Forge.
Source: Kelly's Directory of Devonshire & Cornwall, 1906, p. 218.

302. 1884-5. The Priory, Repton School, Repton, Derbyshire. New boarding house for John Henry Gurney, chief science master. Brick with stone tracery and mullions to some windows and doorways. Two storeys plus attics. Master's accommodation and service wing to S, dining hall (with later extension), studies and dormitories for 34 boys to N. Large tiled entrance hall with massive staircase and stone arcade, typical canted bays with window seats, some original window furniture, one fireplace and serving hatch survive. Extensive alterations and additions.
Source: Plans, Estates Bursary, Repton School.

303. 1884-86. St Peter, Shirwell, Devon. Restoration. *Incumbent:* Rev. James John Chichester. Stone. £1,336. Repair of walls, new roofs, floors and windows. Removal of W gallery, new benches on wood-block flooring, alteration and refitting of pulpit, new stalls, altar and rails.
Sources: Report, plans, specification and correspondence, DRO DD35398B/1-11. Canon Clarke's notebooks, XI, 127-8.

304. 1884-6. Moser's Hall, Shrewsbury School, Shrewsbury, Shropshire. New boarding house for Edward Branthwaite Moser. Brick. Three storeys, with varied gables, crested ridge tiles, star-shaped stacks, traceried staircase window, tile-hung bays, triangular dormer. Principal staircase and free-standing column between two kitchen windows and some stained glass have survived later alterations.
Source: School archives.

305. 1884. St Michael, Sowton, Devon. Design for extension of the churchyard. No evidence that it was ever implemented.
Source: Particulars, including plan, DRO 780A add/PB 216.

306. 1884-6. St James the Great, Torpoint, Cornwall. Enlargement. *Incumbent:* Rev. James Houssemayne Du Boulay (cousin of J.T.H. Du Boulay, see no.147). *Clerk of works:* J. Ambrose Rowse. Stone. £1,600. New chancel with gabled N chancel aisle, cross-gabled S choir vestry with lean-to clergy vestry to E. Most of the fittings swept away in later re-orderings, but pulpit

and lectern survive.
Sources: ICBS 9014. *CB,* 1885, pp. 3-4.

307. 1884-6. Winchester College, Winchester, Hampshire. New sanatorium and associated buildings. Brick. The design won highest award (Silver Medal) for 'School Sanatoria' at 1884 Health Exhibition. Two parallel two-storey ranges raised on shallow arches forming northerly Isolation (12 beds) and southerly Fever (20 beds) Blocks with circular turrets to contain WCs. Fever block with star-shaped chimneys; N projection containing staircase demolished. Isolation block with stone-arched verandahs, some removed, others glazed. Interiors much altered, but some arched doors with simple ironmongery survive. First-floor link building by Edward Cullinan Architects, 1980-4, to create College Art Department.
Administrative Residence: brick, two storeys plus attics, attached to W side of Isolation block provided accommodation for nurses. Demolished 1980s.
Sources: Drawings, 3.3.1884, college archives. *CBells,* 15.10.1886, p. 1107.
Laundry, brick, single-storey with gabled porch. Disinfection, washing, drying and ironing in logical sequence. Alterations to windows and doors, loss of chimneys and attached WC.
Source: Drawings 2.1.1885, college archives.

308. 1885. St Luke, Ramsden Road, Battersea, London. New church hall adjacent to the church. *Incumbent:* Rev. John Erskine Clarke (see nos 237, 242-4, 250, 261, 276, 281, 309, 325). Demolished 2004.
Sources: Battersea Parish Magazine January 1886. Photo in church.

309. 1885-6. St Stephen, Kersley Street, Battersea, London. New church. Rev. H. Percival Smith, curate-in-charge; rector, Rev. J. Erskine Clarke (see nos 237, 242-4, 250, 261, 276, 281, 308, 325). *Builder:* Holloway Bros. Polychrome brick. £5,320. Nave with W narthex and lean-to N and S aisles, chancel with canted sanctuary raised above vestries in crypt, N and S chancel aisles, the former beneath NE tower with splay-footed spire. Clock faces on each side of upper stage of tower have a pointed brick to mark each hour. Benches on wood-block flooring. Typical pale glazing. Stained glass to E window depicting condemnation and martyrdom of St Stephen below scenes of the Crucifixion and Ascension designed by White. Modern temporary wall to W of chancel, but pulpit, crocketted sedilia and aumbry survive.
Sources: Drawings, TNA WORK 16/9/4. ICBS 9047. EC 66836. *CB,* 1885, p. 6; 1887, pp. 8-11. *CBells,* 19.11.1886, p. 1217.

310. 1885-6. St John the Baptist, East Down, Devon. Restoration and reseating. *Incumbent:* Rev. William Edward Durham. Stone. £1,260. Restoration of roofs, most walls, S porch, new windows throughout. New benches, lectern, altar rail and stone reredos.
Sources: ICBS 9060. *CB,* 1886, p. 64.

311. 1885-6. St Peter, Little Comberton, Worcestershire. Restoration and enlargement. *Incumbent:* Rev. Edward Spencer Lowndes. *Builder:* Collins, Tewkesbury. Polychrome stone. £1,700. Restoration of N porch with new door, three lancet windows inserted in N wall of nave, new roofs to W tower, nave and chancel, new wooden chancel arch with six small stained glass windows, lean-to N chancel aisle, cross-gabled S chancel aisle and S transept. New benches

on wood-block flooring, pulpit, wooden eagle lectern, chancel rail, tiled floor, choir stalls, altar rails and altar.
Sources: AASRP, 18, 1885-6, pp. lc-lci. Canon Clarke's notebooks, Glos, 21.

312. 1886-8. St Brannoc, Braunton, Devon. Restoration. *Incumbent:* Rev. William Genn Morcom. £1,220. Repairs to tower, bell cage and roofs, particularly of the 34ft wide nave, where White inserted iron ties.
Sources: ICBS 9107. *CBells,* 27.7.1888, p. 840. *TEDAS*, 5, 1892, pp. 186-7.

313. 1886-7. St Leonard, Sandridge, Hertfordshire. Repairs and enlargement. *Incumbent:* Rev. John Griffith. *Builder:* Thomas Gregory & Co., Clapham Junction. Flint with stone; concrete. £3,600. 'Flimsy' 1837 rebuilt tower replaced by a concrete one, faced with flint outside and brick inside, with low splay-footed shingled spire. Lean-to N and S aisles extended W to enclose tower. New nave roof and clerestory, half-timbering with narrow windows to E gable of nave, repairs to gabled N and S porches and window tracery. Retiling of chancel roof. Walling above Norman chancel arch replaced with timberwork. New benches on wood-block flooring, old encaustic tiles placed in chancel, carved stone pulpit, wooden eagle lectern, choir stalls, typical pale glazing.
Sources: Faculty, HertsRO DSA1/15/4. ICBS 9074. *CB,* 1886, p. 61. *CBells,* 17.6.1887, p. 694. Canon Clarke's notebooks, XIX, 36.

314. 1887. St Clement, Leigh-on-Sea, Essex. Stained glass window, 'designed and drawn' in memory of Bishop Robert Eden of Moray and Ross, a former rector, and his wife Emma. Below depiction of St Andrew, a medallion featuring a small ship to commemorate Eden's gift of the mission ship *Hawk* to Bishop Feild of Newfoundland, whose chaplain had been White's elder brother, Francis Gilbert White (see no. 279).
Sources: CBells, 22.4.1887, p. 501. G, 27.4.1887, p. 640.

315. 1887-8. Vicarage, Stow-cum-Quy, Cambridge. New house, stables, etc. *Incumbent:* Rev. Frederick Watson. *Builder:* J.H. Prime, Cambridge. Brick. £1,560. Two storeys plus attics and cellar. Principal and service staircases, characteristic glazing, sinuous door and window ironmongery, fireplaces, shutters to reception rooms, shallow arched recesses with cupboards beneath in drawing room. Modern glazed door to entrance porch.
Sources: EC 8174. Specification, CamRO P146/3/3. Copies of drawings, now lost, kindly given to the author by Brenda Watkin.

316. 1888-9. St James the Great, Greenstead Green, Essex. New oak chancel screen for the Rev. Edgar Syritt Corrie (see nos 94, 125). *Joiner:* William Dart, Crediton. A memorial to two members of the vicar's family. Light tracery in the upper part is surmounted with ornamental cresting.
Sources: CBells, 18.1.1889, p. 164. Canon Clarke's notebooks, XXIX, 79-80.

317. 1888-9. St Augustine, Heanton Punchardon, Devon. Restoration. *Incumbent:* Rev. Charles Edward Lamb. *Builder:* none, local tradesmen under White's direction. W tower restored and opened into nave, bells re-hung, new windows to nave and chancel with pale glazing. Crested ridge tiles imply work to roofs. W gallery and old pews removed, new benches, pulpit, wooden eagle lectern and choir stalls. Perpendicular screen that had been moved one bay E restored

to original position and extended across N aisle. Whitewash removed from chancel tomb of Richard Coffin (d.1523).
Sources: CBells, 22.3.1889, pp. 380-1. *TEDAS,* 5, 1892, pp. 185-6.

318. 1888-98. St Peter, Hurstbourne Tarrant, Hampshire. Restoration. *Incumbent:* Rev. Francis Henry Sumner. Flint with brick and stone. £1,020. Repair of roofs, removal of one clerestory window, addition of shingled splay-footed spire to W tower. Installation of heating apparatus, re-flooring and reseating nave, new wooden chancel screen, and reredos (now used to store hymn books), all executed as funds became available. S porch rebuilt 1908 to modified version of White's plan.
Sources: ICBS 9390. Drawings, faculty petition, etc., HRO 21M65/205F/1. *CB,* 1890, p. 3.

319. 1888-90. St Mary, Littlehampton, W. Sussex. Rebuilding. *Incumbent:* Rev. Charles Rumball (see no. 268). Brick. Less than £1,000. For lack of funds, only the chancel, N organ aisle and lean-to SE vestry built. Very large five-light geometrical E window set high to accommodate existing altar and reredos. Chancel arch of three orders of moulded brick, pulpit, low wooden screen, choir stalls with three-branched candelabra. Church completely rebuilt to design of Randoll Blacking, 1934.
Sources: ICBS 9282. *CB,* 1888, pp. 18-20. Photos, WSRO PH4363, PH680. D. Robert Ellery, *Littlehampton, A Pictorial History* (1991), fig. 70.

320. 1888-90. St Alban's Cathedral, Pretoria, South Africa. Design for new cathedral. First Anglican bishop, Henry Brougham Bousfield (see no. 221). *Builder:* Munro. *Superintending architect:* F. Emley. Brick. Foundation stone laid 27.3.1890 for extension E of existing church to cost *c.*£2,000. Plan to be cruciform with central tower and spire, chancel and transepts with apsidal ends. Not built, presumably because of lack of funds and political upheavals. Foundation stone destroyed by fire, 1956.
Sources: The Press, Pretoria, 28.3.1890, p. 2. *BN,* 1890, pp. 569-70. B.F.L. Clarke, *Anglican Cathedrals Outside the British Isles* (1958), pp. 31-2.

321. 1888. All Saints, Finchley Road, St John's Wood, London. Design for parish room and Sunday school on N side of the church. *Incumbent:* Rev. A. Spencer. Estimate £3,000. Not built.
Source: ECE/7/1/17408.

322. 1889. Christ Church, Battersea Park Road, Battersea, London. Design for small houses on unconsecrated part of churchyard. *Incumbent:* Rev. Patrick Watson. Not built.
Source: EC 15137.

323. 1889. St Peter, Mount Park Road, Ealing, London. Design for limited competition for new church. Sir Arthur Blomfield and Ewan Christian declined to enter. F.G. Knight (*Quis*) and White (*Fundamentaur*) unsuccessful, the commission awarded to J.D. Sedding (*New and Old*).
Source: Minutes of Church Building Committee, LMA DRO/101/064.

324. Pre-1890. Public Steam Laundry, Hertford, Hertfordshire. Laundry with associated lodge and stables. No further documentary or physical evidence found.

Sources: 'Contemporary British Architects', *BN* 31.1.1890, p. 169. Obituary *B,* 27.1.1900, p. 91.

325. 1890–97. St Luke, Ramsden Road, Battersea, London. Marble and oak fittings. *Incumbent:* Rev. John Erskine Clarke (see nos 237, 242–4, 250, 261, 276, 281, 308–9). *Stone carving:* Farmer & Brindley. *Wood carving:* Harry Hems, Exeter.
1890. Alabaster and marble pulpit, the gift of J.S. Jarvis.
1894. Alabaster and marble chancel screen (the agate balls were added later).
1896. Oak sedilia in memory of Robert Francis and Mary Emma Cook, donated by their friends.
1897. Oak choir stalls and bishop's throne.
A fine wooden eagle lectern is surely also to White's design.
Sources: CBells, 28.5.1897, 539. B.F.L. Clarke, *Parish Churches of London* (1966), 197. Gordon Huelin, *St Luke's Battersea* (1989).

326. 1890–3. Bishop's Palace (Bishopgarth), Westfield Road, Wakefield, W. Yorkshire. New house, stables, lodges, etc. to accommodate the first bishop, William Walsham How. Brick. Three storeys in characteristic L-shaped plan around a top-lit central hall, with brick vaulted entrance below four-storey tower. Individual bedrooms for ten trainee priests necessitated large dining hall, as well as 'Examination Hall' above the chapel. Fine galleried principal staircase, some fireplaces, doors and stained glass have survived sweeping alterations since sale to local authority, 1940. Now West Yorkshire Police Training School.
Sources: Drawings, WYAS WMD5/2/13 box 43, no. 2952. *CBells,* 15.8.1890, p. 661; 6.11.1891, p. 924; 14.4.1893, p. 366. *Wakefield Diocesan Gazette,* vols 1–2.
Trowel, designed by White, presented to Mrs Boyd Carpenter, wife of bishop of Ripon, for laying foundation stone, 24.10.1891, not found.

327. 1890–2. St Anne, Wandsworth, London. Reseating and repairs. *Incumbent:* Rev. Edward Grainger Hall (see no. 297). £994. Organ moved from W gallery to E bay of N gallery, fronts of galleries lowered and splats inserted for openness. New benches to nave, and choir stalls to very shallow chancel. The latter appear to have been swept away when chancel extended to designs of E.W. Mountford, 1895–6.
Sources: ICBS 9516. *CB,* 1891, p. 70.

328. 1891–2. St Luke's Chapel, Brompton Hospital, South Kensington, London. Enlargement of E.B. Lamb's 1849–50 chapel. *Builder:* B.E. Nightingale, Albert Embankment. Stone. £4,000. New gabled N aisle, enlargement of chancel and N organ aisle, new slate roofs and copper-covered ventilation flèches to nave and aisle. Re-use of stone and windows, although some simplification of E window tracery. Alterations to pinnacles and details of W front perhaps the result of decay and later repairs. Hammer-beam roof with figures of angels. Typical pale glazing to E window of organ transept. Altar enlarged. Sedilia and all other fittings E.B. Lamb's originals.
Sources: B, 9.4.1892, p. 294. *G,* 26.10.1892, p. 1614. *CBells,* 28.10.1892, p. 892. *Survey of London,* 41, pp. 136–7.

329. 1891–2. St Michael, Waddesdon, Buckinghamshire. Rebuilding of tower, repairs and restoration. *Incumbent:* Rev. Thomas John Williams (see nos. 211, 266). *Builder:* H.H. Sherwin, Waddesdon. *Clerk of works:* John Beer. Stone. £1,810. Demolition of decayed tower and rebuilding

using the old stones with addition of new W door and four-light window with typical pale glazing with spots of colour to tracery lights, and new SE staircase turret. Repair and restoration of the exterior of the church and removal of accumulated soil in SW corner of churchyard.
Sources: ORO ODP.c.1646. *CBells,* 24.6.1892, p. 540. Canon Clarke's MSS 'Churches in the 19th Century', list of architects in Buckinghamshire.

330. 1892–5. St Oswald, Ashbourne, Derbyshire. Rebuilding of the spire. *Incumbent:* Rev. Francis Jourdain (see no. 183). *Building foreman and clerk of works:* Ralph Clifton. Stone, concrete and 'Delta' metal ties. £4,750.
Source: CBells, 10.5.1895, p. 463.

331. 1892–3. St Andrew, Foxton, Leicestershire. Restoration of nave and aisles. Rev. John McPherson Cunnynghame, curate. *Builder:* H.H. Sherwin, Waddesdon. *Clerk of works:* Mr Beer. Stone. £2,000. Repairs to windows, roofs and walls, including underpinning, heating furnace in vestry created in W bay of S aisle. Removal of W gallery and box pews, new benches on wood-block floor, oak pulpit and lectern.
Sources: Faculty, LeicsRO DE 3378/14. ICBS 9646. *CB,* 1892, p. 81. *Market Harborough Advertiser,* 30.5.1893, p. 5.

332. 1893. Gilbert White Memorial, Selborne, Hampshire. Design for piping water from well-head to drinking fountain in the village to celebrate centenary of death of the Rev. Gilbert White. Stone, surmounted by a cross with oak seat either side. Not built.
Source: Selborne Society, *Nature Notes,* September 1893, p. 172.

333. 1893–5. Shrewsbury School, Shrewsbury, Shropshire. Design for a new boarding house for 42 boys adjacent to Churchill's Hall (no. 273) commissioned by the Governing Body. £8,000. In December 1893 Local Committee demanded alternative three-storey plans to 'amended plans' for two-storey building. Although a year later instructed to prepare a contract, the annual accounts for 1895 show White was paid £201 10s. 0d. for drawings and specification only. Not built.
Sources: Drawings, school archives. Minutes of the Governing Body 1882-1900, Minutes of Local Committee of Governing Body 1 June 1886-8 April 1899, Bailiff Calvert's Papers box A/5/8, school archives.

334. 1894–5. St Philip's Mission Hall, Tennyson Road, Battersea, London. Mission room. *Incumbent:* Rev. E. Herbert Jones. *Builder:* J. Bloomer, Brentford. Brick. £580. Demolished.
Sources: EC 40160. Canon Clarke's MSS 'Demolished & Desecrated Churches of London'.

335. 1895–8. All Saints, Deane, Hampshire. Restoration. *Incumbent:* Rev. William Francis Dashwood Lang (see no. 232). New doors and gates to N porch, new S window to chancel to replace 'sham' one. New floors and stalls to chancel, heating apparatus, oak screen with characteristic pale stained glass to W tower to form vestry. £300.
Sources: HRO 21M65/109F/2; *Winchester Diocesan Calendar,* 1897-9, 21M65/K1/4-6.
1898. Oak pulpit, lectern and chancel screen, all with typical gouged patterning, and 'Many other articles for the due celebration of public worship', £35.

336. 1895. School, Westbury Leigh, Wiltshire. New National School. Stone with brick. £950. Demolished 1990s.
Sources: CBells, 4.10.1895, p. 83. Photo, WRO F8/320/256.

337. 1896. All Saints, Hartley, Kent. Design of stained glass E window in memory of Adam Tait of Hartley Court. Three-lights with figurative panels, the central one of the risen Christ in a mandorla, very similar to that at Brighstone (no. 293). Tait was elected to the board of P&O in 1895; the window was a tribute from his colleagues. Although he died at La Comballaz and was buried at Territet, Switzerland, Tait was not a member of the Alpine Club. The rich geometrical patterned glass above and below the figurative panels was replaced by brown quarries in the 1987 re-ordering.
Source: Faculty, Medway Archives P174_HARTLEY_1712_1984/P174_06_01.

338. 1896-9. St Silas' Clergy House, 74 Penton Street, Pentonville, London. New clergy house and parish hall. *Incumbent:* Rev. Robert Leach. *Builder:* Dove Bros, Islington. Polychrome brick. £4,672. An awkward triangular site. Four storeys plus semi-basement clergy house with crow-stepped gable to entrance front. Large parish hall with triangular dormers, classrooms beneath. Iron columns and rolled steel girders and joists specified. Detail drawings for pivoting windows, stained glass, etc. Demolished.
Sources: Drawings, BAL/V&A Dove Bros collection PB1415/3 (1-77); specification DB/41/3/1. David Braithwaite, *Building in the Blood* (1981), p. 127.

339. 1896(?). Arnos Grove, Southgate, London. Repairs and alterations of mansion for Vyell Edward Walker. *Builder:* Thomas Gregory, Clapham Junction. Since Herbert W. Newby's *Old Southgate* (1949), 75, recounts that electricity and bathrooms were installed in 1896, I have presumed this was the date of White's work. New roof and cupola, repairs to drawing room bay, new entrance portico of brick and stone. Alterations to principal staircase, installation of dinner staircase and lift, repair with copper wire and pierced halfpennies (still visible!) of hall ceiling painted by Gerard Lanscroon, 1723, coffering of dining room ceiling and additions of pilasters to upper part of walls, repairs to panelling of rooms and passages. Much altered and extended in C20 as offices. Now Westminster Beaumont retirement home.
Source: AAN, 13, September 1898, pp. 116-18.

340. 1898-9. St Dionis' Vicarage, Parsons Green, Fulham, London. New house. *Incumbent:* Rev. William Samuel Carter. *Builder:* Dove Bros, Islington. Polychrome brick. £2,375. Two storeys with characteristic stained glass over entrance door, staircase, shutters, fireplaces, pivoting windows. The only surviving White parsonage house still inhabited by the incumbent.
Sources: EC 62380. Drawings, BAL/V&A, Dove Bros collection PB1415/1 (1-5). *Parsons Green, Fulham, Parish Magazine* September 1898–July 1899.

341. Pre-1900. 'Scholastic houses and buildings', Barnet, (Middlesex) London. No further documentary or physical evidence found.
Source: Obituary, *RIBAJ,* 7, 1900, p. 146.

PRESUMED TO BE BY WHITE

342. *c*.1854. School and estate cottages, Scholar Green, Rode Heath, Cheshire. Old School House, Lunts Moss, and a pair of cottages opposite appear to be further commissions for Randle Wilbraham of Rode Hall (see nos. 44-5).

343. *c*.1860. Vicarage, Hatherden, Hampshire. New house, stables, etc. adjacent to the church (no. 65). *Incumbent:* Rev. Carston Dirs Kebbel. Polychrome brick. All White's hallmarks, including

staircase, fireplaces, ironmongery to windows. Double-height bay (not to White's design) added at SW. A subscriptions list dated 13.9.1858 in ICBS 4954, Smannell. Now Michaelmas House.

344. *c*.1862-84. Rectory, Kingston, Kent. Rebuilding [?] and additions. *Incumbent:* Rev. Percy James Croft (see no. 27). Brick. All White's hallmarks: red crested ridge tiles, crow-stepped chimneys, pent-roofed bays, gabled timbered porch, typical door hinges. Central section, with angled buttress to W, appears to have been built first, followed by W wing, and lastly large drawing room to E. Extensions reputed to have been necessary to accommodate Croft's 22 children. Undated photographs show bay window of SW bedroom under wide bell-cast eaves before modern additions and alterations, and shingled flèche to roof ridge. Now The Old Rectory and St Giles Lodge.

345. *c*.1867. Almshouses, Churchgate Street, Harlow, Essex. Polychrome brick. Group of four almshouses with characteristic crested ridge tiles, notched joinery and ironwork. (Identified by Brenda Watkins)

346. 1870(?). St Laurence, Lurgashall, W. Sussex. Alterations. *Incumbent:* Rev. Septimus Fairles (see no. 21). Entrance gates and gateposts to churchyard are characteristic. Brass altar rail almost identical to that at Andover (no. 221). Steps and handrail to pulpit also very typical.

347. *c*.1873. Vicarage, West Wittering, W. Sussex. New two and three-storey house, coach house, etc. east of the church. *Incumbent:* Rev. William Underwood (see no. 240). Brick and flint. All White's hallmarks, including irregular brick banding, gabled north porch with plate-traceried staircase window above, secondary entrance with pent porch. Principal staircase with handrails with leaf-decorated roundel ends. Many modern alterations and additions. Now West Lodge, Brick Rose House, Gable End House, The Coach House.

348. 1885. St Mary the Virgin, Brighstone, Isle of Wight. Chancel reseating. *Incumbent:* Rev. William Edward Heygate (see nos 251, 293). £141.10s. Although not ascribed to White by Canon Heygate in Brighstone Parish Record, 'Special Expenditure on the Church since 1870', 1893, the wooden stalls display all his characteristics.

OTHER ATTRIBUTIONS

1849. St George, City Road, Truro, Cornwall. It has been suggested that a temporary wooden church (*E*, 9, 1849, 395), might have been to White's design. It was replaced in 1855 by a permanent church designed by the Rev. William Haslam (see no. 1). No documentary evidence of White's involvement found.

***c*.1852. St Michael & All Angels, Sowton, Devon.** Lych-gate erected in memory of Sarah Garratt, wife of John Garratt of Bishop's Court, who died in 1852. Listed building description suggests it may have been designed by White, but no documentary or physical evidence found.

1854. Rectory, Tregonna, Little Petherick, Cornwall. Listed building description suggests White designed this for the incumbent, the Rev. Sir Hugh Molesworth (see nos 74, 82). No documentary or physical evidence found. Now Molesworth Manor.

1856. St Mary the Virgin, Selborne, Hampshire. Listed building description states that the chancel arch 'is 1856 by William White'. No documentary or physical evidence found.

1860. Holy Trinity, Walton Street, Aylesbury, Buckinghamshire. Pevsner's *BoE: Buckinghamshire* (1994), p. 153, states that White added a vestry N of the chancel. No documentary or physical evidence for White's involvement has been discovered. Perhaps this was confused with his work at St Michael, Walton (no. 114).

1871. Rosemellyn House, St Columb Major, Cornwall. The listing description reports that the house was 'said to be by William White', but no documentary or physical evidence found.

1871. School, Smannell, Hampshire. The listing description assumes it to be a White design, but no documentary or physical evidence found.

1873. School, Hatherden, Hampshire. The listing description assumes the C19 schoolroom to be a White design *c.*1860, but Education Dept. correspondence indicates a date of 1873, and no documentary or physical evidence of White's involvement found.

ASSESSOR OF COMPETITION

1893. St Paul, Westham, Weymouth, Dorset, 1893.
Source: B, 1893, p. 453.

Catalogue of Works by County

Catalogue of Works outside the UK

Select Bibliography

Published writings by William White

'On the Draining and Drying of Churches', a letter of 6.8.1850, published in *E*, 11, 1850, pp. 153-5.

'Window Tax', a letter of 6.8.1850, published in *E*, 11, 1850, pp. 212-13.

'High Screens', a letter published in *E*, 12, 1851, p. 304.

'On Some of the Principles of Design in Churches', a paper read 8.5.1851 and published in *TEDAS*, 4, 1853, pp. 176-80.

'Upon some of the Causes and Points of Failure in Modern Design', a paper read 22.5.1851 and published in *E*, 12, 1851, pp. 305-13.

'Symbolism, its Practical Benefits and Uses', a paper read 25.7.1852 and published in *TEDAS*, 4, 1853, pp. 304-22.

'Modern Design. Neglect of the Science of Architecture', a paper read 2.6.1853 and published in *E*, 14, 1853, pp. 313-30.

'The Geometrical Proportions of Gothic Churches', a letter published in *B*, 5.11.1853, p. 683.

'Modern Design. On Proportion in Architectural Design', a letter published in *E*, 15, 1854, pp. 291-7.

Is Symbolism Suited to the Spirit of the Age?, a booklet published by Thomas Bosworth, London, 1854.

'Symbolism in Art', a letter published in *CEAJ*, 17, 1854, p. 136.

The Palace, An Artistic Sketch of the 10th of June, 1854, a pamphlet published by Thomas Bosworth, London, 1855.

'Apses and Vestries', letters published in *E*, 16, 1855, pp. 135, 259-61.

'Sacristies', a letter published in *E*, 17, 1856, p. 80.

'Modern Design. On Windows', a paper prepared for the Anniversary Meeting of the Ecclesiological Society, 23.4.1856 and published in *E*, 17, 1856, pp. 319-32.

'Architecture, and its Practical Benefits to Man', a paper read at the Annual Meeting of the Worcester Diocesan Architectural Society 1856 and published in *AASRP*, 3, 1854-6, pp. 37-49.

'So Called Mediæval v. So Called Classic', a letter published in *B*, 14.2.1857, p. 90.

'Fraternities for the Development of Architecture', a letter published in *B*, 27.6.1857, pp. 361-2.

'Style', a letter published in *B*, 18.7.1857, p. 402.

'Communion', a letter published in *E*, 18, 1857, p. 200.

'Architectural Uniformity and its Claims', a lecture for members and friends of the Architectural Museum delivered at the South Kensington Museum and published in *BN*, 17.2.1860, pp. 132-5.

'A Plea for Polychromy', a lecture for members and friends of the Architectural Museum delivered at the South Kensington Museum and published in *BN*, 18.1.1861, pp 50-5.

'Colour in Sacred Art', a letter published in *E*, 22, 1861, pp. 141-7.

'Basilican Arrangement of Churches', letters published in *E*, 23, 1862, pp. 347-51; 24, 1863, pp. 80-6.

'The Wrought-Iron Work of the Great Exhibition of 1862', a paper read at the Architectural Museum and published in *BN*, 22.5.1863, pp. 390-391; 29.5.1863, pp. 410-12.

'Modern Wrought Iron Work', a letter of 14.11.1863 published in *E*, 24, 1863, pp. 343-4.

'Notes on Newland Church, Gloucestershire, with Remarks on Church Restoration and Arrangements' a paper read at the RIBA 30.11.1863 and published in *TRIBA*, 14, 1863-4, pp. 29-44.

'Cathedral Restoration', a letter of 12.5.1864 published in *E*, 25, 1864, pp. 140-2.

'Ironwork: its Legitimate Uses and Proper Treatment', a paper read at the RIBA 20.11.1865 and published in *TRIBA*, 16, 1865-6, pp. 14-30.

'A Report on the Damage Done at Little Torrington Church by Dry Rot', a paper read 11.1.1866 and published in *TEDAS*, 2nd ser., 2, 1872, pp. 13-17. Although not prepared for the Exeter Diocesan Architectural Society, this paper was felt to be so useful that it was read at the College Hall and inserted in the *Transactions*.

'On the Measurement of the Obstruction of Ancient Lights: Further Investigation', a paper read 19.11.1866 and published in *TRIBA*, 17, 1866-7, pp. 17-38

'Systematic Proportion in Architecture', a paper published in *CEAJ*, 31, 1.1.1868, pp. 1-6.

'Descriptive Sketch of a Mansion at Humewood, County Wicklow, in the Course of Erection for Mr. W. Wentworth Fitzwilliam Dick, Member for the County', a paper read at the RIBA 4.1.1869 and published in *TRIBA*, 19, 1868-9, pp. 78-84.

'Color [sic], its Use and Abuse', a paper read 29.4.1869 and published in *TEDAS*, 2nd ser., 2, 1871, pp. 193-204.

'Lighting a Village Church at Night', a letter published in *CBells*, 7.10.1871, p. 647.

'Hammer-Beam Roofs', a paper read to the Architectural Association 29.12.1871 and reported in *B*, 6.1.1872, p. 5.

'Position of the Celebrant', letters published in *CBells*, 8.6. 1872, p. 330; 29.6.1872, p. 366.

'Confirmation Candidates', letter published in *CBells*, 7.9.1872, p. 486.

'Notes and Queries', a letter published in *CBells*, 7.12.1872, p. 18.

'On Church Restoration', a paper on Adisham Church read to the Architectural Association and published in *CB*, 1873, pp. 92-94

'What are Triples?', a letter published in *CBells*, 11.4.1874, p. 223.

'A Brick and Concrete Church, St Mark's Battersea Rise', a paper read to the Architectural Association 8.1.1875 and published in *A*, 16.1.1875, pp. 39-42; *B*, 16.1.1875, pp. 48-50; *BN*, 15.1.1875, pp. 64, 77-8; 22.1.1875, pp. 105-6.

Church Arrangement and Congregational Worship, a pamphlet published by W. Wells Gardner, London, 1875.

The Tourist's Knapsack and Its Contents, a booklet published by W.J. Adams, London, 1875.

'Artisans' Dwellings Improvement Company', a letter published in *CBells*, 17.7.1875, pp. 390-1.

'Revision of the present Translation of the Bible', a letter published in *CBells*, 17.2.1877, p. 135.

'"Restoration" v. "Conservation"', a paper read at the Architectural Association and published in *B*, 2.2.1878, p. 115.

'On the Restoration of the Church at Witham', a description published in *Somersetshire Archaeological and Natural History Society's Proceedings*, 24, 1878, pp. 25-32.

'Chapel of Ease (or future District Church), Hanwell, Middlesex', a description published in *CB*, 1879, pp. 78-81.

'Position of the Celebrant', letters published in *CBells*, 28.6.1879, p. 354; 23.8.1879, p. 449; 20.9.1879, p. 498.

'A Church Mission in a Yorkshire Village', a letter published in *CBells*, 8.11.1879, p, 593.

'"Restoration" at St Alban's and New College', a letter published in *B*, 1.11.1879, p. 1218 and in *CBells*, 15.11.1879, p. 602.

'The Corbel-Table at St Alban's', letters published in *B*, 15.11.1879, p. 1273; 29.11.1879, p. 1327.

Domestic Plumbing and Water Service, a booklet published by Crosby Lockwood & Co., London, 1880.

'Cheap Churches', letters published in *CBells*, 5.6.1880, p. 435; 14.8.1880, p, 593; 4.9.1880, p. 642.

'The *Congé d'Elire*', a letter published in *CBells*, 26.6.1880, p. 482.

'Sanitary Legislation', a letter published in *T*, 8.10.1880, p. 6.

'Styles in Church Building', a letter published in *CBells*, 16.10.1880, p. 750.

'Lecterns and Architects', a letter published in *CBells*, 5.2.1881, p. 154.

'Cheap Churches', a paper read at the Architectural Association and published in *BN*,

11.3.1881, pp, 258-260; *B*, 12.3.1881, pp. 319–321; *CB*, 1881, pp. 70-3, 92-9

'Aesthetical Sanitation', three papers published in *BA*, 22.7.1881, pp. 363-4; 27.1.1882, pp. 37-8; 6.4.1883, pp. 162-3.

'The Right to Reject the Lowest Tender', a paper published in *BA*, 2.2.1883, pp. 49–50.

'Warming of Churches', a letter published in *CBells*, 3.2.1883, p. 169.

'Heating Apparatus', a letter published in *CBells*, 4.3.1883, p. 310.

'Residential Clubs for Clerks and Students', a letter published in *BA*, 1.6.1883, p. 269.

'The Fitting-up of Mission-rooms' a letter published in *CBells*, 1.9.1883, p. 769.

'Heredity', a letter published in *CBells*, 15.9.1883, p. 808.

'Bell-tower Vibration', a letter published in *CBells*, 22.9.1883, p. 828.

'Admiralty and War Office Competition', a letter published in *T*, 14.11.1883, p. 8.

Knapsack Handbook; or Pedestrian's Guide, a booklet published by Edward Stanford, London, 1883

'Church Seats', a paper published in *CB*, 1884, pp. 108-115.

'Could we but see ourselves as others see us', a paper published in *BA*, 28.3.1884, pp. 145-6.

'Hygienic Value of Colour in the Dwelling', a paper published in *B*, 19.7.1884, pp. 99-100.

'Narrow-mindedness', a letter published in *CBells*, 2.8.1884, p. 828.

'Chestnut v. Oak', a letter published in *CBells*, 11.10.1884, p. 1068.

'The Fire-proof Closing of Openings under the Metropolitan Building Act', a paper read at the RIBA 19.1.1885 and published in *TRIBA*, new ser., 1, 1885, pp. 65-72.

'Non-acceptance of Lowest Tender', a letter published in *B*, 7.2.1885, p. 217.

'Arsenic and Architects', a letter published in *B*, 4.4.1885, p. 498.

'The Lowest Tender', a letter published in *B*, 11.4.1885, p. 530.

'R.A. Exhibition', a letter published in *CBells*, 1.5.1885, p. 519.

'Bigotry', a letter published in *CBells*, 22.5.1885, p. 592.

'"Of" and "In"', a letter published in *CBells*, 27.11.1885, p. 1247.

'Wisby in the Island of Gotland', a paper read at the RIBA 14.12.1885 and published in *TRIBA*, new ser., 2, 1886, pp. 66-79.

'Brickwork, and the Leaning Towers of Bologna', a paper read at the Architectural Association 26.2.1886 and published in *BN*, 5.3.1886, pp. 365-7, and in *B*, 6.3.1886, pp. 368-70; 13.3.1886, pp. 422-3.

'The Leaning Towers of Bologna', a re-working of the previous paper, and published in *BA*, 12.3.1886, p. 266; 19.3.1886, pp. 295-6; 26.3.1886, p. 322.

'Parochial Councils', a letter published in *CBells*, 26.3.1886, p. 399.

'Nuisance of Church Bells', letters published in *CBells*, 4.6.1886, p.639; 2.7.1886, pp. 734-5; 20.8.1886, p. 904.

'Church Restoration', a paper published in *The Literary Churchman*, 32, 24.9.1886, pp. 383-6.

'The Planning of a Building', an article published in *BA*, 25.3.1887, p. 224.

'The "Ter Sanctus"', a letter published in *CBells*, 3.6.1887, p. 652.

'Ritual Solutions', a letter published in *CBells*, 17.6.1887, p. 699.

'New Departures', letters published in *CBells*, 15.7.1887, p. 796; 29.7.1887, p. 843.

'The Dilapidation Difficulty', a letter published in *CBells*, 24.2.1888, pp. 319-20.

'Architects', Surveyors' and Engineers' Registration Bill', a letter published in *CBells*, 16.3.1888, p. 391.

'The Reredos at St Paul's', letters published in *CBells*, 6.4.1888, p. 464; 1.6.1888, p. 656.

'The Marriage Bill', a letter published in *CBells*, 11.5.1888, p. 583.

'Ecclesiastical Colours', a letter published in *CBells*, 29.6.1888, p. 751.

'Free and Open Churches in the Country', a letter published in *CBells*, 6.7.1888, p. 776.

'Stack or Rain-pipes', a letter published in *CBells*, 13.7.1888, p. 800.

'Free and Open – All Saints', Notting Hill', a letter published in *CBells*, 31.8.1888, p. 968.

'Church Music', a letter published in *CBells*, 21.12.1888, p. 75.

'Reform in Church Music', letters published in *CBells*, 25.1.1889, p. 195; 15.2.1889, p. 267.

'Kneel or Sit?', a letter published in *CBells*, 24.5.1889, p. 603.

'The Ornaments Rubric and "Comprehension"', a letter published in *CBells*, 19.7.1889, p. 795.

'St Michael's Church, Coventry, Tower and Spire', a letter published in *CBells*, 18.10.1889, p. 1123.

'Church Congregational Music Association', a letter published in *CBells*, 18.7.1889, p. 595.

'The Parson's View of Acoustic Churches', articles published in *BA*, 3.1.1890, pp. 3-4; 17.1.1890, pp. 38-9.

'Wood-Block Floor', a letter published in *BN*, 7.2.1890, p. 224.

'The Galilee of Durham Cathedral: its Name and its Nature', a paper read at the RIBA and published in *TRIBA*, new ser., 6, 1890, pp. 141-52

'Uncongregational Singing', a letter published in *CBells*, 5.9.1890, p. 721.

'Ross Church', a letter published in *CBells*, 12.9.1890, p. 739.

'An Anti-Protest', a letter published in *CBells*, 24.10.1890, p. 891.

'Harvest Festivals', a letter published in *CBells*, 21.11.1890, p. 963.

'Funerals in Inclement Weather', letters published in *CBells*, 24.12.1890, p. 73; 9.1.1891, p. 110.

'Church Warming', a letter published in *CBells*, 30.1.1891, p. 163.

'Early Celebrations', a letter published in *CBells*, 10.4.1891, p. 351.

'Church Music', a letter published in *CBells*, 29.5.1891, p. 477.

'Pews', a letter published in *CBells*, 26.6.1891, p. 549.

'Banns of Marriage', a letter published in *CBells*, 17.7.1891, p. 603.

'Architecture – A Profession or an Art?', a letter published in *T*, 1.11.1891, p. 3.

'The New Century', letters published in *CBells*, 27.11.1891, p. 982; 11.12.1891, p. 29.

'Funeral Reform', a letter published in *CBells*, 5.2.1892, p. 181.

'Congregational Singing', a letter published in *CBells*, 17.6.1892, p. 526.

'Church Music', a letter published in *CBells*, 22.7.1892, p. 618.

'The Lincoln Judgement', a letter published in *CBells*, 18.11.1892, p. 952.

'St Mary's, Oxford', a letter published in *CBells*, 20.1.1893, p. 149.

'Old Fonts', a letter published in *CBells*, 3.3.1893, p. 264.

'Evangelicals and the Lincoln Judgement', a letter published in *CBells*, 17.3.1893, p. 299.

'Wanted, a Font', a letter published in *CBells*, 8.9.1893, p. 750.

'A Serious Weakness', letters published in *CBells*, 1.12.1893, p. 991; 22.12.1893, p. 55; 26.1.1894, p. 145; 23.2.1894, p. 217; 16.3.1894, p. 278; 6.4.1894, p. 331.

'Church Music', a letter published in *CBells*, 11.5.1894, p. 425.

'The Lessons of Holidays', a letter published in *CBells*, 21.9.1894, p. 813.

'Spain and Mexico', a letter published in *CBells*, 28.9.1894, p. 833.

'Congregational Singing', a letter published in *CBells*, 5.10.1894, p. 853.

'Usury and Interest', a letter published in *CBells*, 30.11.1894, p. 1031.

'Mistaken Meanings – Congregational Singing – "Vicar" and "Curate"', a letter published in *CBells*, 7.12.1894, p. 10.

'Mistaken Meanings – Prayer of St Chrysostom', a letter published in *CBells*, 4.1.1895, p. 97.

'Genius v. Hard Work', a letter published in *AAN*, 9, Feb. 1895, pp. 134-5.

'Departmental Doors', a letter published in *CBells*, 15.2.1895, p. 217.

'Noisy Bells', a letter published in *CBells*, 11.4.1895, p. 378.

'Church Congregational Music Association', a letter published in *CBells*, 24.5.1895, p. 497.

'Repairs of Chancel', a letter published in *CBells*, 14.6.1895, pp. 557-8.

'Ecclesiastical Conclusions', a letter published in *CBells*, 12.7.1895, p. 638.

'Turning to the East', a letter published in *CBells*, 29.11.1895, p. 262.

'"Offertories" and "Collections"', a letter published in *CBells*, 2.4.1896, p. 630.

'Private Patronage', a letter published in *CBells*, 15.5.1896, p. 754.

'Reunion', a letter published in *CBells*, 10.7.1896, p. 918.

'Leper Windows', letters published in *CBells*, 24.12.1896, p. 85; 1.1.1897, p. 106.

'Church Bells for Ever!', a letter published in *CBells*, 12.3.1897, p. 310.

'The Communion Table', letters published in *CBells*, 14.1.1898, p. 149; 28.1.1898, p. 189; 11.2.1898, p. 229; 4.3.1898, p. 289; 7.4.1898, p. 397.

'Communion Bread', a letter published in *CBells*, 15.4.1898, p. 418.

'Holy Table/Altar', letters published in *CBells*, 3.6.1898, p. 565; 24.6.1898, p. 625; 29.7.1898, p. 725; 16.9.1898, p. 865; 21.10.1898, p. 990.

'Mattins [sic] and Evensong', a letter published in *CBells*, 24.6.1898, p. 625.

'Disturbances in Church', a letter published in *CBells*, 26.8.1898, p. 805.

'Vivisection', letters published in *CBells*, 2.9.1898, p. 825; 7.10.1898, p. 941.

'Arnos Grove', account of his work at the mansion of Vyell Edward Walker prepared for AA visit, 20.8.1898 and published in *AAN*, 13, Sept. 1898, pp. 116-18.

'Why not the Cat?', a letter published in *CBells*, 28.10.1898, p. 1010.

'Unfaithful Clergy', a letter published in *CBells*, 20.1.1899, p. 173.

'E.[nglish]C.[hurch]U.[nion] and Rome', letters published in *CBells*, 17.2.1899, p. 257; 10.3.1899, p. 317.

'About Numerals', a letter of 3.2.1899 published in *AAN*, 14, Mar. 1899, p. 38.

'Crisis in the Church', letters published in *CBells*, 24.3.1899, p. 356; 21.4.1899, p. 449.

'Anti-vivisection', letters published in *CBells*, 23.6.1899, p. 638; 28.7.1899, p. 738; 11.8.1899, p. 778.

'Grim's (or Graeme's) Dyke', report of AA visit to W.S. Gilbert's house published in *AAN*, 14. Aug. 1899, p. 106.

'Federation of Moderate Churchmen', letters published in *CBells*, 17.11.1899, pp. 1093-4; 15.12.1899, p, 74; 5.1.1900, p. 134.

'Obituary of Sir Arthur W. Blomfield', published in *AAN*, 14, Dec. 1899, p. 164.

'Francis (Bacon), Lord High Chancellor of England', a paper published in *Baconiana*, new ser., 8, 1900, pp. 5-27.

'Cypher writing', a letter published in *Baconiana*, new ser., 8, 1900, p. 51.

Poem

'Un Chat Fidèle', date and publication unknown (copy supplied by the librarian, Gilbert White's House, Selborne, Hampshire).

Unpublished letters and reports by William White

Report on the fees of S.S. Teulon for work carried out in connection with the proposed restoration of Lynton church and additions to Lynton schools, 19.10.1868, DRO, 2579A add/PW30B.

Five letters to Canon A. Codd, Beaminster vicarage, of 31.10.1881, 7.11.1881, 16.11.1881, 18.11.1881, 19.12.1881 concerning the design of the grave for Cecilia Mary Codd, DHC, PE/BE/IN/10/6.

Letter to the secretaries, RIBA, 13.12.1882, concerning the regulations relating to the rotation of the higher offices of the Institute, RIBA Library, Box 21, folder 9, letter 10.

Report on proposed restoration of St Mary the Virgin, Bishops Cannings, Wiltshire, 23.2.1883, ICBS 8783, LPL.

Report on proposed restoration of St James, Avebury, Wiltshire, 23.1.1884, ICBS 8305, LPL.

Letter to the Secretary, RIBA, Mar. 1885 with copy of 'Church Seats' paper published in *CB*, 1884, RIBA Library, WhW/pam 78, fols. 441-3.

Letter to the secretaries, RIBA, 2.7.1885, proposing to speak on 'A week in Wisby', RIBA Library, Box 23, folder 7, Letter 7.

Report on proposed enlargement of St James, Milton Abbas, Dorset, 13.4.1888, ICBS 9227, LPL.

Three letters to the Secretary, RIBA, 4.3.1891, 8.6.1891 and n.d., concerning the architect Giampietri, RIBA Library, Box 33, folder 1, letters 5-7.

Remarks on proposed reseating and repairs of St Cynog, Penderyn, (Brecon) Glamorgan, 7.11.1894, ICBS 9825, LPL.

Remarks on proposed enlargement of St Clement, Rhayader, (Radnorshire) Powys, 2.2.1898, ICBS 10046, LPL.

William White's contributions to debates and discussions

Discussion on design of churches, report published in *E*, 25, 1864, pp. 228-30.

'Art Foliage', report published in *TRIBA*, 16, 1865-6, pp. 42-3.

'On Painting in Connection with Architecture', report published in *TRIBA*, 16, 1865-6, p. 60.

'On the Problem of Providing Dwellings for the Poor', report published in *TRIBA*, 17, 1866-7, pp. 68-70.

'Remarks upon Failures in Construction', report published in *TRIBA*, 17, 1866-7, pp. 187-90.

'On Pedantry in Architecture', report published in *TRIBA*, 17, 1866-7, p. 154.

'Iron Architecture', report published in *A*, 29.5.1880, pp. 363, 369.

'Historical Documents', report published in *TRIBA*, 31, 1880-1, pp. 188-9.

'Minutes of Evidence taken before the Select Committee on Westminster Hall Restoration', 13.3.1885, published in *Reports from Committees*, 7, 1884-5, vol. 13, pp. 121-4.

Discussion on architectural education, *B*, 31.10.1885, p. 623.

'Musical Requirements in Church Planning', report published in *TRIBA*, new ser., 5, 1889, p. 51.

'Architecture in Provence', report published in *TRIBA*, new ser., 6, 1890, p. 85.

'Notes on Church Fittings', notes read in White's absence at the discussion of J.P. Seddon's paper and published in *TRIBA*, new ser., 6, 1890, pp. 184-185

Nineteenth-century writings about White

Criticism of White's paper 'Upon Some of the Causes and Points of Failure in Modern Design', *E*, 12, 1851, p. 354.

'The Crystal Palace', a review of White's pamphlet, *The Palace: an Artistic Sketch of the 10th of June, 1854*, published in *E*, 16, 1855, pp. 162-3.

'Symbolism in Art', a review of White's pamphlet, *Is Symbolism Suited to the Spirit of the Age*, published in *CEAJ*, 17, 1854, pp. 98-100

'Natural Colour in Sacred Architecture', a letter from 'A Member of the Oxford Architectural Society' remarking on White's 'A Plea for Polychromy', published in *E*, 22, 1861, pp. 67-9.

Charles L. Eastlake, *A History of the Gothic Revival* (London, 1872).

'Our Architects and Their Works, No. 2, William White, F.S.A.', a report in *BA*, 16.9.1881, pp. 464-6.

Profile of William White, F.S.A. published in *BN*, 31.1.1890, pp. 168-9.

Profile of William White, F.S.A. published in *CBells*, 29.1.1892, pp. 155-6.

Obituaries and later writings about White

AAN, 15, 1900, p. 20 (ed. G.H. Fellowes Prynne).

BA, 2.2.1900, pp. 73-4 (anon.).

B, 27.1.1900, p. 91 (anon.).

B, 3.2.1900, p. 104 (chairman, AA).

BN, 26.1.1900, p. 123 (anon.).

BN, 26.1.1900, p. 187 (Alexander Graham, hon. sec., RIBA).

Forest School Magazine, Lent 1900, p. 298 (anon.).

RIBAJ, 3rd ser., 7, 1900, pp. 145-6 (Thomas Henry Watson).

TEDAS, 3rd ser., 2, 1908, pp. 3-4 (Anon., possibly Robert Medley Fulford).

Gordon Barnes' notebooks, Cathedrals and Church Buildings Library, Church House, London.

Chris Brooks, 'Bishop's Court, Devon', *Country Life*, 15.2.1990, pp. 54-8.

Basil F.L. Clarke, *Church Builders of the Nineteenth Century* (London, 1938).

 Notes and MSS, Cathedrals and Church Buildings Library, Church House, London.

Christopher Dalton, 'Parsons' Pleasures', *Country Life*, 16.4.1987, pp. 150-2.

Graham Daw, 'William White at St Ive', *Cornish Buildings Group Proceedings*, 1982, pp. 6-9.

Mark Girouard, 'Humewood Castle, Co. Wicklow', *Country Life*, 9.5.1968, pp. 1212-15; 16.5.1968, pp. 1282-5; and in *The Victorian Country House* (London, 1979), pp. 252-62.

Clive Glover, 'The Churches of William White 1825-1900', AA Diploma Thesis, 1982, RIBA Library.

Gill Hunter, 'Cheap and Cheerful: William White in Hampshire', *Ecclesiology Today*, April 2000, pp. 28-32.

 'William White: the Early Years', *The 1840s*, The Victorian Society, Studies in Victorian Architecture and Design, 1, 2008, pp. 106-16.

 '"Inventive and Ingenious": Designs by William White', *Ecclesiology Today*, 2010, forthcoming.

Paul Thompson, 'The Writings of William White' in John Summerson (ed.), *Concerning Architecture* (London, 1968), pp. 226-37.

Clive Wainwright, 'Ardent Simplicity', *Country Life*, 18.10.1990, pp. 150-4.

Brenda Watkin, 'William White 1825-1900, The Architect and Philosopher', AA Diploma Thesis, 1994, RIBA Library.

Miss H.M. White, *Cameos*, Sept. 1960, Bishops College Archive, Cape Town.

Illustration Credits

Frontispiece Royal Institute of British Architects, photograph collection. **1.1, 1.3, 1.6, 2.18, 3.13, 3.14, 4.13, 4.18, 4.31, 5.17, 6.10. 9.16** Peter Hunter. **1.8** Royal Institution of Cornwall, TRURI:1000.339. **1.9, 1.15, 4.8** Christopher Dalton. **1.12** V&A, W.63-1979. Clive Wainwright. **1.13, 1.14** Cornwall Record Office, D/R uncatalogued. **1.16, 4.9, 4.12, 5.12** Josephine Collingwood. **1.18** Graham Daw. **2.1, 3.19, 3.20, 7.3, 7.4, 7.7, 7.8, 7.9, 7.10** National Monuments Record. **2.2** *Building News*, 15.9.1876. **2.3** *The Builder*, 13.10.1855. **2.5, 2.10** Bishops Diocesan College, Cape Town. **2.6** St Andrew's College, Grahamstown. **2.7** Charles Gray (ed.), *Life of Robert Gray, Bishop of Cape Town* (London, 1876), courtesy of Alex Bremner. **2.8** B. Weinreb, *Catalogue 14, The Gothic of Gothick*, 1966. **2.9** St Mark's College, Plymouth. **2.15** Frank van der Riet collection, copied from photos of Dr W.G. Atherstone, etc; original copy in Albany Museum (History), Grahamstown. **2.17** Diocesan Archives Deposit, Cory Library for Historical Research, Rhodes University, Grahamstown, PIC 3280/1. **3.1** *The Ecclesiologist*, 12, 1851. **3.2** T.T. Carter, *A Memoir of John Armstrong* (Oxford, 1875), courtesy of Alex Bremner. **3.4** Martin Charles. **3.5** Arley Hall Archive, courtesy of Jane Foster. **3.6** Arley Hall Archive. **3.9** Diocese of Lincoln, Lincolnshire Archives, MGA 379. **3.10** Centre for Digital Library Research, University of Strathclyde. **3.11** Sir John Soane's Museum, undated. **3.12** Private collection, undated. **3.15** Winchester City Museum, PWCM 2706. **3.18** *The Builder*, 27.7.1867. **4.1** Lloyds TSB Archive, 1902-18. **4.2** *The Builder*, 11.8.1855. **4.3** Stuart Levens. **4.15** Lambeth Palace Library, ICBS 4953. **4.16** Lambeth Palace Library, ICBS 4954. **4.19, 6.2** C.L. Eastlake, *A History of the Gothic Revival* (London, 1872). **4.24** John Wise, *The New Forest* (1880), courtesy of Angela Trend. **4.25** Collection of Angela Trend. **4.26, 4.28** Hampshire Record Office, 20M65/6. **4.29** Berkshire Record Office, D/EX 268/17. **4.30** Selborne Society, *Nature Notes*, September 1893. **5.1** Bishop's Court, 1833 Estate Plan. **5.2** Tim Grevatt. **5.5, 5.6** *Country Life*, 15.2.1990. **5.7, 5.8, 5.9** Clive Wainwright. **5.10, 5.11** Church of England Record Centre, QAB E1. **5.18** West Sussex Record Office, UD/LH/16/1. **6.1** *The Builder*, 8.8.1868. **6.4** *Country Life*, 16.5.1968. **6.5** Wiltshire & Swindon Record Office, 947/2182. **6.9** Charlotte Dale. **6.11** Paul Reeves. **6.13** Christopher Dresser, *The Art of Decorative Design* (London, 1862). **7.1** Sven Tester. **7.2** *Building News*, 15.1.1875. **7.12** Undated photograph in the church. **7.13** Perspective in the church. **8.2** Petrie Collection no. 285, Kent Archaeological Society. **8.3** Bodleian Library, a.67, 282, reproduced in *VCH Oxfordshire*, vol. 10. **8.6** *The Ecclesiologist*, 25, 1864, courtesy of Geoff Brandwood. **8.9** The Victorian Society. **9.1** *Church Bells*, 3,6.1876. **9.2** Martin Harrison. **9.6** *Illustrated London News*, 11.1.1890. **9.7** René Lachal. **9.9** *Church Builder*, 1884. **9.11** *Church Builder*, 1891. **9.13** West Yorkshire Archive Service, Wakefield WMD5/2/13.

Index

Numbers in bold refer to pages where illustrations are to be found.